Boosting Dynamic Capacity for SMEs in Volatile Environments

José De Jesús Reyes Sanchez
https://orcid.org/0000-0002-3866-2363

TECNM Instituto Tecnológico Superior De Fresnillo, Mexico

Mario Alberto Garcia-Camacho
https://orcid.org/0000-0002-9645-3199

TECNM Instituto Tecnológico Superior De Fresnillo, Mexico

Jannet Maricela Barrientos Luján
https://orcid.org/0009-0009-3244-5016

TECNM Instituto Tecnológico Superior De Fresnillo, Mexico

IGI Global
Scientific Publishing
Publishing Tomorrow's Research Today

Vice President of Editorial	Melissa Wagner
Director of Acquisitions	Mikaela Felty
Director of Book Development	Jocelynn Hessler
Production Manager	Mike Brehm
Cover Design	Jose Rosado

Published in the United States of America by
IGI Global Scientific Publishing
701 East Chocolate Avenue
Hershey, PA, 17033, USA
Tel: 717-533-8845 | Fax: 717-533-7115
Website: https://www.igi-global.com E-mail: cust@igi-global.com

Library of Congress Cataloging-in-Publication Data

Names: Reyes Sanchez, José De Jesús, 1978- editor | García-Camacho, Mario Alberto, 1986- editor | Barrientos Luján, Jannet Maricela, 1979- editor
Title: Boosting dynamic capacity for SMEs in volatile environments / [edited by] José De Jesús Reyes Sanchez, Mario Alberto García-Camacho, Jannet Maricela Barrientos Luján.
Description: Hershey, PA : IGI Global Scientific Publishing, [2026] | Includes bibliographical references and index. | Summary: "This book explores how small and medium-sized enterprises (SMEs) can build dynamic capabilities to navigate volatile, uncertain, complex, and ambiguous environments and sustain long-term growth. Through a multidisciplinary lens, it analyzes strategies and innovations used by SMEs to enhance resilience, competitiveness, and alignment with sustainability goals"-- Provided by publisher.
Identifiers: LCCN 2025034249 (print) | LCCN 2025034250 (ebook) | ISBN 9798337360539 hardcover | ISBN 9798337360546 paperback | ISBN 9798337360553 ebook
Subjects: LCSH: Small business | Strategic planning | Organizational change
Classification: LCC HD2341 .B595 2026 (print) | LCC HD2341 (ebook) | DDC 338.6/42--dc23/eng/20260122
LC record available at https://lccn.loc.gov/2025034249
LC ebook record available at https://lccn.loc.gov/2025034250

British Cataloguing in Publication Data
A Cataloguing in Publication record for this book is available from the British Library.

Table of Contents

Preface x

Chapter 1
Digital Transformation for Better SME Performance Through Frugal Management 1
Geetha Manoharan, SR University, India
Harish Kumar Chikuru, SR University, India
Subhashini Durai, LEAD College of Management, India

Chapter 2
Dynamic Capabilities for SMEs in Volatile Environments: The Role of ISO 9001:2026 in Supply Chain Transformation 27
Omar A. Guirette-Barbosa, Universidad Politécnica de Zacatecas, Mexico & Broward International University, Mexico
Selene Castañeda-Burciaga, Universidad Politécnica de Zacatecas, Mexico & Broward International University, Mexico

Chapter 3
Entrepreneurial Leadership Effect on Participatory Governance Through Change-Oriented Organizational Culture 69
Vikki Sharma, Shri Ram College of Commerce, University of Delhi, India
Wako Jio, Bule Hora University, Ethiopia
Shashi Kant, St. Joseph University In Tanzania, Tanzania
Shashank Mittal, O.P. Jindal Global University, India
Pawan Kumar, Lovely Professional University, India
Antoniammal Manual, DMI-St.Eugene University, Zambia

Chapter 4
Frugal Innovation and Knowledge Management in Resource-Constrained Environments 99
Satya Subrahmanyam, Holy Spirit University of Kaslik, Lebanon

Chapter 5
Intellectual Capital-Enhanced Dynamic Capabilities: A Multi-Dimensional Performance Framework for SMEs in VUCA Environments 125
Göran Roos, Adelaide University, Australia

Chapter 6
Minimal Resources, Maximum Impact A Knowledge-Based Approach to Frugal Innovation 159
Gurpreet pal Kaur, Lovely Professional University, India
Mushtaq Ahmed Shah, Lovely Professional University, India

Chapter 7
Rural-Urban Disparities in SME Access to Non-Banking Financing in Colombia Post COVID-19 187
Hector Botello, Washington State University, USA

Chapter 8
Strengthening Micro and Small Enterprises' (MSEs) Dynamic Capabilities Through Digital Transformation in the VUCA Era 205
Lucky Nugroho, Universitas Mercu Buana, Indonesia

Compilation of References 233

About the Contributors 275

Index 279

Detailed Table of Contents

Preface x

Chapter 1
Digital Transformation for Better SME Performance Through Frugal Management 1
Geetha Manoharan, SR University, India
Harish Kumar Chikuru, SR University, India
Subhashini Durai, LEAD College of Management, India

This chapter examines how digital transformation and economical management might boost SMEs' success. Digital transformation empowers SMEs by simplifying processes, improving data-driven decision-making, and improving customer experiences. Frugal management emphasizes cost-effective and resource-efficient methods, which are crucial for budget-constrained SMEs. Combining these tactics allows SMEs to acquire cutting-edge technology without high expenses, boosting productivity and competitiveness. The study shows how digital technology and lean management have improved operations and cut costs in several real-world cases. It also discusses managerial attitudes and strategic adoption issues, emphasizing the need for realistic and scalable digital solutions for small and medium-sized enterprises (SMEs) to achieve sustainable growth and better business results.

Chapter 2
Dynamic Capabilities for SMEs in Volatile Environments: The Role of ISO 9001:2026 in Supply Chain Transformation 27
Omar A. Guirette-Barbosa, Universidad Politécnica de Zacatecas, Mexico & Broward International University, Mexico
Selene Castañeda-Burciaga, Universidad Politécnica de Zacatecas, Mexico & Broward International University, Mexico

The ISO 9001:2026 standard represents a critical evolution in quality management systems, particularly relevant for SMEs operating in volatile environments. This chapter examines, from a strategic and multidimensional approach, how the new version of the standard enhances dynamic capacity by redefining quality beyond compliance, and by integrating tools such as artificial intelligence (AI), blockchain, and the Internet of Things (IoT) to optimize processes, anticipate risks, and create value. Through conceptual, technical, and practical analysis of real-world cases and literature review, the chapter highlights the benefits of ISO 9001:2026 implementation for SMEs seeking to strengthen resilience, agility, and competitiveness in increasingly interconnected and demanding supply chains. Furthermore, common barriers to adoption are identified, and strategies for overcoming them are proposed, emphasizing cultural, technological, and human transformation. Ultimately, ISO 9001:2026 will not only improve business performance but also act as a catalyst for SMEs to build ethical, sustainable, and intelligent business ecosystems, boosting their dynamic capacity to thrive under volatility.

Chapter 3
Entrepreneurial Leadership Effect on Participatory Governance Through Change-Oriented Organizational Culture 69
Vikki Sharma, Shri Ram College of Commerce, University of Delhi, India
Wako Jio, Bule Hora University, Ethiopia
Shashi Kant, St. Joseph University In Tanzania, Tanzania
Shashank Mittal, O.P. Jindal Global University, India
Pawan Kumar, Lovely Professional University, India
Antoniammal Manual, DMI-St.Eugene University, Zambia

This chapter addresses the contextualized interaction between entrepreneur leadership and participatory governance moderated by change oriented organizational culture over the Ethiopian context. The study with the sample size of 394 respondents uses a quantitative methodology to evaluate the dynamics of these variables. The results indicate that leadership of the entrepreneur greatly affects the participatory governance because it leads to a change-oriented organizational culture. This culture which is flexible, innovative and involves employee interaction takes on a mediating role of improving practices of governance. The chapter makes a contribution towards understanding of the influence of leadership style in governing. It underlines the need to develop an organizational culture that will have embraced change towards enhancing participatory governance. The implication of these findings implies that the leaders of organizations must focus more on entrepreneurial leadership and cultural transformation to realize effective governance.

Chapter 4
Frugal Innovation and Knowledge Management in Resource-Constrained Environments 99
Satya Subrahmanyam, Holy Spirit University of Kaslik, Lebanon

In resource-constrained environments, Small and Medium Enterprises (SMEs) face mounting challenges due to limited capital, infrastructure, and formal knowledge systems. This chapter explores how frugal innovation and knowledge management (KM) together enhances SME resilience and adaptability. Frugal innovation—rooted in simplicity, affordability, and resource-efficiency—aligns with the needs of volatile, low-income markets. KM enables SMEs to harness internal and external knowledge through informal practices like storytelling, peer learning, and digital platforms. Using the dynamic capabilities framework, the chapter illustrates how SMEs develop agility through integrated innovation and KM. Real-world case studies from Africa, Asia, and Latin America highlight successful low-cost innovations in healthcare, education, and manufacturing. Challenges such as limited digital access and tacit knowledge loss are addressed with practical strategies. The chapter concludes with policy implications and future research directions.

Chapter 5
Intellectual Capital-Enhanced Dynamic Capabilities: A Multi-Dimensional Performance Framework for SMEs in VUCA Environments 125
Göran Roos, Adelaide University, Australia

This chapter develops the IC-Enhanced Dynamic Capabilities Framework for SMEs operating in VUCA environments. The framework integrates intellectual capital theory with dynamic capabilities theory, positioning human capital, structural capital, and relational capital as foundational resources that enable sensing, seizing, and transforming capabilities. These capabilities drive multi-dimensional performance across profitable growth, productivity enhancement, human capital retention and development, and environmental footprint reduction. The framework operates through bidirectional transformation mechanisms where intellectual capital enables capability development whilst being enhanced through capability deployment, creating reinforcing cycles. Implementation follows a four-phase approach: assessment and preparation, capability development, implementation and integration, and continuous adaptation. The theoretical contribution demonstrates how SMEs can leverage knowledge-based assets to build adaptive capabilities for sustained competitive advantage in turbulent environments.

Chapter 6
Minimal Resources, Maximum Impact A Knowledge-Based Approach to Frugal Innovation 159
Gurpreet pal Kaur, Lovely Professional University, India
Mushtaq Ahmed Shah, Lovely Professional University, India

The chapter examines how frugal innovation has been combined with knowledge management in settings where financial, infrastructural, institutional and human resource conditions are acute. It underlines the idea that the force of impactful innovation may be motivated by expertise instead of resources. It corroborates on Knowledge-based View (KBV) of the firm and stresses the value of tacit skills, local knowledge, collective experience and general-access internet-based spaces and platforms. The chapter demonstrates the development of the frugal innovation over time using a conceptual and case-based approach and discusses creation, sharing and application of knowledge in low-resource environments. It presents a model that describes how knowledge input, knowledge management processes and collaborative effort in stakeholders are key to attaining socially relevant innovation at minimum cost. It illustrates through global and Indian case studies including Aravind Eye Care, M-Pesa, SELCO Solar, and Goonj, how radically different knowledge intensive frugal innovation is able to provide cost and scalable solutions to pertinent problems in a variety of arenas including healthcare, finance, energy, and grassroots development. A subsequent theoretical contribution of the chapter is to lend plausibility to KBV as an extension of frugal innovation, furnishing practical resources and policy insights on how to nurture and develop inclusive knowledge environments. This study suggested the direction of future research opportunities, among others, on AI-enabled knowledge integration, cross-sectoral relations, and longitudinal evaluations as possible ways to sustain and spread frugal innovation.

Chapter 7
Rural-Urban Disparities in SME Access to Non-Banking Financing in Colombia Post COVID-19 187
Hector Botello, Washington State University, USA

This chapter examines the impact of the COVID-19 pandemic on small and medium-sized enterprises' (SMEs) access to financing in Colombia, focusing on the disparities between rural and urban areas. The purpose is to understand how these businesses adapted to financial constraints by leveraging non-banking financing sources. The analysis reveals that in the post-pandemic period, SMEs were significantly more likely to utilize non-banking financing, such as microfinance and fintech, compared to traditional banking. A key finding is the existence of significant rural-urban disparities, with rural SMEs being 30.4% less likely than their urban counterparts to access non-banking financing in 2021. Younger firms and male-owned businesses demonstrated a higher likelihood of securing financing. The chapter concludes by discussing the policy implications of these findings, highlighting the need for targeted financial inclusion strategies to support rural and underserved SMEs and promote a more resilient and equitable financial ecosystem in Colombia.

Chapter 8
Strengthening Micro and Small Enterprises' (MSEs) Dynamic Capabilities Through Digital Transformation in the VUCA Era 205
Lucky Nugroho, Universitas Mercu Buana, Indonesia

Digital transformation is a strategic imperative for Micro and Small Enterprises (MSEs) in the VUCA era, marked by volatility, uncertainty, complexity, and ambiguity. This chapter addresses the gap between the urgency for digital adaptation and MSEs' readiness in technology, behavior, and policy by applying Dynamic Capabilities Theory (DCT) to explain how sensing, seizing, and transforming processes enhance adaptability. Using a qualitative synthesis of literature and field practices, the study identifies key success determinants: adoption of AI, IoT, and Big Data; digital behavioral readiness; inclusive public policy; and integration of ESG and CSR values. Findings highlight that effective transformation requires synergy between internal capacity and external ecosystem support through partnerships, funding, and training. The study extends DCT's application to MSEs, offering data-driven, behavioral, and policy strategies for sustainable transformation, and recommends a community-based, inclusive approach to bridge the digital divide and foster equitable growth in Indonesia.

Compilation of References 233

About the Contributors 275

Index 279

Preface

INTRODUCTION

Small and medium-sized enterprises (SMEs) are widely recognized as the backbone of global economies, yet they are increasingly challenged by volatile, uncertain, complex, and ambiguous (VUCA) environments. Rapid technological change, shifting market demands, supply chain disruptions, and global crises have intensified the need for SMEs to move beyond traditional operational efficiency toward adaptive, resilient, and forward-looking capabilities. This edited volume emerges from the recognition that "dynamic capacity"—the ability to sense, seize, and transform in response to change—is no longer optional but essential for SME survival and growth.

As editors, we have curated this collection to bridge theory and practice by bringing together diverse scholarly perspectives and empirical insights from across continents. The contributions reflect a multidisciplinary approach, integrating fields such as strategic management, digital transformation, quality systems, entrepreneurship, innovation, and knowledge management. Collectively, the chapters provide a comprehensive understanding of how SMEs can leverage both tangible and intangible resources to remain competitive under conditions of uncertainty.

This book also emphasizes inclusivity in context and application. By drawing on evidence from emerging and developed economies alike, it highlights that while the challenges SMEs face may be global, the pathways to resilience are often local and context-specific. The volume therefore offers both universal frameworks and adaptable strategies that scholars, practitioners, and policymakers can employ to strengthen SME ecosystems worldwide.

CHAPTER OVERVIEW

This volume is structured to progressively explore the foundations, enablers, and applications of dynamic capacity in SMEs operating in volatile environments.

Chapter 1 examines the intersection of digital transformation and frugal management, demonstrating how SMEs can achieve improved performance through cost-effective technological adoption. It highlights the importance of scalable and resource-efficient innovation strategies.

Chapter 2 explores the strategic implications of ISO 9001:2026, illustrating how evolving quality management standards enhance dynamic capabilities through the integration of emerging technologies such as AI, blockchain, and IoT in supply chains.

Chapter 3 investigates the role of entrepreneurial leadership in fostering participatory governance, emphasizing the mediating influence of a change-oriented organizational culture in shaping effective governance practices.

Chapter 4 focuses on the synergy between frugal innovation and knowledge management, offering insights into how SMEs in resource-constrained environments can build resilience through low-cost, knowledge-driven solutions.

Chapter 5 introduces a multi-dimensional framework linking intellectual capital to dynamic capabilities, illustrating how human, structural, and relational capital contribute to sustainable performance in VUCA contexts.

Chapter 6 extends the discussion on frugal innovation through a knowledge-based perspective, showcasing how tacit knowledge and collaborative ecosystems enable impactful innovation with minimal resources.

Chapter 7 examines post-pandemic financing trends in Colombia, highlighting rural-urban disparities in access to non-banking financial resources and their implications for SME resilience and inclusivity.

Chapter 8 addresses digital transformation in micro and small enterprises (MSEs), identifying key determinants such as technological readiness, policy support, and ecosystem collaboration for successful adaptation.

CONCLUSION

This volume underscores that dynamic capacity is not a singular capability but a composite of interrelated competencies that enable SMEs to navigate and thrive amid uncertainty. From digital transformation and quality management to leadership, innovation, and financial access, the chapters collectively demonstrate that resilience emerges from the integration of strategy, culture, and capability development.

A key takeaway from this collection is the critical role of context in shaping SME strategies. Whether operating in emerging markets with resource constraints or in highly competitive global industries, SMEs must tailor their approaches to their unique environments while maintaining a forward-looking orientation. The frameworks and case studies presented herein provide actionable insights that can inform both strategic decision-making and policy formulation.

As editors, we hope this book serves as a valuable resource for academics, practitioners, and policymakers seeking to understand and enhance SME performance in turbulent times. More importantly, we envision it as a catalyst for continued research and dialogue on building resilient, adaptive, and innovative SME ecosystems capable of sustaining growth in an ever-changing world.

Chapter 1
Digital Transformation for Better SME Performance Through Frugal Management

Geetha Manoharan
http://orcid.org/0000-0002-8644-8871
SR University, India

Harish Kumar Chikuru
SR University, India

Subhashini Durai
LEAD College of Management, India

ABSTRACT

This chapter examines how digital transformation and economical management might boost SMEs' success. Digital transformation empowers SMEs by simplifying processes, improving data-driven decision-making, and improving customer experiences. Frugal management emphasizes cost-effective and resource-efficient methods, which are crucial for budget-constrained SMEs. Combining these tactics allows SMEs to acquire cutting-edge technology without high expenses, boosting productivity and competitiveness. The study shows how digital technology and lean management have improved operations and cut costs in several real-world cases. It also discusses managerial attitudes and strategic adoption issues, emphasizing the need for realistic and scalable digital solutions for small and medium-sized enterprises (SMEs) to achieve sustainable growth and better business results.

DOI: 10.4018/979-8-3373-6053-9.ch001

1 INTRODUCTION: THE SME'S DIGITAL DILEMMA

Small and medium-sized businesses, often known as SMEs, are the fundamental building blocks of economies all over the world. According to the World Bank, they are responsible for about 90 percent of enterprises and more than fifty percent of employment throughout the globe. As a result, the viability and vitality of these firms are essential to the stability and expansion of the economy (World Bank, 2021). Their contributions to the fabric of our communities, as well as the engines of innovation and the producers of local jobs, are invaluable. Nevertheless, these essential organizations are confronted with a threat to their very existence that simultaneously presents them with the greatest opportunity: the unrelenting advance of digital transformation.

The pressure to "go digital" is enormous currently, when the expectations of customers are moulded by the seamless experiences provided by digital giants, and when operational efficiency is determined by data-driven automation. According to Rogers (2016), digital transformation is no longer about making a strategic decision; rather, it is a fundamental requirement for both survival and improvement. It promises a tantalizing array of benefits, including increased productivity through automated workflows, deeper customer relationships through data analytics and personalized marketing, expanded market reach through e-commerce, and greater resilience through agile, cloud-based operations (Westerman et al., 2014). These benefits are all a promise. On the other hand, the narrative that predominates in situations involving digital transformation is frequently one of endeavours that are enormous, complicated, and prohibitively expensive. It conjures up visions of expensive enterprise resource planning (ERP) systems, teams of data scientists, and bespoke software development projects, all of which are well beyond the financial and operational capability of the ordinary small and medium-sized firm (SME). Consequently, this results in a perilous abyss known as the SME Digital Dilemma. They are aware that they need to bridge the digital gap, yet it seems as though the bridge is constructed for multi-national corporations who have huge funds.

That narrative is called into question in this chapter. According to this argument, the limitations that small and medium-sized enterprises (SMEs) confront, such as fewer finances, smaller teams, and less bureaucracy, are not insurmountable obstacles; rather, they have the potential to serve as catalysts for a more intelligent, agile, and successful approach to digital transformation. A strong management philosophy that is frequently ignored is frugal management, and it is this philosophy that holds the key to unleashing this whole potential.

1.1 Defining Frugal Management

It is a mentality and a strategic approach that is centered on accomplishing more with less (Radjou & Prabhu, 2015). Frugal management is also known as frugal innovation or jugaad innovation in its Indian context. Also known as jugaad innovation. To be "cheap" does not mean to take shortcuts or to compromise on quality. This is not the case. Being resourceful, intelligent, and value-focused are more important than anything else. By eliminating elements that are not needed and focusing on the capabilities that are vital, it promotes the art of designing solutions to complicated issues that are straightforward, efficient, and economical.

Fundamental principles of frugal management include the following:

1. Embracing Constraints: Rather than viewing restrictions in resources as disadvantages, viewing them as creative fire that encourages creativity and concentration has been suggested by Bound and Thornton (2012).
2. Prioritizing basic, "good-enough" solutions that efficiently tackle a fundamental problem above complicated, feature-rich systems that are expensive and difficult to build is the definition of the preference for simplicity over complexity.
3. Leveraging Existing Resources refers to the process of discovering novel and creative methods to make use of the resources, capabilities, and assets that are already available to an individual.
4. Instead, then focusing on technology innovation for its own sake, customer-centric value creation involves putting a strong emphasis on finding solutions to the most pressing challenges faced by customers.
5. Iterative and Agile Progress: Making modest, incremental changes and learning from feedback, rather than trying a single, high-risk "big bang" transformation (Ries, 2011).

1.2 The Synergy of Frugality and Digital Transformation for SMEs

A significant synergy is created when this mindful approach to saving money is applied to the process of digital transformation. Instead of striving to mimic the digital strategies of major businesses, small and medium-sized enterprises (SMEs) can chart their own path—one that is practical, relatively inexpensive, and well suited to their scale and agility. Starting with the query, "What is the most recent technology that we ought to purchase?" is not the first step in a thrifty digital transformation. Questions such as "What is our biggest business bottleneck or customer pain point?" serve as the starting point for this process.

"What is the simplest, most affordable digital tool that can solve 80% of this problem right now?"

"How can we use free or low-cost platforms to test our ideas before committing significant capital?"

By taking this approach, the intimidating idea of digital transformation is transformed into a set of actions that are both realistic and value-driven, making it more doable. It makes it possible for small and medium-sized organizations (SMEs) to take use of the democratizing potential of contemporary technology, such as cloud computing, Software-as-a-Service (SaaS), open-source software, and no-code platforms, to accomplish targets that were previously the sole purview of major corporations. To implement this thrifty strategy, this chapter will serve as a guide. We are going to go from the theoretical to the practical, beginning with the establishment of the fundamental principles of frugal management in the context of digital technology. We will then construct a "Frugal Digital Toolkit," which will consist of a collection of specialized technologies that are inexpensive and applicable to major business sectors. Following this, we will develop a comprehensive, step-by-step roadmap for implementation, with an emphasis on the cultural and human factors that are necessary for success. Finally, we will illustrate that the way to improved performance in the digital era is not paved with gold for small and medium-sized enterprises (SMEs), but rather with inventiveness, resourcefulness, and dedication to cost-effective and sensible action. This will be accomplished via the use of illustrative case studies and an honest evaluation of the possible hurdles.

2 THE CONCEPTUAL FRAMEWORK: CORE PRINCIPLES OF FRUGAL DIGITAL MANAGEMENT

Developing a strong conceptual basis is a vital step that must be taken before delving into tools and methodological approaches. First and foremost, frugal management is a mentality, and then it is a collection of strategies. This will result in disjointed efforts and unsatisfactory outcomes if you adopt a few low-cost tools without also internalizing the mindset that underlies them. With a consistent set of principles that govern every choice, from the selection of technology to the administration of projects, a successful frugal digital transformation may be achieved.

2.1 Principle 1: The 80/20 Rule in Technology Adoption

The Pareto Principle, sometimes known as the 80/20 rule, is the fundamental principle that underpins thrifty internet management. The theory, which was initially noticed by Vilfredo Pareto and later popularized in the business world by Joseph Juran, proposes that a small minority of causes are responsible for a vast majority of consequences (about 80%) (Koch, 2008). About the field of technology, this indicates that a sizeable amount of the value that is derived from a software platform is frequently taken from a limited subset of the platform's fundamental characteristics.

According to the conventional method, a small or medium-sized enterprise (SME) can be enticed to buy a complete software package that includes everything since it claims to tackle every imaginable problem. The consequence of this is that users frequently must pay a large membership fee for hundreds of functions, of which they only make use of a small number. This is a misapplication of technology.

Thrifty Approach: The thrifty small and medium-sized enterprise (SME) begins by determining 20% of an issue that is responsible for 80% of the suffering. By way of illustration, rather of looking for a major customer relationship management system to completely revamp the entire sales process, they can determine that manually tracking follow-ups is the most significant bottleneck. Afterwards, they look for a straightforward and inexpensive application that is good at automating reminders and keeping track of conversations. In the first place, they fix the fundamental issue, which allows them to achieve a substantial effect for a fraction of the expense. To prioritize the "must-have" functionality, they made a conscious decision to disregard the "nice-to-have" aspects.

2.2 Principle 2: The Primacy of SaaS and Cloud Computing

Cloud computing and the Software-as-a-Service (SaaS) model are arguably the greatest enablers of frugal digital transformation. They fundamentally shift the economic model of technology from high upfront capital expenditure (CapEx) to low, predictable operational expenditure (OpEx), a move seen as highly strategic for agile businesses (Armbrust et al., 2010).

CapEx Model (Traditional): Buying software licenses outright, purchasing and maintaining on-premises servers, and hiring IT staff to manage the infrastructure. This model is capital-intensive, inflexible, and carries a high risk of obsolescence.

OpEx Model (Frugal/Cloud): Subscribing to software on a monthly or annual basis. The provider handles all server maintenance, security, and updates. This offers several frugal advantages:

- Low Barrier to Entry: SMEs can access enterprise-grade software for a small monthly fee, avoiding a large initial investment.
- Scalability: Plans can be scaled up or down as the business grows or needs change. You only pay for what you use.
- Reduced Overhead: Eliminates the need for physical servers and dedicated IT maintenance staff.
- Accessibility: Cloud-based tools can be accessed from anywhere with an internet connection, enabling remote work and operational flexibility.
- The frugal SME defaults to a "cloud-first" and "SaaS-first" policy for any new technology consideration.

2.3 Principle 3: The MVP (Minimum Viable Product) Mindset for Processes

The lean startup model, which was famously described by Eric Ries (2011), is where the idea of a Minimum Viable Product (MVP) was taken from. A minimum viable product (MVP) is a version of a new product that enables a team to collect the greatest amount of verified learning about consumers with the least amount of work. The application of this approach to the enhancement of internal processes may be quite beneficial.

The traditional approach involves designing a "perfect," all-encompassing digital process on paper, then spending months selecting and deploying the technology, and then applying it throughout the whole organization. If it turns out that the initial assumptions were incorrect, then the entire time and money that was invested is just squandered.

Instead of focusing on a "Minimum Viable Product," the small and medium-sized enterprise prefers to concentrate on a "Minimum Viable Process." They first identify a problem, then they come up with a basic digital solution, and last, they test it with a single person or a small team utilizing tools that are either free or very inexpensive.

An example of this would be a small or medium-sized enterprise (SME) that, rather of purchasing a full-fledged human resource management system, could construct a straightforward process by utilizing a free Google Form for submissions, a shared Google Sheet to monitor requests, and an automatic email using a program such as Zapier. This MVP process requires only a few hours of setup time, and it does not cost anything. The small and medium-sized enterprise (SME) has verified the requirement if it is successful and demonstrates its value. As the firm grows, the SME may then consider making an investment in a more robust and specialized solution.

2.4 Principle 4: Integration and Interoperability over Monolithic Systems

Large corporations often favor monolithic, all-in-one ERP systems that promise a single source of truth. For SMEs, these systems are often overkill—too complex, too rigid, and too expensive. The frugal alternative is to build a flexible "digital ecosystem" of best-in-class, specialized applications that can communicate with each other through Application Programming Interfaces (APIs) (Brynjolfsson & McAfee, 2014). The Frugal Tech Stack: An SME might use:

- QuickBooks Online for accounting.
- Shopify for e-commerce.
- Mailchimp for email marketing.
- Trello for project management.

Individually, these are affordable and excellent at their specific functions. The magic happens when they are connected. Using integration platforms like Zapier or Make (formerly Integromat), the SME can create automated workflows without writing a single line of code. For example: "When a new sale is made on Shopify (Trigger), automatically create an invoice in QuickBooks (Action 1) and add the customer to a specific Mailchimp mailing list (Action 2)."

This modular approach allows the SME to swap out tools as better or more affordable options become available, avoiding vendor lock-in and maintaining maximum flexibility.

2.5 Principle 5: Open-Source Software as a Strategic Asset

Open-source software (OSS) is software with source code that anyone can inspect, modify, and enhance. Once seen as a niche for hobbyists, OSS has become a cornerstone of modern IT infrastructure and a significant strategic asset for businesses seeking to reduce costs and increase flexibility (Fitzgerald, 2006).

Areas where OSS shines for SMEs:

Website & E-commerce: WordPress combined with the WooCommerce plugin is a powerful, endlessly customizable, and free alternative to subscription-based platforms like Shopify. The SME only pays for web hosting. Operating Systems & Office Suites: Using Linux on company computers and LibreOffice instead of Microsoft Windows and Office 365 can eliminate significant licensing fees. CRM & ERP: Systems like Odoo and ERPNext offer comprehensive, open-source business management suites that can be self-hosted, providing immense power for a fraction of the cost of their proprietary counterparts. The frugal SME does not dismiss OSS as being only for tech companies. They strategically assess where the trade-off between the "sweat equity" of implementation and the long-term cost savings makes the most sense. By internalizing these five principles—the 80/20 rule, a cloud-first policy, an MVP mindset, a focus on integration, and the strategic use of open-source software—SMEs can build a robust intellectual framework to guide their digital transformation journey. This framework ensures that every decision is filtered through the lens of value, efficiency, and resourcefulness.

3 THE FRUGAL DIGITAL TRANSFORMATION TOOLKIT: HIGH-IMPACT, LOW-COST TECHNOLOGIES

With the guiding principles established, we can now explore the specific digital tools and platforms that form the frugal SME's toolkit. This section is organized by core business function, highlighting how accessible technologies can be deployed to solve common problems, enhance efficiency, and drive growth.

3.1 Operations and Productivity: The Digital Engine Room

Efficient operations are the foundation of any successful business. Digital tools can automate repetitive tasks, improve communication, and streamline project management, freeing up valuable human time for higher-value activities.

Collaboration and Communication:

The problem is that delays and errors are caused by disjointed communication through email chains, misplaced data, and unclear ownership of what tasks are being performed.

A tiered strategy that makes use of freemium collaborative hubs will be the frugal solution.

No cost for Level 1: It is possible to concentrate team communication into channels using Slack or Microsoft Teams (free version), which would significantly reduce the amount of internal email. File-sharing platforms such as Google Drive and Dropbox are included into their functionality.

At the Level 2 (Low-Cost): When you upgrade to a subscription plan, you have access to additional services such as group video calls, unlimited message history, and other integrations.

Project and Task Management:

The issue is that there is a lack of visibility in the development of the project, missing deadlines, and workloads that are not balanced. Visual, Kanban-style project management solutions are the solution to this frugal problem. Trello provides a card-based system that is both easy to use and straightforward. The free tier is quite liberal and offers enough features for many smaller companies. By providing more powerful functionality, Asana makes it possible to manage complicated projects that involve dependencies. The free version may accommodate up to 15 people at a time. ClickUp is a formidable all-in-one rival that offers a great free plan in addition to priced premium levels that are cheap.

Document Management and Office Suite:

The problem is that there are high license prices for office software (like Microsoft Office), and there are difficulties with version control when documents are sent back and forth. A cost-effective solution is to use cloud-based office suites. Email, calendar, cloud storage (Drive), and collaboration tools (Docs, Sheets, and Slides) are all included in Google Workspace, which is offered for a cheap monthly charge according to the number of users. Versioning problems are eliminated when real-time cooperation is used. LibreOffice is a desktop alternative that is highly compatible with the file formats used by Microsoft Office. It is also free and open source.

Automation without Code:

Several manual and repetitive procedures, such as data entering across various apps, occupy a significant amount of time each week. Inexpensive solution: integration platforms that need no coding. Integration of Zapier and Make (Integromat): In other words, these are "digital glue" services. Small and medium-sized enterprises (SMEs) can construct automated workflows (also known as "Zaps" or "Scenarios") between thousands of online applications. The free tiers are ideal for automating a few specific tasks that are of crucial importance. As an illustration: "When a customer fills out a contact form on my WordPress website, create a new card in Trello and add a row to a Google Sheet."

3.2 Marketing and Customer Engagement: Reaching More for Less

Marketing is often perceived as a major cost center, but digital channels have leveled the playing field, allowing SMEs to compete with larger players on a limited budget.

Website and Online Presence:

The problem is that many have the impression that professional web creation is quite expensive.

User-friendly website builders and open-source content management systems are the frugal solutions. WP.org is the most widely used content management system (CMS) in the world. It is a free and self-hosted version of WordPress. When combined with a low-cost hosting plan and a premium theme that costs between $50 and $80 for a one-time purchase, a small or medium-sized enterprise (SME) may construct a website that is very professional and customized. Carrd: Carrd provides professional templates for as little as $19 per year for websites that are straightforward and consist of a single page (for example, sites for service businesses or landing pages).

Search Engine Optimization (SEO):

Search engine optimization (SEO) firms may be rather pricey. Budget-Friendly Solution: Concentrate on fundamental SEO by doing it yourself using free tools. Google's Keyword Planner is a tool that may be used to investigate what prospective clients are looking for. These free plugins for WordPress, known as Yoast SEO and Rank Math, are designed to assist users in improving on-page content, titles, and descriptions. For local small and medium-sized businesses (SMEs) to be visible in local search results and on Google Maps, Google Business Profile is a vital and free tool.

Content and Social Media Marketing:

The issue at hand is the expense involved in producing graphics of a professional standard and administering many social media sites. Freemium design and scheduling tools are the solution to the frugal problem. Canva: The free edition of this graphic design tool is a game-changer since it enables anybody to make social media posts, posters, and presentations that seem professional via the use of templates. Freemium services offered by Buffer and Hootsuite enable small and medium-sized enterprises (SMEs) to schedule posts across various social media platforms in a single dashboard, therefore saving a substantial amount of time.

Email Marketing and CRM:

The issue is the high cost of sophisticated customer relationship management (CRM) and marketing automation technologies. Cost-Effective Method: Get started with freemium products that are generous. MailChimp is an excellent choice for beginning a newsletter because it provides a free plan that allows for up to 500 contacts and 1,000 emails each month respectively. When it comes to managing contacts, tracking transactions, and logging sales activity, HubSpot CRM provides a CRM that is both robust and completely free of charge. This offers a tremendous amount of value and may be expanded even further as the company expands.

3.3 Sales and E-commerce: Digitizing the Transaction

For many SMEs, the most direct path to growth is through selling online. The barriers to entry for e-commerce have never been lower.

E-commerce Platform:

One of the issues is the difficulty and expense involved in constructing a bespoke internet store. Turnkey e-commerce systems are such a cost-effective solution. ify's basic plan is a cost-effective, all-in-one solution that covers everything from the storefront to payment processing and shipping integration. Although it is not free, Shopify's basic plan is an impressively comprehensive solution. It is the most convenient option for users. One of the most widely used open-source e-commerce solutions is called WooCommerce, which is a WordPress plugin. The installation process is completely free, and it provides an unprecedented level of freedom; nevertheless, it demands more hands-on supervision of hosting and security.

Payment Processing:

The Problem: The difficulty of setting up traditional merchant accounts. Frugal Solution: Modern, integrated payment gateways. Stripe / PayPal: These services are easy to integrate into any website or e-commerce platform. They charge a simple, transparent percentage-plus-flat-fee per transaction, with no monthly fees, making the cost directly proportional to sales.

Customer Support:

The Problem: A dedicated support agent is a significant cost. Frugal Solution: Implement self-service options and consolidated communication channels. FAQ Page: A well-written Frequently Asked Questions page can deflect a large percentage of common inquiries. Tawk.to: A free live chat widget that can be easily added to a website, allowing SMEs to provide real-time support to customers.

3.4 Finance and Administration: Streamlining the Back Office

While back-office operations are necessary, they do not contribute to income generation. The objective of thrifty digital transformation in this context is to achieve maximal automation and precision at the lowest possible cost. The Accounting Process and Billing: What's the Issue: Keeping books manually, which takes a lot of time and involves utilizing spreadsheets, is prone to mistakes. Cloud-based accounting software is a cost-effective solution. What is Xero and QuickBooks Online? A nominal monthly membership cost is required to use these systems, which automate tasks such as reconciling bank feeds, invoicing, tracking expenses, and producing financial reports. Because of the time that is saved and the precision that is obtained, the return on investment is quite high. Wave is a fantastic starting point for service-based enterprises and freelancers because it provides free software for accounting, invoicing, and scanning receipts.

Human Resources (HR):

The issue pertains to the manual management of payroll, leave, and employee onboarding activities. HR platforms that are integrated and low-cost are the frugal solution. When it comes to payroll, benefits, and basic human resources, Gusto offers a platform that is both user-friendly and economical. Additionally, it automates tax filings and compliance. In addition to being a component of the larger Zoho ecosystem, Zoho People offer a free plan that allows for up to five users and includes features such as personnel database administration and leave monitoring. A small or medium-sized enterprise (SME) may construct a digital infrastructure that is robust, integrated, and cost-effective by making deliberate selections from this toolkit. The most important thing is to begin on a small scale, concentrating on the tools that provide solutions to the most major pain points first, and then gradually growing the ecosystem as the company expands and its requirements change.

4 THE STRATEGIC IMPLEMENTATION ROADMAP: A PHASED FRUGAL APPROACH

Adopting technology is one thing; successfully integrating it into the fabric of the business is another. A haphazard approach, even with frugal tools, leads to wasted effort and low adoption. A structured, phased roadmap, similar in spirit to the Plan-Do-Check-Act cycle of continuous improvement (Deming, 1986), is critical. This roadmap is a cycle, not a linear path, emphasizing continuous improvement.

Phase 1: Assess and Strategize (The "Why" and "What")

This foundational phase is about introspection and planning, not purchasing. Skipping this step is the most common reason for failure.

Step 1: Identify the Core Pain Points. Forget about technology for a moment. Gather your team and ask fundamental questions:

- What is the most repetitive, time-consuming task we do every week?
- Where do our customers experience the most friction when dealing with us?
- What information do we wish we had but can't easily access?
- What process is most prone to human error?
- Why did we lose our last three potential customers? The goal is to generate a list of real business problems, not a Wishlist of technologies.

Step 2: Map Existing Processes. Before you can improve a process, you must understand it. Create simple flowcharts for the key workflows identified in Step 1. How does sales lead become a customer? How is an invoice generated and paid? This visual map will reveal bottlenecks and opportunities for digital intervention.

Step 3: Define "SMART" Frugal Goals. For each pain point, define a specific, measurable, achievable, relevant, and time-bound (SMART) goal. The framework is widely attributed to George T. Doran's work on effective management objectives (Doran, 1981). The frugal constraint is crucial here.

- *Bad Goal:* "Improve marketing."
- *Good, Frugal Goal:* "Increase qualified leads from our website by 15% within three months without increasing our marketing ad spending." This goal forces a focus on low-cost solutions like SEO or improving the website's contact form, rather than just buying more ads.

Step 4: Audit Existing Technology. SMEs often have more digital assets than they realize. Are you using all the features of your Google Workspace subscription? Could a simple spreadsheet macro automate a reporting task? Leveraging what you already have is the essence of frugality.

Phase 2: Prioritize and Pilot (The "Low-Hanging Fruit")

With a clear understanding of the problems and goals, the next phase is about making strategic choices and testing them on a small scale.

Step 1: The Impact/Effort Matrix. Plot the identified problems on a simple 2x2 matrix. The y-axis is "Business Impact" (High/Low) and the x-axis is "Implementation Effort/Cost" (Low/High). This common strategic tool helps visualize priorities effectively.

- High Impact, Low Effort (Top-Left Quadrant): These are your "Quick Wins" or "low-hanging fruit." This is where you must start. Examples might include setting up a free CRM to track leads or using a scheduling tool to reduce back-and-forth emails.
- High Impact, High Effort (Top-Right): These are major strategic projects. Tackle these later, after you've built momentum.
- Low Impact, Low Effort (Bottom-Left): Do these if you have spare time, but don't prioritize them.
- Low Impact, High Effort (Bottom-Right): Avoid these entirely.

Step 2: Research Frugal Solutions. Focusing only on the Quick Wins, research potential tools. Use the toolkit from Section 3 as a starting point. Look for platforms with free trials or generous freemium tiers. Read reviews on sites like Capterra or G2, paying close attention to comments from other small businesses.

Step 3: Run a Minimum Viable Pilot. Do not roll out a new tool for the entire company. Select one or two tech-savvy and open-minded employees to run a small-scale pilot project for a defined period (e.g., two weeks), embodying the iterative principles of the lean startup (Ries, 2011).

Example: To test a new project management tool, create a pilot project with a single client. Use the tool exclusively for that project. This contains risk and provides a real-world test.

Step 4: Gather Feedback. At the end of the pilot, gather honest feedback from the participants. Was the tool intuitive? Did it solve the problem? Did it create new problems? This feedback is invaluable for making a final adoption decision.

Phase 3: Adopt and Scale (The "How")

Once a pilot has proven successful, it's time to roll out the solution more broadly. This phase is all about managing change and ensuring user adoption.

Step 1: Develop Simple Standard Operating Procedures (SOPs). Create a short, simple document or video (using a free tool like Loom) that explains how to use the new tool for the specific process it's intended for. Don't just point employees to the tool's generic help section. Show them *your* company's way of using it.

Step 2: Champion-Led Training. The employees from the successful pilot are now your champions. Ask them to lead a short training session for their colleagues. Peer-to-peer learning is often more effective and relatable than a top-down mandate from management.

Step 3: Focus on the "WIIFM" (What's In It For Me?). When introducing the new tool, focus on how it will make employees' jobs easier, not just how it will benefit the company. This is a core principle of effective change management (Kotter, 1996). Frame it to eliminate tedious tasks, reduce errors, or make collaboration smoother.

Step 4: Integrate and automate. As the tool becomes part of the daily workflow, look for opportunities to connect it to other systems using integration tools like Zapier. This is where you multiply the efficiency gains. For example, once the team has adopted a new form builder, automate the process so that form submissions create tasks in your project management tool.

Phase 4: Measure and Iterate (The "What's Next?")

Digital transformation is not a one-time project. This final phase closes the loop and sets the stage for the next cycle of improvement.

Step 1: Revisit Your SMART Goals. Go back to the goals you defined in Phase 1. Did you achieve them? Use the analytics provided by the new tool or track metrics manually to measure the outcome. Did you reduce invoice processing time by 20%? Did qualified leads increase by 15%?

Step 2: Quantify the ROI. The return on investment (ROI) for frugal solutions is often immense. Calculate it, even if it's a simple "back-of-the-napkin" calculation. Example: "This $20/month scheduling tool saves each of our three consultants two hours a month. At a billable rate of $100/hour, that's $600 in recovered time for a $20 cost—a 30x ROI." Celebrating these wins reinforces the value of the frugal approach.

Step 3: Solicit Ongoing Feedback. Create a simple channel (e.g., a dedicated Slack channel or a Google Form) for employees to suggest further improvements or flag issues. This fosters a culture of continuous improvement, a key trait of a "learning organization" (Senge, 1990).

Step 4: Return to Phase 1. With the first Quick Win successfully implemented, return to your Impact/Effort matrix and select the next priority. The business is now more efficient, the team is more confident with digital tools, and you have momentum to tackle the next challenge.

This iterative, four-phase cycle de-risks digital transformation builds momentum through small wins & ensures that every technological investment is tied directly to a tangible business outcome.

5 CULTIVATING A FRUGAL INNOVATION CULTURE: THE HUMAN ELEMENT

Technology is merely an enabler. A successful and sustainable digital transformation, especially a frugal one, is fundamentally dependent on the people within the organization. The most brilliant toolkit and roadmap will fail if the company culture resists change, fears experimentation, or lacks digital literacy. Cultivating a frugal innovative culture is not a separate step but an ongoing process that underpins the entire transformation journey.

5.1 Leadership as the Frugal Champion

Change must start at the top. The SME owner or leadership team must not only approve the frugal strategy but actively embody and champion it. As John P. Kotter (1996) argued, a powerful guiding coalition is essential for any successful change initiative.

Leading by Example: If leadership insists on using a simple tool like Google Sheets for a report instead of demanding a complex dashboard, it sends a powerful message. When a leader openly discusses a failed pilot project as a valuable learning experience rather than a mistake, it creates psychological safety for others to experiment.

Empowerment over Micromanagement: A frugal culture thrives on employee ingenuity. Leaders must empower their teams to identify problems and propose solutions. This requires establishing a high degree of psychological safety, where employees feel safe to take interpersonal risks like suggesting a new idea (Edmondson, 2018). A manager says, "I've heard great things about Asana for task management. Can you take two days to see if it could solve our deadline issue and report back?" is fostering a frugal culture. One who dictates a solution without consultation is stifling it.

Celebrating Resourcefulness: Publicly recognize and reward employees who find clever, low-cost ways to solve problems. This could be as simple as a shout-out in a team meeting for an employee who automated a report or a small bonus for a team that saved money by switching to an open-source alternative. This reinforces the idea that resourcefulness is a highly valued trait.

5.2 Fostering Digital Literacy and a "Tinkerer's" Mindset

For many employees in non-tech roles, new software can be intimidating. Overcoming this requires a deliberate effort to build confidence and curiosity.

Investing in "Just-in-Time" Learning: Instead of expensive, generic training courses, encourage the use of free, high-quality online resources. Platforms like YouTube, supplier-provided tutorials, and blogs are treasured troves of practical, task-specific knowledge. The goal is to teach employees *how to find answers* and build the personal mastery described by Senge (1990).

Creating a "Sandbox": Set up a safe, non-critical environment where employees can "play" with new tools without the fear of breaking a live system. This could be a dummy account in a new CRM or a test project in a management tool. This encourages exploration and learning by doing.

Promoting the "Tinkerer's" Mindset: A tinkerer is someone who isn't afraid to try things, connect A to B, and see what happens. Encourage employees to spend a small amount of their time (e.g., an hour every Friday) exploring the features of the tools they already use or trying out a new app that might improve their workflow. This is the R&D department of a frugal company.

5.3 Breaking Down Silos for Cross-Functional Innovation

In many SMEs, departments operate in silos. The marketing team uses their tools, and the operations team uses theirs, with little interaction. Frugal digital transformation thrives on breaking down these walls and encouraging systems thinking (Senge, 1990).

The Power of Integration: As discussed in the toolkit, the greatest efficiencies are often found at the intersection of different functions. When the sales, marketing, and service teams all have access to a shared, free CRM, they gain a 360-degree view of the customer. This can only happen if they collaborate on the selection and implementation of the tool.

Problem-Solving "Sprints": Gather a small, cross-functional team (e.g., one person from sales, one from operations, one from finance) to focus on solving a single, specific problem in a short timeframe (a "sprint"). Their diverse perspectives will often lead to more creative and holistic solutions than if a single department tackled it alone. For example, in solving the problem of slow invoices, the sales perspective (when to trigger the invoice) is as important as the finance perspective (what information is needed).

5.4 Embracing "Good Enough" and Overcoming Perfectionism

Perfectionism is the enemy of frugal innovation. The pursuit of a flawless, all-encompassing solution leads to "analysis paralysis" and prevents action.

The MVP Culture: The Minimum Viable Product/Process mindset must be a cultural norm. The team needs to be comfortable with launching an internal solution that is 80% perfect and iterating based on feedback. The mantra should be "progress over perfection."

Celebrating Speed and Learning: The success of a project should be measured not just by the outcome but by the speed of learning. A pilot that quickly proves a tool is *not* a good fit is a huge success—it has saved the company time and money that would have been wasted on a full-scale implementation. This reframing of "failure" as "validated learning" is a core tenet of the lean startup approach (Ries, 2011).

By focusing on these human elements—leadership, employee skills, collaboration, and mindset—an SME can create fertile ground for frugal digital tools to take root and flourish. This cultural foundation transforms digital adoption from a series of disjointed projects into a sustainable, self-reinforcing engine of continuous improvement.

6 CASE STUDIES: FRUGAL DIGITAL TRANSFORMATION IN ACTION

To illustrate how these principles and tools come together in the real world, let's examine three hypotheticals but realistic case studies of SMEs from different sectors. (These case studies are illustrative and do not require formal citations).

Case Study 1: "Artisan Bakes," a Local Bakery

Business: A small bakery with one retail location, known for its high-quality bread and pastries. It also has a growing side business catering for local offices.

Pain Points: The owner spends hours each week managing catering orders from a notebook. They have no way to communicate with repeat customers, and invoicing is manual and slow.

The Frugal Transformation Strategy: They create an online catering order form using Jotform (free plan) embedded on a simple website from Carrd ($19/year). Using Zapier (free plan), form submissions populate a Google Sheet and create a task in Trello. They build a customer email list with Mailchimp (free plan) and handle invoicing with Wave (free).

The Outcome: The owner saves 6-8 hours weekly, order errors are reduced, and a loyal customer base is cultivated through email marketing. Total Monthly Software Cost: ~$2.

Case Study 2: "ConstructRight," a Small Construction Contractor

Business: A team of 10 specializing in residential renovations.

Pain Points: Inefficient on-site to office communication, chaotic project tracking, and a manual, time-consuming payroll process.

The Frugal Transformation Strategy: They adopt Asana (free plan) for project management, using the mobile app for on-site photo updates. A shared Google Drive folder centralizes documents. They send clients short video updates using Loom (free plan). Payroll is completely automated with a subscription to Gusto.

The Outcome: Communication-related delays are cut by 30%, client satisfaction soars, and payroll administration time is reduced by over 90%. Total Monthly Software Cost: ~$50-$60.

Case Study 3: "Innovate Legal," a Boutique Law Firm

Business: A 3-person law firm specializing in intellectual property for startups.

The Pain Points: Slow, manual client onboarding, inefficient meeting scheduling via email, and no systematic lead tracking.

The Frugal Transformation Strategy: They use Calendly (free plan) to eliminate scheduling friction. HubSpot's Free CRM is implemented for lead tracking. Client intake is handled by Google Forms, and engagement letters are sent via a basic DocuSign plan for e-signatures. A Zapier automation connects Calendly bookings to HubSpot.

The Outcome: Client onboarding time is cut from one week to 48 hours, lawyers save hours each week on admin tasks, and lead conversion increases by 20% due to systematic follow-up. Total Monthly Software Cost: ~$15-$25.

These case studies demonstrate that frugal digital transformation is not about buying complex software, but about creatively applying simple, affordable tools to solve specific, high-value business problems.

7 CHALLENGES AND PITFALLS OF THE FRUGAL APPROACH

The strategy of being thrifty is powerful; nonetheless, it is not without its difficulties and the possibility of falling into traps. Recognizing and taking preventative measures to manage these risks is essential for achieving success over the long run. Being thrifty should not be synonymous with being reckless.

7.1 The "Cheap" vs. "Frugal" Trap: Ignoring Total Cost of Ownership (TCO)

Getting real frugality confused with short-sighted cheapness is the major risk that may be identified. When there are additional expenses associated with a free tool, it is not necessarily the most cost-effective choice.

Ward Cunningham (1992) was the first person to propose the notion of technical debt, which argues that selecting a solution that is simple but limited might result in the requirement of more expensive reworking in the future time. There is a possibility that a free tool might address an immediate problem; but, when the company outgrows the tool, the cost of moving the data and retraining the workforce can be significantly more than the cost of paying for a solution that is more scalable from the beginning.

Unreported Time Expenses: It is possible to buy open-source software at no cost; nevertheless, it may need a substantial amount of effort and technical ability to install, configure, provide maintenance, and ensure its security. An honest evaluation of whether the time spent may be better spent on core company operations is required of a small or medium-sized enterprise (SME). Paying for the convenience of software as a service (SaaS) solution is always the more cost-effective option.

The Total Cost of Ownership (TCO) Equation: an economic decision considers the Total Cost of Ownership, which encompasses not only the expenses of purchasing but also the costs of implementation, training, maintenance, and the possibility of migration costs in the future.

7.2 Security and Data Privacy Risks

Using a patchwork of free or low-cost cloud services requires a vigilant approach to security, a major concern for SMEs who are increasingly targeted by cyberattacks (ENISA, 2021).

Vetting Providers: It's crucial to use reputable providers who are transparent about their security practices (e.g., SOC 2 compliance) and data privacy policies.

Password Management: With more tools comes a greater number of accounts. Implementing a mandatory password manager and enabling two-factor authentication (2FA) wherever possible is non-negotiable.

Data Governance: SMEs must be aware of where their data is being stored and who has access to it, especially to comply with regulations like the General Data Protection Regulation (GDPR).

7.3 The Problem of "App Sprawl"

The ease of adopting new SaaS tools can lead to "app sprawl" or "SaaS sprawl"a chaotic and disconnected collection of applications that can hinder rather than help productivity (Gartner, 2020).

Fragmented Data: When different departments use different, unintegrated tools, it creates data silos, making a holistic view of the business impossible.

Subscription Creep: Many small monthly subscriptions can add up to a significant expense. A regular audit of all software subscriptions is necessary to cancel unused services.

Loss of a Common "Digital Workplace": When employees must jump between a dozen different apps, it can lead to confusion. A strategy to centralize notifications and work in a primary hub (like Slack or Teams) becomes critical.

7.4 Scalability and Integration Challenges

A tool that is perfect for a 3-person team may be completely inadequate for a 15-person team.

Thinking One Step Ahead: When selecting a tool, even a free one, it's wise to look at its paid tiers and upgrade path. How easy is it to export your data if you need to leave?

The Limits of No-Code: While no-code automation tools like Zapier are incredibly powerful, they have their limits. On a certain scale, a more robust, custom-coded integration or a more unified software suite may become necessary. The frugal SME must recognize when they have reached the limits of their initial toolkit and be prepared to invest in the next level of technology.

By being aware of these pitfalls, SMEs can navigate their frugal digital transformation with greater wisdom, ensuring that their resourceful approach builds lasting value rather than future problems.

8 THE FUTURE TRAJECTORY: FRUGALITY AS A SUSTAINABLE COMPETITIVE ADVANTAGE

The fundamentals of frugal digital management are not only a means of coping for small and medium-sized enterprises (SMEs) that are limited in their resources; rather, they are the basis for constructing an organization that is robust, flexible, and future-proof. The mentality and abilities that are created throughout a frugal transformation, such as resourcefulness, iterative problem-solving, and a relentless emphasis on value, become a deeply established competitive advantage.

8.1 Preparing for the Next Wave: AI and Low-Code

The next frontier of digital technology, particularly Artificial Intelligence (AI) and No-Code/Low-Code platforms, is perfectly aligned with the frugal ethos.

Frugal AI: SMEs can benefit from the democratization of AI, which is now being embedded directly into affordable SaaS tools (Iansiti & Lakhani, 2020). From AI-powered suggestions in email marketing to automated expense categorization in accounting software, these features augment team capabilities without requiring specialized hires.

The Rise of the Citizen Developer: No-Code/Low-Code platforms empower non-technical employees to build custom applications and internal tools. This trend, identified by technology analysts as a major shift in software development (Gartner, 2021), allows SMEs to create perfectly tailored solutions for their unique workflows without the cost of hiring developers.

8.2 Sustainability and the Frugal Mindset

There is a natural and profound intersection between the concepts of "doing more with less" and the ideals of environmental and financial sustainability. Waste Reduction: A digital strategy that is frugal helps to decrease waste in all its varied forms. According to Masanet et al. (2013), cloud computing is significantly more energy-efficient than the maintenance of servers located on on-premises locations. By digitizing workflows and automating processes, we can minimize the amount of time that is wasted by humans and the number of physical resources that are used. Adaptability as a means of resilience: The digital infrastructures of small and medium-sized enterprises (SMEs) that are flexible and modular are intrinsically more robust. The agility that was generated by a cloud-based strategy that was inexpensive was directly responsible for their capacity to pivot fast, which was exhibited during the COVID-19 pandemic.

8.3 Conclusion: Frugality is Strategy

It is the core thesis of this chapter that the limits that appear to be a disadvantage for small and medium-sized enterprises are their greatest strategic asset in the digital era. This is the argument that is presented in this chapter. Inability to lavishly spend money on technology compels smaller businesses to exercise discipline and concentration, which larger businesses frequently lack. SMEs are compelled to ask the appropriate questions, to prioritize with a merciless approach, and to emphasize the pursuit of value above all else. When viewed through the lens of economic management, digital transformation is not a lesser, compromised version of the "real thing." This route is one that is more intelligent, more robust, and more sustainable. It is about combining the ageless knowledge of resourcefulness with the power of modern technology to make it more accessible to more people. The attention is shifted from the tools themselves to the issues that they answer because of this.

It is possible for leaders of small and medium-sized enterprises (SMEs) to remove the mystery around digital transformation by adopting the ideas of the 80/20 rule, cloud-native solutions, an MVP attitude, and a culture of empowered experimentation. Rather than being a cause of concern, they can transform it into a path of improvement that is ongoing, controllable, and thrilling. By doing so, they will not only improve their performance and ensure their future, but they will also demonstrate that in the digital economy, the most effective inventions frequently originate not from those with the largest finances, but rather from those with the most inventive brains.

REFERENCES

Armbrust, M., Fox, A., Griffith, R., Joseph, A. D., Katz, R., Konwinski, A., Lee, G., Patterson, D., Rabkin, A., Stoica, I., & Zaharia, M. (2010). A view of cloud computing. *Communications of the ACM*, *53*(4), 50–58. DOI: 10.1145/1721654.1721672

Bound, K., & Thornton, I. (2012). *Our Frugal Future: Lessons from India's Innovation System*. Nesta.

Brynjolfsson, E., & McAfee, A. (2014). *The Second Machine Age: Work, Progress, and Prosperity in a Time of Brilliant Technologies*. W. W. Norton & Company.

Cunningham, W. (1992). *The WyCash portfolio management system. Addendum to the proceedings of the OOPSLA '92 conference on Object-oriented programming systems, languages, and applications*. ACM.

Deming, W. E. (1986). *Out of the Crisis*. MIT Press.

Doran, G. T. (1981). There's a S.M.A.R.T. way to write management's goals and objectives. *Management Review*, *70*(11), 35–36.

Edmondson, A. C. (2018). *The Fearless Organization: Creating Psychological Safety in the Workplace for Learning, Innovation, and Growth*. John Wiley & Sons.

ENISA (European Union Agency for Cybersecurity). (2021). *ENISA Threat Landscape for SMEs*. ENISA Publications.

Fitzgerald, B. (2006). The transformation of open-source software. *Management Information Systems Quarterly*, *30*(3), 587–598. DOI: 10.2307/25148740

Gartner, Inc. (2020). *Managing SaaS Costs and Risks in the Age of App Sprawl*. Gartner Research.

Gartner, Inc. (2021). *Gartner Forecasts Worldwide Low-Code Development Technologies Market to Grow 23% in 2021*. Gartner Press Release.

Iansiti, M., & Lakhani, K. R. (2020). *Competing in the Age of AI: Strategy and Leadership When Algorithms and Networks Run the World*. Harvard Business Review Press.

Koch, R. (2008). *The 80/20 Principle: The Secret to Achieving More with Less*. Crown Business.

Kotter, J. P. (1996). *Leading Change*. Harvard Business School Press.

Masanet, E., Shehabi, A., Ramakrishnan, L., Liang, J., Ma, X., Walker, B., & Mantha, P. (2013). *The Energy Efficiency Potential of Cloud-Based Software: A U.S. Case Study*. Lawrence Berkeley National Laboratory. DOI: 10.2172/1171159

Radjou, N., & Prabhu, J. (2015). *Frugal Innovation: How to Do More with Less*. PublicAffairs.

Ries, E. (2011). *The Lean Startup: How Today's Entrepreneurs Use Continuous Innovation to Create Radically Successful Businesses*. Crown Business.

Rogers, D. L. (2016). *The Digital Transformation Playbook: Rethink Your Business for the Digital Age*. Columbia Business School Publishing. DOI: 10.7312/roge17544

. Senge, P. M. (1990). *The Fifth Discipline: The Art & Practice of The Learning Organization*. Doubleday/Currency.

Westerman, G., Bonnet, D., & McAfee, A. (2014). *Leading Digital: Turning Technology into Business Transformation*. Harvard Business Review Press.

World Bank. (2021). *Small and Medium Enterprises (SMEs) Finance*. Retrieved from https://www.worldbank.org/en/topic/smefinance

Chapter 2
Dynamic Capabilities for SMEs in Volatile Environments:
The Role of ISO 9001:2026 in Supply Chain Transformation

Omar A. Guirette-Barbosa
http://orcid.org/0000-0003-1336-9475
Universidad Politécnica de Zacatecas, Mexico & Broward International University, Mexico

Selene Castañeda-Burciaga
http://orcid.org/0000-0002-2436-308X
Universidad Politécnica de Zacatecas, Mexico & Broward International University, Mexico

ABSTRACT

The ISO 9001:2026 standard represents a critical evolution in quality management systems, particularly relevant for SMEs operating in volatile environments. This chapter examines, from a strategic and multidimensional approach, how the new version of the standard enhances dynamic capacity by redefining quality beyond compliance, and by integrating tools such as artificial intelligence (AI), blockchain, and the Internet of Things (IoT) to optimize processes, anticipate risks, and create value. Through conceptual, technical, and practical analysis of real-world cases and literature review, the chapter highlights the benefits of ISO 9001:2026 implementation for SMEs seeking to strengthen resilience, agility, and competitiveness in increasingly interconnected and demanding supply chains. Furthermore, common barriers to adoption are identified, and strategies for overcoming them are proposed,

DOI: 10.4018/979-8-3373-6053-9.ch002

emphasizing cultural, technological, and human transformation. Ultimately, ISO 9001:2026 will not only improve business performance but also act as a catalyst for SMEs to build ethical, sustainable, and intelligent business ecosystems, boosting their dynamic capacity to thrive under volatility.

1. INTRODUCTION

In the evolution of business thinking, quality has ceased to be viewed as a simple verification of technical specifications (compliance with requirements) to become a fundamental piece of business strategy. From the early days of the Industrial Revolution, where standardization and efficiency prevailed, to the complex global environments of today, the concept of quality has evolved to respond to increasingly dynamic markets and consumers with higher demands, directly influencing the ability of organizations to satisfy and even anticipate their needs.

The first approaches, strictly focused on productivity (mass production), were promoted by pioneers like Frederick Taylor, whose models, although revolutionary for their time, treated work as a sum of disconnected parts. Over time, the need for a more integrated view of the production system arose, which led to initiatives such as Statistical Process Control (SPC), led by Walter A. Shewhart, and the Total Quality Management (TQM) approach by W. Edwards Deming and Joseph Juran. These work structures established that quality should permeate every corner of the organization, promoting employee involvement, continuous improvement (Kaizen), customer focus, and the use of data as a basis for decision-making. The implementation of the TQM approach allowed for the unification of processes and the standardization of criteria across the entire company, including the supply chain, which consolidated a culture focused on continuous improvement.

Similarly, continuing along the evolutionary thread, methodologies such as the Toyota Production System, with its principles of "zero defects" and "Just-in-Time" (JIT), as well as the American Six Sigma strategy, marked a milestone by focusing on efficiency and variability reduction, setting new standards for organizational quality.

In today's market, where supply chains span from the initial supplier to post-sale service (even including returns), effective management becomes key to creating value, reducing costs, satisfying customers, and maintaining competitiveness, even permanence. To this end, the upcoming update of the ISO 9001 standard, scheduled for 2026, takes on strategic importance. This version is expected to reinforce the fundamental principles of quality management and expand its focus toward sustainability (across its 3 pillars), digital transformation (AI), and a deeper integration with the supply chain. This chapter offers an approach to how the next revision of the ISO

9001 standard will transform standards of excellence and strengthen the operational capacity of companies in a challenging and constantly changing environment.

Recent studies reinforce this urgency. For example, the International Organization for Standardization reported that over one million companies are currently ISO 9001 certified, yet adoption rates for digital quality tools remain below 30% (ISO, 2023). Research highlights that ISO 9001:2015 struggles to address sustainability metrics and digital supply chain risks (Gabriel et al., 2021; Hekneby & Olsen, 2024).

This creates a research gap: the lack of frameworks connecting ISO 9001 with emerging technologies such as AI, Blockchain, and IoT, and their role in fostering resilience and sustainability. If this gap is not addressed, organizations risk inefficiencies, rising costs, and reduced competitiveness in global markets (Echeverría, 2024). By explicitly linking these trends with the forthcoming 2026 revision, the introduction positions this study as both urgent and necessary within the scholarly conversation.

2. PROBLEM STATEMENT

The rapid transformation of global supply chains, driven by digitalization, sustainability pressures, and unexpected disruptions (pandemics, geopolitical instability, climate change), exposes limitations in the current ISO 9001:2015 framework. While the 2015 revision introduced risk-based thinking and a stronger integration of stakeholder context, it does not adequately address the scale and urgency of today's challenges.

Sustainability Integration: ISO 9001:2015 lacks explicit requirements to embed environmental and social sustainability across the supply chain lifecycle (Gabriel et al., 2021).

Technological Gaps: The standard does not fully incorporate advanced tools such as AI, Blockchain, and IoT, which are increasingly critical for quality control, traceability, and predictive risk management (Shovon et al., 2024).

Resilience Deficit: Organizations certified under ISO 9001:2015 often report difficulties in maintaining operational continuity during disruptions, revealing a lack of robust resilience metrics. A useful measure would be the "total recovery time," encompassing restoration of critical functions such as production, deliveries, and financial operations (Barasa et al., 2018).

Collaboration Barriers: The success of digital models depends on data sharing, yet reluctance persists due to security, competition, or privacy concerns (Lee et al., 2025).

Exposure to Emerging Risks: Digitalization has increased exposure to cyberattacks, geopolitical conflicts, and natural disasters (Ibiyemi & Olutimehin, 2024).

Global Competitiveness: Emerging economies adopting ISO 9001 face added challenges aligning certification with digital transformation and sustainability, potentially widening the gap with advanced economies (Hekneby & Olsen, 2024).

Problem Definition. This situation underscores the research problem: How can ISO 9001:2026 evolve into a framework that not only ensures compliance with quality requirements but also enables organizations to build sustainable, resilient, and technologically integrated supply chains? Addressing this gap is crucial for both scholarly discourse and practical implementation, as failure to do so risks inefficiencies, reputational losses, and competitive disadvantages globally.

3. PURPOSE / IMPORTANCE OF THE STUDY

Purpose Statement. The purpose of this study is to analyze and anticipate how ISO 9001:2026 can redefine quality management systems by addressing the shortcomings of the 2015 version and aligning them with the contemporary realities of global supply chains. This is designed as a conceptual and applied qualitative study, oriented toward reviewing recent literature, analyzing case examples, and synthesizing best practices. The population of interest includes organizations across global supply chains, with emphasis on manufacturing and logistics sectors where ISO 9001 certification is most prevalent. The variables of interest are sustainability integration, digital transformation, and resilience, examined in relation to organizational performance.

Intended Outcomes. The study aims to contribute to both theory and practice by clarifying how ISO 9001:2026 can:

- Enable firms to embed sustainability in processes and decision making.
- Leverage advanced technologies (AI, Blockchain, IoT) for improved traceability, predictive quality, and risk anticipation.
- Enhance resilience metrics that support business continuity in volatile environments.

• Importance of the Study.

Scholarly Relevance: Contributes to academic discourse by filling the gap between ISO 9001's current provisions and the demands of Industry 4.0 and sustainability-driven supply chains. The study provides evidence-based insights that connect quality management with emergent technologies and risk management strategies.

Practical Value: Offers organizations guidance on preparing for the upcoming ISO 9001:2026 revision, ensuring they are not only compliant but also strategically positioned to thrive in volatile, uncertain, complex, and ambiguous (VUCA) environments.

Societal Impact: Underlines the broader implications of supply chain resilience and sustainability for economic stability, environmental protection, and social responsibility. This makes the research not only operationally significant but also socially urgent.

Supporting Evidence. ISO 9001:2026 will not only improve business performance but will act as a catalyst for building ethical, sustainable, and intelligent business ecosystems, especially in emerging contexts seeking global competitiveness. The global adoption of ISO 9001 has proven to bring real and tangible value to organizations, enabling them to differentiate themselves and earn trust among their stakeholders. The most notable benefits of certification include (Guirette-Barbosa et al., 2025):

Strengthened corporate image: Compliance with the standard translates into a solid reputation based on reliability.
Customer loyalty: Consistent quality and enhanced customer experience create long-term relationships.
Effective communication: Improved information flows both internally and externally.
Employee satisfaction: Clarity in processes and active participation in continuous improvement.
Productivity and operational efficiency: Optimization of resources and elimination of unnecessary activities.
Financial benefits: Reduced costs, increased revenues, and access to new markets.

These benefits should not be viewed in isolation but as components of broad sustainability encompassing environmental, financial, reputational, and human dimensions. The inclusion of ESG (environmental, social, and governance) criteria in ISO 9001:2026 will make these contributions clearer. ISO 9001:2026 will be a powerful tool in this process, as it will enable emerging economies to consolidate international standards without compromising their identity and provide them with the necessary foundations to compete with integrity in global markets.

4. NATURE OF THE STUDY / METHODOLOGY

This study adopts a qualitative and conceptual methodology supported by a systematic literature review and a case based analytical approach. The rationale for selecting this methodology is grounded in the need to integrate theoretical insights with practical applications of ISO 9001 in diverse supply chain contexts. A qualitative approach is justified because the aim is to explore concepts, frameworks, and organizational practices rather than to generate statistically generalizable findings. Quantitative or mixed-method approaches were considered but set aside, since the available evidence is more conceptual and illustrative in nature.

Research Design. Literature Review: Recent scholarship (2020–2025) on ISO 9001, quality management, and supply chain digitalization was systematically reviewed to identify emerging trends, unresolved issues, and gaps in the literature. Selection criteria included peer-reviewed status, publication within the last five years, and direct relevance to ISO 9001 or supply chain resilience. Exclusion criteria removed non-academic sources lacking methodological transparency.

Case Study Approach. The study incorporates the real-world case of JDE Peet's, a global coffee and tea company, to illustrate how organizations are adapting quality management practices to digital transformation, sustainability, and resilience demands.

Comparative Analysis. Cross-case synthesis with industry reports and ISO surveys allows for identifying patterns and divergences between theoretical propositions and practice.

Scope of Data. The data analyzed include peer-reviewed journal articles, industry white papers, ISO reports, and publicly available corporate sustainability/quality reports. These sources provide triangulation to ensure credibility and reliability of insights.

Analytical Orientation. The analysis emphasizes three interrelated dimensions: (1) sustainability integration into quality management systems, (2) digital transformation through AI, Blockchain, and IoT, and (3) resilience-building in global supply chains. Arguments were constructed by synthesizing evidence across sources, comparing conceptual insights with practical applications. Findings are interpreted through the lens of continuous improvement and stakeholder theory.

Limitations of the Methodology (to be expanded in Chapter 9). While the study provides rich conceptual synthesis and illustrative case evidence, it does not include original quantitative data collection. This limits the ability to generalize findings statistically, though it strengthens their conceptual and practical relevance.

5. THEORETICAL FRAMEWORK

The ISO 9001 standard represents the fundamental pillar internationally for quality management in organizations of all types, and it is no surprise that it is the most widely used/certified standard (Bravi & Murmura, 2021). In a global scenario marked by rapid technological advancements, increasingly personalized markets, and shorter product life cycles, the need for management systems capable of addressing this complexity in a structured and flexible manner arises (Pylypchuk et al., 2025). Process-based management thus becomes a key tool that transforms environmental challenges into competitive advantages by enabling greater operational efficiency, a reduction in variability, and a better capacity to respond to customer requirements (Ahmed & Ruth, 2024).

The pursuit of organizational excellence requires much more than techniques and procedures; it demands a culture focused on constant learning, critical reflection, and systematic improvement (Hekneby & Olsen, 2024). Organizations that adopt this philosophy are better positioned to detect internal weaknesses and seize emerging opportunities (Pirrone & Milotta, 2024). Decision-making based on reliable data and the strategic approach to operational processes allows the construction of robust management systems with a high capacity to adapt to environmental changes and a tangible economic impact (Varatharaj, 2024).

The survival of a product or service in the market increasingly depends on a company's ability to offer differentiated value (Ayub, 2022). This value comes not only from innovation but from the operational quality and efficiency that sustain this differentiation (Latan et al., 2020). For this reason, the ISO 9001 standard provides a clear framework to design, implement, and maintain systems that ensure quality and can evolve alongside the demands of the competitive environment (Quevedo et al., 2022).

In this context, the ISO 9001:2026 standard is positioned as a fundamental guide not only to establish quality standards but also to create a true system of organizational intelligence (Osho & Shiyanbola, 2024). Companies that manage to integrate this standard with analytical tools, strategic thinking, and collaborative structures will be able to not only meet current requirements but also anticipate future changes, thus consolidating their position in the global market (Chavan et al., 2024).

5.1. Continuous improvement, evolution of the iso 9001 requirements until the 2026 version

Since its foundation in 1947, the International Organization for Standardization (ISO) has established global references for standardization across multiple sectors. Among its most influential standards, ISO 9001 has become the most widely adopted standard for quality management (Chowdhary & Kumar, 2023). Since its initial release in 1987 and through successive updates (1994, 2000, 2008, and 2015), this standard has evolved to adapt to transformations in the business environment, technological advancements, and the new expectations of stakeholders (Bravi & Murmura, 2021).

The current version, ISO 9001:2015, was designed for contexts characterized by volatility, uncertainty, complexity, and ambiguity (VUCA environments) (Naveen et al., 2022). This edition introduced a high-level structure known as Annex SL, which promoted greater integration between different management systems (Stefanova-Stoyanova & Danov, 2022). Furthermore, it established the need to understand the organizational context and that of stakeholders as a foundation for defining strategic objectives (Dziedzic et al., 2023). It represented a substantial shift towards a preventive management approach, based on risk analysis rather than merely correcting past errors (Martins et al., 2021).

5.2 From Document Compliance to Proactive Management

Originally, the ISO 9000 family emerged with the goal of standardizing processes and improving quality in international organizations (Anwer, 2024). In its early editions, the focus was on document compliance, but with the 2000 revision, a radical change emerged: the adoption of the process-based management approach, which considers the organization as a system of interconnected activities (Gueorguiev, 2024). This approach was strengthened with the continuous improvement cycle PDCA (Plan, Do, Check, Act), promoting the ongoing review of processes (Stovpnyk, 2024).

The 2015 edition consolidated this model, considering globalization, digitalization, and the growth of increasingly complex supply chains. The standard shifted focus from technical compliance to strategic adaptation capability (Singh, 2020).

5.3 Advances in ISO 9001:2015 and Projections for the 2026 Revision

The most recent edition, ISO 9001:2015, introduced a conceptual shift by replacing the term "quality assurance" with "quality management," indicating a more holistic view (Simão et al., 2020). It incorporated risk management as the basis for all strategic decisions, requiring organizations to understand their environment and anticipate threats (Gabriel et al., 2021). Additionally, it expanded the focus beyond customers, also considering employees, suppliers, government, and communities as relevant stakeholders (Bravim et al., 2020).

The concept of quality then became a holistic strategic function, supported by leadership, dynamic planning, and effective communication (Özkan, 2021). This vision fosters a culture of prevention, innovation, and continuous improvement (Torcică & Georgescu, 2022).

Projections for the 2026 Version: Supply Chain and Sustainability as Pillars

It is anticipated that the next edition of the standard will have two main pillars: advanced supply chain management and a thorough integration of sustainability (Singh, 2024). The supply chain will be viewed as an interdependent system, where traceability, transparency, collaboration, and the use of technologies such as Blockchain will gain greater importance (Yekeen et al., 2024). Explicit social and environmental sustainability criteria will also be included, from the design to the final disposal of products and services (Boçe & Hoxha, 2024).

Thus, ISO 9001:2026 will not only raise operational standards but will encourage organizations to take an active role in building responsible, digital, and resilient business models (Ijiri et al., 2025).

Digital Supply Chains: The Integration of Quality, Technology, and Sustainability

The digital revolution has profoundly transformed the business landscape, enabling the emergence of models such as Industry 4.0 and the so-called Supply Chain 4.0 (Milovanović et al., 2022). These trends revolve around a new concept: Digital Supply Chains (DSC), which are based on technological integration and constant connectivity across all stages of the production process (Rimmer & Kam, 2022). This digitalization enables faster, customizable, and adaptable logistics networks, where both suppliers and consumers must have a high level of technological maturity to fully leverage their potential (Prameswari et al., 2025), (Avilés-Sacoto et al., 2021).

The success of this digital model depends on full collaboration between all the links in the chain, which is hindered by reluctance to share strategic data due to security, competition, or privacy concerns (Lee et al., 2025). However, despite these limitations, the benefits of an interconnected and real-time supply chain are undeniable, enabling organizations to overcome the limitations of conventional systems with isolated and fragmented information (Thakur, 2024).

Along the way to the end consumer, each agent in the chain (from manufacturers to distributors) generates and utilizes crucial data for logistics efficiency. The true value of DSC lies in their ability to collect, process, and act upon real-time data across the entire network, representing a qualitative leap compared to traditional models (Nagy & Szentesi, 2024).

5.4 Nature of Digital Supply Chains

DSC are dynamic and collaborative networks where multiple actors interact through the exchange of products, services, and digitized information (Thakur, 2024). These networks rely on interconnected systems that allow data to be captured at all stages of the logistical and production process, achieving seamless integration between autonomous units linked by common platforms (Mullapudi, 2025).

The key characteristics of DSC include (Barnhart, 2023), (Dey, 2022), (Abdul-Azeez et al., 2024), (Radke et al., 2021):

- Comprehensive Connectivity: Suppliers, customers, and processes are digitally linked in real-time.
- Total Visibility: Shared information enables faster and more accurate decision-making.
- Smart Data Analysis: Big data, artificial intelligence, and machine learning are used to anticipate problems and optimize resources.
- Adaptability: The system can quickly adjust to unexpected events.
- Progressive Automation: Repetitive tasks are managed by systems that learn and improve over time.
- Real-Time Collaboration: Immediate availability of information strengthens cooperation between actors.
- Customization of Offerings: The final customer's preferences are analyzed to offer tailored products.

5.5 Digitalization, The Key to Competitiveness and Sustainability

In the face of current economic challenges, digitalization is no longer an optional advantage but a necessity to survive and thrive (Owusu-Berko, 2025). The most competitive companies today invest in technologies such as digital twins to simulate their operations, generate scenarios, and optimize their performance with up-to-date data (Pal et al., 2025) (Mahankali, 2025).

Digital transformation involves rethinking traditional processes and redesigning them under a logic focused on value, efficiency, and scalability (Kotte et al., 2025). It is not just about automating what already exists but about innovating from the ground up (Egbumokei et al., 2024). This digital vision enables operation with real-time analytics platforms capable of absorbing and acting on enormous volumes of information to make faster and more accurate decisions (Singh, 2025) (Agho et al., 2025).

The main benefits include (Farazi & Zahidur, 2024), (Tiwari et al., 2024):

- Increased operational efficiency and error reduction.
- Better decisions through real-time data.
- Flexibility in changing or unpredictable environments.
- Personalized customer experience.
- Promotion of new data-driven business models.
- Full traceability in the supply chain.

Monitoring of environmental impacts, promoting social responsibility and transparency.

6. LITERATURE ANALYSIS / REVIEW

The upcoming edition of the ISO 9001 standard for 2026 will explicitly strengthen the integration of sustainability criteria into quality management systems (Stovpnyk, 2024). This approach will transform the role of the quality coordinator into a key agent of sustainable change, with a mission that goes beyond technical compliance with requirements and products, also actively promoting ethical, environmental, and social values both inside and outside the organization (Bondarenko, 2024). Therefore, sustainability will be positioned as a guiding principle of business performance (Haouat Essalih, 2025).

Although some current regulations are advancing in this direction, many still fail to fully capture the deep connections between quality, processes, and sustainability (Glogovac et al., 2020). A representative example is the section on the "organizational context," which could be enriched by incorporating elements from the Fourth Industrial Revolution, such as smart manufacturing, cyber-physical systems, the Internet of Things, Big Data, or artificial intelligence (Shovon et al., 2024). For an organization to be truly sustainable and digital, it must adopt this integration from its foundations, expanding digital and responsible logic throughout its value chain (Gitau, 2025), (Ma et al., 2022).

6.1. Fundamentals of Sustainability Applied to ISO 9001:2026

The concept of sustainable development, formalized in the Brundtland Report (1987), posits that it is possible to meet current needs without compromising the ability of future generations to meet their own needs. This implies promoting equity, reducing poverty, and improving quality of life in a systemic and balanced way (Scanlan, 2021).

To align with this paradigm, organizations must adopt a strategic and conscious approach that reconfigures their operations towards sustainable practices:

- Ethical Supplier Selection: Prioritizing those who guarantee responsible practices in social and environmental matters (Basiru et al., 2025).
- Sustainable Product and Service Design: Creating solutions that reduce negative impacts, favor efficiency, and are recyclable or reusable (Sun, J. 2024).
- Commitment to Organizational Culture: Including sustainable principles at all levels and functions within the company (Magallanes, 2020).

Various methodologies can support this integration, such as Lean Manufacturing, 5S, Six Sigma, Zero Defects, Just in Time, energy efficiency, carbon footprint calculation, and green logistics (Saygılı & Çığal, 2022). In addition, Corporate Social Responsibility (CSR) provides a holistic view of the organizational impact on the environment.

In this sense, ISO 9001:2026 will offer a coherent framework to achieve competitive organizations that are also ethical and sustainable (Rahardjo et al., 2023).

6.2. Intersection of Quality, Sustainability, and the Supply Chain

Sustainability should be conceived as a transversal principle throughout an organization, permeating every area and strategic decision. An effective way to achieve this is through the life cycle approach, which analyzes the environmental and social impact of a product from its inception to its disposal or recycling (Puglieri et al., 2024).

The ISO 9000 family of standards (quality) and ISO 14000 family (environment) already apply the continuous improvement approach through the PDCA cycle. Both require evaluating risks and impacts, considering both internal factors and external events such as climate change or global crises (Haouat & Essalih, 2025).

In the 2026 version of ISO 9001, it is expected that this convergence between quality and sustainability will be consolidated through concrete actions such as (Haouat Essalih et al., 2025), (Galkaduwa, 2024):

- Life Cycle Analysis: Comprehensive consideration of impacts from design to end of use.
- Evaluation of Responsible Suppliers: Requirement for sustainable criteria in the supply network.
- Environmental Indicators in QMS: Inclusion of metrics on energy, water, waste, etc.
- Measurement of Sustainable Resilience: Assessment of adaptability in adverse social and ecological contexts.
- Transparent Communication of Results: Clear disclosure of sustainability progress to stakeholders.

This evolution positions sustainability not as a voluntary appendix but as an essential dimension of operational excellence.

The future of organizational management demands a mindset that transcends traditional performance indicators. ISO 9001:2026 will drive this change by recognizing that quality can no longer be dissociated from the social and environmental impact each product or process generates. Companies that adopt this holistic vision, with strategies that simultaneously integrate efficiency, ethics, and ecology, will not only be more competitive but also more relevant and respected in a society that demands commitment and transparency (Figueirêdo et al., 2024).

6.3 Risk Management and Resilience in the Digital Era

In today's globalized context, risk management (ISO 31000) has become an indispensable strategic tool to ensure the stability and continuity of supply chains (Orzáez & Moreno, 2021). This approach requires a structured process that allows for the identification, classification, and prioritization of both threats and opportunities, in order to design effective mechanisms that reduce their probability of occurrence or their impact (Widianti et al., 2024).

Although digitalization has enhanced connectivity among logistics actors, it has also amplified exposure to emerging risks such as geopolitical conflicts, cyberattacks, or natural disasters (Ibiyemi & Olutimehin, 2024). Therefore, organizations must develop early monitoring capabilities, ongoing analysis, and strategic response mechanisms to make quick and informed decisions in complex scenarios (Echeverría, 2024).

The risks in the supply chain can be grouped into several key categories (Echeverría, 2024):

- Operational and capacity risks: Production interruptions, equipment failures, talent shortages, or quality issues.
- External risks: Natural disasters, pandemics, political instability, or risks associated with climate change.
- Technological and innovation risks: Cybersecurity failures, technological obsolescence, or lack of digital skills.
- Legal and regulatory risks: Non-compliance with labor, environmental, or health regulations.
- Macroeconomic risks: Financial crises, currency fluctuations, or global economic phenomena.

Once identified, risks can be addressed through various strategies (Rosa & Lita, 2020):

- Elimination: Completely removing the cause of the risk.

- Mitigation: Reducing its impact or probability through specific actions.
- Transfer: Shifting the management of the risk to third parties (insurance, contracts).
- Acceptance: Accepting the risk when its impact is tolerable or the cost of mitigation is not viable.

6.4 Proactive Risk Prevention in Digital Environments

To achieve sustained improvement, risks must be continuously analyzed and controlled at each point in the supply chain. This requires strengthening detection and response capabilities through technical and methodological tools that allow action before a disruption occurs (Meena et al., 2024).

Within Sustainable Digital Supply Chains (SDSC), risk is defined as any potential event that negatively impacts the quality, efficiency, or sustainability of the system. Therefore, risk management must rely on multiple sources of information and remain up-to-date. Some effective tools (Curkovic et al., 2013), (Kilic et al., 2023), (Sharma & Pratap, 2023) include:

- FMEA (Failure Modes and Effects Analysis).
- Value chain mapping.
- Scenario simulation and vulnerability analysis.
- Big Data and predictive analytics.
- Audits of key suppliers.
- Geopolitical and economic monitoring of the environment.
- Organizational risk culture diagnostics.

These tools help identify weak points, improve anticipation capabilities, and formulate more agile responses (Rodrigues et al., 2022).

6.5. Mitigation Strategies and the Role of ISO 9001:2026

Mitigating a risk involves implementing a coherent set of specific measures to reduce it to acceptable levels. Fesobi et al. (2024) emphasize that this process must be systematic, with designated responsibilities, defined deadlines, and monitoring mechanisms. Chowdhury (2025) concludes that, in practice, mitigation and acceptance strategies are the most commonly used, as eliminating or transferring a risk entirely is often difficult.

Risk management should not be viewed as a one-time activity but as a dynamic and cyclical process that adapts to new conditions. The cycle includes the phases of identification, analysis, planning, execution, and monitoring. The earlier action is taken, the greater the efficiency in prevention (Karminska-Bielobrova & Shmatko, 2021).

The 2026 version of ISO 9001 will establish a solid regulatory framework that will consolidate this integrated risk management, highlighting aspects such as:

- Inclusion of risk in the QMS: Covering quality, continuity, and sustainability (Simão et al., 2020).
- Risk-based strategic planning: Proactive approach to key decisions (El Khatib et al., 2020).
- Use of digital technologies for monitoring: AI, IoT, and real-time advanced analytics (Shiyanbola, 2024).
- Risk management performance evaluation: Measurement through indicators (KPIs) (Silvério & Pestana, 2022).
- Collaboration with suppliers: Shared management and transparent communication (Alherian et al., 2021).
- Risk-oriented organizational culture: Promotion of anticipatory thinking at all levels (Parra et al., 2025).

Thus, the standard will not only encourage prevention but will strengthen the ability of organizations to adapt and thrive in volatile contexts (Al-Balushi, 2024).

In an interconnected and digitalized economy, resilience is not only achieved through technology but through an organizational culture that values anticipation and adaptability (Malhotra, 2023). ISO 9001:2026 will position risk as a transversal axis of business performance, transforming how operations are planned and change is managed (Yazo-Cabuya et al., 2025). Companies that learn to live with uncertainty and turn it into a competitive advantage will be better prepared to lead in uncertain environments (Malhotra, 2023).

6.6. Smart Quality and Resilience in the Supply Chain

The ISO 9001 standard has historically been a key support for strengthening organizational resilience, providing guidelines for structuring knowledge, optimizing resources, and promoting a proactive attitude (Guirette-Barbosa et al., 2025). However, the standard does not include an explicit resilience metric. A useful measure would be the "total recovery time," which includes the restoration of critical functions after a disruption, such as production, communications, deliveries, financial operations, and business activity, as well as its impact across the entire value chain (Barasa et al., 2018).

The ISO 9001:2026 update will bring an innovative approach that will integrate "smart quality," allowing products and services to be managed through autonomous systems that anticipate, control, and optimize outcomes (Gosan & Kosasih, 2020). This model goes beyond mere regulatory compliance and incorporates dynamic control tools aligned with performance variables, defects, energy consumption, and risks (Sârb et al., 2021). These will be predictive, adaptive systems focused on continuous learning (Lončarević et al., 2024).

6.7 What is Smart Quality and What is its Scope?

Smart quality is based on capturing, modeling, and managing intangible assets that influence organizational performance, such as reputation, loyalty, innovation culture, and work environment (Ito et al., 2020). These elements, although not always visible, are decisive in the sustained success of an organization (Ramos-González et al., 2021). To manage them, it is essential to have a deep understanding of the business model, integrate data from multiple sources, and develop tools that turn this data into meaningful decisions (Escot-Domínguez & Quiñones, 2025).

This approach enables the creation of Intelligent Quality Systems, where data stops being just records and becomes strategic inputs (Siougle et al., 2023). Thus, it strengthens the ability to adjust processes in real-time and respond agilely to unexpected events (Ahmed & Ruth, 2024). The ISO 9000 family of standards will remain the foundation, but certifications will evolve towards validating not only the system but also the individual skills of those responsible for each process (Aguenza, 2024).

The incorporation of Artificial Intelligence, Big Data, and Machine Learning will enhance this transformation, allowing for continuous monitoring, predictive analysis, and automated learning (Solonytska et al., 2024). Every piece of data generated will feed the system, increasing its self-regulation and continuous improvement capacity (Jarrett, 2022).

6.8 Strengthening Resilience: Beyond Recovery Capacity

Organizational resilience is redefined in this digital era as the ability not only to recover after a disruption but to anticipate, resist, adapt, and grow despite adversities (Ţîmbaliuc, 2024). This approach requires developing specific competencies in three key areas:

- Proactive process management centered on people and resources: This involves clearly defining critical processes, assigning responsibilities, establishing contingency plans, and providing appropriate tools to staff. Real-time monitoring systems, such as dashboards, should be used to make data-driven decisions (Rodríguez, 2020).

- Diversification and sustainability of supplies: It is unsustainable to depend on a single source for key materials. Alternatives must be in place to ensure operational continuity, considering factors such as raw materials, transportation, legal requirements, and sustainability standards. A truly resilient supplier operates with environmental and social responsibility, in addition to having their own contingency plans (Medina et al., 2020).

  The ISO 9001:2026 standard will drive this transformation toward more resilient organizations through practices such as:

- Identification of critical points and bottlenecks (SPOF) (Cadavid et al., 2021).
- Integrated business continuity plans within the quality management system (Fares, 2024).
- Systematic management of incidents and lessons learned (Buenrostro & Domínguez, 2023).
- Use of emerging technologies such as AI, IoT, and Blockchain (Gamboa et al., 2020).
- Promotion of collaborative networks with suppliers and strategic partners (Cerroblanco-Vázquez et al., 2021).

In this new paradigm, quality will no longer just be compliance but intelligence applied to sustainability and continuous adaptation (Stovpnyk, 2024).

In the coming years, organizations that wish to thrive must understand that resilience is not simply a reaction to crisis, but a strategic competency built with anticipation, data, and leadership (Yazo-Cabuya et al., 2025). Smart quality will be the key to navigating this change, allowing companies to design systems that learn from the past, operate efficiently in the present, and actively prepare for the future (Martusewicz et al., 2024). ISO 9001:2026 will consolidate this vision by merging technology, strategy, and human value into a single management model (Osho et al., 2024).

6.9. Emerging Technologies in ISO 9001:2026 and the Supply Chain

Technological innovation has become a decisive factor for organizations to evolve and stay competitive. In the realm of quality and supply chain management, the incorporation of emerging technologies has transformed processes, improving their accuracy, efficiency, traceability, and adaptability (Toromade et al., 2024), (Sah et al., 2024), (Xu, 2025). These technologies not only strengthen relationships with various stakeholders but also reinforce sustainability as a strategic priority (Xue, Li & Ivanov, 2025). The ISO 9001:2026 version will actively promote the integration of key technologies such as Artificial Intelligence (AI), Blockchain, and the Internet of Things (IoT) (Muruganandham et al., 2022).

6.9.1 Artificial Intelligence: The Core of Smart Quality

AI refers to systems capable of performing complex functions that previously required human intelligence, such as learning, inference, and decision-making. These systems use algorithms to process large volumes of data, identify patterns, predict outcomes, and improve their performance autonomously (Sheth et al., 2023).

In the context of quality management and the supply chain, AI allows simultaneous monitoring of multiple processes with unprecedented precision (Chen, 2025). It can identify potential failures, analyze customer feedback in natural language, and generate immediate decisions based on data (Nweje & Taiwo, 2025). These capabilities are essential for improving response times, reducing errors, and making decisions based on unbiased analysis (Khoa et al., 2024).

Additionally, ISO 9001:2026 is expected to require organizations to understand and clearly document the capabilities of their AI systems, especially in regard to quality control, defect prediction, and risk assessment (Mohan, 2025).

Possible Applications of AI in ISO 9001:2026:

- Demand prediction and inventory optimization.
- Automated quality control with computer vision.
- Predictive diagnostics of machinery failures.
- Customer feedback analysis.
- Optimization of logistical routes.
- Predictive risk management.
- Process automation in warehouses and production.

6.10 Blockchain: Trust and Traceability in Real-Time

Blockchain is a distributed ledger technology that guarantees the immutability and transparency of information. Initially used in cryptocurrencies, its use has expanded to business management, particularly to ensure traceability and authenticity in value chains (Liu et al., 2025).

This technology allows for securely recording each movement of products, certifications, audits, or transportation conditions. ISO 9001:2026 will promote its implementation in scenarios where data accuracy is critical to maintaining trust among actors in the chain (Khairunnisa et al., 2024).

Key uses of blockchain in ISO 9001:2026 (Muruganandham et al., 2022; Andita & Nugraha, 2022):

- Full traceability of products.
- Digital certification of tests and audits.
- Decentralized control of suppliers and their credentials.
- Smart contracts to automate quality conditions.
- Product life cycle tracking in circular economy models.

Although its immutability can represent rigidity in managerial decisions that require flexibility, this can be resolved by using private chains or carefully designed hybrid systems (Le et al., 2022).

6.11 IoT (Internet of Things): Sensors Connecting the Physical World to Quality

The Internet of Things (IoT) consists of a network of physical devices equipped with sensors that collect, process, and send real-time data. These sensors enable the monitoring of key conditions such as temperature, vibration, humidity, or location, improving traceability, quality control, and logistical efficiency (Bedi et al., 2024).

IoT allows companies to react immediately to deviations in their processes, generate automatic alerts, and adjust their operations in real-time. Its integration with management systems will provide comprehensive performance visualization and improve strategic decision-making (Sallam et al., 2023).

Main IoT applications in ISO 9001:2026 (Sallam et al., 2023; Soori et al., 2023):

- Monitoring storage and transportation conditions.
- Automated inventory control.
- Predictive asset maintenance.
- Optimization of production processes.
- Real-time tracking of deliveries.
- Environmental performance evaluation.
- Improvement in operational safety.

The implementation of IoT, like AI and Blockchain, will be recognized by ISO 9001:2026 as a key tool to advance toward data-driven quality models, resilience, and sustainability.

The integration of emerging technologies should not be limited to their acquisition but requires a clear, ethical, and purposeful strategy. ISO 9001:2026 will open a new chapter in business management, where machines, algorithms, and sensors will be allies of quality, but the true differentiator will be the human intelligence that knows how to interpret, guide, and turn them into sustainable competitive advantages. Technology should be an extension of the vision, not its replacement (Business Management Systems, 2025).

7. CASE STUDIES

The international growth of multinational corporations has led to supply chains that are vast, interdependent, and increasingly complex. While this expansion has generated unprecedented economic opportunities, it has also increased the vulnerability of organizations to disruptions caused by natural phenomena, health crises, or political instability. A disruption at any point in the chain can create large-scale domino effects, impacting reputation, customer trust, and operational continuity.

The case study presented in this section illustrates how certification under the ISO 9001 standard has been an effective tool for enhancing sustainability, traceability, and operational resilience in global companies, particularly in their supply chains. For this analysis, a review of academic and technical literature published since 2019, along with reports from governmental and non-governmental organizations, was used, focusing on the role of quality in strengthening sustainable supply chains.

In particular, the case of Jacobs Douwe Egberts (JDE Peet's), a company that implemented quality management systems to strengthen operational robustness in their value chains, was examined. The benefits observed include:

- Greater alignment of suppliers with common policies and standards.
- Clear definition of responsibilities throughout the chain.
- Reduction of asymmetric power and opportunistic practices.
- Systematic performance evaluation through internal audits.
- Transparency in procurement and contracting processes.

These results demonstrate that the implementation of ISO 9001 can be a decisive factor in transitioning from reactive models to strategic, resilient approaches in logistics management.

7.1. Success Case: Jacobs Douwe Egberts

JDE Peet's, one of the leading companies in the coffee and tea industry globally, developed a supply chain characterized by its high degree of complexity and technological dependence. With the rapid advancement of digitalization, the company faced the challenge of integrating its quality management (QMS), environmental, and sustainability systems with new digital platforms (EPAM, 2023).

To address this challenge, JDE conducted a comprehensive simulation based on digital twins, aiming to evaluate the real performance of their logistics network. The analysis revealed that, although each component operated optimally, the lack of synchronization and integration between areas led to bottlenecks, resource waste, and impacts on environmental performance (JDE, 2024).

For example, an efficiency improvement at one plant could cause saturation in transportation or storage systems. Similarly, a change in the quality of raw materials from a supplier had secondary effects on the total carbon footprint or recycling costs. The study concluded that the key lies not only in optimizing isolated processes but in achieving a systemic, coordinated vision of the supply chain (WTA, 2023).

ISO 9001:2026, by requiring a broader approach based on risks, sustainability, and digitalization, will provide the necessary framework for companies like JDE Peet's to overcome such challenges.

Additionally, JDE Peet's exemplifies how a global organization can integrate quality management, sustainability, and operational digitalization systems. Their structured and responsible approach, supported by advanced technologies and collaborative digital platforms, aligns with the anticipated ISO 9001:2026 model, where resilience, real-time monitoring, and sustainability converge in a single management system.

7.2. Collaboration, Digitalization, and Sustainability as Strategic Pillars

Recent global crises, such as the COVID-19 pandemic, geopolitical tensions, and energy shifts, have exposed the fragility of traditional supply chains and the urgency of adopting new operational paradigms (Nathany, 2022). Three major learnings emerge from these scenarios:

Pillar 1: Strategic Cooperation Between Companies (Lotfi & Larmour, 2021)

The pandemic highlighted that even competitors can collaborate to survive. In sectors such as food or automotive, rival companies shared transport or joint purchases to cope with shortages and maintain operations. This model of "coopetition" is key to building more stable and resilient networks and can be driven by the principles of ISO 9001:2026, which recognizes external stakeholders as strategic partners.

Pillar 2: Deep Digitalization and Intelligent Data Management (Javed et al. 2024)

Having large volumes of data is not enough: there is a need to convert it into useful knowledge. Digitalization, combined with technologies like AI or digital twins, allows for modeling scenarios, anticipating failures, and making evidence-based decisions. ISO 9001:2026 will encourage this approach by consolidating a data-driven quality management system.

Pillar 3: Sustainability as a Long-Term Differentiator (Attanayake & Ratnayake, 2024)

Organizations that adopt sustainable practices and circularity not only comply with regulations but position themselves as responsible leaders. Traceability, transparency, and investment in clean technologies become sources of competitive advantage. The new ISO standard will include these criteria as a central part of organizational performance.

8. RECOMMENDATIONS / IMLPICATIONS

Quality Management Systems (QMS) based on the ISO 9001 standard are an essential tool for achieving the sustainable growth of organizations. Their application not only guarantees high-quality products and services but also promotes safer work environments, fosters inclusion, and encourages corporate responsibility (Guirette-Barbosa et al., 2025). With the anticipated update for 2026, this standard will make a qualitative leap by more explicitly incorporating sustainability and integrated supply chain management as central elements of organizational performance (Fu et al., 2022).

Organizations that can quickly adapt to technological changes, environmental demands, and the expectations of more informed and demanding customers will be better positioned to lead their respective sectors. The COVID-19 pandemic accelerated this process, pushing companies to reinvent themselves digitally, adapt their operational models, and create new ways to engage with their key stakeholders (George, 2025).

Companies that can provide superior customer experiences, supported by advanced digital tools, data analysis, and automated processes, will stand out significantly in the new environment. The ISO 9001:2026 version will recognize and enhance these capabilities, fostering a new generation of intelligent, user-centered quality management systems (Alshahrani & Husain, 2023).

8.1. Global Adoption and Strategic Benefits

The global adoption of ISO 9001 has proven to bring real and tangible value to organizations, enabling them to differentiate themselves and earn trust among their stakeholders. By having a validated management system, companies project consistency, responsibility, and commitment.

The most notable benefits of certification include (Guirette-Barbosa et al., 2025):

- Strengthened corporate image: Compliance with the standard translates into a solid reputation based on reliability.
- Customer loyalty: Consistent quality and enhanced customer experience create long-term relationships.
- Effective communication: Improved information flows both internally and externally.
- Employee satisfaction: Clarity in processes and active participation in continuous improvement.
- Productivity and operational efficiency: Optimization of resources and elimination of unnecessary activities.
- Financial benefits: Reduced costs, increased revenues, and access to new markets.

These benefits should not be viewed in isolation but as components of broad sustainability encompassing environmental, financial, reputational, and human dimensions. The inclusion of ESG (environmental, social, and governance) criteria in ISO 9001:2026 will make these contributions clearer.

It should be noted that the impact of the standard also extends to the macroeconomic level. A European report from 2020 analyzed over 500 standards and concluded that standardization has a direct positive effect on economic development, innovation, and quality of life, especially in emerging countries (ISO, 2023).

8.2. Impact on Emerging Economies

In the current global scenario, eco-efficiency is positioned as a key differentiator for developing countries. Regions such as Asia, Latin America, and Africa are emerging with more flexible and sustainable models, in contrast to advanced economies that still depend on resource-intensive production schemes (Rodríguez-García et al., 2022).

The expansion of digitalized supply chains and the reduction of technological barriers enable emerging countries to adopt clean solutions from early stages, avoiding the environmental and structural costs of obsolete models. This ability to "leapfrog" opens new possibilities for sustainable, competitive, and inclusive development (Tim et al., 2020).

Moreover, new social and environmental demands are transforming the criteria for accessing international markets. Those who fail to align with sustainable practices will be left behind. Conversely, nations and organizations that develop digital, traceable, and circular supply chains from the outset will gain relevance in a world increasingly regulated by ethical and ecological standards (Ezekwu, 2025).

ISO 9001:2026 will be a powerful tool in this process, as it will enable these economies to consolidate international standards without compromising their identity and provide them with the necessary foundations to compete with integrity in global markets.

9. SCOPE AND LIMITATIONS

9.1 Scope of the Study

Focus: Anticipatory and analytical review of how ISO 9001:2026 can address the shortcomings of the 2015 version within global supply chains.
Unit of analysis: Organizational quality management systems (QMS) and their interaction with sustainability, digital transformation (AI, Blockchain, IoT), and resilience practices.
Sectors emphasized: Manufacturing and logistics, given their prevalence of ISO 9001 certification and supply-chain criticality; insights are relevant to adjacent sectors through conceptual transfer.
Temporal window: Core literature from 2020–2025 (with selective inclusion of seminal, pre-2020 sources for theoretical grounding). Case evidence reflects practices reported up to 2025.
Geographical reach: Global perspective with attention to challenges in emerging economies (e.g., capability gaps for digital/ESG integration).

9.2 Delimitations

Design delimitation: The study is qualitative and conceptual; it does not conduct primary quantitative testing, surveys, or experiments.
Standards scope: References to related standards (e.g., ISO 14001, ISO 45001, ISO 31000) are used for triangulation only; they are not analyzed exhaustively.
Technology depth: Mentions of AI, Blockchain, IoT illustrate integration pathways; no vendor/product benchmarking or algorithmic performance testing is undertaken.

Case coverage: The JDE Peet's case is illustrative, not intended as a sector-wide evaluation.

9.3 Limitations (Threats and Constraints)

Generalizability: Findings are analytical/transferable, not statistically generalizable, due to the non-probabilistic, qualitative design.
Evidence availability & bias: Reliance on published sources may introduce publication, language (English-centric), and recency biases; fast-moving topics (cyberrisks, AI adoption) risk obsolescence.
Standards transparency: Details of ISO 9001:2026 prior to final release may limit specificity; some inferences are based on trends and authoritative commentary.
Case specificity: Single-case depth constrains breadth; organizational idiosyncrasies may affect transferability across sectors/regions.
Construct overlap: Interdependence among sustainability, digitalization, and resilience can complicate attribution of effects to any single dimension.

9.4 Rigor, Validity, and Reliability Measures

Triangulation: Cross-checking insights across peer-reviewed literature, ISO reports/surveys, and industry white papers.
Transparent selection: Inclusion/exclusion criteria specified in Chapter 4 (peer-reviewed, 2020–2025, direct relevance; exclusion of non-transparent sources).
Chain of evidence: Theoretical claims anchored to recognized frameworks (TQM, RBV, Stakeholder, Resilience, Institutional).
Reflexivity: Acknowledgment of the authors' conceptual stance (constructivist), with explicit delimitations to reduce interpretive drift.

10. CONCLUSIONS

The upcoming revision of the ISO 9001 standard, scheduled for 2026, is shaping up to be a comprehensive and advanced guide for companies to transform their quality management systems into more efficient, resilient structures aligned with the challenges of the 21st century. Its central objective is to optimize processes, reduce waste, promote continuous improvement, and, above all, respond with agility and responsibility to the expectations of all stakeholders.

The current business environments, marked by health, geopolitical, economic, and climate uncertainty, have tested companies' ability to adapt to unforeseen scenarios (VUCA). This new landscape has forced a reevaluation of strategic priorities, placing risk management, sustainability, and digitalization as fundamental pillars for operational continuity (all integrated within supply chains).

In this context, the new version of ISO 9001 will not merely be a compendium of technical requirements but an organizational transformation model that articulates ethical principles, operational intelligence, and a systemic vision. Organizations that adopt it with a strategic approach will not only elevate their internal performance but also position themselves as agents of positive change within their communities and productive sectors.

Technologies such as artificial intelligence (AI), blockchain, and the Internet of Things (IoT) will not replace humans but will complement them, enhancing their capabilities, improving the quality of the work environment, and recognizing talent as a key asset. In this sense, the true evolutionary leap will not only be technological but deeply human.

Organizations that choose to integrate ISO 9001:2026 with conviction, strategic vision, and openness to change will be building more than just efficient processes: they will be laying the foundations for a more ethical, resilient, and sustainable future. This standard represents a modern compass guiding companies towards an economy where quality translates into trust, innovation, equity, and collective well-being.

11. FUTURE RESEARCH

Future inquiry should move from conceptual anticipation to empirical demonstration of how ISO 9001:2026 reshapes supply-chain performance through sustainability integration, digital enablement, and resilience. We propose a concise agenda centered on four priorities: (1) Sustainability effects—estimate whether embedding ESG criteria within QMS improves environmental and social outcomes across multi-tier networks; (2) Digital quality mechanisms—identify how AI, Blockchain, and IoT capabilities mediate impacts on traceability, defect rates, and decision speed; (3) Resilience operationalization—validate practical metrics (e.g., Total Recovery Time, service fill-rate during disruption) and test their predictive value for continuity and recovery; and (4) Adoption economics and equity—quantify cost–benefit profiles for SMEs versus large firms and examine capability gaps in emerging economies.

Methodologically, evidence should combine quasi-experimental designs (e.g., Difference-in-Differences around certification windows, matched controls), panel models with firm-level KPIs (quality, ESG, risk), and mixed-methods (surveys, interviews, and digital trace data) to explain mechanisms, complemented by structured case-comparative analysis for configuration insights (leadership × digital maturity × supplier programs). Key data sources include ISO Survey microdata, audit findings, supplier scorecards, recall/incident logs, ERP/MES records, sustainability reports, and logistics/cyber events. Cross-regional samples (Latin America, EU, North America, Asia) and cross-sector designs (automotive, food & beverage, electronics, mining/materials, healthcare) will strengthen external validity.

Expected contributions are threefold: (i) validate the causal linkages posited in this study; (ii) operationalize resilience and ESG within ISO 9001:2026 through reliable indicators and dashboards; and (iii) deliver evidence-based guidance for managers and policymakers on context-sensitive adoption pathways. Attention to ethics and data governance (privacy-preserving analytics, cyber-resilience-by-design) remains essential to ensure that performance gains do not compromise trust or inclusion.

REFERENCES

Abdul-Azeez, O., Ogadimma, A., & Idemudia, C. (2024). Optimizing supply chain management: strategic business models and solutions using SAP S/4HANA. *Magna Scientia Advanced Research and Reviews*. .DOI: 10.30574/msarr.2024.11.1.0097

Agho, M., Eyo-Udo, N., Onukwulu, E., Sule, A., & Azubuike, C. (2025). Digital Twin Technology for Real Time Monitoring of Energy Supply Chains. *International Journal of Research and Innovation in Applied Science*. .DOI: 10.51584/IJRIAS.2024.912049

Aguenza, B. (2024). *Readiness of Local Educational Institution for ISO 9001:2015 Quality Management System Certification: A Comprehensive Analysis*. Education Policy and Development., DOI: 10.31098/epd.v2i1.1804

Ahmed, S., & Ruth, D. (2024). *The benefits of iso 9001 certification for small to medium-sized engineering firMS*. Performance Improvement Journal., DOI: 10.56811/PFI-24-0010

Al-Balushi, M. (2024). The impact of quality management systems on organizational resilience. *International Journal of Quality & Reliability Management*. Advance online publication. DOI: 10.1108/IJQRM-05-2023-0169

Alherian, N., Spasojević-Brkić, V., Perišić, M., & Alsharif, A. (2021). *Integrated risk management model implementation's contextual dependence on company size*. Tehnika., DOI: 10.5937/tehnika2103361A

Alshahrani, M., & Husain, K. (2023). The effectiveness of the implementation of ISO 9001 on SMEs performance: The case of an emerging economy. *International Journal of Quality & Reliability Management*. Advance online publication. DOI: 10.1108/IJQRM-08-2022-0233

Anwer, A., 2024. ISO 9000: (1987-2016) A trend's Review. *Journal of Policy Research*. .DOI: 10.61506/02.00236

Attanayake, A., & Ratnayake, R. (2024). Transitioning to Circular Economy in Power Distribution Utilities: A Framework Integrating ISO 9001 Quality Management Standards. *2024 IEEE International Conference on Industrial Engineering and Engineering Management* (IEEM), 760-764. DOI: 10.1109/IEEM62345.2024.10857066

Avilés-Sacoto, H., Avilés-González, J., & García-Reyes, S. (2021). A Model to Become a Supply Chain 4.0 Based on a Digital Maturity Perspective. 1058-1067. .DOI: 10.1016/j.procs.2022.01.305

Ayub, A. (2022). Motivation and benefits of iso 9001:2015 implementation and maintenance in a Malaysian legal firm. https://www.qjssh.com/index.php/qjssh/article/view/107

Barasa, E., Mbau, R., & Gilson, L. (2018). What Is Resilience and How Can It Be Nurtured? A Systematic Review of Empirical Literature on Organizational Resilience. *International Journal of Health Policy and Management*, *7*(6), 491–503. DOI: 10.15171/ijhpm.2018.06 PMID: 29935126

Barnhart, C. (2023). Data and connectivity as key building blocks for effective collaboration with supply chain partners. *Journal of Supply Chain Management, Logistics and Procurement*. .DOI: 10.69554/FTSR7867

Basiru, J., Ejiofor, C., Onukwulu, E., & Attah, R. (2025). Sustainable Procurement in Multinational Corporations: A Conceptual Framework for Aligning Business and Environmental Goals. *International Journal of Multidisciplinary Research and Growth Evaluation*. .DOI: 10.54660/.IJMRGE.2023.4.1.774-787

Bedi, K., Singh, P., Kohli, N., Kaur, H., Angra, P., & Cheema, G. (2024). Effectiveness of IoT (Internet of Things) in Real-Time Supply Chain Monitoring and Management. *2024 Second International Conference Computational and Characterization Techniques in Engineering & Sciences (IC3TES)*, 1-5. DOI: 10.1109/IC3TES62412.2024.10877555

Boçe, M., & Hoxha, J. (2024). *Blockchain Technology as a Catalyst for Sustainable Development: Exploring Economic, Social, and Environmental Synergies*. Academic Journal of Interdisciplinary Studies., DOI: 10.36941/ajis-2024-0041

Bondarenko, S. (2024). Quality management of business processes in the context of achieving sustainable development of fashion industry enterprises. *Management*, *37*(1), 94–105. Advance online publication. DOI: 10.30857/2415-3206.2023.1.9

Bravi, L., & Murmura, F. (2021). Evidences about ISO 9001:2015 and ISO 9004:2018 implementation in different-size organisations. *Total Quality Management & Business Excellence*, *33*(11-12), 1366–1386. DOI: 10.1080/14783363.2021.1954900

Bravim, M., Lira, T., De Freitas, R., & Xavier, T. (2020). A evolução nos estudos da gestão da qualidade baseado na norma iso 9001:2015: um estudo bibliométrico: the evolution in quality management studies based on iso 9001: 2015 standard: a bibliometric study. *Brazilian Journal of Production Engineering* - BJPE, 88-106. https://dialnet.unirioja.es/servlet/articulo?codigo=8698522

Buenrostro, H., & Domínguez, N. (2023). *Propuesta de Categorías Para la Medición de la Sustentabilidad Portuaria a Través de la Metodología FuzzyDelphi. European Scientific Journal.* ESJ., DOI: 10.19044/esj.2023.v19n37p174

Business Management Systems. (2025). What might be changed in ISO 9001:2026? Business Management Systems Ltd. https://businessmanagementsystems.ltd.uk/what-might-be-changed-in-iso-90012026/

Cadavid, V., Duque, D., & Carabalí, L. (2021)... *Modelo Multicriterio para el Diseño de Cadenas de Suministro Considerando Opciones Reales para el Tratamiento de la Incertidumbre.*, *26*, 159–166. DOI: 10.22517/23447214.24543

Cerroblanco-Vázquez, V., López-Mateo, C., & Macías, D. (2021). Asociatividad y cadenas de valor: estudio de caso de una marca colectiva de mezcal en Guanajuato, México (Associativity and Value Chains: A Case Study of a Collective Brand of Mezcal in Guanajuato, México). *PSN: Other International Political Economy: Trade Policy (To*pic). .DOI: 10.29393/RAN7-2ACCL20002

Chavan, V., Joshi, A., & Jha, D. 2024. Strategic Integration of HR, Organizational Management, Big Data, IoT, and AI: A Comprehensive Framework for Future-Ready Enterprises. *2024 Ninth International Conference on Science Technology Engineering and Mathematics (ICONSTEM*), pp. 1-6. DOI: 10.1109/ICONSTEM60960.2024.10568704

Chen, S. (2025). Research on Supply Chain Logistics Prediction and Decision Optimization Driven by Artificial Intelligence. *Academic Journal of Business & Management.* .DOI: 10.25236/AJBM.2025.070218

Chowdhary, Y., & Kumar, B., 2023. Advancement and benefits associated with ISO 9000 series. Asian Journal of Pharmaceutical Research. .DOI: 10.52711/2231-5691.2023.00008

Chowdhury, A. (2025). A systematic review of risk-based procurement strategies in retail supply chains: sourcing flexibility and vendor disruption management. *American Journal of Advanced Technology and Engineering Solutions.* .DOI: 10.63125/jr03rv07

Curkovic, S., Scannell, T., & Wagner, B. (2013). Using FMEA for Supply Chain Risk Management. *Using FMEA for Supply Chain Risk Management.*, *1*, 251. DOI: 10.1201/b18610-3

Dey, A. (2022). Network wide visibility and Orchestration for Supply Chain. https://www.sciencedirect.com/science/article/pii/S2667344422000081

Dziedzic, S., Warmińska, A., & Wyrwa, D., 2023. Perspectives of the analysis of organisation's context in the light of the ISO 9001:2015 standard and the subject literature. *Scientific Papers of Silesian University of Technology. Organization and Management Series*. .DOI: 10.29119/1641-3466.2023.181.7

Echeverría, E. (2024). Supply Chain Resilience And Risk Management: Strategies For Mitigating Global Supply Chain Disruptions. *Educational Administration: Theory and Practice*. .DOI: 10.53555/kuey.v30i6.5680

Egbumokei, P., Dienagha, I., Digitemie, W., Onukwulu, E., & Oladipo, O. (2024). The role of digital transformation in enhancing sustainability in oil and gas business operations. *International Journal of Multidisciplinary Research and Growth Evaluation*. .DOI: 10.54660/.IJMRGE.2024.5.5.1029-1041

Escot, L. Domínguez-Quiñones, I., & Aliende. (2025). Application of data science for building corporate reputation strategy: An analysis in business intangibles scoping review. *Corporate and Business Strategy Review*. .DOI: 10.22495/cbsrv6i2art10

Ezekwu, E. (2025). Sustainable supply chain practices: Driving efficiency, reducing waste, and promoting circular economy models. *International Journal of Science and Research Archive*. DOI: 10.30574/ijsra.2025.14.1.0206

Farazi, R., & Zahidur, M. (2024). Designing circular supply chains with digital technologies for competitive sustainability: An operation management perspective. *International Journal of Science and Research Archive*. .DOI: 10.30574/ijsra.2024.13.1.1928

Fares, O. (2024). *Falta de seguridad en la gestión de la cadena de suministros en la agroindustria ecuatoriana*. Revista Científica Sapientia Technological., DOI: 10.58515/028RSPT

Fesobi, B., Fesobi, M., & Ogungbeje, O. (2024). Implementing agile supply chain strategy for improved response to market volatility: a systematic literature review. *South Florida Journal of Development*. .DOI: 10.46932/sfjdv5n12-057

Figueirêdo Da, S. M. (2024, September 08). S., De Araujo Filho, J., Rocha, T., De Paula Filho, F., & Cavalcanti, M. (2024). Sustainability Indicators in the Integrated Management of Industries with Galvanic Activities. *Journal of Management and Sustainability*, *14*(2), 53. Advance online publication. DOI: 10.5539/jms.v14n2p53

Fu, Q., Rahman, A., Jiang, H., Abbas, J., & Comite, U. (2022). Sustainable Supply Chain and Business Performance: *The Impact of Strategy, Network Design, Information Systems, and Organizational Structure*. https://www.mdpi.com/2071-1050/14/3/1080

Gabriel, L., Da Silva, C., Sampaio, P., & Martins, Y. (2021). ISO 9001:2015 and risk-based thinking: scientific research insights. *Total Quality Management & Business Excellence*, *33*(11-12), 1326–1343. DOI: 10.1080/14783363.2021.1954898

Gamboa, J., Castro, J., & Mantilla, C. (2020). The Sustainable Supply Chain: Concepts, Optimization and Simulation Models, and Trends. . .DOI: 10.14483/23448393.16926

George, E. (2025). *Business model innovation in a post-pandemic world: How companies are redefining value creation.* International Journal For Multidisciplinary Research., DOI: 10.36948/ijfmr.2025.v07i01.36703

Gitau, T. (2025). The Role of Industry 4.0 Technologies in Shaping Sustainable Digital Business Models: An Integrated Approach to Innovation and Strategic Capability Development: An Empirical Literature Review. *The International Journal of Humanities & Social Studies*. .DOI: 10.24940/theijhss/2025/v13/i1/HS2501-004

Glogovac, M., Ruso, J., & Maričić, M. (2020). ISO 9004 maturity model for quality in industry 4.0. *Total Quality Management & Business Excellence*, *33*(5-6), 529–547. DOI: 10.1080/14783363.2020.1865793

Gosan, M., & Kosasih, W. (2020). Quality Management System in Automatic Machine Construction Based on ISO 9001. *IOP Conference Series. Materials Science and Engineering*, *1007*(1), 012064. Advance online publication. DOI: 10.1088/1757-899X/1007/1/012064

Gueorguiev, T. (2024). *The PDCA cycle in innovation management systems based on ISO 56001:2024*. Unitech – Selected Papers., DOI: 10.70456/UIFI9691

Guirette-Barbosa, O. A., Castañeda-Burciaga, S., Ramírez-Salazar, M. A., Cruz-Domínguez, O., Carrera-Escobedo, J. L., Velázquez-Macías, J. D. J., Lara-Torres, C. G., Celaya-Padilla, J. M., & Durán-Muñoz, H. A. (2025). Transforming Quality into Results: A Multivariate Analysis with Hotelling's T2 on the Impact of ISO 9001. *Systems*, *13*(4), 226. DOI: 10.3390/systems13040226

Haouat, Z., Essalih, S., Bennouna, F., & Amegouz, D. (2025). Development of a Global Framework for an Integrated Life Cycle Assessment (LCA) Model in Quality, Safety and Environmental (QSE) Management Systems: Improving Environmental, Social and Economic Sustainability Performance. *Sustainability (Basel)*, *17*(8), 3521. Advance online publication. DOI: 10.3390/su17083521

Hekneby, T., & Olsen, T. (2024). The role of leadership in organizational learning in multinational companies. *The Learning Organization*, *31*(2), 141–162. Advance online publication. DOI: 10.1108/TLO-09-2022-0101

Ibiyemi, M., & Olutimehin, D. (2024). Cybersecurity in supply chains: Addressing emerging threats with strategic measures. *International Journal of Management & Entrepreneurship Research*. .DOI: 10.51594/ijmer.v6i6.1241

Ijiri, G., Chilicaus, G., Licapa-Redolfo, G., Ballesteros, M., Otazú, C., Miranda, S., Castillo, M., De Los Ángeles Guzmán Valle, M., & Castillo, J. (2025). Digital Transformation and Sustainability in Post-Pandemic Supply Chains: *A Global Bibliometric Analysis of Technological Evolution and Research Patterns (2020–2024). Sustainability (Basel), 17*(7), 3009. Advance online publication. DOI: 10.3390/su17073009

ISO. (2023). *The ISO Survey of Management System Standard Certifications (latest available results for ISO 9001)*. International Organization for Standardization.

Ito, K., Umeda, S., & Sekiya, H. (2020). Impact of Intangibles on Corporate Value. *Journal of Human Resource and Sustainability Studies*, *8*(2), 131–150. Advance online publication. DOI: 10.4236/jhrss.2020.82008

Jarrett, J. (2022). Update and Acceleration of Health Care Using Artificial Intelligence in Medical Treatments and Diagnostics. *Advances in Social Sciences Research Journal*, *8*(12), 394–400. Advance online publication. DOI: 10.14738/assrj.812.11425

Javed, A., Basit, A., Ejaz, F., Hameed, A., Fodor, Z., & Hossain, M. (2024). The role of advanced technologies and supply chain collaboration: During COVID-19 on sustainable supply chain performance. *Discover Sustainability*, *5*(1), 46. Advance online publication. DOI: 10.1007/s43621-024-00228-z

Karminska-Bielobrova, M., & Shmatko, N. (2021). Risk-management as an aspect of operational management. *Bulletin of the National Technical University "Kharkiv Polytechnic Institute" (economic sciences)*. DOI: 10.20998/2519-4461.2021.1.36

Khairunnisa, N., Christiani, F., & Prawiyogi, A. (2024). Supply Chain Transparency: Exploring Blockchain Solutions for Enhanced Traceability and Efficiency. *Blockchain Frontier Technology*. .DOI: 10.34306/bfront.v4i1.569

Khatib, M., Zeyoudi, A., & Shaqar, S. (2020). The Influence of Integrating ISO and TQM on Project Risk Management. *American Journal of Industrial and Business Management*. .DOI: 10.4236/ajibm.2020.1012118

Khoa, B., Nguyen, H., Anh, D., & Ngoc, N. (2024). Impact of Artificial Intelligence's Part in Supply Chain Planning and Decision Making Optimization. *International Journal of Multidisciplinary Research and Growth Evaluation*. .DOI: 10.54660/.IJMRGE.2024.5.6.837-856

Kilic, H., Canbakis, S., Karabas, M., Koseoglu, S., Unal, E., & Kalender, Z. (2023). Integrated Supply Chain Risk Assessment Methodology Based on Modified FMEA. *Journal of Risk Analysis and Crisis Response*, *13*(2). Advance online publication. DOI: 10.54560/jracr.v13i2.359

Kotte, K., Thammareddi, L., Kodi, D., Anumolu, V. K. A., & Joshi, S. (2025). Integration of Process Optimization and Automation: A Way to AI Powered Digital Transformation. *2025 First International Conference on Advances in Computer Science, Electrical, Electronics, and Communication Technologies (CE2CT)*, 1133-1138. DOI: 10.1109/CE2CT64011.2025.10939966

Latan, H., Jabbour, C., Jabbour, A., Fiorini, P., & Foropon, C. (2020). Innovative efforts of ISO 9001certified manufacturing firms: Evidence of links between determinants of innovation, continuous innovation and firm performance. *International Journal of Production Economics*, *223*, 107526. Advance online publication. DOI: 10.1016/j.ijpe.2019.107526

Le, T., Hsu, C., & Chen, W. (2022). A Hybrid Blockchain-Based Log Management Scheme With Nonrepudiation for Smart Grids. *IEEE Transactions on Industrial Informatics*, *18*(9), 5771–5782. DOI: 10.1109/TII.2021.3136580

Lee, C., Sohn, D., Sang, M., & Lee, C. (2025). Empirical Analysis of Barriers to Collaborative Information Sharing in Maritime Logistics Using Fuzzy AHP Approach. *Sustainability (Basel)*, *17*(4), 1721. Advance online publication. DOI: 10.3390/su17041721

Lita, P., & Rosa, I. (2020). Perbandingan ISO 31000 dan COBIT 5 for Risk sebagai framework risk management pasca implementasi Enterprise Resource Planning (Studi kasus: PT Pupuk Indonesia (Persero)) [Tesis sarjana, Universitas Negeri Padang]. Repository Universitas Negeri Padang. http://repo.unp.ac.id/31018/

Liu, W., Zhang, X., & Chen, H. (2025). Improving Supply Chain Transparency through Blockchain Technology. *Optimizations in Applied Machine Learning*. .DOI: 10.71070/oaml.v5i1.89

Lončarević, Z., Rebersek, S., Sela, S., Skvarč, J., Ude, A., & Gams, A. (2024). Adaptive Visual Quality Inspection Based on Defect Prediction From Production Parameters. *IEEE Access : Practical Innovations, Open Solutions*, *12*, 93899–93910. DOI: 10.1109/ACCESS.2024.3424664

Lotfi, M., & Larmour, A. (2021). Supply chain resilience in the face of uncertainty: how horizontal and vertical collaboration can help?. *Continuity & Resilience Review*. .DOI: 10.1108/CRR-04-2021-0016

Ma, S., Ding, W., Liu, Y., Ren, S., & Yang, H. (2022). Digital twin and big data-driven sustainable smart manufacturing based on information management systems for energy intensive industries. *Applied Energy, 326*, 119986. Advance online publication. DOI: 10.1016/j.apenergy.2022.119986

Magallanes, M. (2020). Impacto de la gestión de sustentabilidad empresarial en la cultura organizacional. 12, 45-56. .DOI: 10.20983/novarua.2020.20.3

Mahankali, R. (2025). *Digital twins and enterprise architecture: a framework for real time manufacturing decision support*. International Journal Of Computer Engineering And Technology., DOI: 10.34218/IJCET_16_01_049

Malhotra, Y. (2023). Augmented AI-Knowledge Driven Intelligent Systems for Adversarial-Dynamic Uncertainty and Complexity. SSRN *Electronic Journ*al. DOI: 10.2139/ssrn.4380524

Martins, Y., Da Silva, C., Sampaio, P., & Gabriel, L. (2021). ISO 9001:2015 and risk-based thinking: scientific research insights. *Total Quality Management & Business Excellence, 33*(11-12), 1326–1343. DOI: 10.1080/14783363.2021.1954898

Martusewicz, J., Wierzbic, A., & Łukaszewicz, M. (2024). Strategic Transformation and Sustainability: Unveiling the EFQM Model 2025. *Sustainability (Basel), 16*(20), 9106. Advance online publication. DOI: 10.3390/su16209106

Medina, E., Lara, M., Dávila, J., & Velarde, R. (2020). Gestión eficiente de las economías locales a través de estrategias administrativas/Efficient management of local economies through administrative strategies., 654–673-654–673. .DOI: 10.18502/keg.v5i2.6288

Meena, M., Mishra, Y., Dusad, C., Dangayach, G., Sarkar, P., & Singh, A. (2024). Navigating Uncertainty: Cutting Edge Approaches in Process Control and Monitoring for Risk Mitigation in Supply Chain Management. *The 3rd International Electronic Conference on Processes*. DOI: 10.3390/engproc2024067074

Milovanović, G., Milovanović, S., & Popović, G. (2022). The role of Industry 4.0 in digitalization of production and supply chains. *Ekonomika (Nis), 68*(2), 1–14. Advance online publication. DOI: 10.5937/ekonomika2202001M

Mohan, V.Vijay Mohan, Keerthana N. (2025). Integrated AI Models for Simultaneous Quality Improvement and Risk Reduction in Production Processes. *Journal of Information Systems Engineering & Management, 10*(18s), 499–512. Advance online publication. DOI: 10.52783/jisem.v10i18s.2935

Mullapudi, L. (2025). Optimizing Supply Chain Management with Real Time Data Integration Platform. *International Journal of Scientific Research in Computer Science, Engineering and Information Technology*. .DOI: 10.32628/CSEIT25111243

Muruganandham, R., Venkatesh, K., Devadasan, S., & Harish, V. (2022). TQM through the integration of blockchain with ISO 9001:2015 standard based quality management system. *Total Quality Management & Business Excellence*, *34*(3-4), 291–311. DOI: 10.1080/14783363.2022.2054318

Nagy, G., & Szentesi, S. (2024). *Collaborative logistics: An innovative strategy to address future logistics challenges*. Advanced Logistic Systems Theory and Practice., DOI: 10.32971/als.2024.031

Nathany, D. (2022). Impact of COVID-19 on Supply Chain: A Comprehensive Analysis. *Interantional journal of scientific research in engineering and management*. .DOI: 10.55041/IJSREM16967

Naveen, K., Selvan, C., & Senanayake, R. (2022). Assessment of Risk and Opportunity in Accordance With ISO 9001. *International Journal of Social Ecology and Sustainable Development*, *13*(5), 1–16. Advance online publication. DOI: 10.4018/IJSESD.292037

Nweje, U., & Taiwo, M. (2025). Leveraging Artificial Intelligence for predictive supply chain management, focus on how AI- driven tools are revolutionizing demand forecasting and inventory optimization. *International Journal of Science and Research Archive*. .DOI: 10.30574/ijsra.2025.14.1.0027

Orzáez, H., & Moreno, G. (2021). Risk management methodology in the supply chain: A case study applied. *Annals of Operations Research*, *313*(2), 1051–1075. DOI: 10.1007/s10479-021-04220-y

Osho, G., J., & Omisola, J., Shiyanbola., 2024. A Systems-Based Framework for ISO 9000 Compliance: Applying Statistical Quality Control and Continuous Improvement Tools in U.S. Manufacturing. *International Journal of Advanced Multidisciplinary Research and Studies*. .DOI: 10.62225/2583049X.2024.4.6.4052

Owusu-Berko, L. (2025). Advanced supply chain analytics: Leveraging digital twins, IoT and blockchain for resilient, data-driven business operations. *World Journal of Advanced Research and Reviews*. .DOI: 10.30574/wjarr.2025.25.2.0572

Özkan, B. (2021). Analysing Effects of ISO 9001:2015 Quality Management System on Organizational Communication Structure. *Open Journal of Social Sciences*, *9*(10), 85–96. Advance online publication. DOI: 10.4236/jss.2021.910006

Pal, P., Hens, A., Behera, N., & Lahiri, S. (2025). Digital twins: Transforming the chemical process industry A review. *Canadian Journal of Chemical Engineering, 103*(8), 3611–3636. Advance online publication. DOI: 10.1002/cjce.25611

Parra, Y., Veloz, M., Ávila, G., Veloz, M., Rochina, P., & Parra, E. (2025). Risk Management in Process Management in the Contemporary Organization that Meets Sustainable Development Goals (SDG). *Journal of Lifestyle and SDGs Review*. .DOI: 10.47172/2965-730X.SDGsReview.v5.n02.pe04175

Peet's, J. D. E. (2024). Supplier Self-Assessment Form 2024. https://www.jdepeets.com/siteassets/home/sustainability/responsible-sourcing/jde-peets-supplier-self-assessment-form-2024.pdf

Pirrone, G., & Milotta, M. (2024). Entrepreneurial Culture and Continuous Improvement to Handle Environmental Turbulence. *Proceedings of the International Conference on Business Excellence*, 18, 1465 - 1476. DOI: 10.2478/picbe-2024-0120

Prameswari, A., Riezky, R., & Sudrajat, D. (2025). Supply chain 4.0 maturity, agility, resilience and absorptive capacity: an empirical study in Indonesia. *Jurnal Teknik Industri*. .DOI: 10.14710/jati.20.1.33-41

Puglieri, F., Ferreira, M., Júnior, A., Piekarski, C., & Silva, D. (2024). How to consider life cycle thinking into ISO 14001? A step-by-step method for small and medium sized companies and a case study in waste management. *Gestão & Produção*. DOI: 10.1590/1806-9649-2024v31e8723

Pylypchuk, V., Holitsyn, A., & Vasilkova, N. (2025). *International standards of the ISO 9000-9004 series in the system of marketing management*. Marketing and Digital Technologies., DOI: 10.15276/mdt.9.1.2025.7

Radke, A., Wuest, T., & Romero, D. (2021). Developing Digital Supply Network's Visibility Towards Transparency and Predictability. 13-21. .DOI: 10.1007/978-3-030-85902-2_2

Rahardjo, B., Wang, F., Lo, S., & Chu, T. (2023). A Sustainable Innovation Framework Based on Lean Six Sigma and Industry 5.0. *Arabian Journal for Science and Engineering*. Advance online publication. DOI: 10.1007/s13369-023-08565-3

Ramos-González, M., Rubio-Andrés, M., & Sastre-Castillo, M. (2021). Effects of socially responsible human resource management (SR-HRM) on innovation and reputation in entrepreneurial SMEs. *The International Entrepreneurship and Management Journal, 18*(3), 1205–1233. DOI: 10.1007/s11365-020-00720-8

Rimmer, P. & Kam, B., (2022). Consumer connectivity: forging supply chain success in the digital ecosystem. . .DOI: 10.4337/9781789905731.00012

Rodríguez, J. (2020). La gestión de recursos humanos en contextos de individualización., 16, 15. .DOI: 10.15332/22563067.5551

Rodríguez-García, M., Galindo-Manrique, A., Cortez-Alejandro, K. A., & Méndez-Sáenz, A.-B. (2022). Eco-efficiency and financial performance in Latin American countries: An environmental intensity approach. *Research in International Business and Finance*, *59*, 101547. Advance online publication. DOI: 10.1016/j.ribaf.2021.101547

Sah, B., Hasan, M., Shofiullah, S., & Faysal, S. (2024). AI-Driven IoT And Blockchain Integration In Industry 5.0 A Systematic Review Of Supply Chain Transformation. *Innovatech Engineering Journal*. .DOI: 10.70937/itej.v1i01.12

Sallam, K., Mohamed, M., & Mohamed, A. (2023). Internet of Things (IoT) in Supply Chain Management: Challenges, Opportunities, and Best Practices. S*ustainable Machine Intelligence Journal*. .DOI: 10.61185/SMIJ.2023.22103

Sârb, A., Udrea, C., Onita, D., Itul, L., & Popa, M. (2021). Prediction of defects using machine learning techniques in order to improve quality management system A case study. *MATEC Web of Conferences*. DOI: 10.1051/matecconf/202134305010

Saygılı, M., & Çiğal, E. (2022). Using Lean Six Sigma for Sustainability in Inbound Logistics: An Application in The Automotive Industry. *International Journal of Environment and Geoinformatics*, *9*(2), 108–119. Advance online publication. DOI: 10.30897/ijegeo.975066

Scanlan, M. (2021). *Sustainable by Design*. Prosperity in the Fossil-Free Economy., DOI: 10.12987/yale/9780300253993.003.0006

Sharma, S., & Pratap, R. (2023). A case study of risks prioritization using FMEA method. International Journal of Engineering Research and, 12(5), 449–453. DOI: 10.17577/IJERTV12IS050170

Sheth, A., Roy, K., Gaur, M., & Sheth, A. (2023). Neurosymbolic Artificial Intelligence (Why, What, and How). *IEEE Intelligent Systems*, *38*(3), 56–62. DOI: 10.1109/MIS.2023.3268724

Shiyanbola, J., Omisola, J., & Osho, G. (2024). A Systems Based Framework for ISO 9000 Compliance: Applying Statistical Quality Control and Continuous Improvement Tools in U.S. Manufacturing. *International Journal of Advanced Multidisciplinary Research and Studies*. .DOI: 10.62225/2583049X.2024.4.6.4052

Shovon, M., Amjad, M., & Hasan, A. (2024). Examining the integration of industry 4.0 technologies in manufacturing. *Academic journal on science, technology, engineering & mathematics education*. .DOI: 10.69593/ajsteme.v4i04.137

Silvério, J., & Pestana, G. (2022). Integrated Risk Monitoring in the Quality Management System., 3-12. .DOI: 10.1007/978-3-031-04829-6_1

Simão, V., Bonina, N., Lima, G., & Gonçalves, O. (2020). Comparative analysis between ABNT NBR ISO 9001:2015 and ABNT NBR ISO 31000:2009: The risk mindset in quality management systems. *Brazilian Journal of Development*, *6*(3), 10872–10887. DOI: 10.34117/bjdv6n3-320

Singh, G. (2020). Developing a maintenance management system based on integrated approach of ISO 9001:2015 and TQM philosophy. *Industrial Engineering and Management*, *9*(1), 1–4. DOI: 10.4172/2169-0316.1000295

Singh, P. (2024). Measuring the Broader Value Proposition of Digital Transformation in Supply Chains. *International. The Journal of Supply Chain Management*, *13*(1), 16–24. Advance online publication. DOI: 10.59160/ijscm.v13i1.6222

Singh, R. (2025). Transforming humanitarian supply chains with digital twin technology: A study on resilience and agility. *International Journal of Logistics Management*, *36*(4), 1119–1135. Advance online publication. DOI: 10.1108/IJLM-08-2024-0504

Siougle, E., Dimelis, S., & Malevris, N. (2023). Does personal data protection matter for ISO 9001 certification and firm performance? *International Journal of Productivity and Performance Management*. Advance online publication. DOI: 10.1108/IJPPM-07-2022-0345

Solonytska, I., Popel, O., Mardar, M., & Ganchev, S. (2024). *Evolution of quality control systems: from taylor to modern standards*. Scientific Works., DOI: 10.15673/swonaft.v88i2.3055

Soori, M., Arezoo, B., & Dastres, R. (2023). Internet of things for smart factories in industry 4.0, a review. *Internet of Things and Cyber-Physical Systems*, *3*, 192–204. Advance online publication. DOI: 10.1016/j.iotcps.2023.04.006

Stefanova-Stoyanova, V., & Danov, P. 2022. Comparative Analysis of Specialized Standards and Methods on Increasing the Effectiveness and Role of PDCA for Risk Control in Management System*s*. 2022 10th International Scientific Conference on Computer Science (COMSCI), pp. 1-4. DOI: 10.1109/COMSCI55378.2022.9912583

Stovpnyk, O., 2024. Building integrated management systems: achieving synergy and sustainability in modern organizations. *Вісник Східноукраїнського національного університету імені Володимира Даля*. .DOI: 10.33216/1998-7927-2024-284-4-89-95

Study, I. S. O. (2021). *International Organization for Standardization. (2021). Economic impact of standards – Methodological guidance* [PDF]. ISO.

Sun, J. (2024). How to Green the Supply Chain Through Daily Necessities Packaging Management from the Perspective of Consumers' Habits. *Advances in Economics, Management and Political Science*s. .DOI: 10.54254/2754-1169/66/20241216

Systems, E. P. A. M. (2023). Driving sustainable impact for JDE Peet's. https://www.epam.com/services/client-work/driving-sustainable-impact-for-jde-peets

Thakur, V. (2024). Collaborative supply chain network: Confusion or way ahead. International *Journal of Multidisciplinary Research and Growth Evaluation*. .DOI: 10.54660/.IJMRGE.2024.5.4.688-694

Tim, Y., Cui, L., & Sheng, Z. (2020). Digital resilience: How rural communities leapfrogged into sustainable development. *Information Systems Journal*, *31*(2), 323–345. DOI: 10.1111/isj.12312

Ţîmbaliuc, N. (2024). Organizational resilience in conditions of uncertainty. *EcoSoEn*. .DOI: 10.54481/ecosoen.2023.3.14

Tiwari, M., Bidanda, B., Geunes, J., Fernandes, K., & Dolgui, A. (2024). Supply chain digitisation and management. *International Journal of Production Research*, *62*(8), 2918–2926. DOI: 10.1080/00207543.2024.2316476

Torcică, G., & Georgescu, D. (2022). Analysis of the Quality-Risk Correlation in the Educational Organization. *LUMEN Proceedings*. DOI: 10.18662/lumproc/gidtp2022/04

Toromade, A., Soyombo, D., Kupa, E., & Ijomah, T. (2024). Technological innovations in accounting for food supply chain management. *Finance & Accounting Research Journal*. .DOI: 10.51594/farj.v6i7.1315

Varatharaj, M. (2024). *Enterprise Data-Driven Decision Making: A Framework for Digital Transformation and Organizational Excellence*. International Journal For Multidisciplinary Research., DOI: 10.36948/ijfmr.2024.v06i06.34279

Widianti, T., Firdaus, H., & Rakhmawati, T. (2024). Mapping the landscape: A bibliometric analysis of ISO 31000. *International Journal of Quality & Reliability Management*, *41*(7), 1783–1810. Advance online publication. DOI: 10.1108/IJQRM-09-2023-0287

Xu, J. (2025). Research on the Strategies and Methods for Improving the Efficiency of Logistics Supply Chain. *Advances in Economics, Management and Political Sciences*. .DOI: 10.54254/2754-1169/2024.GA19140

Xue, J., Li, G., & Ivanov, D. (2025). Digital transformation in the blockchain era: Balancing efficiency and resilience in operations management. *International Journal of Production Economics*, *282*, 109525. Advance online publication. DOI: 10.1016/j.ijpe.2025.109525

Yazo-Cabuya, E., Ibeas, A., & Rey-Caballero, R. (2025). Multi-Criteria Decision Making for Risk Management in Quality Management Systems. *Sustainability (Basel)*, *17*(3), 1092. Advance online publication. DOI: 10.3390/su17031092

Yekeen, A., Ewim, C., & Sam-Bulya, N. (2024). Enhancing supply chain security and transparency with ai and blockchain integration for future-proof solutions. *International Journal of Frontline Research in Science and Technology*. .DOI: 10.56355/ijfrst.2024.4.1.0052

Chapter 3

Entrepreneurial Leadership Effect on Participatory Governance Through Change-Oriented Organizational Culture

Vikki Sharma
http://orcid.org/0009-0003-5985-0667
Shri Ram College of Commerce, University of Delhi, India

Wako Jio
http://orcid.org/0009-0003-6192-459X
Bule Hora University, Ethiopia

Shashi Kant
http://orcid.org/0000-0003-4722-5736
St. Joseph University In Tanzania, Tanzania

Shashank Mittal
http://orcid.org/0009-0007-8643-4350
O.P. Jindal Global University, India

Pawan Kumar
http://orcid.org/0000-0001-7501-3066
Lovely Professional University, India

Antoniammal Manual
DMI-St.Eugene University, Zambia

ABSTRACT

This chapter addresses the contextualized interaction between entrepreneur leadership and participatory governance moderated by change oriented organizational culture over the Ethiopian context. The study with the sample size of 394 respondents uses a quantitative methodology to evaluate the dynamics of these variables. The results indicate that leadership of the entrepreneur greatly affects the participatory gov-

DOI: 10.4018/979-8-3373-6053-9.ch003

ernance because it leads to a change-oriented organizational culture. This culture which is flexible, innovative and involves employee interaction takes on a mediating role of improving practices of governance. The chapter makes a contribution towards understanding of the influence of leadership style in governing. It underlines the need to develop an organizational culture that will have embraced change towards enhancing participatory governance. The implication of these findings implies that the leaders of organizations must focus more on entrepreneurial leadership and cultural transformation to realize effective governance.

INTRODUCTION

With the world becoming an increasingly globalized world the importance of participatory governance has been highlighted across the globe given that societies are looking for more accommodating processes in decision making (Diakova et al., 2024; Karnsomdee & Phongkaew, 2023). Participatory governance enables citizens to be empowered, improve transparency and mistrust of buildings (Abawari et al., 2024) . It is a theory that formed out of the democratic ideas of involving the citizenry in the operation of governance and it has developed in different political situations and movements (Vivona, 2024; Demircioglu & Chowdhury, 2021). It has its origin in the late 20th century when the necessity of collaborative governance structures that go beyond classical hierarchical structures became clear to scholars and practitioners alike (Potipiroon & Thawornprasert, 2024). As the literature discusses, empirically, the leadership is an influential factor in determining the organizational culture and government (Lee & Shin, 2024). The body of literature demonstrates that the status of entrepreneurial leadership as innovation, flexibility, and risk-taking can play an essential role in altering organizational relations and governance rules (Maula et al., 2025). Nevertheless, the relationship among entrepreneurial leadership, that of change-oriented organizational culture and participatory governance is an insufficiently explored issue, at least in the context of developing countries, (Kumari et al., 2025). Most of the existing studies neglect to pay enough attention to the contextual influences of these relationships and therefore there is a lack of understanding regarding how entrepreneurial leadership can become an effective way of instilling participatory governance in various cultures (Campbell, 2025).

There are also practical issues that hinder the implementation of participatory governance in Ethiopia such as bureaucracy, lack of participation by the masses, and opposition to change in institutions (Jinga et al., 2024). These obstacles indicate the necessity of a diversified framework that will combine leadership patterns and cultural processes to promote a better approach to governance (Chen & Mandiberg, 2024). It is against this backdrop that the chapter attempts to address these research gaps by exploring how participatory governance is being impacted using an entrepreneurial leadership that is oriented towards change in organizational culture (Masih et al., 2025). Through answering the question, *how does entrepreneurial leadership influence participatory governance by Ethiopians and what is the role of change-oriented organizational culture in the relationship?*, the researcher, therefore, aims to establish the position of entrepreneurial leadership participatory governance in Ethiopia, and the role that change-oriented organizational culture plays in the relationship. we are trying to present the knowledge, which can reunite future researchers and policymakers.

BACKGROUND OF STUDY

Participatory governance has been experiencing increased popularity as societies are realizing the value of involving citizens in the governance mechanisms that Apprehension them (Lee & Shin, 2024; Demircioglu & Chowdhury, 2021). The model in question encourages transparency, accountability, and responsiveness, the key traits necessary to encourage trust between citizens and their governments (Kumari et al., 2025). Nevertheless, the use of participatory governance is not devoid of difficulties, especially in developing countries, where the political, social and economic context affect the nature of governance exercise (Maula et al., 2025). The governance environment in Ethiopia has greatly evolved over time since the early 1990s and it has shifted to a more decentralized governance system with the view of promoting the local autonomy (Potipiroon & Thawornprasert, 2024). Despite the attempts, participatory governance is mostly idealistic, and most of the initiatives have totally failed to attract meaningful citizen engagement (Vivona, 2024). In one example, a case study introduction at the local governmental level in Addis Ababa shown that although citizen forums had been developed as a way to solicit the citizen views, the attendance in these forums has been dwindling because of lack of awareness and optimism in the forums (Abawari et al., 2024; AlAnazi et al., 2022). Most citizens viewed such forums as formalities and not real sources of influence and this led to a gap in the government structures and the needs of the community (Diakova et al., 2024). The Productive Safety Net Program (PSNP) is another feasible case study where the issues that are involved in participatory governance have been signified (Campbell, 2025). The program was started due to food insecurity and was to make communities part of the process of planning and decision-making (Jinga et al., 2024). It was however reported that local leaders tended to dominate the proceedings to the exclusion of community Apprehensions and existing power relations were entrenched (Chen & Mandiberg, 2024). This was the top-down approach which caused frustrations amongst the citizens as they felt that their input was not valued and people became ineffective to the program (Masih et al., 2025).

Moreover, organizational culture can hardly be overestimated. Bureaucratic tendencies and threats of change are deep-rooted in most Ethiopian institutions, and present major challenges to implementing participatory governance (Kant et al., 2025). A case study of the Ministry of Agriculture revealed that even though there are training programs to encourage the use of participatory techniques in the department, deep-rooted hierarchical systems remained, limiting the application of collaborative approaches in policy formulation (Jio et al., 2025). Behind the above case studies lies the analytical details of the complexities of attempting to engage participatory governance in Ethiopia (Tuga et al., 2025). They stress the necessity to have a better comprehension on how entrepreneurial leadership can have a transformational effect when coping with such problems (Loukopoulos et al., 2025). Leaders by establishing a change-based organizational culture can establish those environments to promote real citizen engagement, to fill the gap between governance structures and community demands (Deresso et al., 2026). This chapter seeks to discuss such dynamics that can be very useful in the studies of researchers and policymakers who attempt to improve Participatory Governance in Ethiopia and other places like it.

STATEMENT OF PROBLEM

Participatory governance, though envisaged in Ethiopia comes with numerous challenges that prevent optimal realization (Jinga et al., 2024; Adula et al., 2025). Participatory governance in the ideal form would create an inclusive atmosphere in which all the citizens are involved in the process of decision making resulting to a more accountable and effective policies (Kant et al., 2025; Demircioglu & Chowdhury, 2021). Nevertheless, this situation in its modern form is described by low citizen engagement, professional bureaucracy and distrust in the system of governance (Jio et al., 2025). This gap between the desired and the reality presents a noteworthy issue, which might need intensive research (Kumari et al., 2025). There is some counter-intuitive evidence in the empirical literature on whether participatory governance initiatives are effective (Maula et al., 2025). Although there is evidence in certain studies that, with greater citizen involvement can come better governance results, other studies report that when one meets the challenges of greater involvement, much more rarely do the efforts turn out to provide substantive involvement (Potipiroon & Thawornprasert, 2024). The inconsistent outcomes present a conflicting picture to the policymakers and the researchers indicating a lack of cautious analyses that take into account the interactions of diverse influences in participatory governance

(Diakova et al., 2024). Even gaps in theory are numerous in the literature (Lee & Shin, 2024). Entrepreneurial leadership and its ability to create a change-oriented organizational culture that can benefit participatory governance is not properly captured in most frameworks (Abawari et al., 2024). This neglect reduces our knowledge as to how to ensure that the leadership styles may effectively fill in the gap between the structures of governance and those of community expectations (Vivona, 2024).

There is also the considerable shortage of knowledge on the nature of contextual factors which influence the participatory governance (Campbell, 2025). Much existing research has been general on principles of governance and has not fully taken into consideration the differing socio-cultural dynamics involved (Masih et al., 2025). Such contextual faults hamper the possibility of designing context-specific-solutions that connect with the local realities (Chen & Mandiberg, 2024). Viable obstacles to the practice of participatory governance also exist. The promotion of citizen engagement in the community is commonly encouraged by bureaucratic opposition, deficient training, and a lack of resources (Loukopoulos et al., 2025). The priorities of local leaders might be more significant than the interest of the community preserving the prior existing inequalities and disappointment in citizens (Tufa et al., 2025). This chapter attempts to address these pertinent research gaps by investigating the impact of participatory governance using entrepreneurial leadership as an organizing culture that is geared toward change.

THEORETICAL FOUNDATION

Participatory Governance Theory: It considers the importance of citizen participation in the decision making process. It emerged due to the theory of democratic forms of governance and promotes the inclusion and transparency as the necessary features of efficient governance. According to this theory, active participation of citizens in the government process will result in better outcomes, higher levels of accountability and institutional trust. The theory is also applied in Ethiopia as a fundamental guide Apprehensioning how the citizens can affect the nature of governance and policymaking by showing that mechanisms that can ensure that the citizenry actively participate in the governance process are required (Lee & Shin, 2024).

Transformational Leadership Theory: It is Apprehensioned with leaders that influence and encourage the subordinates to move beyond their limited self-interests to serve or benefit the organization or the community. James MacGregor Burns developed this theory and Bernard Bass expanded on it, therefore, putting emphasis on the aspects of vision, inspiration, and change. Transformational leaders are regarded as force of change in the sense in which they create an environment that is attractive to innovation and group goals. Within the domain of participatory governance studies, this theory highlights the importance of entrepreneurial leaders that have the ability of developing a change-oriented culture in organizations, thereby stimulating citizen participation and effectiveness of governance (Campbell, 2025).

Change Management Theory: It is Apprehensioned with the management and transition of change in an organization. This theory was formulated by theorists like Kurt Lewin, John Kotter; it describes procedures that are to be followed in effective implementation of change within organizations. It also makes clear that it is necessary to recognize resistance to change and support in adapting to it. This theory is applicable in participatory governance since it emphasizes on the need of organizations to change their structures and cultures in order to allow citizen participation. Leaders in transformation governance by comprehending the nature of change will navigate easier in the intricacies that are involved in change processes (Vivona, 2024).

Social Capital Theory: It attaches importance to the value of social networks and relations. Ordained by such sociologists as Pierre Bourdieu and Robert Putnam, the theory states that the collectivity of action and cooperation may be achieved by means of social connections and trust between the individuals. With regards to administration, social capital would prove to be critical in acting as a facilitator of interaction and co-ordination between the citizens and the institutions. The theory can also be used to understand the subtlety of an ethnography based on communities and the importance of trust in boosting participatory government within settings where post-historical impediment could be present (Potipiroon & Thawornprasert, 2024).

The *Transformational Leadership Theory* is the primary theoretical lens in viewing this study. The reason behind this decision is the desire to examine how this practice recognizes the role of entrepreneurial leadership in changing people due to which they are ready to develop a culture that favors participatory governance. Through the use of the qualities and characteristics of transformational leaders, the research intends to explain how such leaders are well positioned to close the divide between systems of governance and the involvement of the community.

DEFINITION AND ORIGIN OF CONCEPT

Participatory Governance: It entails practices employed by people who take part in the decision-making and the making of policy decisions so that their voices are heard and taken into account. Appearing on the basis of the democratic theories of citizen input, participatory governance entails numerous mechanisms, including, but not limited to, citizens consultations, community forums, and participatory policymaking. It has its origins to the 20th century civil rights movements and the social justice programs where the significance of inclusive systems of governance was highlighted (Abawari et al., 2024).

Entrepreneurial Leadership: The capacity to identify opportunities, innovate and inspire others to work towards the same end is always an attribute of an entrepreneurial leadership. This business idea puts together some of the fundamentals of entrepreneurship and application of principles of leadership, where vision, taking risks, and being flexible is vital. The term was formed as the result of research on effective leadership within entrepreneurial endeavors wherein leaders are to create an environment where creativity and change responsiveness is encouraged (Potipiroon & Thawornprasert, 2024).

Change-Oriented Culture of Organization: It is the type of working environment meant to spread the idea of flexibility, innovativeness, and progressive thinking. The culture helps to motivate the employees towards adapting to change, risk taking as well as cooperating with each other in the pursuit of shared objectives. This concept dates back to the organizational behavior research where scholars have established the role played by culture in the engagement of employees and efficiency of the organizations. The ability to implement new strategy in an organization like participatory governance requires a change oriented culture (Vivona, 2024).

Social Capital: it defined as networks, relationships and trust that allow people and groups to cooperate with one another. An idea borrowed on sociological research, the term emphasizes the importance of social ties in facilitating community-based action and social engagement. Participatory governance highly depends on social capital because it encourages cooperation and mutual trust amongst the citizens and allows meaningful participation in governance structures (Lee & Shin, 2024).

EMPIRICAL LITERATURE REVIEW

Entrepreneurial leadership and participatory governance

The confluence between the entrepreneurial leadership and participatory governance has attracted growing interest in empirical research especially since organizations have been striving to increase citizen participation with a view of improving the outcomes pertaining to governance (Diakova et al., 2024). It has been emphasized that in the context of organizations, the issue of entrepreneurial leadership, which is about innovation, risk-taking and vision of change, is a key driver in establishment of organizational culture as well as in participation of governance (Abawari et al., 2024). A notable study stream is the research on how entrepreneurial leaders can create an atmosphere in the society that will encourage the citizen participation (Vivona, 2024). As an example, a research study has been conducted on local government initiatives of different countries which showed that cities under entrepreneurial leadership performed more successfully in applying participatory governance procedures (Potipiroon & Thawornprasert, 2024). Such leaders have been keen on involving citizen participation on new fronts considering innovative consultation mechanisms, including, but not limited to, digital consultations and community workshops which has not only enhanced citizen engagement in the process but also democratic trust in the governance (Lee & Shin, 2024). The other empirical literature that is important examines organizational culture as a mediator of relationship between entrepreneurial leadership and participatory governance (Piwowar-Sulej & Iqbal, 2025). The literature on the organizational culture of change places a high level of importance on a change-oriented culture within a company to achieve the application of the vision of the entrepreneurial leaders into measurable participatory practices (Maula et al., 2025). According to their results organizations with positive culture of flexibility and open communication reduce the probability of unsuccessful attempts to involve citizens in processes of governance (Kumari et al., 2025). This concurs with the fact that the concept of organizational culture has the potential to either accommodate or impede implementation of participatory governance strategies (Campbell, 2025).

Further, the challenges accompanying the undertaking of participatory governance in restrictive institutional settings are also discussed (Jinga et al., 2024). As an example, one might cite a study that has raised the challenges encountered by local governments (Ling et al., 2025), where the attempts of engaging citizens in meaningful ways were hampered by the existing bureaucratic procedures and the bureaucratic culture of opposing change even in the face of the presence of entrepreneurial leaders (Chen & Mandiberg, 2024). The relevance of this study is in its emphasis of the need to take local circumstances into consideration regarding the effectiveness of participatory governance initiatives and that leadership is not enough to achieve the expected result without an appropriate organizational culture (Masih et al., 2025). The issue of social capital has also been discussed against entrepreneurial leadership and participatory governance (Loukopoulos et al., 2025). It has been found that the presence of good social networks and faith in community members will increase collective action and involvement in governance (Fang et al., 2024). Within the Ethiopian context it has been established that through building on social capital, the entrepreneurial leadership can make the trying environment more conducive with regard to participatory governance (Ling et al., 2024). This relationship brings out the mutual relationship between community involvement and the leadership styles that foster the same (Sørensen & Lindholst, 2025). Also, empirical studies have attempted to measure the role played by entrepreneurial leaderships in the outcome of corporate governance (Karnsomdee & Phongkaew, 2023). Meta-analysis synthesized the studies and concluded that organizations with entrepreneurial leaders can not only report higher levels of citizen participation but also report higher governance outcomes satisfaction (Adula et al., 2025). This point stresses the entrepreneurial leadership has the possibility to change the practice of governance and increase overall delivery of the services provided to people (Karo et al., 2025).

H1: Entrepreneurial leadership and participatory governance having empirical association

Entrepreneurial leadership and change-oriented organizational culture

Empirical studies have always underscored a point at which entrepreneurial leaders are able to foster the dose of change, innovation and adaptability that are critical in the business atmospheres of organizations that must strive to excel in the environment (Karnsomdee & Phongkaew, 2023; Lemi et al., 2025). The role brought on by entrepreneurial leaders in determining organizational culture is one of the major themes in the literature (Sørensen & Lindholst, 2025). One study identified that entrepreneurial leaders proactively develop a culture of innovation harnessing risk-taking and experimentation on the part of employees (Ling et al., 2025). They found out that such leaders yield a high employee engagement and creativity in their organizations (Fang et al., 2024). This is in line with the idea that a leader of an entrepreneur does not Apprehension decision making alone, but he is also a cultural designer who establishes values and behaviors that help in the creation of a proactive attitude towards change (Masih et al., 2025). Furthermore, the article under consideration supports the centrality of communication in the process of creating a change-driven organizational culture (Chen & Mandiberg, 2024). Their results indicate that open communication and feedback systems enabled by the decision makers of the company are essential in depicting perceptions of empowerment among workers to provide ideas in relation to the organizational change (Jinga et al., 2024). Such participation does not only contribute to the promotion of the culture of innovation but also makes employees more committed to the organizational objectives, which highlights the relationship between leadership style and cultural results (Diakova et al., 2024).

The influence of change-oriented culture on the performance of the organization has been studied as well (Vivona, 2024). As an example, one study showed that organizations that had a strong culture of change and it was developed through the entrepreneurial leadership showed stronger adaptability to the changes in the market and increased performance ratios (Abawari et al., 2024). They demonstrated that these types of organizations were more appropriate to introduce strategic changes quickly, thus, creating competitive advantage in corresponding industries (Potipiroon & Thawornprasert, 2024). This is evidence that a supportive culture plays a paramount role in facilitating the ability of any organization to respond to the external challenges successfully (Lee & Shin, 2024). Also that mediating effects of change oriented culture have been expressed in the literature on the relationship between entrepreneurial leadership and organizational outcome (Piwowar-Sulej & Iqbal, 2025). Based on a study, the existence of change-oriented culture plays a serious role of mediating the effects of entrepreneurial leadership on performance in innovations (Maula et al., 2025). They have found out that though entrepreneurial leaders can act as engines of innovation vision, it is through the organizational culture that is ultimately determined whether the vision is achieved wholly or not (Kumari et al., 2025). This implies that the creation of a culture of change is critical in transforming the leadership intentions into actual results (Campbell, 2025). There are, nevertheless, empirical studies which show difficulties in creating an organizational culture which is oriented toward change (Loukopoulos et al., 2025). Such obstacles have been found out through research, like resistance to change and the traditional practices that have structural roots, which can hinder the initiatives of entrepreneurial leaders (Kant et al., 2025). They proved that leaders should approach such cultural inertia problems in a manner that proactively serves to support change programs in a way that values and expectations of the employees are supported (Dereso et al., 2025.

> H2: Entrepreneurial leadership and change-oriented organizational culture having empirical association

Change-oriented organizational culture and participatory governance

The dynamics between the participatory culture of organizations and their organizational cultures that are focused on change have emerged as a subject of greater interest especially as organizations seek to integrate citizen participation and the outcomes of the governance (Potipiroon & Thawornprasert, 2024). As empirical studies have indicated, a change oriented culture may be used in substantially enhancing participatory governance involving participatory scheme of things and encouraging innovative environment (Abawari et al., 2024). Among the major findings of the literature is the fact that an organizational culture that reinforces change orientation promotes flexibility and responsive behavior that forms a critical element in effective participatory governance (Diakova et al., 2024). As an example, one study revealed that organizations that had a strong culture of change realized better success in adopting participatory practices of governance (Vivona, 2024). In their study, they show thus linked cultures positively affect open communication and make the employees and citizens themselves engaged in decision-making as well (Lee & Shin, 2024). This follows the fact that through embracing change, the organizations stand in better position to address needs and preferences of their constituents leading to more effective governance (Piwowar-Sulej & Iqbal, 2025). In addition, change-oriented cultures are empirically shown to increase trust and cooperation among stakeholders, which is also an essential part of participatory governance (Piwowar-Sulej & Iqbal, 2025). Some studies pointed to the importance of building relations with the external community and among the civic organizations through fostering a culture of change as organizations that implement this system effectively not only enhance their relationships with the outside community members and other civic organizations, but also enhance collaboration within the organizations (Maula et al., 2025). Their results displayed that trust established on the routes of change-oriented culture enables increased citizen input in the process of governance as people will feel more appreciated and heard in decision-making (Kumari et al., 2025).

In addition, the literature provides mediated relationship between leadership and participatory governance through change-oriented organizational culture (Campbell, 2025). In one study, the leaders who embraced a change oriented organizational culture were observed to have greater effects on participatory governance output by making the processes of feedback, encouraging feedback and property innovation (Jinga et al., 2024). Their study revealed that in the organizations that were governed by such leaders, the citizen participation and contentment with the governance process rose, which indicated that leadership and culture are both interrelated variables that determine the success of participatory governance (Chen & Mandiberg, 2024). Still, the issues of developing a change-minded culture that will endorse participatory governance occur (Masih et al., 2025). Existing research has seen impediments that include change resistance, fear of the loss of control and deep-seated bureaucratic processes which may throttle attempts to foster citizen engagement (Loukopoulos et al., 2025). They have highlighted that it is significant to work with such barriers by education leaders and policymakers in specific ways, i.e. through offering training programs and awareness activities to create a culture of accepting change and fostering governance efforts (Fang et al., 2024). As well, the social capital concept is usually associated with a change oriented culture and participatory governance (Kyeong, 2025). Research has revealed that when organizations have good social capital, which is defined by trust and cooperation, then chances are high that the practices of participatory governance would be implemented adequately (Ling et al., 2025). As an example, one study showed that societies that had much social capital actively participated in the governance process (Sørensen & Lindholst, 2025). This implies that the creation of a change-oriented culture has the potential of promoting social capital hence enabling more of the citizen participation and cooperation in the governance process (Karnsomdee & Phongkaew, 2023).

H3: Change-oriented organizational culture and participatory governance having empirical association

Entrepreneurial leadership, participatory governance, change-oriented OC

It has been of great interest in empirical research to focus on the mediation role of change-oriented organizational culture in the linkage between enterprise leadership and participatory governance (Karnsomdee & Phongkaew, 2023). This literature base aims at unraveling the application of participatory governance that can be manipulated by entrepreneurial leaders by the development of a culture that focuses on change and innovation (Chen et al., 2024). An early research study examined the direct impact of entrepreneurial leadership on participatory governance and concluded that entrepreneurial leaders-that is, leaders able to display entrepreneurial behaviors (including, taking risks, articulation of a vision and able to promote innovation) are more successful in enhancing citizen input (Sørensen & Lindholst, 2025). Nonetheless, they also gave the fact that the key mediating change-oriented organizational culture plays an essential role (Ling et al., 2025). The study showed that with the entrepreneurial leaders that make their culture more adaptive and having open communication, they stand a higher chance of successfully engaging in participatory governance between them (Dereso et al., 2025). This implies that the effects of entrepreneurial leadership have an additional support in being accompanied by an organizational culture. Additional empirical support is given to this mediation hypothesis (Jio et al., 2025). In one study, diverse local government efforts were examined and researchers found that change-oriented cultures dramatically improve the efficacy of the participatory-governance-practices (Kant et al., 2025). Their results showed that the organization having the high culture of change had more credibility of adopting an innovative participatory mechanism, i.e. community-based projects and participatory policymaking mechanism, which resulted in increased satisfaction and participation by the citizen in turn (Kyeong, 2025). This is an indicator of the need to inculcate a culture that does not only tolerate but more so promotes change as a window towards better results in governance (Loukopoulos et al., 2025).

Besides, the literature emphases the relationship between change-oriented culture and entrepreneurial leadership of breaking the hurdles of participatory governance (Masih et al., 2025). A study established that an entrepreneurial leadership that is keen on cultural changes will be able to avert the resistance to participating among citizens and stakeholders (Chen & Mandiberg, 2024). These leaders can use a culture to create a system that promotes input and feedback and turn the skepticism into participation (Jinga et al., 2024). They found in their work that mediating role of change-oriented culture plays a crucial role in acting on the intentions of entrepreneurial leaders in bringing discussions into the action that involves participatory governance (Campbell, 2025). Also, the issue of social capital is frequently discussed in this regard (Kumari et al., 2025). A change oriented organizational culture has been found by a study and subsequent research to contribute to social capital in terms of increasing trust and cooperation among the members of the community (Maula et al., 2025). Having such social capital is essential in participatory governance because that will motivate the people to participate in collective action and decision-making (Piwowar-Sulej & Iqbal, 2025). The culture of change orientation, mediated in such a way as to enhance effective leadership, does not only assist in bringing about a high level of leadership affectation but also enhances social networks essential in a successful governance (Lee & Shin, 2024). Nonetheless, there are still issues of setting up this mediation pathway (Potipiroon & Thawornprasert, 2024). Studies have also noted that established organization routines and organizational cultural lethargy may undermine the endeavors of entrepreneurial leaders to inject the organization with change oriented culture (Abawari et al., 2024). They conclude that unless the systemic obstacles can be resolved, then the possibilities of introducing entrepreneurial leadership and thereby improving participatory governance by way of cultural transformation could be low (Vivona, 2024). This brings out the necessity of combining evaluation of leadership capabilities and integration of cultures in the strategies to promote successful participatory governance (Diakova et al., 2024).

H4: Entrepreneurial leadership, participatory governance and change-oriented organizational culture Mediation having empirical association

FRAMEWORK

Figure 1. Conceptual Framework

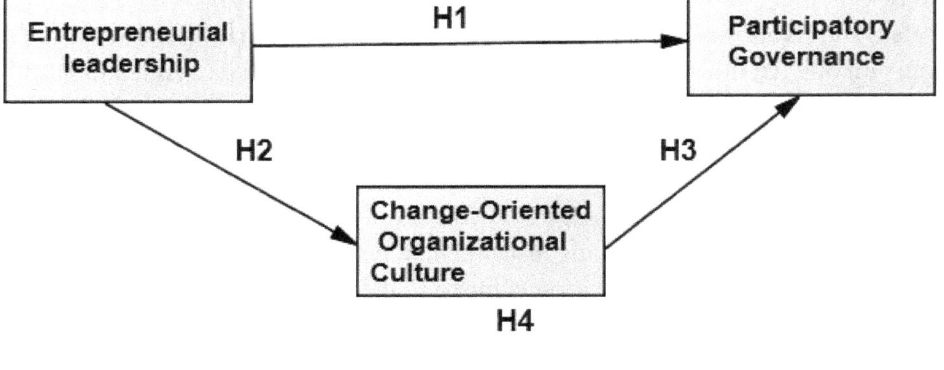

METHODOLOGY

Three hundred and ninety-four (394) samples were taken across different organizations in Ethiopia and the questionnaire used to collect this sample was structured and aimed to measure the constructs of interest. Sample size was calculated on statistical suggestions to ascertain the sufficient power of the study in analyzing the information and drawing significant conclusions out of the data. Data analysis began by evaluating the appropriateness of the data in the factor analysis by measuring the KMO. The value of KMO was over 0.70, which implies that the sample size was sufficient and further analysis could be used. After this, EFA was run to illustrate the latent structure of data and to test the measurement scales. EFA enabled to determine the crucial aspects the sphere of entrepreneurial leadership, change-away organizational culture, and participatory governance, helping to modify the elements of the measurements. After identifying the factors, the structure of the factors as read in the EFA was validated by establishing CFA in AMOS software. The data fitting showed that match was good implying that the constructs were clearly defined and were fit to proceed with the analysis. In order to examine the hypothesized relationships between the constructs they were used SEM to examine them. It helped to examine the direct and indirect impact of the relationships between entrepreneurial leadership, change-oriented organizational culture, and participatory governance. The analysis was able to give an understanding of the mediating effect of change-oriented culture between leadership and the outcomes of governance.

Scale Development

The scale development process was based on sufficient review of literature relevant to measurement development and this informed development of measurement items under each of the construct. In the case of, entrepreneurial leadership, items were based off of already existing frameworks that prioritize traits of vision, innovation, and risk-taking. The research adapted scales that were used in earlier surveys, e.g., by Bass and Avolio (1994) and Gupta and Singh (2019), with modifications to make them pinpoint the Ethiopian setting. In terms of change-oriented organizational culture, researchers, such as Wang and Hu (2020), emphasized the role of adaptability, open communication, and empowerment of employees, which is why the scale was created on the basis of their ideas. The products were designed to measure these dimensions as they were sensitive to the context of organizational culture that was fast evolving. Lastly, the surveying instrument of participatory governance was created based on the identified constructs found in the literature with the focus on the engagement of the people involved, transparency, and accountability. Data collected by Kahn and Sethi (2018) and Turner and Baker (2020) thoroughly informed the measurement items, since they were aimed at understanding the ways in which the practice of governance can be improved with the active participation of citizens.

RESULT

Table 1. Data competence

Sampling Suitability		.906
Bartlett's Assessment	Chi-Square	2095.96
	Df	126
	Sig.	.000

Source: Authors

The findings on the sampling competence reported in Table 1. The KMO value of 0.906 depicts sufficient level of sampling adequacy, indicating that the data would be suitable in determining underlying factors. A value of KMO of more than 0.70 is still acceptable, and higher results imply better sampling adequacy, like 1.0. This outcome suggests that the variables covered by the study are correlated enough such that factor analysis should be considered. The suitability of the data supports with Chi-square =2095.96 and a significant level (P-value) of> 0.000. The large p-value ($p<0.05$) shows that there is a strong correlation to exist among the variables and thus the factor analysis procedure is indeed justifiable. Basically, both tests confirm the appropriateness of data gathered to proceed with further evaluation, and it is possible to identify underlying constructs of entrepreneurial leadership, change-oriented organizational culture, and participatory governance. The same findings can be used to justify the further analyses in that the findings of the study would be dependable and true.

Table 2. Variance Explicated

C	Initial Eigenv			Extraction Sums			Rotation Sums		
	Total	% of Variance	Cumulative %	Total	% of Variance	Cumulative %	Total	% of Variance	Cumulative %
1	4.1	32.5	32.5	4.1	32.5	32.5	3.0	21.1	21.1
2	2.3	9.7	42.2	2.3	9.7	42.2	2.6	15.1	40.4
3	2.3	9.7	63.5	2.3	9.7	63.5	1.8	14.8	63.5
4	.99	6.2	57.2						

continued on following page

Table 2. Continued

C	Initial Eigenv			Extraction Sums			Rotation Sums		
	Total	**% of Variance**	**Cumulative %**	**Total**	**% of Variance**	**Cumulative %**	**Total**	**% of Variance**	**Cumulative %**
5	.81	6.3	64.5						
6	.73	5.9	69.4						

Source: Authors

Table 2 shows the outcomes of the Total Variance Explained as the outcome of the exploratory factor analysis with the Principal Component Analysis as the extraction method. Initial eigenvalues, extraction sums of squared loadings, and rotation sums of squared loadings have been reported in the table for the identified factors. The first eigenvalues show that the first component provides information about 4.1 of the greater amount of variance, 32.5 percent of the entire variance in the data group. This is quite a large amount, indicating that there is some substantial measurement of the underlying structure in the first factor. Components 2 and 3 show significant results as well with each explaining 2.3 eigenvalues, with 9.7 percent of the variance, adding up to a cumulative 63.5 percent of the variance at the three components. It is interesting to note that the fourth, fifth, and sixth components have the diminishing returns with eigenvalues of 0.99, 0.81, and 0.73 respectively. These elements elaborate 6.2%, 6.3%, and 5.9 percent of the variance which totals to 69.4 percent.

Table 3. Covariances

Covariance			Estimate	S.E.	C.R.	P	Hy.
change-oriented organizational culture	<-->	Entrepreneurial leadership	.274	.032	8.073	.00	H2
change-oriented organizational culture	<-->	participatory governance	.303	.029	7.989	.00	**H3**
Entrepreneurial leadership	<-->	participatory governance	.254	0.34	7.741	.00	**H1**

Source: Authors

The covariance estimates of the major constructs are manifested in table 3). The level of covariance between change-oriented organization culture and entrepreneurial leadership is 0.274 and the S.E. = 0.032. A p-value of 0.00 and C.R of 8.073 show that the positive relationship between knowledge and cognition is very significant, justifying the H2. Such implies that effective entrepreneurial leadership is closely related to an impressive change oriented organizational culture, meaning that cultures that have adaptive cultures have higher chances of exposing entrepreneurial behaviors. In the same context, the fitted estimates value between change-oriented organizational culture and participatory governance is 0.303, with S.E. =0.029, C.R. = 7.989, p-value = 0.00, which implies that this relationship is significantly important, and this supports Hypothesis 3 (H3). This finding supports the notion of organizations having a strong culture of change are most likely to involve the citizens in the governance processes as this improves the participatory systems of governance.

Finally, covariance value between entrepreneurial leadership and participatory governance is 0.254 with S.E. = 0.34, CR = 7.741; p-value = 0.00, which confirms H1.

Table 4. Validity Apprehension

	CR	AVE	MSV	MaxR(H)	EL	COOC	PG
EL	0.732	0.643	0.219	0.852	**0.654**		
COOC	0.758	0.657	0.132	0.763	0.171	**0.665**	
PG	0.793	0.603	0.274	0.797	0.383	0.193	**0.684**

Note: EL= Entrepreneurial leadership; COOC= change-oriented organizational culture; PG= participatory governance

Source: Authors

The validity issues are provided in Table 4. The CR values are 0.732 for entrepreneurial leadership, 0.758 for change-oriented organizational culture and 0.793 with participatory governance. Regarding the CR, as a rule, values higher than 0.7 can be regarded as acceptable, which indicates that all constructs have sufficient reliability. This is backed by the validity of constructs because the AVE are 0.643, 0.657, and 0.603 of the measures of entrepreneurial leadership, change-oriented organizational culture and a participatory governance respectively. The AVE of more than 0.5 shows that a significant percentage of variance in the indicators is due to the latent construct making it true that the constructs being valid were actually studying the theoretical concepts. The MSV indicate the strongest correlations of all constructs, where EL and COOC are (0.219), COOC and PG (0.132) and EL and PG (0.274). These values indicate that the constructs are not equivalents as the MSV of each construct is even smaller than AVE, which supports the discriminant validity. Lastly, the ranges of MAXR(H) values within the constructs are in the good limits of 0.763-0.852. These values too confirm the strength of the scales applied to the study.

Figure 2. Structural Equation Model

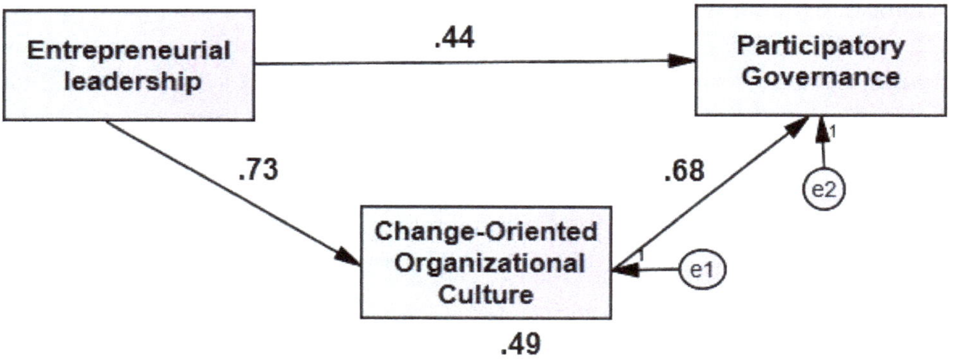

Table 5. Model Appropriate

Sig.	Chi-Sq	RMR	Goodness	Confirmatory	TLI	RMSEA
0.006	1.073	.036	0.930	0.912	0.911	.028

Source: Authors

Table 5 shows model fit. The Sig. of 0.006 implies the model is statistically significant therefore implying that the proposed relationships have a meaning. Such a value of Chi-Square in the results is relatively small at 1.073 and this reflects positively on the model fit since lower values would imply that the model fits better with the observed and expected data. Under the goodness of fit measures, the RMR is found at 0.036 which is less than the standard value of 0.05 thus proving the reliability of the model further. When classifying the goodness of fit indices, the model appears to be strongly fit such that GFI is 0.930 and CFI 0.912. The two values are above the widely-used level of 0.90, which predicts the data can be fitted to the model. Moreover, TLI is indicated as 0.911, which also supports the conclusion that the model offers a good fit. The RMSEA 0.028 is very significant, where values of less than 0.05 indicate a close fitting. This low value of RMSEA is indicative of the fact that the model is a good representation of the data and the postulated relationships are well-grounded.

Table 6. Regression

Relative			Approx.	S.E.	C.R.	P	Ass.
change-oriented organizational culture	<---	Entrepreneurial leadership	.864	.143	7.583	.00	H2
participatory governance	<---	change-oriented organizational culture	.328	.131	2.853	.00	H3
participatory governance	<---	Entrepreneurial leadership	.957	.192	7.958	.00	H1

Source: Authors

The outcome of the regression analysis is offered in Table 6 The coefficient of the dependence of entrepreneurial leadership and the change-oriented organizational culture is 0.864 and SE is 0.143. CR of 7.583 and p-value of 0.00, imply high significance of a positive effect in support of H2. The high coefficient value implies that entrepreneurial leadership plays a significant role in developing an organizational culture that is oriented towards change. In addition, the regression result indicates that the organizational culture of change has a substantial implication to participatory governance, whose coefficient is 0.328 and S.E. is 0.131. The statistic that shows the significance of this relationship verified through the critical ratio of 2.853 and p-value = 0.00 defends the H3. This observation implies that a sound change-oriented culture has a positive effect on the development of participatory governance practices. Finally, direct influence of entrepreneurial leadership on participatory governance is modeled with a coefficient of 0.957 and an S.E. of 0.192). The p-value of 0.00 and critical ratio of 7.958 proves the significance of this relationship, and it supports the H1 well. The finding means that participatory governance is a direct conduit of effective entrepreneurial leadership, and the leader of an organization plays a very key role as far as the establishment of participatory governance in organizations is manifested.

Table 7. Mediation

	substance
Entrepreneurial leadership → participatory governance	.44
Entrepreneurial leadership → change-oriented organizational culture → participatory governance	.73*.68=.49
	.94

Source: Authors

Table 7 shows how the change-oriented organizational culture intervenes between entrepreneurial leadership and participatory governance. This table outlines the direct and indirect effects that entrepreneurial leadership both has on participatory governance and a broader understanding of exactly what is occurring. The direct effect of the impact of the entrepreneurial leadership on the participatory governance is given as 0.44, which is significant and large. This implicit approach implies that successful entrepreneurship leadership can make direct contributions to better participatory governance processes, justifying the significance of leadership the driving force in the engagement of citizens and cooperation. Besides, the table reflects the indirect contribution of the entrepreneurial leadership to the participatory governance, i.e. through the change oriented organizational culture. This is obtained as a product of the two path coefficients between entrepreneurial leadership and change-oriented organizational culture (0.73) and change-oriented organizational culture and participatory governance (0.68). This gives a resulting indirect effect of 0.49, which shows that a significant percentage of the influence that the entrepreneurial leadership of the organization has on participatory governance is mediated by a change-oriented culture. When the overall effect is addressed, the entire effect of the entrepreneurial leadership on the participatory governance that involves the direct as well as the indirect routes is 0.94. This overall impact is quite high, which affirms the significant contribution of entrepreneurial leadership to determining the outcomes of participatory governance. This relationship is reported to be mediated by the change-oriented organizational culture making the designation of partial mediation, the impact of which is that the concept of leadership, namely the entrepreneurial leadership, has a strong direct impact on participatory governance. All in all, Table 7 substantiates the role of change-oriented organizational culture as an essential mechanism of effectuation of entrepreneurial leadership into active participatory governance, and thus depicts the interdependence of these constructs in effecting good governance practices.

DISCUSSION

The results of the present research can support the evidence of the close connections between entrepreneurial leadership, the organizational culture that focuses on change, and participatory governance. The pronounced positive results indicate that the entrepreneurial leaders apply key effort in the mobilization of an organizational culture that is friendly to change, that in itself boosts participatory governance exercises. This is in line with what is already present in literature that points to the relevance of leadership to the establishment of organizational culture and innovation. The fact that the direct impact of entrepreneurial leadership is significant shows that leaders with entrepreneurial traits, including vision, risk-taking and adaptability have better chance to engage citizens in the processes of governance effectively. Additionally, its role as mediator is further explained by the change-oriented organizational culture that also underlines its significance as a mediator between leadership and governance outcomes. The robust indirect effect implies that, besides magnifying the effect of entrepreneurial leadership, a positive culture can establish an environment, in which participatory governance is actually possible. The finding is especially effective in the modern quick dynamic organization environments where flexibility and citizen involvement is the key to success. The results of the study also show that change-oriented organization culture partially mediates the connection between entrepreneurial leadership and participatory governance but the direct impact of leadership also cannot be underestimated. This indicates that, on the one hand, it is important to instill an orientation on the change in culture but, on the other hand, the direct impact of the entrepreneurial leaders in governing the practices cannot be ruled out.

CONCLUSION

This research brings into the fore the inherent interrelationship between the organizational culture of change and the participatory governance as well as entrepreneurial leadership. The results indicate that the role of entrepreneurial leaders is critical towards imbuing a culture of not only accommodating changes, but also strengthen citizen participation in the governance activities. This high positive correlation between the two concepts namely, entrepreneurial leadership and participatory governance portrays the significance of one aspect which in this case is entrepreneurial leadership in achieving good governance practices. The mediating effect of change-oriented organizational culture, further refutes this finding that investing in the change oriented organizational culture is critical in enhancing the effectiveness of the leadership on the outcomes of governance. These lessons imply that to enhance participatory governance in organizations, there is a need to develop entrepreneurial leader character as well as develop a favorable organizational culture. Through this, they are able to develop environments that promote innovativeness, flexibility and participation of citizens. In general, the research fills the gap in available sources of information as it is the first to draw empirical evidence of interrelatedness of the given constructs, which serve as the kind of framework that future researchers can use, as well as practitioners, which can be applied to governance.

MANAGERIAL IMPLICATIONS

The results of the research in question have enlightening managerial meanings to the organizations striving to improve participatory governance. To begin with, there is a necessity to invest in facilitating the entrepreneurial leadership potential of the managers. The presence of entrepreneurial leadership in terms of vision, openness, and risk taking ability within an organization may contribute greatly to the organizational culture and the creation of an environment where change and innovation thrives. Leadership development programs and training should be aimed at instilling such traits in leaders, so that they are ready to reach out to stakeholders and pursue participatory governance. Additionally, it is expected that organizations give a priority to the establishment of a change oriented organizational culture. Part of this entails the promotion of an uninhibited dialogue, teamwork, and the responsiveness to novel ideas and techniques. This can be enabled by managers, who create an inclusive environment in which employees feel respected and encouraged to share knowledge and get involved in decision-making procedures. In this way, the organizations will not only boost the morale among internal members of the organization but will also get to interact with the surrounding community. Also, leaders should see the need in correlating their vision with the objectives of participatory governance. The alignment will be facilitated by frequent feedback systems and the strategies of the stakeholders that allow input form both employees and the community at large.

PRACTICAL IMPLICATIONS

First, companies ought to initiate special training programs that nurture entrepreneurial leadership styles in the organization managers. The same skill development can be brought about through workshops and mentorship programs that are dedicated to teaching aspects of innovation, risk analysis, and future/strategic thinking, which help leaders overcome difficult obstacles of governance trends. Moreover, to promote an organizational culture of changes, one needs to have tangible approaches, i.e., to incorporate cross-functional teams that may promote unity and exchange of ideas. Organizations can foster engagement and commitment among employees by creating a culture in which workers have power to express their views and be part of any decision making process. This in its turn establishes a culture enabling the participatory governance to thrive. In addition, companies are supposed to engage the use of feedback mechanisms that include stakeholders in the process of governance. Periodic surveys, town meetings and focus groups will allow open discussions between community and leader in a manner where multiple voices are addressed in the decision-making process. The practice will not only enhance relationships with stakeholders, but also increase transparency and accountability. Lastly, leaders of organizations ought to create an ongoing loop of performance measurement and feedback to determine the success of their leadership and cultural efforts. Monitoring progress and undertaking data-driven adaptations can help organizations make sure their action plans are updated and work to facilitate participatory governance.

THEORETICAL IMPLICATIONS

The study helps us in understanding the manner in which leadership dynamics affect organizational culture thus, leading to modes of governance by confirming the relationships among the said constructs through empirical evidence. The combination of theories brings into the fore the significance of distinct multidimensional perception of organizational effectiveness, which can no longer regard leadership as an independent parameter but rather as influencer affecting cultural and governance outcomes. Besides, the results imply that the change-oriented business culture is the main mediator on the relationship between entrepreneurial leadership and participatory government. The given insight is valuable to the theoretical models that aim to describe the process of the translation of leadership practices to governance efficacy with the focus on culture as a facilitating instrument of engagement and innovation. As well, the research promotes further study the contextual situations that can mediate these relations. The possibility of future research includes the study of the influence of different organizational contexts, circumstances in the industry, and cultural settings on leadership-culture-governance relationships. This would not only add to the theoretical views but also present a complex picture of how to work on participatory governance in the various contexts.

RECOMMENDATION

The development of entrepreneurial leadership should be given first priority in organizations as organizations should invest in elaborate training programmers. Such programs ought to be geared towards instilling skills on leaders that are related to innovation, strategic thinking and flexible management so that they can effectively steer through the complexity of governance and effectively achieve organizational change once they are in an organization. Also, it should be a strategic priority to develop a change-oriented organizational culture. Organizations are also encouraged to introduce more initiatives which encourage team work and open communication like staff team-building events and cross department projects. The establishment of mechanisms of collaboration on ideas, i.e. innovation workshops or suggestion systems will help employees become actively engaged in governance processes and more committed to the mission of the organization. Besides this, there is a need to put in place effective feedback mechanisms which involve active participation of stakeholders in governance. It is through a survey, focus groups and community forums that organizations need to seek the input of employees, community members and other stakeholders on a regular basis. Not only does this improve transparency, but it increases trust and accountability, so the opinions of anybody can be taken into account during decision-making procedures. Lastly, companies must make themselves to continuous review and reformation of their leadership and cultural endeavors. Evaluating how well their strategies are working on a regular basis using the standard of performance and satisfaction regarding their stakeholders, institutions are placed in a position to make the necessary changes that will better align their strategies to participate in participatory governance.

FUTURE DIRECTIONS

A research avenue that needs to be addressed is longitudinal analysis of these constructs to see how their dynamics change with time especially when the organization is under different pressures. Such a study can inform a lot about the sustainability of participatory governance practices and the long-term effects of the practices of entrepreneurial leadership. The other key aspect that should be examined is the situational elements that drive these relations. In future research, one might explore the influences of industry-specific attributes, dimension of size of organizations, and culture settings on the relationship between leadership, culture, and governance. This may assist in highlighting best practices that fit various contexts, which will improve cross-setting applicability of results. Also, they might explore the involvement of technology in enabling participatory governance, and organization culture. This growing dependence on electronic instruments in the management and coordination of behaviors provides a possibility of examining the role that technology can play in boosting or undermining the success of leadership and culture programs aimed at fostering interaction. Last but not least, discussing the possible difficulties that leaders have to encounter when attempting to foster a culture of change and participatory governance would further help to understand the obstacles to implementation in a more complete way. Having identified these barriers, it may be possible to develop specific strategies to overcome them and the end result is more effective practices in governance.

REFERENCES

Abawari, A. M., Debela, K. L., & Abegaz, M. B. (2024). The effects of organizational culture on change management in Oromia public sectors: The mediating role of leadership styles. *Cogent Business & Management, 11*(1), 2375623. DOI: 10.1080/23311975.2024.2375623

Adula, M., Kant, S., Badi, S., & Kumari, M. (2025). Abusive Work Environment Effect on Female Entrepreneurs' Emotional Wellbeing by Mediation of Social and Moral Values in the Horn of Africa. In *Supporting Psychological and Emotional Wellbeing Among Entrepreneurs* (pp. 1-22). IGI Global Scientific Publishing.

AlAnazi, A. A., Kura, K. M., Suleiman, E. S., & Abubakar, R. A. (2022). Mediating effect of organisational innovation in the prediction of change-oriented leadership on organisational performance. *International Journal of Innovation Science, 14*(1), 138–156. DOI: 10.1108/IJIS-03-2021-0051

Campbell, J. W. (2025). Change management, performance feedback, and public service motivation: Cultivating change-oriented behaviour in public organisations. *Asia Pacific Journal of Public Administration, 47*(2), 140–164. DOI: 10.1080/23276665.2024.2382092

Chen, C., Duan, J., & Peng, Y. (2024). How does sense of power influence change-oriented organizational citizenship behavior? Evidence from China. *Public Performance & Management Review, 47*(3), 732–760. DOI: 10.1080/15309576.2023.2298414

Chen, K. K., & Mandiberg, J. M. (2024). Legitimizing organizations via research: Facilitating possibilities through the study of relational, emergent, transformative, and change-oriented organizations (RETCOs). *Public Integrity, 26*(3), 360–373. DOI: 10.1080/10999922.2023.2262212

Demircioglu, M. A., & Chowdhury, F. (2021). Entrepreneurship in public organizations: The role of leadership behavior. *Small Business Economics, 57*(3), 1107–1123. DOI: 10.1007/s11187-020-00328-w

Deresso, J. W., Karo, C. A., & Kant, S. (2026). Organizational Culture Effect on Employees' Learning and Growth by Mediation of Employee Commitment in the Ethiopian Public Sector. In *Leading Inclusive Workplaces Through Digital Transformation and Organizational Change* (pp. 251-280). IGI Global Scientific Publishing.

Diakova, A., Bagrationi, K., & Gordienko, O. (2024, November). Change-oriented Leadership in the Context of Transitioning to Strategic Autonomy. In *European Conference on Management, Leadership & Governance* (pp. 114-123). Academic Conferences International Limited. DOI: 10.34190/ecmlg.20.1.2962

Fang, Y., Liu, Y., Yu, P., & Chen, N. (2024). How does narcissistic leadership influence change-oriented organizational citizenship behavior? Empirical evidence from China. *Humanities & Social Sciences Communications*, *11*(1), 1–11. DOI: 10.1057/s41599-024-03159-2

Jinga, A. A., Hussen, J. O., Negash, H. G., & Estifanos, A. B. (2024). Leadership behavior and organizational change management in selected public universities of Ethiopia: Exploring the impact of leadership influences and change processes. *Heliyon*, *10*(19), e37149. DOI: 10.1016/j.heliyon.2024.e37149 PMID: 39398013

Jio, W., Kant, S., & Lemi, K. (2025). Ethical Leadership: Effect on Future of Organizational Citizenship Behavior by Mediation of Organizational Culture in Ethiopia. In *Generation Alpha and Next Generation Leadership for Greener Futures* (pp. 41-62). IGI Global Scientific Publishing.

Kant, S., Niguse, T., Terefe, A., Jio, W., & Adula, M. (2025). Ethical Leadership's Role in Promoting Resilience Among Employees by Mediation of Building a Resilient Organizational Culture in the Horn of Africa. In *Enhancing Resilience in Business Continuity Management* (pp. 219–244). IGI Global Scientific Publishing. DOI: 10.4018/979-8-3693-8809-9.ch007

Kant, S., Terefe, A., Alemu, Z. K., & Takaro, G. S. (2025). Unlocking the Potential of Smart Logistics by Enhancing Business Leadership Through Human Capital in the Horn of Africa. In *Understanding Human Decision-Making in Economic Models* (pp. 81–110). IGI Global Scientific Publishing. DOI: 10.4018/979-8-3693-8166-3.ch004

Karnsomdee, P., & Phongkaew, P. (2023). The influence of entrepreneurial leadership and public entrepreneurship on organizational performance of local administrative organizations in the northeastern region of Thailand. *Russian Law Journal*, *11*(6S), 238–252.

Karo, C. A., Deresso, J. W., & Kant, S. (2025). Organizational Culture Effect on Enhancing Workplace Productivity Through Women Employees' Normative Commitment in the Ethiopian Public Sector. In *Enhancing Workplace Productivity Through Gender Equity and Intergenerational Communication* (pp. 137-166). IGI Global Scientific Publishing.

Kumari, V., Tiwari, A., & Mendiratta, A. (2025). Does Inclusive Leadership Promote Rule Breaking for Positive Change? Exploring Psychological Empowerment and Change-oriented Citizenship Behavior. *Business Perspectives and Research*, 22785337251357736.

Kyeong, K. (2025). Do Transformational Leadership and Innovative Climate Always Enhance Employees' Innovative Behavior? Focusing on the Moderated Mediating Role of Innovative Climate on Change-Oriented Organizational Citizenship Behavior. *Public Personnel Management*, *54*(4), 00910260251325269. DOI: 10.1177/00910260251325269

Lee, J., & Shin, H. (2024). Effects of Inclusive leadership on the diversity climate and change-oriented organizational citizenship behavior. *Behavioral Sciences (Basel, Switzerland)*, *14*(6), 491. DOI: 10.3390/bs14060491 PMID: 38920823

Lemi, K., Kant, S., & Jio, W. (2025). Greener Hospital Future in the Horn of Africa by Transactional Leadership: Outcome on Altruism Through Adaptability. In *Generation Alpha and Next Generation Leadership for Greener Futures* (pp. 1-22). IGI Global Scientific Publishing.

Ling, B., Yao, Q., Liu, Y., & Chen, D. (2024). Fairness matters for change: A multilevel study on organizational change fairness, proactive motivation, and change-oriented OCB. *PLoS One*, *19*(10), e0312886. DOI: 10.1371/journal.pone.0312886 PMID: 39480783

Loukopoulos, A., Papadimitriou, D., & Glaveli, N. (2025). Rising to the challenge: Job stress, role overload, and change-oriented organizational citizenship behavior in the public sector. *International Public Management Journal*, •••, 1–20. DOI: 10.1080/10967494.2025.2513369

Masih, S., Punchanathan, U. E., Naqshbandi, M. M., & Ahmed, F. (2025). How inclusive leadership drives change-oriented extra-role behaviors via leader-member exchange and trust in leadership. *Global Knowledge, Memory and Communication*. Advance online publication. DOI: 10.1108/GKMC-05-2024-0276

Maula, S. S. A. Z., Syurofa, S. S., Aulia, S., Aulia, P., & Fauzi, R. Z. (2025). Adaptive Leadership and Organizational Agility: Managing Change and Fostering Entrepreneurship in Uncertain Times. *Oikos*, *17*(2), 303–322.

Piwowar-Sulej, K., & Iqbal, Q. (2025). Workplace envy as an inhibitor of change-oriented organizational citizenship behavior: The role of sustainable leadership. *Journal of Organizational Change Management*, *38*(1), 103–122. DOI: 10.1108/JOCM-02-2024-0086

Potipiroon, W., & Thawornprasert, W. (2024). Local government managers' change-oriented leadership and employees' change-supportive behaviour during COVID-19: Utilizing the theory of planned behaviour. *Asia Pacific Journal of Public Administration, 46*(2), 139–158. DOI: 10.1080/23276665.2023.2207833

Sørensen, P., & Lindholst, A. C. (2025). Does long-term management education change behaviors? A study of change in self-perceived leadership behaviors among participants in a three-year Danish diploma program. *International Journal of Public Sector Management, 38*(4), 507–523. DOI: 10.1108/IJPSM-05-2023-0167

Tufa, G., Kinde, Z., & Kant, S. (2025). Strategic Leadership: Effect on Employee Performance With Mediation of Dynamic Capabilities in Case of Ethiopian Public Organizations. In *Generation Alpha and Next Generation Leadership for Greener Futures* (pp. 115-138). IGI Global Scientific Publishing.

Vivona, R. (2024). The new era leadership for the public sector? Entrepreneurship, effectiveness, and democracy. *Public Management Review, 26*(6), 1566–1582. DOI: 10.1080/14719037.2022.2162957

KEY TERMS AND DEFINITIONS

Change-Oriented Organization Culture: An organizational culture, which promotes innovation, flexibility, and proactive response to change at the workplace. The given form of a culture will foster an atmosphere of empowerment where workers will feel free to innovate, advocate new ideas and participate in the process of ongoing improvement.

Direct effect: It is the impact of a variable to another one in which there are no intermediate variables between them. In the spirit of this research chapter, it entails immediate effect of entrepreneurial leadership to participatory governance.

Entrepreneurial Leadership: An innovation-driven, risk-taking and problematic solving approach to leadership. Leaders in the field of entrepreneurship encourage and engage teams to change and go after new opportunities to ensure the organizational growth and adaptability.

Indirect Influence: The influence of one variable merged on another which happens by means of one or additional mediating variables. The idea plays a vital role in explaining why organizational culture may act as an intermediary in connecting the leadership with the outcomes of governance.

Mediation: Mediation in research is a type of interaction in which one variable (identified as the mediator) intervenes between other two variables. It assists to clarify how or why a specific effect happens giving information about systems that underlie relations.

Organizational Effectiveness: How well an organization is fulfilling its goals and objectives as measured in terms of the many criteria used which include efficiency, stakeholder's satisfaction and capability to respond to changes. The idea revolves around the assessment of success of leadership and governance.

Participatory Governance: This is a form of governance where it would include the stakeholders (such as employees, community members, and any other Apprehensioned parties) in the decision-making processes. Transparency, collaboration and accountability are featured in this model and they create a sense of ownership and participation amidst the participants.

Chapter 4
Frugal Innovation and Knowledge Management in Resource-Constrained Environments

Satya Subrahmanyam
http://orcid.org/0000-0003-0441-2742
Holy Spirit University of Kaslik, Lebanon

ABSTRACT

In resource-constrained environments, Small and Medium Enterprises (SMEs) face mounting challenges due to limited capital, infrastructure, and formal knowledge systems. This chapter explores how frugal innovation and knowledge management (KM) together enhances SME resilience and adaptability. Frugal innovation—rooted in simplicity, affordability, and resource-efficiency—aligns with the needs of volatile, low-income markets. KM enables SMEs to harness internal and external knowledge through informal practices like storytelling, peer learning, and digital platforms. Using the dynamic capabilities framework, the chapter illustrates how SMEs develop agility through integrated innovation and KM. Real-world case studies from Africa, Asia, and Latin America highlight successful low-cost innovations in healthcare, education, and manufacturing. Challenges such as limited digital access and tacit knowledge loss are addressed with practical strategies. The chapter concludes with policy implications and future research directions.

DOI: 10.4018/979-8-3373-6053-9.ch004

1. INTRODUCTION

Anyone who has spent time working with small businesses in Lagos, Dhaka, or Ho Chi Minh City quickly notices something that does not fit neatly into the innovation textbooks. Entrepreneurs with limited capital, patchy electricity, and no research and development budget regularly produce solutions that are genuinely useful, often elegant, and sometimes transformative. A mechanic fabricates a fuel injection cleaner from local materials that costs a fraction of the imported alternative. A village pharmacist devises a cold chain workaround using clay pots and wet sand that keeps vaccines viable for hours beyond their rated window. A textile cooperative in rural Bangladesh redesigns its dyeing process to use a third of the water after a drought cuts supply. These are not accidents. They are the product of accumulated contextual knowledge, social networks, and a particular orientation toward problems that turns scarcity into specification.

The academic literature has a name for this phenomenon. Frugal innovation refers to the deliberate process of creating products, services, or business models that are affordable, functional, and accessible to people who have been priced out of or structurally excluded from conventional markets (Hossain, 2018; Rehman et al., 2024). The concept has roots in the Indian notion of jugaad, a term that captures creative improvisation under constraint, but it has since expanded well beyond its geographic origin to describe a universally relevant mode of innovation that is increasingly attractive even in high-income economies grappling with sustainability and social equity imperatives (Weyrauch & Herstatt, 2021).

What the literature has been slower to address is the question of sustainability. A brilliant improvisation is not the same as a reliable organisational capability. For frugal innovation projects and strategically rather than episodically, there must be systems in place to capture what was learned, share it across the organisation, build on it in future projects, and protect it from the attrition that comes with staff turnover and competitive pressure. This is precisely where knowledge management enters the frame.

Knowledge management refers to the set of practices and systems through which organisations identify, capture, organise, distribute, and apply knowledge to achieve their objectives (Dalkir, 2017). For SMEs operating in volatile environments, knowledge management is not a luxury function associated with corporate knowledge centres and enterprise software. It is the informal but structured accumulation of what works, held in procedures, relationships, stories, and routines that allow the organisation to learn from experience and act on that learning. When knowledge management and frugal innovation are aligned, the result is a capability that is both adaptive and cumulative.

This chapter makes three contributions. First, it synthesises the emerging post-2020 literature on frugal innovation and knowledge management to establish their theoretical intersection. Second, it proposes an integrated conceptual model, the FIKM model, that maps the mechanisms through which knowledge management processes enable and sustain frugal innovation in SMEs. Third, it derives practical implications for managers and policymakers based on evidence from three regional contexts. The chapter proceeds through seven sections covering theoretical foundations, the knowledge management and frugal innovation interface, the FIKM model, empirical evidence, challenges, implications, and conclusions.

2. THEORETICAL FOUNDATIONS

2.1 Understanding Frugal Innovation

The term frugal innovation has been in academic circulation for roughly two decades, but its theoretical footing has become considerably firmer since 2020 as a new generation of scholars has moved beyond description toward explanation. Hossain (2018) conducted a systematic review of 135 frugal innovation studies and found that the field had converged around three core attributes: affordability, meaning a price point accessible to low-income users; functionality, meaning a product or service that performs its core purpose reliably; and sustainability, meaning both environmental responsibility and the capacity for long-run commercial viability. These three attributes are not simply marketing criteria. They encode deep decisions about what knowledge the innovator needs, what tradeoffs are acceptable, and what kind of user relationship will sustain the innovation over time.

Rehman and others (2024) offer a useful distinction between frugal innovation as a market strategy and frugal innovation as a social practice. The market strategy perspective, dominant in management scholarship, tends to frame frugal innovation as a tool for serving the bottom of the pyramid, a term coined by Prahalad (2004) to describe the approximately four billion people living on less than eight dollars a day. The social practice perspective, more prominent in development studies and science and technology studies, emphasises frugal innovation as a form of grassroots knowledge production that challenges the assumption that innovation flows from rich countries to poor ones. This chapter draws on both perspectives while remaining anchored in the management literature, because SMEs are simultaneously commercial actors and embedded social institutions.

Weyrauch and Herstatt (2021) argue that frugal innovation is best understood not as a category of product but as a process of constraint-driven design that can occur in any context where resources are scarce relative to the problem to be solved.

This processual view is important because it connects frugal innovation directly to organisational capabilities rather than treating it as a property of outputs. If frugal innovation is a process, then it can be managed, and the question becomes: what managerial practices make it more reliable?

2.2 The Knowledge-Based View and Dynamic Capabilities

Two theoretical pillars support the argument of this chapter. The first is the knowledge-based view of the firm, which holds that knowledge is the most strategically significant resource an organisation possesses and that competitive advantage rests on the capacity to generate, integrate, and apply knowledge more effectively than rivals (Grant, 1996). The knowledge-based view has been extended and refined by numerous scholars, but its core insight remains relevant: what a firm knows and what it can do with that knowledge are the primary determinants of what it can achieve.

The second pillar is the dynamic capabilities framework, which Teece et al. (1997) introduced to explain how firms sustain competitive advantage in environments characterised by rapid technological change. Dynamic capabilities are defined as the organisational routines and processes by which firms sense opportunities and threats, seize upon promising opportunities, and reconfigure their resource base when necessary. Subrahmanyam et al. (2024) have revisited the dynamic capabilities framework in the context of SMEs in volatile environments and argued that the reconfiguration dimension is particularly salient for smaller firms, because they cannot rely on scale or market power and must instead rely on speed and adaptability. Knowledge management, in this reading, is the operational infrastructure of dynamic capability: it is how organisations reconfigure their knowledge assets in response to environmental change.

Zollo and Winter (2002) argued that dynamic capabilities develop through three mechanisms: experience accumulation, knowledge articulation, and knowledge codification. This sequential logic maps closely onto the knowledge management processes discussed in this chapter and provides a theoretical justification for treating knowledge management not merely as administrative housekeeping but as a driver of strategic capability development. Recent work by Orelj and Torfason (2022) has confirmed this connection empirically in a sample of Spanish SMEs, finding that firms with more developed knowledge management systems were significantly more likely to demonstrate the adaptive and reconfiguration dimensions of dynamic capability.

2.3 SMEs and the Resource-Constrained Context

SMEs account for more than 90% of businesses worldwide and approximately 70% of employment in most economies, yet they consistently report facing greater barriers to innovation than large firms (OECD, 2023). These barriers are not simply financial. Agyapong & Attram (2019) found in a study of Ghanaian SMEs that the most debilitating constraints were not the absence of money per se but the absence of systems for learning from experience, retaining organisational knowledge, and accessing the external knowledge that would make better use of available resources. In other words, the binding constraint was often a knowledge management deficit rather than a capital deficit.

Volatile environments compound these challenges. Volatility here refers to the compounded effect of macroeconomic instability, institutional uncertainty, infrastructure deficits, and rapid competitive change that characterise many emerging market contexts but are also increasingly visible in developed economies following the disruptions of the COVID-19 pandemic and global supply chain fragmentation (Homayoun et al., 2023). In volatile environments, the knowledge that allowed an SME to operate effectively last year may be obsolete or misleading this year. The adaptive capacity to continuously update, reframe, and apply knowledge becomes as important as the stock of knowledge itself.

Table 1. Theoretical Frameworks Underpinning the FIKM Model

Theoretical Framework	Core Proposition	Relevance to Frugal Innovation in SMEs
Knowledge-Based View (Grant, 1996)	Knowledge is the primary source of competitive advantage	Explains why contextual and tacit knowledge held by SME employees constitutes a strategic asset in frugal innovation
Dynamic Capabilities (Teece et al., 1997; Fainshmidt et al., 2019)	Firms sustain advantage by sensing, seizing, and reconfiguring resources	Frames frugal innovation as a reconfiguration capability built through knowledge management routines
Organisational Learning (Zollo & Winter, 2002)	Capabilities develop through experience accumulation, articulation, and codification	Provides a process model linking knowledge management practices to the development of frugal innovation routines
Resource-Based View (Wernerfelt, 1984)	Idiosyncratic resources and capabilities create sustained advantage	Supports the argument that frugal know-how, being tacit and context-specific, is difficult to imitate
Bottom of Pyramid Framework (Prahalad, 2004)	Large underserved markets exist at low-income levels and require different value propositions	Contextualises the market motivation for frugal innovation and the knowledge demands it creates

Note. The table synthesises five theoretical traditions that jointly explain the relationship between knowledge management and frugal innovation in SME contexts.

3. THE KNOWLEDGE MANAGEMENT AND FRUGAL INNOVATION INTERFACE

3.1 Why Frugal Innovation Is Knowledge-Intensive

There is a tendency in popular discourse to associate frugal innovation with simplicity, as though removing features from a product also reduces the cognitive demands of creating it. This is a significant misconception. Frugal innovation is, if anything, more knowledge-intensive than conventional innovation precisely because it cannot rely on financial resources as a substitute for insight. When a pharmaceutical SME in Nigeria reformulates a drug to use locally available active ingredients at a fraction of the imported cost, it draws on pharmacological knowledge, knowledge of local supply chains, knowledge of regulatory pathways, and knowledge of the economic behaviour of its intended users. Each of these knowledge domains must be integrated, and each must be current and contextually accurate to produce a product that is both safe and commercially viable.

Research on innovation embeddedness shows that the intensity of knowledge and its effects on innovation outcomes are shaped by the specific material, social, and institutional conditions in which innovation occurs, a phenomenon often discussed under the concept of contextual embeddedness (Wigren-Kristoferson et al., 2022). Frugal innovations are typically highly contextually embedded, which means that the knowledge required to produce them cannot simply be imported from more resource-abundant settings. It must be generated locally, from observation, interaction, and experimentation. This positions frugal innovation as a fundamentally local knowledge practice, even when the resulting product eventually travels to other markets.

Bisha (2025) extends this argument by showing that successful frugal innovators in the Indian medical devices sector engaged in what they call reverse knowledge engineering, a process of working backwards from the constraints of the target user to the specifications of the product. This is not the same as conventional user-centred design, which typically starts from an existing product and asks how it might be improved. Reverse knowledge engineering starts from the constraints themselves and asks what kind of knowledge is needed to produce something that works within them. The implication is that frugal innovation requires a distinctive knowledge orientation, one that treats constraints as design specifications rather than barriers.

3.2 Knowledge Acquisition in Resource-Constrained Settings

For SMEs in resource-constrained environments, the question of where knowledge comes from is far from trivial. Large corporations can fund research and development departments, commission market research, and acquire knowledge-bearing firms.

SMEs have none of these options at scale. Their knowledge acquisition tends to rely on three primary channels: direct user interaction, peer networks, and opportunistic access to external knowledge sources such as universities, non-governmental organisations, and development agencies.

Direct user interaction is perhaps the most underappreciated knowledge source in the SME innovation literature. De Marchi et al. (2022) studied 47 frugal innovation projects in Bangladesh and found that in the most successful cases, entrepreneurs had invested significantly in what the authors call immersive learning, a sustained and often informal process of living with and observing the intended users of the innovation. This is not ethnographic research in the academic sense, but it produces something functionally equivalent: a rich, tacit understanding of how users experience problems and what solutions they would actually adopt.

Peer networks function as a particularly efficient knowledge transfer mechanism in SME clusters, where firms producing similar or complementary products coexist in geographic proximity. Adu-Gyamfi & Adjei, (2018) found that SMEs in the Suame manufacturing cluster in Ghana regularly exchanged technical knowledge through informal apprenticeship, joint problem solving, and the movement of skilled workers between firms. This constitutes a form of distributed knowledge management that operates at the ecosystem level rather than the firm level, and it has significant implications for how frugal innovation capabilities develop and spread.

3.3 Knowledge Codification and Organisational Memory

Knowledge acquisition is only valuable if the knowledge acquired can be retained and reused. This is where many SMEs in resource-constrained environments face their most acute challenge. When the entrepreneur who developed a frugal solution leaves the firm, takes on a different role, or simply becomes overwhelmed by the demands of running a growing business, the knowledge that produced the innovation can disappear with them. This is the organisational memory problem, and it is far more severe in SMEs than in large organisations because there are fewer people among whom critical knowledge is distributed.

Codification is the process of converting tacit, experience-based knowledge into explicit, transferable form. This might mean writing down a production process, creating a visual diagram of a service workflow, recording a video of a skilled craftsperson performing a task, or developing a simple checklist that captures the key decision points in an innovation project. The purpose is not to eliminate tacit knowledge, which is often impossible, but to create anchors that help others reconstruct it. Shao et al. (2024) found in a study of manufacturing SMEs that firms which invested in even minimal codification practices, including process maps and brief project debriefs, demonstrated significantly higher innovation persistence, defined as the ability to continue innovating beyond the first generation of a product or process.

There is, of course, a real tension between the informality that characterises many successful frugal innovators and the discipline required for effective codification. SMEs in low-income environments often operate under significant time pressure, and the leaders who possess the most valuable knowledge are precisely the ones who are most stretched. Successful codification in these contexts tends to be lightweight, embedded in practice rather than imposed as an additional administrative burden, and connected to tangible rewards such as recognition or training opportunities.

3.4 Knowledge Sharing and Transfer

Even when knowledge has been acquired and codified, it does not automatically flow to the people who need it. Knowledge sharing is an active process that requires both structural conditions, meaning channels through which knowledge can flow, and motivational conditions, meaning reasons for individuals to share rather than hoard what they know. Both are more difficult to establish in SME contexts than is commonly recognised.

Structural conditions for knowledge sharing in SMEs tend to be informal but can be deliberately shaped. Medase & Abdul-Basit (2020) found that organised regular informal gatherings, such as end-of-week team debriefs, shared meal breaks, or joint visits to customer sites, achieved significantly higher rates of cross-functional knowledge transfer than those that relied on formal reporting structures. The gatherings created conversational contexts in which tacit knowledge could surface naturally rather than being forced into a report that would not capture its richness.

Motivational conditions are shaped by organisational culture. Where leaders model knowledge sharing by being open about what they have learned from failures as well as successes, employees are more likely to share. Where knowledge is treated as a source of individual power, hoarding is rational from the employee perspective even if it is dysfunctional for the organisation. Ode and Ayavoo (2020) found that transformational leadership style was one of the strongest predictors of effective knowledge sharing in SMEs across three sub-Saharan African countries, largely because transformational leaders created psychological safety conditions in which sharing knowledge, including knowledge of mistakes, was seen as an act of organisational contribution rather than personal exposure.

3.5 Knowledge Application and Value Creation

The ultimate purpose of knowledge management is not to accumulate knowledge but to apply it. In the frugal innovation context, knowledge application means converting insights from users, market conditions, and prior innovation experience into products, processes, and business models that create value under conditions of resource constraint. This application process is iterative and rarely linear.

Orelj and Torfason (2022) describe what they call the knowledge management innovation loop, a cyclical process in which knowledge application in one innovation project generates new experiential knowledge that feeds back into the knowledge management system and enhances the quality of future innovation efforts. This loop is the mechanism through which frugal innovation becomes a capability rather than an event. Each iteration deposits a layer of organisational learning that makes the next iteration faster, cheaper, and more likely to succeed. SMEs that have completed several turns of this loop develop what Zollo and Winter (2002) call higher-order routines, stable patterns of behaviour that allow them to innovate efficiently without having to reinvent the process from scratch each time.

Table 2. Knowledge Management Processes and Their Roles in Frugal Innovation

KM Process	Definition in SME Context	Role in Frugal Innovation	Representative Mechanisms
Knowledge Acquisition	Sourcing new knowledge from users, peers, and external partners	Builds the contextual intelligence needed to design constraint-driven solutions	Immersive user observation, cluster networks, university linkages
Knowledge Codification	Converting tacit know-how into explicit, reusable artefacts	Protects organisational memory and enables replication of frugal practices	Process maps, video tutorials, project debriefs, checklists
Knowledge Sharing	Distributing knowledge across individuals and teams within and beyond the firm	Prevents knowledge silos and accelerates problem solving under resource pressure	Informal team debriefs, apprenticeship, peer mentoring
Knowledge Application	Using stored and shared knowledge in the design of new products, processes, or models	Converts knowledge management investment into frugal innovation outputs	Rapid prototyping, iterative testing, lean experiment cycles
Knowledge Integration	Combining knowledge from diverse sources into coherent innovation inputs	Enables the cross-domain synthesis that distinguishes effective frugal innovation	Cross-functional teams, boundary-spanning roles, open innovation partnerships

Note. Mechanisms listed are illustrative; the actual mechanisms used by any SME will depend on its sector, scale, and operating environment.

Figure 1. The KM–Frugal Innovation Interface

Author, (2026)

4. THE FRUGAL INNOVATION KNOWLEDGE MANAGEMENT MODEL

4.1 Model Overview

The Frugal Innovation Knowledge Management (FIKM) model proposed in this chapter synthesises the theoretical foundations and knowledge management process analysis presented in the preceding sections into an integrated framework that can guide both research and practice. The model has four components: environmental triggers, knowledge management enablers, frugal innovation outputs, and feedback loops that sustain capability development over time. It is important to emphasise that the model is not sequential in the sense that each component must be fully developed before the next can begin. In practice, the components interact continuously and recursively.

The FIKM model draws most directly on Fainshmidt et al. (2019), who call for dynamic capabilities research that takes seriously the specific institutional and resource conditions of emerging market SMEs, and on Lim and Fujimoto (2019), who argue that frugal innovation frameworks need to incorporate explicit attention to knowledge processes rather than treating the knowledge dimension as implicit. The model also incorporates the learning cycle logic of Zollo and Winter (2002), positioning the feedback loop as the mechanism through which repeated frugal innovation experience builds deeper and more reliable organisational capability.

4.2 Environmental Triggers

Environmental triggers are the conditions that make frugal innovation both necessary and possible. Resource scarcity is the most fundamental trigger: when capital, skilled labour, infrastructure, and market access are all constrained relative to the problem to be solved, frugal innovation is not a strategic choice but a practical necessity. Institutional voids, a term developed by Khanna and Palepu (1997) and recently revisited by Ur Rehman et al. (2024) in the context of innovation ecosystems, refer to the absence of the market-supporting institutions that firms in high-income contexts can take for granted. These include reliable contract enforcement, transparent regulatory frameworks, accessible financial services, and functioning logistics infrastructure. Where these institutions are absent or unreliable, SMEs must generate the knowledge to navigate around them, and this knowledge becomes a critical frugal innovation input.

Market volatility constitutes a third major trigger. When demand patterns shift rapidly, when input costs are unpredictable, or when competitive landscapes change faster than conventional product development cycles allow, the capacity to innovate frugally, meaning quickly and cheaply, becomes a competitive survival mechanism. Homayoun et al. (2023) found that SMEs in volatile environments that had developed frugal innovation capabilities were significantly more likely to survive economic shocks than those relying on conventional innovation strategies, precisely because their lower cost base gave them more room to adapt.

4.3 Knowledge Management Enablers

Knowledge management enablers are the organisational practices and systems that allow SMEs to acquire, retain, share, and apply the knowledge needed for frugal innovation. The five knowledge management processes discussed in Section 3 constitute the core enablers, but two additional factors deserve specific attention: absorptive capacity and knowledge leadership.

Absorptive capacity, originally developed by Cohen and Levinthal (1990) and recently applied to SME frugal innovation contexts by Agyapong & Attram (2019), refers to the firm's ability to recognise the value of new external knowledge, assimilate it, and apply it to commercial ends. Absorptive capacity is itself knowledge-dependent: firms with a broader prior knowledge base are better able to identify and integrate new knowledge. This creates a path dependency that is both an opportunity and a challenge for SMEs: those that have invested in building a knowledge base, even informally, are better positioned to benefit from external knowledge sources, while those that have not may find themselves unable to exploit the knowledge that is theoretically available to them.

Knowledge leadership refers to the role that senior managers and founders play in creating and sustaining the conditions for effective knowledge management. Ode and Ayavoo (2020) found that in SME contexts, the behaviour of the top leader was the single most powerful predictor of knowledge management effectiveness, because SMEs lack the bureaucratic structures that enforce knowledge practices in large organisations. When founders model knowledge sharing, invest even modest resources in codification, and treat learning from failure as valuable rather than embarrassing, these orientations cascade through the organisation.

4.4 Frugal Innovation Outputs

The FIKM model distinguishes three categories of frugal innovation output: product and service innovations, process innovations, and business model innovations. Product and service innovations are the most visible: the low-cost diagnostic device, the affordable sanitation system, the simplified financial product. Process innovations are equally important but less visible: the reconfigured supply chain that eliminates a costly intermediary, the production method that substitutes a locally available material for an imported one, the service delivery system that leverages community trust networks to reduce distribution costs. Business model innovations may be the most transformative of all, because they can change the economics of an entire sector: pay-per-use models that convert capital purchases into affordable operating expenditures, micro-franchise models that distribute risk and knowledge simultaneously, or platform models that aggregate dispersed informal producers into a market-facing entity.

Escudero-Cipriani and others (2024) argue that the most durable frugal innovations typically involve all three output types simultaneously: a product innovation that is cost-effective, a process innovation that makes it producible at scale, and a business model innovation that makes it commercially sustainable in the target market. This integration across output types is itself a knowledge management challenge, because it requires synthesising knowledge from domains, including product design, operations, and business model design, that are often held by different people and rarely combined in the same conversation.

4.5 Feedback Loops and Capability Building

The distinguishing feature of the FIKM model, compared to simpler input-output frameworks, is its explicit attention to the feedback mechanisms through which frugal innovation experience builds knowledge management capability, which in turn makes future frugal innovation more effective. This is not a theoretical abstraction. Shao et al. (2024) documented this dynamic empirically in SMEs, showing that firms that had completed two or more frugal innovation projects with structured debriefing processes achieved their third project in significantly less time and at significantly lower cost than their first, whereas firms without structured debriefing showed no such improvement trajectory.

The feedback loop operates at two levels. At the project level, each frugal innovation project generates experiential knowledge that, if captured and shared, becomes a resource for the next project. At the capability level, the accumulated experience of multiple projects builds what might be called frugal innovation literacy: a shared organisational understanding of how to approach constraint-driven innovation, what traps to avoid, and what practices reliably generate good outcomes. This literacy is the closest thing an SME can have to a sustainable innovation advantage in a resource-constrained environment.

Table 3. Components of the FIKM Model and Their Practical Implications

FIKM Component	Key Elements	Implications for SME Practice
Environmental Triggers	Resource scarcity, institutional voids, market volatility, sustainability pressures	SMEs should conduct periodic environmental scans to identify which triggers are most acute and calibrate their knowledge management investment accordingly
KM Enablers	Knowledge acquisition, codification, sharing, application, integration; absorptive capacity; knowledge leadership	Leaders should model knowledge sharing and invest in lightweight codification tools that fit SME operational realities
Frugal Innovation Outputs	Product and service innovations, process innovations, business model innovations	SMEs should aim for integration across all three output types to maximise the sustainability and commercial viability of frugal innovations
Feedback Loops	Project-level learning, capability-level learning, frugal innovation literacy	Structured post-project debriefs and cross-project knowledge reviews are the practical mechanisms through which feedback loops are activated

Note. FIKM = Frugal Innovation Knowledge Management. The model is integrative and recursive; components do not operate in sequence but interact continuously.

Figure 2. The Integrated Frugal Innovation–Knowledge Management (FI-KM) Framework

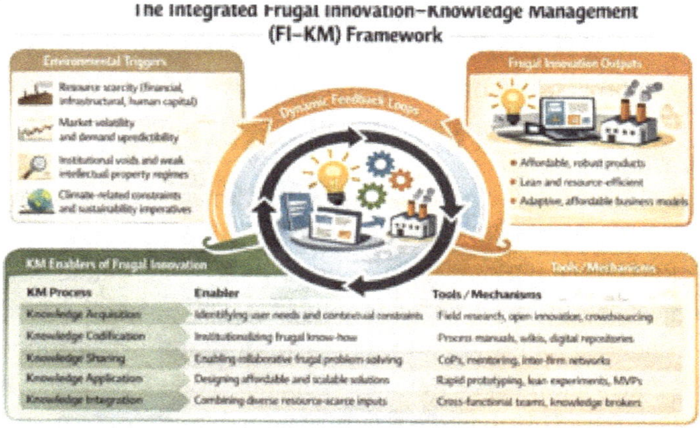

Author, (2026)

5. EMPIRICAL EVIDENCE FROM THREE REGIONAL CONTEXTS

5.1 Sub-Saharan Africa: Knowledge Networks and Agricultural Innovation

The agricultural SME sector in sub-Saharan Africa provides some of the richest evidence for the FIKM model in action, precisely because the constraints are so severe and the stakes so high. Adu-Gyamfi & Adjei (2018) studied a cluster of smallholder processing cooperatives in Ghana that had collectively developed a low-cost cassava flour processing method requiring no imported equipment and using waste heat from a neighbouring bakery to reduce drying time. The innovation was not the product of a single entrepreneur's insight but of an extended period of peer knowledge exchange within the cluster, facilitated by a cooperative association that held regular meetings and maintained a shared record of processing experiments.

What is striking about this case from a knowledge management perspective is that the knowledge infrastructure was entirely informal but highly functional. The cooperative association was the codification mechanism: meeting minutes and shared logbooks served as organisational memory. The regular meetings were the sharing mechanism. The rotation of technical leads across member firms was the acquisition mechanism, ensuring that knowledge generated in one firm was exposed to others. And the shared goal of reducing processing costs for all members was the application motivator. None of these mechanisms required significant financial investment, but they collectively constituted a knowledge management system that enabled sustained frugal innovation.

Agyapong & Attram (2019) draw a similar conclusion from a broader study of 234 manufacturing SMEs in Ghana, finding that network-based knowledge management practices, defined as those relying on inter-firm knowledge exchange rather than internal documentation systems, were the strongest predictor of frugal innovation output among firms with low internal knowledge management investment. This suggests that where individual SMEs lack the resources for internal knowledge management infrastructure, ecosystem-level knowledge networks can partially substitute, particularly for knowledge acquisition and sharing, though the codification gap typically remains.

5.2 South Asia: Healthcare Innovation and Tacit Knowledge Codification

The Indian healthcare sector has long been a reference point for frugal innovation scholars, with landmark cases including the Jaipur Foot prosthesis and the Aravind Eye Care system representing frugal innovation at its most impressive. More recent evidence from the post-2020 period documents how knowledge management practices have enabled the scaling and adaptation of these models.

Bisha and Krishnan (2014) studied a network of low-cost diagnostic device manufacturers in Tamil Nadu and found that the firms with the highest rates of product iteration and market adaptation were those that had invested in what the authors call structured tacit knowledge capture: a set of practices designed to make the experiential knowledge of senior technicians accessible to younger workers without requiring those technicians to reduce the complexity of what they knew. Techniques included video recording of repair and calibration processes, paired working arrangements in which a novice shadowed an expert for a defined period, and regular problem-solving sessions in which difficult cases were discussed collectively and solutions recorded. These practices were not expensive, but they were consistent and deliberate.

The Bangladesh context adds a complementary dimension. De Marchi et al. (2022) studied frugal innovation in the ready-made garment sector and found that the most innovative SMEs in the sector were those that had developed systematic mechanisms for capturing and applying knowledge about international buyer requirements, local regulatory changes, and process efficiency improvements simultaneously. These firms operated in a sector characterised by extreme external knowledge pressure, with technical specifications changing frequently and regulatory compliance requirements evolving rapidly. Their knowledge management practices were sophisticated relative to firm size because the cost of not managing knowledge in this environment was evident and immediate.

5.3 Southeast Asia: Digital Knowledge Management and Frugal Service Innovation

Southeast Asia presents a distinct variation on the FIKM model because the region has experienced rapid mobile technology diffusion over the past decade, creating a new set of low-cost knowledge management tools accessible even to very small firms. Díaz-Arancibia et al. (2024) found that SMEs in the logistics and transport sector were using smartphone-based communication platforms as de facto knowledge management systems, sharing route optimisation insights, customer preference data, and regulatory updates through group messaging channels. While these channels lacked the structure of formal knowledge management systems, their near-universal adoption created a knowledge-sharing infrastructure that effectively replaced more expensive alternatives.

The interesting finding in Díaz-Arancibia et al. (2024) is not simply that informal digital tools can support knowledge management but that firms which had established shared norms around their use, such as an expectation that useful information would be shared proactively, that messages containing actionable insights would be tagged for easy retrieval, and that important lessons from customer interactions would be summarised weekly, significantly outperformed those that used the same tools without these norms. Technology was a necessary but not sufficient condition for effective digital knowledge management; the organisational norms were the critical differentiator. This finding echoes the broader point about knowledge leadership: systems without culture produce little.

Table 4. Regional Evidence for the FIKM Model: Selected Cases

Region	Sector	Primary KM Mechanism	Frugal Innovation Output
Sub-Saharan Africa (Ghana)	Agricultural processing	Cooperative knowledge networks and shared logbooks	Low-cost cassava flour processing using waste heat
Sub-Saharan Africa (Ghana)	Manufacturing SMEs	Inter-firm knowledge exchange in industrial clusters	Incremental process innovations reducing input costs
South Asia (India)	Medical devices	Structured tacit knowledge capture through video and paired working	Iterative low-cost diagnostic device development

continued on following page

Table 4. Continued

Region	Sector	Primary KM Mechanism	Frugal Innovation Output
South Asia (Bangladesh)	Ready-made garments	Multi-domain KM systems tracking buyer, regulatory, and process knowledge	Rapid adaptation to changing buyer specifications
Southeast Asia (Vietnam)	Logistics and transport	Smartphone-based knowledge sharing with organisational norms	Frugal route optimisation and service personalisation

Note. All cases are drawn from post-2020 empirical literature. Sectors and KM mechanisms are specific to each study; the table does not claim these are the only relevant cases in each region.

6. CHALLENGES AND BARRIERS TO FIKM IMPLEMENTATION

6.1 The Codification Dilemma

Perhaps the most persistent challenge in implementing effective knowledge management for frugal innovation is what might be called the codification dilemma. On one side of this dilemma is the organisational imperative to capture and retain knowledge so that it can be reused. On the other side is the genuine difficulty of codifying knowledge that is fundamentally tacit, contextual, and relational. The knowledge that allows a skilled artisan to know that a mixture is ready, or that allows an experienced community health worker to assess a patient's condition without diagnostic equipment, cannot be fully captured in a written procedure. Attempts to codify it too precisely can produce documents that are technically accurate but practically useless, because they omit the judgment and perception that give the original knowledge its value.

The solution is not to abandon codification but to pursue it with appropriate humility. Effective codification in SME contexts tends to be partial rather than comprehensive, capturing the structural elements of a practice while acknowledging that the tacit elements must be transmitted through demonstration and supervised practice. Dzenopoljac et al. (2025) found that the most effective codification artefacts in their study were those that functioned as memory triggers rather than complete instructions, prompting knowledgeable practitioners to recall the full tacit knowledge rather than attempting to replace it.

6.2 Knowledge Retention Under High Turnover

Staff turnover is a chronic problem for SMEs in resource-constrained environments, and its implications for knowledge retention are severe. Skilled employees who have been central to frugal innovation projects are often the most attractive to larger firms or to international opportunities, and the knowledge they carry may be poorly codified precisely because they were too valuable and too busy to document it. Medase & Abdul-Basit (2020) found that in their sample of Ghanaian SMEs, the average knowledge retention loss from the departure of one key employee was estimated by managers to set the firm back by the equivalent of eighteen months of learning. This figure suggests that knowledge retention is not simply a knowledge management nicety but a strategic priority with material financial consequences.

Strategies for addressing this challenge include deliberate knowledge succession planning, in which senior practitioners are expected to designate and mentor knowledge successors as part of their routine responsibilities; cross-training programmes that distribute critical knowledge across multiple individuals; and exit interview protocols designed to capture the most valuable knowledge from departing employees before they leave. None of these strategies perfectly prevents knowledge loss, but in combination they significantly reduce its impact.

6.3 Power Dynamics and Knowledge Hoarding

In many SME contexts, knowledge is power in a very literal sense. An employee who possesses unique knowledge that the organisation depends on enjoys job security, higher wages, and organisational influence that they would lose if that knowledge were widely shared. This creates a rational incentive for knowledge hoarding that knowledge management systems must actively counteract. The challenge is that the most effective countermeasures are cultural rather than structural, and cultural change is slow and difficult to engineer in organisations operating under day-to-day survival pressure.

Subrahmanyam (2025) found that the most effective approach to reducing knowledge hoarding in SME contexts was not to eliminate the incentive but to redirect it: rather than penalising hoarding, successful firms created alternative sources of status and reward for knowledge sharing. Employees who shared valuable knowledge became recognised as organisational experts, sought out for advice by colleagues and managers, and rewarded with the kind of relational capital that was more durable than the temporary advantage of holding knowledge exclusively. This reframing of knowledge sharing as a form of professional identity rather than a sacrifice of competitive advantage proved more effective than compliance-based approaches.

6.4 Technological Barriers and the Digital Divide

The potential of digital tools to support knowledge management in SME contexts is real, as the Vietnamese evidence demonstrates, but it is not uniformly accessible. Significant portions of the SME population in sub-Saharan Africa and South Asia continue to face barriers including unreliable electricity, limited internet access, low digital literacy among employees, and inability to afford even modest software subscriptions. Where these barriers exist, digital knowledge management solutions are not viable, and organisations must rely on analogue alternatives.

This is not necessarily a fatal limitation. Lim and Fujimoto (2019) argue that many of the most effective knowledge management practices for frugal innovation are inherently low-technology: regular team meetings, storytelling practices in which experienced practitioners share case narratives, physical displays of process documentation in workshop spaces, and the deliberate organisation of workspaces to facilitate knowledge-sharing conversations. The risk is that when digital tools do become available, organisations may adopt them without the cultural and procedural foundations that make them effective, investing in technology rather than in the practices that give technology its value.

7. IMPLICATIONS FOR PRACTICE AND POLICY

7.1 Implications for SME Managers

The central practical message of this chapter is that knowledge management need not be expensive, complex, or technologically intensive to be effective. What it must be is intentional. SME managers who approach knowledge management as a set of deliberate practices, however simple, rather than as something that happens naturally in the course of doing business, will develop frugal innovation capabilities that are more reliable, more scalable, and more resilient to disruption than those who do not.

Three priorities stand out from the evidence reviewed. First, invest in knowledge acquisition from users. The most powerful source of frugal innovation insight is direct, sustained engagement with the people whose problems the innovation is designed to solve. This does not require formal ethnographic methods or significant budget. It requires curiosity, time, and a genuine orientation toward learning from observation rather than from assumption. Managers who regularly visit customers, who encourage front-line employees to report what they hear and see in the field, and who create forums in which that information is shared and discussed are building the foundation of frugal innovation capability.

Second, create simple codification habits. A brief written summary after every significant project, a photograph of a novel production setup, a five-minute audio recording of a skilled employee explaining how they solved a problem: these practices cost almost nothing and accumulate into an organisational knowledge base that is genuinely valuable over time. Discipline is more important than sophistication. A basic logbook kept consistently is worth more than an enterprise knowledge management system that is never used.

Third, model and reward knowledge sharing. The cultural conditions for effective knowledge management are set by leaders. When senior managers are visibly open about what they have learned, including from failures, and when they recognise employees who contribute knowledge to the collective rather than hoarding it, the organisational culture shifts in ways that no policy or procedure can achieve.

7.2 Implications for Ecosystem Architects and Development Organisations

Much of the evidence reviewed in this chapter points to the importance of ecosystem-level knowledge management mechanisms: the cooperative associations, cluster networks, and inter-firm exchange relationships that allow knowledge to flow across SME boundaries. Development organisations, industry associations, and business support providers are in a uniquely powerful position to facilitate these mechanisms because they operate at the ecosystem level and can create the connective infrastructure that individual firms cannot build alone.

Practical interventions might include establishing sector-specific knowledge communities of practice, facilitated by a professional coordinator who curates knowledge exchange and maintains shared records of innovation experiments across member firms. They might include knowledge translation programmes that help SMEs access the applied research produced by universities and public research institutions in forms that are directly usable. They might include peer learning visits, in which managers from one firm observe the practices of another, one of the simplest and most effective forms of tacit knowledge transfer available. Adu-Gyamfi & Adjei (2018) found that peer learning visits were rated by Ghanaian SME managers as the most valuable support activity offered by their cooperative association, more valuable than financial support, training, or market access assistance.

7.3 Implications for Policymakers

Policymakers concerned with SME innovation in volatile and resource-constrained environments have tended to focus their attention on financial instruments: grants, loans, and tax incentives that reduce the cost of investment. This chapter suggests that these instruments address only one dimension of the frugal innovation challenge. The knowledge dimension is equally important and is addressed by a different set of policy tools.

Policies that support SME knowledge management capacity might include funding for cluster-level knowledge coordination roles, which are currently under-resourced in most emerging market economies. They might include requirements that public innovation support programmes include a knowledge management component, so that firms receiving innovation grants are also supported to capture and retain the knowledge generated. They might include the development of simple, accessible knowledge management frameworks and tools designed specifically for SMEs in low-resource contexts, rather than the scaled-down versions of enterprise knowledge management systems that are typically offered. And they might include investment in the university-SME linkages that allow frugal innovation knowledge to flow in both directions: from universities to SMEs through applied research, and from SMEs to universities through the industry-embedded learning that enriches research with contextual reality.

Ur Rehman et al. (2024) argue that the institutional void problem will not be solved by individual SME-level interventions alone. Sustained frugal innovation capacity in resource-constrained environments requires what they call innovation ecosystem governance: deliberate, sustained public investment in the shared knowledge infrastructure from which all firms draw, including quality standards, testing facilities, regulatory guidance, and technology diffusion services. In this sense, the policy implications of the FIKM model go beyond SME support to encompass the broader architecture of the innovation ecosystem in which SMEs operate.

Table 5. Summary of Implications for Key Stakeholders

Stakeholder	Key Challenge Addressed	Recommended Action
SME Managers	Knowledge loss from staff turnover and informal practice	Establish lightweight codification habits; implement knowledge succession planning; conduct structured post-project debriefs
SME Managers	Knowledge hoarding undermining collective capability	Model knowledge sharing from the top; create recognition mechanisms for knowledge contributors; link sharing to career development
Ecosystem Architects	Fragmented knowledge base across SME clusters	Facilitate sector-specific communities of practice; organise peer learning visits; support shared knowledge repositories for cluster members
Development Organisations	Limited access to applied research and technical knowledge	Fund knowledge translation programmes; support university-SME partnerships; provide facilitated access to public research outputs
Policymakers	Absence of KM infrastructure in public innovation support programmes	Require KM components in innovation grant programmes; fund cluster KM coordinator roles; invest in ecosystem-level knowledge infrastructure

Note. Recommendations are derived from the empirical evidence reviewed and the FIKM model framework. Implementation should be adapted to the specific institutional context of each country or sector.

8. CONCLUSION

The argument developed in this chapter can be stated plainly: frugal innovation and knowledge management are not separate concerns that happen to overlap occasionally in the experience of resource-constrained SMEs. They are deeply interdependent, and the relationship between them is the primary explanation for why some SMEs in volatile environments develop durable innovation capabilities while others remain perpetually dependent on individual genius and fortunate circumstance.

The FIKM model presented here is a conceptual framework rather than a fully tested empirical model, and future research should develop and validate its components with greater precision. The five knowledge management processes identified in Table 2 require individual examination in relation to specific frugal innovation output types. The feedback loop mechanism needs longitudinal research designs to trace capability development over time. And the model needs testing in contexts beyond the three regional cases examined here, including in the SME sectors of transitional economies in Eastern Europe and the Middle East, which face their own distinctive forms of resource constraint and institutional uncertainty.

Several contributions emerge from the analysis. Theoretically, the chapter demonstrates that frugal innovation is most productively understood as a knowledge-intensive dynamic capability rather than as a property of low-cost products. This framing connects frugal innovation research to the broader dynamic capabilities literature and opens productive avenues for theory development. Empirically, the synthesis of post-2020 evidence from sub-Saharan Africa, South Asia, and Southeast Asia documents the variety of knowledge management mechanisms that support frugal innovation in different institutional contexts and confirms that no single mechanism is universally sufficient. Practically, the chapter offers managers, ecosystem architects, and policymakers a grounded set of recommendations that can be implemented without significant financial resources.

There is something quietly important about the fundamental premise of frugal innovation and knowledge management as complementary disciplines. Both are ultimately about doing more with less, not through wishful thinking but through disciplined practice. Knowledge management in resource-constrained SMEs is not about knowledge management systems in the enterprise software sense. It is about the human practices through which organisations learn from experience, remember what they have learned, and put that learning to use. These practices are within reach of any organisation that is serious about building sustainable innovation capability, regardless of its size or the richness of its resource environment. In a world where the challenges of sustainability, inclusion, and resilience demand that we innovate smarter rather than simply more expensively, that is a genuinely encouraging conclusion.

REFERENCES

Adu-Gyamfi, Y., & Adjei, B. (2018). *Skills development, knowledge and innovation at Suame Magazine, Kumasi* (Open AIR Working Paper No. 16). Open African Innovation Research. (Working paper discusses how artisans acquire skills through apprenticeships and share knowledge and innovation within the Suame cluster.) https://openair.africa/wp-content/uploads/2020/05/WP-16-Skills-Development-Knowledge-and-Innovation-at-Suame-Magazine-Kumasi.pdf

Agyapong, D., & Attram, A. B. (2019). Effect of owner-manager's financial literacy on the performance of SMEs in the Cape Coast Metropolis in Ghana. *Journal of Global Entrepreneurship Research*, *9*(67), 1–13. DOI: 10.1186/s40497-019-0191-1

Bisha, A. (2025). Frugal innovation – new paradigm in innovation management. *Balkan Journal of Interdisciplinary Research*, *11*(1), 35–47. DOI: 10.2478/bjir-2025-0003

Cohen, W. M., & Levinthal, D. A. (1990). Absorptive capacity: A new perspective on learning and innovation. *Administrative Science Quarterly*, *35*(1), 128–152. DOI: 10.2307/2393553

Dalkir, K. (2017). *Knowledge management in theory and practice* (3rd ed.). MIT Press.

De Marchi, V., Pineda-Escobar, M. A., Howell, R., Verheij, M., & Knorringa, P. (2022). Frugal innovation and sustainability outcomes: Findings from a systematic literature review. *European Journal of Innovation Management*, *25*(6), 984–1007. DOI: 10.1108/EJIM-02-2022-0083

Díaz-Arancibia, J., Hochstetter-Diez, J., Bustamante-Mora, A., Sepúlveda-Cuevas, S., Albayay, I., & Arango-López, J. (2024). Navigating digital transformation and technology adoption: A literature review from small and medium-sized enterprises in developing countries. *Sustainability (Basel)*, *16*(14), 5946. DOI: 10.3390/su16145946

Dzenopoljac, V., Dzenopoljac, A., Ognjanovic, J., Kraus, S., & Puumalainen, K. (2025). From sharing to shaping: Role of knowledge quality and ambidexterity in SME innovation performance. *Journal of Innovation & Knowledge*, *10*(100838), 100838. Advance online publication. DOI: 10.1016/j.jik.2025.100838

Escudero-Cipriani, C., García-del Junco, J., Chafloque-Céspedes, R., & Alvarez-Risco, A. (2024). Frugal innovation in the business environment: A literature review and future perspectives. *Frontiers in Artificial Intelligence*, *7*, 1385522. Advance online publication. DOI: 10.3389/frai.2024.1385522 PMID: 39712468

Fainshmidt, S., Wenger, L., Pezeshkan, A., & Mallon, M. R. (2019). When do dynamic capabilities lead to competitive advantage? The importance of strategic fit. *Journal of Management Studies*, *56*(4), 758–787. DOI: 10.1111/joms.12415

Grant, R. M. (1996). Toward a knowledge-based theory of the firm. *Strategic Management Journal*, *17*(S2), 109–122. DOI: 10.1002/smj.4250171110

Homayoun, S., Velashani, M. A. B., Abbas Alkhafaji, B. K., & Jabbar Mezher, S. (2023). The effect of COVID-19 on the performance of SMEs in emerging markets in Iran, Iraq and Jordan. *Sustainability (Basel)*, *15*(10), 7847. DOI: 10.3390/su15107847

Hossain, M. (2018). Frugal innovation: A review and research agenda. *Journal of Cleaner Production*, *182*, 926–936. DOI: 10.1016/j.jclepro.2018.02.091

Khanna, T., & Palepu, K. G. (1997). Why focused strategies may be wrong for emerging markets. *Harvard Business Review*, *75*(4), 41–51.

Lim, C., & Fujimoto, T. (2019). Frugal innovation and design changes expanding the cost-performance frontier: A Schumpeterian approach. *Research Policy*, *48*(4), 1016–1029. DOI: 10.1016/j.respol.2018.10.014

Medase, S. K., & Abdul-Basit, S. (2020). External knowledge modes and firm-level innovation performance: Empirical evidence from sub-Saharan Africa. *Journal of Innovation & Knowledge*, *5*(2), 81–95. DOI: 10.1016/j.jik.2019.08.001

Orelj, A., & Torfason, M. T. (2022). They didn't ask: Online innovation communities as a latent dynamic capability. *Technological Forecasting and Social Change*, *180*, 121738. Advance online publication. DOI: 10.1016/j.techfore.2022.121738

Organisation for Economic Co-operation and Development. (2023). *OECD SME and entrepreneurship outlook 2023*. OECD Publishing. https://www.oecd.org/content/dam/oecd/en/publications/reports/2023/06/oecd-sme-and-entrepreneurship-outlook-2023_c5ac21d0/342b8564-en.pdf

Prahalad, C. K. (2004). *The fortune at the bottom of the pyramid: Eradicating poverty through profits*. Wharton School Publishing.

Rehman, K. U., Anwar, R. S., Antohi, V. M., Ali, U., Fortea, C., & Zlati, M. L. (2024). Driving frugal innovation in SMEs: How sustainable leadership, knowledge sources and information credibility make a difference. *Frontiers in Sociology*, *9*, 1344704. Advance online publication. DOI: 10.3389/fsoc.2024.1344704 PMID: 38497083

Shao, B., Kuang, X., & Wang, H. (2024). Digital knowledge management and technological innovation of manufacturing enterprises: The perspective of dynamic capabilities. *Keji Jinbu Yu Duice*, *41*(14), 111–121. DOI: 10.6049/kjjbydc.2023030519

Subrahmanyam, S. (2025). Talent Management in Startups and SMEs. In Al Daraai, S., Al Abri, S., & Alhamar Alkathiri, N. (Eds.), *Aligning Talent Management and Organizational Innovation Goals* (pp. 359–392). IGI Global Scientific Publishing., DOI: 10.4018/979-8-3373-0015-3.ch013

Subrahmanyam, S., Aishwaryalaxmi, N. S., Khalife, D., Shaikh, I. A. K., Faldu, R., & Asthana, N. (2024). Impact of Knowledge Management and Big Data Analytics Capabilities on Firm Performance. In *2024 Ninth International Conference on Science Technology Engineering and Mathematics (ICONSTEM)* (pp. 1-5). IEEE. https://doi.org/DOI: 10.1109/ICONSTEM60960.2024.10568874

Teece, D. J., Pisano, G., & Shuen, A. (1997). Dynamic capabilities and strategic management. *Strategic Management Journal, 18*(7), 509–533. https://www.jstor.org/stable/3088148. DOI: 10.1002/(SICI)1097-0266(199708)18:7<509::AID-SMJ882>3.0.CO;2-Z

Ur Rehman, K., Anwar, R. S., Antohi, V. M., Ali, U., Fortea, C., & Zlati, M. L. (2024). Driving frugal innovation in SMEs: How sustainable leadership, knowledge sources and information credibility make a difference. *Frontiers in Sociology, 9*, 1344704. DOI: 10.3389/fsoc.2024.1344704 PMID: 38497083

Wernerfelt, B. (1984). A resource-based view of the firm. *Strategic Management Journal, 5*(2), 171–180. DOI: 10.1002/smj.4250050207

Weyrauch, T., & Herstatt, C. (2016). What is frugal innovation? Three defining criteria. *Journal of Frugal Innovation, 2*(1), 1. Advance online publication. DOI: 10.1186/s40669-016-0005-y

Wigren-Kristoferson, C., Brundin, E., Hellerstedt, K., Stevenson, A., & Aggestam, M. (2022). Rethinking embeddedness: A review and research agenda. *Entrepreneurship and Regional Development, 34*(1–2), 32–56. DOI: 10.1080/08985626.2021.2021298

Zollo, M., & Winter, S. G. (2002). Deliberate learning and the evolution of dynamic capabilities. *Organization Science, 13*(3), 339–351. DOI: 10.1287/orsc.13.3.339.2780

KEY TERMS AND DEFINITIONS

Absorptive Capacity: An organization's capability to identify valuable external knowledge, assimilate it into internal processes, and apply it commercially to support innovation and strategic adaptation.

Dynamic Capabilities: Higher-order organizational abilities that enable firms to sense opportunities, seize them through innovation, and reconfigure resources and competencies to respond effectively to rapidly changing market conditions.

Frugal Innovation: A resource-efficient innovation approach focused on designing affordable, accessible, and robust products, services, or processes by creatively utilizing limited resources and prioritizing essential functionality for underserved or cost-sensitive markets.

Grassroots Innovation: Locally developed innovation initiatives originating from communities, informal networks, or individuals who create context-specific solutions to address social, economic, or environmental challenges.

Knowledge Management (KM): A systematic organizational process involving the creation, acquisition, codification, sharing, and application of knowledge to enhance decision-making, innovation capability, and long-term competitive advantage.

Organizational Learning: A continuous process through which organizations acquire, interpret, and integrate knowledge derived from experience, experimentation, and interaction with stakeholders to improve performance and innovation outcomes.

Resource-Constrained Environments: Economic or institutional contexts where organizations face significant limitations in financial capital, infrastructure, technology, skilled labor, or institutional support, requiring adaptive and cost-efficient operational strategies.

Reverse Innovation: An innovation process in which products or solutions initially developed for emerging or resource-constrained markets are later adapted and introduced into developed markets due to their cost efficiency and simplicity.

Small and Medium-Sized Enterprises (SMEs): Business organizations characterized by relatively small workforce size, limited capital resources, and flexible organizational structures, often operating with constrained financial, technological, and managerial capacities compared to large corporations.

Volatile Environments: Business contexts characterized by high levels of uncertainty, rapid market fluctuations, technological disruptions, and institutional instability that require organizations to maintain flexibility and adaptive capabilities.

Chapter 5
Intellectual Capital-Enhanced Dynamic Capabilities:
A Multi-Dimensional Performance Framework for SMEs in VUCA Environments

Göran Roos
http://orcid.org/0000-0003-0943-3585
Adelaide University, Australia

ABSTRACT

This chapter develops the IC-Enhanced Dynamic Capabilities Framework for SMEs operating in VUCA environments. The framework integrates intellectual capital theory with dynamic capabilities theory, positioning human capital, structural capital, and relational capital as foundational resources that enable sensing, seizing, and transforming capabilities. These capabilities drive multi-dimensional performance across profitable growth, productivity enhancement, human capital retention and development, and environmental footprint reduction. The framework operates through bidirectional transformation mechanisms where intellectual capital enables capability development whilst being enhanced through capability deployment, creating reinforcing cycles. Implementation follows a four-phase approach: assessment and preparation, capability development, implementation and integration, and continuous adaptation. The theoretical contribution demonstrates how SMEs can leverage knowledge-based assets to build adaptive capabilities for sustained competitive advantage in turbulent environments.

DOI: 10.4018/979-8-3373-6053-9.ch005

INTRODUCTION AND THEORETICAL FOUNDATION

Small and medium-sized enterprises represent over 99% of global business activity, contributing significantly to employment generation, innovation capacity, and economic growth patterns (Kraus et al., 2020). These organisations frequently operate within environments characterised by volatility, uncertainty, complexity, and ambiguity—collectively termed VUCA environments (Millar et al., 2018; Schoemaker et al., 2018). This reality creates substantial challenges as rapid technological shifts, evolving market conditions, changing consumer preferences, regulatory transformations, and intensifying competitive require unprecedented levels of organisational agility and resilience.

Unlike their larger counterparts, SMEs cannot typically leverage extensive financial resources or substantial tangible asset bases to navigate turbulent conditions. These constraints manifest in several distinctive ways. Resource (including available person hours) limitations restrict their ability to pursue multiple strategic initiatives simultaneously, while modest financial reserves provide minimal cushion during economic downturns or limits the investments that can be made. However, SMEs demonstrate certain structural advantages, including flatter organisational hierarchies that enable faster decision-making processes, though these same structures can create capability gaps and frequently a lack of absorptive capacity when it comes to emerging knowledge domains. Additionally, their closer proximity to customers and markets provides significant advantages in environmental sensing and market responsiveness.

A particularly critical characteristic emerges in SMEs' heavy reliance on key individuals, where the departure of essential employees can fundamentally disrupt operations (Senaratne & Wang, 2018). This dependency reflects the fundamental architecture of SME human capital, with knowledge typically concentrated within the owner-manager and a small core team. The centrality of the owner-manager means that organisational sensing capacity becomes heavily dependent on their individual cognitive capabilities for perception, attention, and environmental interpretation (Helfat & Peteraf, 2015). This individual-level foundation of organisational capabilities forms a critical component of the micro-foundations perspective that underpins dynamic capabilities theory.

Given these distinctive characteristics, SMEs' competitive advantage increasingly depends on their ability to effectively leverage intellectual capital resources rather than competing primarily on scale or financial resources. The knowledge, skills, relationships, and innovative capacities embedded within these firms become critical determinants of sustainable success. This reality has made SMEs' intellectual capital essential for understanding how these organisations can build and continuously adapt the dynamic capabilities needed for sustained performance and growth within VUCA environments (Vătămănescu et al., 2019). This relationship between intellectual capital and dynamic capabilities forms the theoretical foundation for the framework presented in this chapter.

Intellectual Capital Theory and Components

The concept of intellectual capital broadly encompasses the non-financial and non-physical assets of an organisation that are not fully captured on traditional balance sheets, including both the knowledge residing in employees' minds and the structures and relationships that enable systematic value creation (Roos & Roos, 1997). Intellectual capital theory emerged from growing recognition that traditional financial measures inadequately captured the value-creating potential of knowledge-based assets in contemporary economies (Edvinsson & Malone, 1997) as well as from broadening the resource based view of the firm (Roos, 2019).

The widely accepted tripartite classification divides intellectual capital resources into three interconnected components that work synergistically. *Human capital* encompasses the knowledge, skills, abilities, experience, and capabilities possessed by employees. *Structural capital* includes organisational knowledge embedded in processes, systems, databases, organisational culture, intellectual property, and operational routines that remain within the organisation even when employees leave. *Relational capital* comprises the value derived from relationships with customers, suppliers, partners, and other external stakeholders, including reputation, trust, and network connections (Edvinsson & Sullivan, 1996; Roos et al., 1997; Bontis, 1998; Nahapiet & Ghoshal, 1998). These three components interact and transform to enable organisational adaptation and performance enhancement.

To understand how intellectual capital differs fundamentally from traditional organisational resources, Table 1 provides a comprehensive comparison of intellectual capital resource categories and their distinguishing attributes. This framework illustrates why intellectual capital resources require fundamentally different management approaches compared to monetary and physical resources, particularly regarding ownership structures, economic behaviour patterns, and value appropriation mechanisms.

Table 1. Resource Categories and Their Distinguishing Attributes (Source: Roos et al., 2005; Roos, 2019)

Attribute	Monetary Resources	Physical Resources	Relational Resources	Organisational Resources	Human Resources
Description	Financial resources that take the form of cash assets (such as marketable securities) that can easily be converted to pure cash	Anything that can be touched, for example has a physical presence (that is what you would normally find under the heading of plant and equipment in the balance sheet)	The relationships held by individuals on behalf of the firm or that are embodied in the form of contracts with the firm as one party	The outcome of desires to hold explicit or implicit relationships with the firm by external parties; The result of human endeavours developed internally in the firm or acquired externally by the firm that is now owned by the firm and that are not physical or monetary in nature	All useful resources that are embodied in people
Ownership & Control	Firm	Firm	Nobody owns; co-controlled	Firm	Individual
Economic Behaviour	Decreasing marginal return	Decreasing marginal return	Network economic behaviour	Network economic behaviour	Increasing marginal return
Known Conversion Rate to Monetary Value	Yes	No	No	No	No
Additive Nature	Yes	Yes	No	No	No
Information Asymmetry	Low	Low	High	High	High
Rivalry Resource	Yes	Yes	No	No	No
Excludability	Yes	Yes	No	Partial	No

continued on following page

Table 1. Continued

Attribute	Monetary Resources	Physical Resources	Relational Resources	Organisational Resources	Human Resources
Examples of Appropriation Mechanisms	Financing structure and cost of capital	IP, Firm specific assets, First mover advantage	Network size, Reputation, Bargaining power, Customer retention	Causal ambiguity, Contracts, Agreement stability, Imperfect mobility, Brand	Shared values/goals, Innovativeness, Absorptive capacity
Drives towards a strategic logic (in the meaning of Stabell & Fjeldstad, 1998) of	Value Chain	Value Chain	Value Network (Although can drive towards a value shop logic in the very early stages of the resource lifecycle and towards value chain in the very late stages of the resource lifecycle)	Value Network (Although can drive towards a value shop logic in the very early stages of the resource lifecycle and towards value chain in the very late stages of the resource lifecycle)	Value Shop

This resource categorisation demonstrates that intellectual capital resource components exhibit fundamentally different characteristics from traditional resources, including network economic behaviour, high information asymmetry, and non-rivalry features that enable simultaneous use by multiple parties without depletion. This explains why intellectual capital resources requires different management approaches and why they can serve as a foundation for a stream of temporary competitive advantages in an SME context (Roos et al., 2025). The network economic behaviour and increasing marginal returns characteristics of relational and human capital resources respectively, become particularly important in the application domains discussed later in this chapter.

The deployment of intellectual capital resources involves significant strategic trade-offs that create management paradoxes for SME leaders. Research reveals that individual intellectual capital resource components can exhibit counterintuitive effects when considered in isolation rather than as integrated systems. Subramaniam and Youndt (2005) found that human capital, when examined independently, demonstrated a negative association with radical innovative capability, contrary to conventional expectations. This paradox suggests that assembling highly skilled experts without appropriate collaborative structures can create cognitive entrenchment, where deep domain expertise leads to rigid mental models that resist paradigm-challenging ideas. This finding reinforces the importance of the integrated approach presented in the framework section below, where all three intellectual capital resource types work synergistically rather than independently and where value creation mean the transformation system that results in the desired value.

A critical distinction must be drawn between resource type and accounting recognisability, as intellectual capital resources are not synonymous with intangible resources. The classification of resources as monetary, physical, relational, organisational, or human reflects their fundamental economic behaviour and strategic logic, not their tangible or intangible expression (Roos, 2019). This distinction becomes important when considering the transformation mechanisms described in the framework development section.

Table 2. Resource Type versus Accounting Recognisability (with examples) (Adapted from Roos, 2019)

Resource Category	**Tangible Expression**	**Intangible Expression**
Monetary Resources	Cash	Borrowing capacity
Physical Resources	Building	Building location value
Relational Resources	Repeat orders	Preferred supplier status
Organisational Resources	Employee contracts	Organisational culture
Human Resources	Physical presence	Problem-solving ability

Dynamic Capabilities Theory

Dynamic capabilities refer to a firm's ability to integrate, build, and reconfigure internal and external competencies to address rapidly changing environments, constituting the fundamental mechanisms through which organisations adapt and evolve over time (Teece et al., 1997). These represent higher-order capabilities that enable an organisation to systematically sense opportunities and threats, seize opportunities by mobilising and orchestrating resources, and continuously reconfigure or transform its resource base as environmental conditions require (Teece, 2007). The three fundamental processes of sensing, seizing, and transforming form the capability layer of the framework presented below.

The development of dynamic capabilities emerges through systematic organisational learning processes that transform ad-hoc responses into reliable, repeatable routines that can be deployed when environmental conditions require adaptation. Zollo and Winter (2002) identified three core learning mechanisms that drive capability evolution - experience accumulation through systematic repetition of activities, knowledge articulation that converts tacit understanding into explicit, and knowledge codification that embeds organisational learning into formal procedures and systems. These learning mechanisms connect directly to the structural capital resource development processes discussed in the intellectual capital section above, creating systematic linkages between knowledge and adaptive capacity.

The development of dynamic capabilities fundamentally depends on specific micro-foundations operating at both individual and team levels within organisations. Micro-foundations represent the individual-level and group-level actions, interactions, and cognitions that underlie and give rise to collective-level organisational constructs and outcomes (Felin et al., 2015). At the individual level, managerial cognitive capabilities provide the foundation for sensing, seizing, and transforming activities within organisations. Helfat and Peteraf (2015) identify specific cognitive capabilities that underpin each dynamic capability viz perception and attention mechanisms for sensing opportunities and threats, problem-solving and reasoning capabilities for seizing opportunities through business model design and resource orchestration, and social cognition and communication skills for transforming organisational structures and processes. These cognitive capabilities together form the micro-foundational basis for the human capital resource contributions to dynamic capabilities described in the framework section.

The Intellectual Capital-Dynamic Capabilities Nexus

Integrating these theoretical perspectives results in intellectual capital emerging as both an antecedent and enabler of dynamic capabilities, with both constructs driving SME performance outcomes through systematic interactions. Dynamic capabilities do not emerge in isolation but is a result of the systematic utilisation of a firm's knowledge assets and intellectual resources (i.e. its human capital resources) (Hsu & Wang, 2012; Zahra et al., 2006). This theoretical integration forms the foundation for the framework presented in the following section.

Consider how an SME's ability to sense new technological trends depends critically on its human capital resources in the form of skilled employees who systematically scan the environment, combined with its relational capital resources through established links to industry networks and information sources (Ali et al., 2023). Similarly, the organisation's ability to seize opportunities by developing new products or entering new markets hinges on structural capital resources including effective research and development processes, organisational cultures that support innovation, and codified knowledge systems that can be shared and acted upon systematically (Agostini et al., 2017). Likewise, the ability to reconfigure and transform business operations relies on the organisation's internal knowledge systems, learning routines, and change-management expertise combined with structural capital resources, as well as leadership skills and employee agility as human capital resources (Teece, 2007; Pasamar et al., 2015). These specific relationships between intellectual capital resources and dynamic capabilities is elaborated upon in the framework description below.

Empirical studies have consistently reinforced this theoretical linkage between intellectual capital resources and dynamic capabilities across various organisational contexts. Firms with higher quality and quantity intellectual capital tend to exhibit stronger dynamic capabilities and superior performance outcomes, whereas those lacking important intellectual capital resources struggle to adapt effectively to environmental changes (Hsu & Wang, 2012; Han & Li, 2015). Hsu and Wang (2012) found that in high-tech firms, the effect of structural capital resources on firm performance was fully mediated by dynamic capability, suggesting that organisational knowledge and systems only translated into performance gains when the firm possessed the adaptive processes to channel those resources into strategic action. Human and relational capital resources demonstrated partially mediated effects, indicating that while talented people and networks boost performance outcomes, they do so more powerfully when combined with strong dynamic capabilities that can systematically leverage these assets.

This creates a continuous improvement loop where enhanced workforce capabilities drive better dynamic processes, which subsequently further develop workforce capabilities and the firm's overall knowledge base through systematic learning and capability building. The mutual reinforcement proves critical for sustained performance in VUCA environments, as it allows SMEs to continuously adapt and evolve rather than merely respond reactively to individual environmental shocks (Ali et al., 2021). This bidirectional relationship forms a key feature of the framework discussed below, where capability deployment generates outcomes that further enhance the organisation's intellectual capital resource base through systematic learning processes.

THE IC-ENHANCED DYNAMIC CAPABILITIES FRAMEWORK

The integration of intellectual capital theory and dynamic capabilities framework requires a comprehensive conceptual model that explains how knowledge-based assets enhance organisational adaptation and performance within SME contexts. Drawing on the theoretical foundations established above, the IC-Enhanced Dynamic Capabilities Framework posits that each component of intellectual capital—human, structural, and relational—plays a distinct yet interconnected role in bolstering the firm's dynamic capabilities across sensing, seizing, and transforming dimensions. These enhanced dynamic capabilities then lead to improved organisational performance across the four interconnected dimensions explored in the application domains section below.

Human Capital Resources and Dynamic Capabilities

Human capital resources serves as the foundational element of many dynamic capabilities in SMEs, building directly on the micro-foundational perspective introduced in the theoretical discussion above. Human capital resources contributes to dynamic capabilities through several different mechanisms that all create competitive advantage.

Human capital resources underpins the sensing capability through pathways that enhance organisational environmental awareness. Skilled and knowledgeable employees demonstrate superior abilities in environmental scanning, recognising emerging market trends, and identifying potential threats or opportunities before they become obvious to competitors (Teece, 2007). An SME with experts in cutting-edge technologies or employees deeply embedded in customer communities possesses superior sensors for relevant environmental changes that can be translated into strategic advantage. Strong human capital resources has been consistently linked to greater absorptive capacity—the ability to absorb, process, and utilise new knowledge—which essentially represents a sensing and learning-oriented dynamic capability (Zahra & George, 2002).

Human capital resources proves crucial for the seizing capability by providing the cognitive and executional resources necessary to capitalise on identified opportunities. Once an opportunity is identified through systematic sensing, it requires competent managers and staff to conceptualise appropriate responses such as new product development or strategic pivots, and to execute these responses effectively within existing resource constraints. Without sufficient expertise and problem-solving ability, an SME might recognise a market gap but lack the capability to capitalise on it. Dynamic capabilities like rapid product development or flexible manufacturing rely fundamentally on engineers, designers, and decision-makers who can innovate and troubleshoot in real time—all functions that depend on the quality and to some extent quantity of human capital resources (Han & Li, 2015).

Human capital resources facilitates the transforming ability by providing the change management skills, learning agility, and cross-functional knowledge necessary for organisational adaptation. Adapting the organisation—whether through adopting new business models, restructuring operational teams, or implementing new processes—requires change management skills, learning agility, and often cross-functional knowledge that resides in human capital resources (Teece, 2007). Employees who demonstrate versatility, continuous learning orientation, and openness to change make it possible for SMEs to realign resources quickly and smoothly when environmental conditions demand transformation. Conversely, less skilled or change-averse workforces can become bottlenecks that slow or actively resist necessary transformation processes. This transforming ability becomes particularly important in the environmental footprint reduction domain discussed later in this chapter.

Structural Capital Resources and Dynamic Capabilities

The structural capital resources provides the organisational mechanisms and institutional knowledge infrastructure that supports dynamic capabilities, connecting directly to the learning mechanisms identified by Zollo and Winter (2002) in the theoretical foundation section above. These embedded organisational resources create capabilities that transcend individual employees and provide the foundation for the creation of a sustainable competitive advantages (or in reality more likely a sequence of temporary competitive advantages) (Roos et al., 2025).

Knowledge management systems, including databases, knowledge repositories, and documented best practice manuals, enable organisations to retain and distribute knowledge, thereby supporting the sensing capability by ensuring information flows efficiently to appropriate decision points (Easterby-Smith & Prieto, 2008). A well-maintained customer relationship management database can help an SME identify shifts in customer preferences, effectively functioning as an early warning system for opportunity and threat sensing that operates continuously rather than episodically.

The firm's processes and routines represent critical structural capital resources that creates dynamic capabilities. Dynamic capabilities often manifest as learned, stable processes that can be deployed when environmental conditions require adaptive responses (Eisenhardt & Martin, 2000). A new product development process represents a structural capital resource that facilitates innovation capability; an SME that has established a proven stage-gate process or agile sprint routine for new product development can more effectively seize innovation opportunities than a firm that approaches each innovation initiative through ad hoc methods. Similarly, a systematic process for periodically reviewing and realigning business models represents a structural capital resource that underpins transforming capability by creating routine mechanisms for strategic adaptation. These processes become particularly important for the productivity enhancement objectives explored in the application domains section.

Organisational culture represents another structural capital resource that influences dynamic capabilities across all three dimensions. A culture that encourages experimentation, tolerates calculated risks, and embraces continuous change facilitates dynamic capabilities by motivating employees to engage in sensing activities (scanning for improvement opportunities), seizing behaviours (taking initiative on identified opportunities), and transforming actions (accepting new roles or modified workflows) (Teece, 2007; Wang & Ahmed, 2007). Conversely, rigid or overly hierarchical cultures can stifle the behaviours needed for dynamic adaptation across all organisational levels. This cultural dimension becomes particularly relevant for human capital resource retention and development applications discussed later in this chapter.

Relational Capital Resources and Dynamic Capabilities

The relational capital resources plays a dual role in the dynamic capabilities' framework, extending the organisation's sensing and resource access capabilities beyond its formal boundaries while creating competitive advantages through network effects. These external relationships create capabilities that individual organisations could not develop independently.

Relational capital resources functions as an extended sensing apparatus that operates beyond the organisation's formal boundaries, creating environmental awareness. Strong relationships with customers provide insights into unmet needs and early warnings of changing demand patterns, effectively extending the SME's sensing capability into market dynamics (Yli-Renko et al., 2001). Close ties with suppliers and industry partners can alert firms to new technologies or shifts in supply chain dynamics before these changes become widely apparent. The high levels of trust and information exchange that characterise strong relational capital resources is important for obtaining timely, quality information that enables superior sensing capabilities (Nahapiet & Ghoshal, 1998).

Relational capital resources contributes to seizing and transforming capabilities by providing access to external resources and complementary capabilities that SMEs lack internally. When opportunities arise that exceed the firm's internal capabilities, well-connected SMEs can leverage partner relationships to seize these opportunities—for instance, through co-developing products with technology allies or quickly adjusting distribution channels through logistics partnerships. This represents a dynamic capability of networking or alliance management that is enabled by strong relational capital resources. These external partnerships become particularly important for SMEs pursuing profitable growth strategies, as discussed in the application domains section.

Regarding transforming capabilities, relational capital resources can ease major organisational transformations by providing access to external expertise and resources. For example, when an SME decides to outsource a function or pivot to a new business model, having established trustworthy relationships with suppliers or subcontractors can make the transition faster and smoother than attempting these transformations independently. In contrast, firms with weak relational capital resources might struggle to find reliable new partners or face resistance from customers when changing value propositions. This transforming function of relational capital resources connects directly to the environmental sustainability applications explored later in this chapter.

Framework Integration and Interactions

The framework recognises that the relationship between intellectual capital resources and dynamic capabilities operates bidirectionally and cumulatively, building on the theoretical integration discussed in the nexus section above. Dynamic capabilities development requires initial investments in intellectual capital resources, but capability deployment generates outcomes that further enhance the organisation's intellectual capital resource base through learning and experience accumulation. Successful innovation projects enhance human capital resources through skill development and experience accumulation, structural capital resources through the creation of new processes and systems, and relational capital resources through enhanced reputation and strengthened stakeholder relationships.

The intellectual capital resource-enhanced dynamic capabilities framework recognises that human, structural, and relational capital resources interact and reinforce each other in contributing to dynamic capabilities, directly addressing the paradox identified by Subramaniam and Youndt (2005) in the theoretical foundation section above. Dynamic capabilities achieve maximum robustness when supported by all three forms of intellectual capital resources working in combination rather than in isolation. A firm's human capital resources might generate novel ideas through superior sensing, but without structural capital resources providing processes to evaluate and fund new ideas, and relational capital resources providing market feedback or partnerships to implement ideas, the opportunity might not be seized effectively. Similarly, an SME might possess rich structural capital resources in the form of patents and operational manuals, but without skilled people (human capital resources) who know how to update and use those assets, and without customers (relational capital resources) to provide strategic direction, that structural capital resources may remain underutilised.

This cumulative aspect of the framework proves particularly important for SMEs, as it suggests that early investments in intellectual capital resources can generate self-reinforcing benefits over time through learning processes. SMEs that develop dynamic capabilities create positive feedback loops that enable accelerated learning and capability enhancement, providing a mechanism for overcoming initial resource disadvantages through superior knowledge accumulation and utilisation. This reinforcing cycle becomes evident across all four application domains discussed in the following section.

The framework also incorporates environmental factors that influence the intellectual capital resource-dynamic capabilities relationship, connecting directly to the VUCA environment characteristics introduced at the beginning of this chapter. VUCA environments create both opportunities and challenges for SME development that must be addressed through integrated approaches. Volatility systematically increases the importance of sensing capabilities supported by diverse human capital resources and extensive relational capital networks. Uncertainty emphasizes the need for robust structural capital resources that can support rapid decision-making and resource reallocation. Complexity requires integrative capabilities that can manage interdependencies across multiple organisational domains. Ambiguity demands sense-making capabilities that draw upon all intellectual capital resources working in coordination.

Framework Summary

The Intellectual Capital Resource-Enhanced Dynamic Capabilities (ICR-EDC) Framework presents a theoretical integration that positions intellectual capital resources as the foundational resource base from which dynamic capabilities emerge and through which SMEs achieve multi-dimensional performance outcomes in VUCA environments. The framework operates through three interconnected theoretical layers that create transformation processes enabling organisational adaptation and competitive advantage development.

The foundational layer comprises three intellectual capital resources as detailed in Tables 1 and 2 above. Human capital resources encompasses the cognitive capabilities, expertise, and learning capacity of individuals within the organisation. Structural capital resources represents the embedded knowledge systems, processes, and organisational routines that enable knowledge capture, storage, and deployment. Relational capital resources constitutes the network relationships and stakeholder connections that provide access to external knowledge resources and collaborative opportunities.

The capability layer transforms intellectual capital resources into dynamic organisational abilities through three fundamental processes that create competitive advantages. Sensing capabilities enable organisations to identify and interpret environmental opportunities and threats through information gathering and analysis processes. Sensing capabilities facilitate the mobilisation and orchestration of resources to exploit identified opportunities through innovation and strategic action. Transforming capabilities support continuous organisational adaptation through learning systems and resource reconfiguration processes.

The performance layer encompasses four interconnected outcome dimensions that reflect contemporary SME requirements, as explored in the application domains section below. Profitable growth emerges through innovation-driven expansion and market responsiveness enabled by enhanced sensing and sensing capabilities. Productivity enhancement results from process optimisation and operational efficiency improvements supported by structural capital resource investments and transforming capabilities. Human capital resource retention and development occurs through enhanced organisational attractiveness and learning environments that leverage all intellectual capital resources. Environmental footprint reduction manifests through sustainability-oriented innovations and resource efficiency improvements that integrate environmental considerations into sensing, seizing, and transforming processes. The framework is illustrated in Figure 1.

Figure 1. Illustration of Synthesized Framework

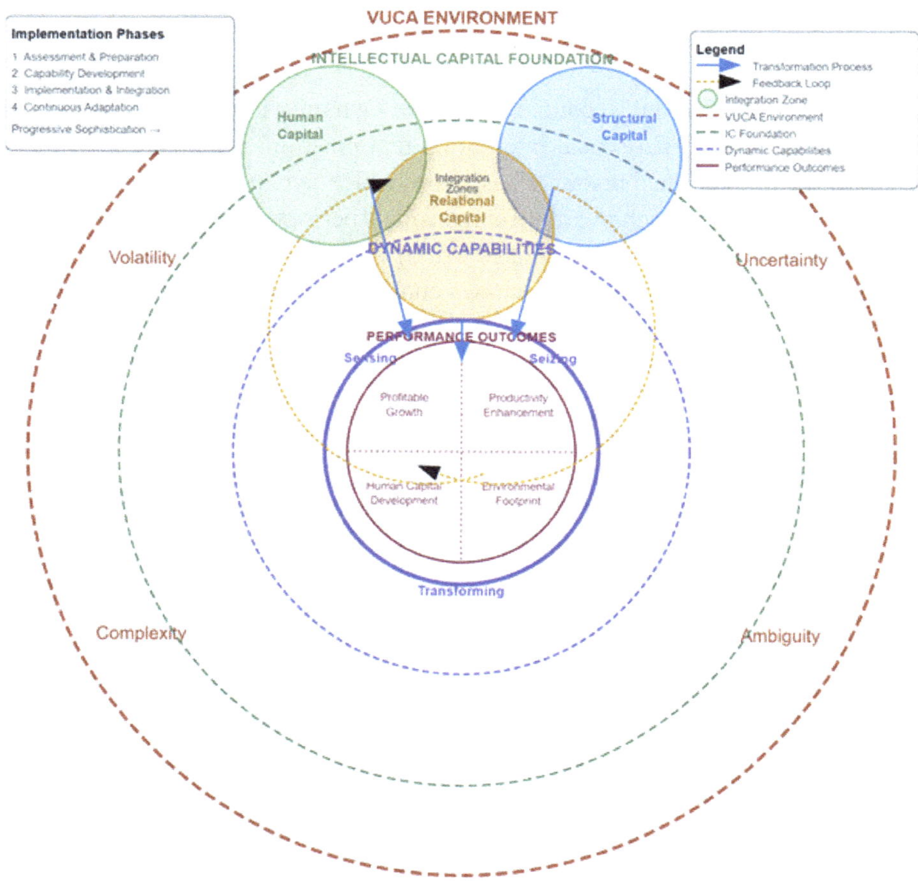

APPLICATION DOMAINS: MULTI-DIMENSIONAL SME PERFORMANCE ENHANCEMENT

The ICR-EDC Framework described above enables SME performance enhancement across four interconnected domains that reflect contemporary business requirements and competitive pressures. Each domain demonstrates how the interaction between intellectual capital resources and dynamic capabilities generates specific performance outcomes, whilst simultaneously contributing to the reinforcing cycles identified in the framework integration section above.

Profitable Growth Through ICR-EDC

Profitable growth represents a fundamental objective for SMEs, requiring the simultaneous achievement of revenue expansion and margin preservation within increasingly competitive market environments. The ICR-EDC Framework provides a systematic approach to growth that leverages the knowledge-based assets described in the theoretical foundation section to identify opportunities, develop capabilities, and create competitive advantages.

Innovation-led expansion represents one pathway through which ICR-EDC drive profitable growth, drawing directly on the human capital resource sensing and sensing capabilities detailed in the framework section above. SMEs that leverage their intellectual capital resources to innovate continuously can introduce new offerings that fuel revenue growth while commanding premium margins (Agostini et al., 2017). Human capital resources provides the systematic foundation through creative and knowledgeable employees who generate product ideas and improvements. However, dynamic capability becomes essential to realise these ideas through processes that develop, test, and market innovations rapidly and efficiently. Structural capital resources, including innovation processes and experimental cultures, becomes essential in this context, connecting directly to the organisational culture aspects discussed in the structural capital section above.

Market agility and opportunity seizing represent another pathway through which intellectual capital resources and dynamic capabilities contribute to profitable growth outcomes. In VUCA markets, opportunities for growth can emerge and disappear rapidly, as established in the introduction section above. SMEs with rich market knowledge (relational capital resource) and analytical skills (human capital resource) can systematically sense emerging customer needs or underserved market segments. Their dynamic market capabilities, such as agile marketing approaches, rapid resource reallocation processes, or systematic partnership formation, allow them to seize these opportunities ahead of competitors (Teece, 2007; Chen & Jaw,

2014). This market agility directly utilises the relational capital sensing mechanisms described in the framework section.

Intellectual capital resources contributes to competitive advantage, which underpins long-term profitable growth in competitive markets. Competitive advantage arises when firms can create more value than competitors in ways that are difficult to imitate over time (Barney, 1991). Intellectual capital resources like knowledge and relationships are often unique to individual firms and path-dependent, reflecting the non-rivalry and excludability characteristics shown in Table 1 above. Dynamic capabilities help firms renew competitive advantages as environmental conditions change (Ambrosini & Bowman, 2009), connecting directly to the transforming capabilities discussed in the framework section.

Productivity Enhancement Through Capability Development

Productivity enhancement represents a critical performance domain for SMEs, particularly given their resource constraints identified in the introduction section and intensifying competitive pressures across industries. The ICR-EDC Framework provides an approach to productivity improvement that leverages intellectual capital resources to optimise operational efficiency whilst maintaining the flexibility and responsiveness that constitute key SME advantages.

Knowledge and process optimisation forms the foundation of productivity improvements within resource-constrained environments. Structural capital resources proves particularly influential in this context since they encompasses the codified knowledge of best practices, systematic use of advanced technologies, and streamlined business processes, as detailed in the structural capital resource section above. SMEs with strong structural capital resources, such as well-documented workflows and robust knowledge databases, are better equipped to eliminate inefficiencies and avoid reinventing processes across different projects or time periods. This connects directly to the knowledge management systems discussed in the framework section above.

Dynamic capabilities enable the firm's capacity to continuously improve and reconfigure processes over time (Wu, 2010), utilising the transforming capabilities described in the framework section above. A dynamic capability in lean management or continuous improvement allows firms to refine operations for greater efficiency over time. This capability is underpinned by human capital resources in the form of employees skilled in problem-solving and process engineering, and structural capital resources through processes to capture improvement ideas and implement changes efficiently. Lin and Wu (2014) found that dynamic capabilities contributed to operational performance, with the authors noting that firms' abilities to integrate and reconfigure resources led to higher productivity and quality outcomes.

Human capital resources affects productivity through its impact on labour efficiency and adaptability, connecting directly to the human capital resources' sensing and transforming capabilities discussed in the framework section above. Well-trained, knowledgeable employees tend to be more productive as they can solve problems faster, make fewer errors, and adapt to new tools or methods more readily than less skilled counterparts. Employees who understand the reasoning behind tasks can suggest improvements, feeding into dynamic improvement capabilities (Snow et al., 2011). This demonstrates the bidirectional relationship between intellectual capital resources and dynamic capabilities identified in the framework integration section above.

Relational capital resources contributes to efficiency by improving coordination with external partners throughout the value chain, utilising the external sensing mechanisms described in the relational capital resources section above. SMEs with strong supplier relationships may receive priority service or collaborative inventory management, reducing lead times and stock level requirements. Close customer relationships might allow SMEs to better forecast demand patterns or customise production runs to actual needs, minimising overproduction or rework requirements. These represent dynamic supply chain capabilities enabled by trust and information sharing across firm boundaries (Mubarik et al., 2022).

Human Capital Resource Retention and Development

Human capital resource retention and development represents a critical performance domain for SMEs, given their documented dependence on key individuals identified in the introduction section and their limited resources for replacement and training activities. The ICR-EDC Framework provides a systematic approach to human capital resource management that creates engaging work environments, develops employee capabilities, and builds organisational loyalty, whilst simultaneously strengthening the human capital resource foundation for dynamic capabilities described in the framework section above.

Intellectual capital resource strategies contribute to retention by enhancing the employee value proposition through learning opportunities and knowledge-sharing culture, connecting directly to the structural capital culture aspects discussed in the framework section above. SMEs that invest in their structural capital resources by establishing training programs, mentoring systems, or knowledge-sharing platforms signal to employees that their growth and development are valued by the organisation. Research demonstrates that opportunities for personal development and learning are primary factors in employee retention, especially for knowledge workers who have alternatives in competitive labour markets (Jia-Jun & Hua-Ming, 2022). When employees perceive that by remaining with the SME, they will accumulate valuable skills and knowledge, they are more likely to remain committed, contributing to the continuous improvement loop identified in the framework integration section above.

Relational capital resources, though usually conceptualised as external, has an important internal analogue in the relationships and social capital among employees within the organisation. Strong internal social networks foster commitment and reduce turnover because they create supportive work environments that employees value beyond purely financial compensation (Nahapiet & Ghoshal, 1998). SMEs can leverage their typically close-knit cultures as a form of relational capital resource that binds employees to the firm through meaningful relationships and shared experiences. This internal relational capital complements the external relational capital mechanisms described in the framework section above.

Human capital resource development represents another important dimension of this performance area that creates advantages. Intellectual capital theory urges continuous enhancement of human capital resources as it directly raises the value-creating potential of the firm through capability building (Bontis, 1998), supporting the increasing marginal returns characteristic shown in Table 1 above. SMEs with strong dynamic learning capabilities can rotate employees through different functions, encourage continuous education, and adopt new tools that upgrade skills across the organisation. Each of these interventions increases employees' competencies and often their job satisfaction, since people generally enjoy growing their skills and capabilities. This development process directly strengthens the human capital resource foundation for sensing, seizing, and transforming capabilities described in the framework section above.

Environmental Footprint Reduction and Sustainability

Environmental footprint reduction represents an increasingly important performance domain for SMEs, driven by regulatory requirements, customer expectations, and cost reduction opportunities within the VUCA environment. The ICR-EDC Framework provides a systematic approach to environmental management that integrates sustainability considerations into organisational decision-making processes through the sensing, seizing, and transforming capabilities described in the framework section above.

Green intellectual capital encompasses knowledge, skills, relationships, and systems specifically oriented towards environmental management and eco-innovation, representing an application of traditional intellectual capital concepts (Yuslisa et al., 2020; Wei et al., 2023). This concept represents a specialised subset of traditional intellectual capital focused on sustainable practices, extending the tripartite classification discussed in the theoretical foundation section above. Green human capital resources includes employees' environmental awareness and expertise in cleaner production or eco-design methodologies. Green structural capital resources comprises databases of environmental regulations, formal sustainability procedures, and patents for green technologies. Green relational capital resources includes relationships with environmental stakeholders, including regulators, non-governmental organisations, and environmentally conscious customers (Asiaei et al., 2023b).

Dynamic capabilities related to environmental management include what researchers' term dynamic eco-capabilities or sustainable dynamic capabilities, representing the firm's ability to integrate environmental considerations into the normal capability processes of sensing environmental risks and opportunities, seizing them by systematically innovating green solutions, and transforming business models to be more sustainable (Kortus & Gutmann, 2023; Ortis-Avram et al., 2024). These capabilities directly utilise the three-layer framework structure presented above, systematically applying sensing, seizing, and transforming processes to environmental challenges and opportunities.

Environmental opportunity sensing involves for example recognising trends in consumer preference for low-carbon products or identifying potential for using waste products as raw materials in circular economy models or identifying new technologies that could reduce the carbon footprint in the production process. Such sensing requires internal knowledge of the firm's environmental footprint and potential improvement areas, supported by structural capital resources such as emissions monitoring systems, and external knowledge through relational capital resources like links to environmental experts or networks that signal new opportunities. This demonstrates the integrated use of all three intellectual capital resource categories described in the framework section above.

Environmental opportunity seizing involves developing eco-friendly products or investing in cleaner technology, utilising the human capital problem-solving capabilities and structural capital innovation processes described in the framework section above. Environmental transformation involves changing processes to reduce waste or shifting to renewable energy sources, drawing on the transforming capabilities and change management aspects discussed above. This application domain demonstrates how the framework can be extended to address contemporary sustainability requirements whilst maintaining the integrated approach to intellectual capital and dynamic capabilities that forms its theoretical foundation.

TECHNOMED SOLUTIONS CASE STUDY - ICR-EDC FRAMEWORK APPLICATION

TechnoMed Solutions, a 150-employee German SME specialising in diagnostic medical equipment, exemplifies the application of the ICR-EDC Framework within a high-technology VUCA environment. The organisation encountered multiple environmental pressures including rapid technological change, evolving regulatory requirements, and intensifying competitive pressure from established multinationals and emerging Asian competitors. These conditions necessitated systematic organisational transformation to maintain competitive position and achieve sustainable growth.

The company's initial resource configuration reflected the characteristics typical of traditional manufacturing SMEs, with heavy emphasis on physical assets and technical expertise whilst demonstrating underdevelopment in relational and structural capital resources. This configuration created vulnerability to environmental turbulence and limited the organisation's capacity for systematic adaptation to changing market conditions.

Initial Assessment Using ICR-EDC Framework

Foundational Layer Analysis - Intellectual Capital Resources.

The assessment of TechnoMed's intellectual capital assets revealed imbalances in the three resource categories presented in the theoretical model. The human capital resources were strong in engineering and technical expertise, reflecting the company's history as a manufacturer and the German educational system in technical fields. However, the assessment identified weaknesses in market sensing capabilities, customer relationship management competencies, and knowledge of international business practices. These weaknesses limited the firm's capacity to sense changes in the environment and respond to new possibilities beyond its traditional domestic market.

Structural capital assets showed concentration in product development and manufacturing processes with no, or minimal, investment in market intelligence systems, customer relationship management infrastructure, or knowledge management capabilities. The processes and systems within the organisation showed traditional manufacturing practices instead of the knowledge management systems necessary for developing dynamic capabilities. Organisational culture continued to be product-oriented with no, or little, focus on customer orientation or environmental scanning activities.

Relational capital resources were concentrated among German suppliers and customers, developing path dependencies that restricted access to global market intelligence and international opportunities. The network relationships within the organisation offered stability in the domestic market but limited sensing capabilities with respect to international trends, new technologies, and changing customer needs in global markets.

Capability Layer Analysis - Dynamic Capabilities Assessment.

The assessment revealed weaknesses across the three dynamic capability dimensions defined in the framework. Sensing capabilities operated primarily through informal mechanisms dependent on individual managers rather than systematic environmental scanning processes. The organisation lacked structured approaches for identifying technological trends, customer preference changes, or competitive developments, limiting its capacity for proactive adaptation.

Seizing capabilities demonstrated functionality within established product categories but showed constraints when addressing new market opportunities or customer requirements. The organisation possessed technical competencies for incremental innovation but lacked systematic processes for radical innovation or market expansion. Resource mobilisation processes remained oriented towards traditional manufacturing approaches rather than knowledge-intensive activities.

Transforming capabilities exhibited limitations in organisational reconfiguration and business model adaptation. The organisation's hierarchical structure and manufacturing-oriented culture created resistance to systematic change processes. Knowledge transfer mechanisms operated informally, constraining the organisation's capacity for systematic learning and capability development.

Framework-Guided Transformation Strategy

Human Capital Resource Development.

The organisation implemented human capital resource enhancement programmes aligned with the framework's emphasis on cognitive capabilities and learning capacity. Training initiatives addressed market analysis competencies, customer relationship management skills, and international business capabilities. Engineering personnel received instruction in customer-centred design methodologies, enhancing their capacity to sense and respond to evolving customer requirements.

Management development programmes focused on strategic thinking capabilities and international business competencies, directly addressing the cognitive microfoundations identified in the theoretical framework. These initiatives enhanced the organisation's sensing capabilities through improved environmental scanning abilities and seizing capabilities through enhanced problem-solving and resource orchestration competencies.

Structural Capital Resource Investment.

Structural capital resource development addressed the embedded knowledge systems and organisational routines required for dynamic capability enhancement. The organisation implemented customer relationship management systems that integrated customer information, technical support data, and market intelligence. These systems created the information infrastructure necessary for sensing and seizing capabilities.

Product development processes underwent enhancement through stage-gate methodologies incorporating customer feedback and market analysis throughout development cycles. Knowledge management systems facilitated capture and sharing of technical expertise, market intelligence, and customer insights across organisational boundaries. These structural capital resource investments created the organisational mechanisms necessary for capability deployment and learning processes.

Relational Capital Resource Expansion

Relational capital resource development emphasised international market entry and collaborative partnerships providing access to new customers, technologies, and market intelligence. The organisation established partnerships with distributors in international markets, creating access to local market knowledge and customer relationships that extended sensing capabilities beyond domestic boundaries.

Collaborative relationships with research institutions enhanced access to emerging technologies and technical expertise, supporting both sensing and seizing capabilities through external knowledge integration. Customer relationship enhancement initiatives developed partnerships with key customers that provided insights into evolving requirements and collaborative development opportunities, creating sources of market intelligence and innovation stimuli.

Performance Outcomes Across Application Domains

Profitable Growth Achievement.

The systematic application of the ICR-EDC Framework generated revenue growth acceleration from 8 per cent annually to 25 per cent annually over a three-year period. This growth resulted primarily from international expansion and new product development capabilities enabled through enhanced sensing and seizing capabilities. The organisation's improved capacity for opportunity identification and resource mobilisation facilitated market entry strategies that leveraged enhanced relational capital resources and innovation processes.

Productivity improvements of 20 per cent emerged through enhanced processes and knowledge management systems, demonstrating the framework's capacity for simultaneous growth and efficiency enhancement. These improvements reflected the optimisation of structural capital resources and their integration with human capital resource capabilities.

Human Capital Resource Retention and Development.

Employee retention improved substantially, with turnover declining from 15 per cent to 6 per cent annually. Employee engagement surveys indicated improvements in job satisfaction, career development opportunities, and organisational commitment. The organisation's enhanced reputation facilitated recruitment in competitive technical labour markets, creating positive feedback loops that further strengthened human capital resources.

These outcomes demonstrate the framework's capacity for addressing the human capital resource challenges identified in the theoretical foundation section, where SME dependence on key individuals creates organisational vulnerabilities. The systematic approach to capability development created engaging work environments that reduced these dependencies whilst enhancing overall organisational capacity.

Environmental Footprint Reduction

Environmental performance improvements resulted from product design initiatives that reduced material consumption and energy requirements. The organisation developed capabilities in eco-design that created competitive advantages in environmentally conscious European markets. These outcomes reflect the application of green intellectual capital concepts within the framework's environmental application domain.

The integration of environmental considerations into sensing, seizing, and transforming processes demonstrates the framework's adaptability to contemporary sustainability requirements whilst maintaining organisational performance across other dimensions.

Theoretical Implications and Framework Validation

The TechnoMed case demonstrates the relationships between intellectual capital resources, dynamic capabilities, and multi-dimensional performance outcomes proposed in the ICR-EDC Framework. The organisation's transformation confirms the foundational role of intellectual capital resources in dynamic capability development and the mediating effect of capabilities in translating knowledge assets into performance improvements.

The case validates the framework's emphasis on integrated approaches rather than isolated resource development. The organisation's attempts to develop individual intellectual capital resource components in isolation proved insufficient for sustained capability enhancement. Performance improvements emerged when all three resource categories operated synergistically through systematic dynamic capability processes.

The transformation demonstrates the bidirectional relationship between intellectual capital resources and dynamic capabilities identified in the theoretical framework. Enhanced capabilities generated outcomes that further developed the organisation's knowledge base through learning processes, creating the positive feedback loops essential for sustained adaptation in VUCA environments.

The case confirms the framework's applicability across the four performance domains identified in the application section. The organisation achieved simultaneous improvements in profitable growth, productivity enhancement, human capital resource development, and environmental performance, demonstrating the framework's capacity for addressing contemporary SME requirements through integrated approaches.

Framework Application Insights

The systematic application of the ICR-EDC Framework reveals several insights relevant for both theoretical development and practical implementation. The framework's three-layer structure provides operational guidance for SME managers seeking to enhance organisational capabilities whilst addressing resource constraints characteristic of smaller organisations.

The emphasis on knowledge-based assets rather than financial or physical resources aligns with the resource categorisation presented in the theoretical framework and demonstrates practical approaches for SMEs to achieve competitive advantages through intellectual capital resource development rather than scale-based strategies.

The case demonstrates the framework's utility for addressing VUCA environment challenges through capability development rather than reactive responses to environmental shocks. The organisation's enhanced sensing, seizing, and transforming capabilities created adaptive capacity that transcended individual environmental changes and established foundations for sustained competitive advantage.

The multi-dimensional performance outcomes achieved through framework application confirm the integrated nature of contemporary SME requirements and the necessity for systematic approaches that address financial, operational, human, and environmental dimensions simultaneously rather than sequentially or independently.

CONCLUSION

This chapter has developed a conceptual framework for making sense of how SMEs can deploy intellectual capital to develop their dynamic capabilities and attain multi-dimensional performance in VUCA contexts. The ICR-EDC Framework offers both theoretical understanding and practical utility in dealing with interconnections among knowledge-based resources, organisational competencies, and performance implications amidst modern business issues.

The discussion shows that intellectual capital forms the foundation for dynamic capabilities, as evidenced by the classification of resources shown in Tables 1 and 2. Human capital resources provide the expertise, creativity, and problem-solving abilities required to identify opportunities and reconfigure operations. Structural capital resources offer the processes, systems, and organisational knowledge enabling the consistent and effective deployment of capabilities over time. Relational capital resources stretch the boundaries of a firm, incorporating external information and resources that improve adaptive responses to environmental pressures. Empirical studies consistently show that SMEs with rich intellectual capital are better positioned to develop capabilities for innovation, agility, and resilience in competitive markets.

Dynamic capabilities are the means through which intellectual capital is converted into tangible outcomes, as supported by the three-layer model shown in Figure 1. Having knowledge assets alone is not sufficient; small and medium-sized enterprises (SMEs) need to systematically utilize these assets through the process of sensing, seizing, and transforming to attain a competitive advantage (Teece, 2007). The combination of qualified manpower, flexible routines, and relational networks allows SMEs to swiftly modify their offerings and increase operations in reaction to abrupt environmental changes. The interaction between intellectual capital and dynamic capabilities systematically enhances different aspects of performance simultaneously, including financial, operational, human, and environmental metrics across the four areas of application identified earlier.

The model's focus on knowledge-based resources and adaptive competencies is in accordance with trends within knowledge-based economies and sustainable development priorities that typify current business contexts. The intellectual capital and dynamic capabilities of SMEs can be developed through manageable strategies instead of depending on innate characteristics or external factors outside of their control. By placing emphasis on what is known, whom they know, and learning and adapting, SMEs are able to develop internal strength and stability that allows them to ride out external turbulence within VUCA conditions while they pursue growth and development agendas.

The ICR-EDC Framework offers a platform for ongoing research and practice innovation capable of improving SME performance and informing wider economic development goals at the inter-industry and regional levels. The practical implications for SME managers are that they should adopt a systemic view to developing capabilities that draw on intellectual capital investments to promote organisational agility and performance across the interrelated areas of profitable growth, productivity improvement, human capital formation, and environmental sustainability. Such integration allows SMEs to develop competitive strengths that go beyond the impact of singular environmental shocks and establish long-term stakeholder value for all.

REFERENCES

Agostini, L., Nosella, A., & Filippini, R. (2017). Does intellectual capital allow improving innovation performance? A quantitative analysis in the SME context. *Journal of Intellectual Capital, 18*(2), 400–418. DOI: 10.1108/JIC-05-2016-0056

Ali, M. A., Hussin, N., Flayyih, H. H., Haddad, H., Al-Ramahi, N. M., Almubaydeen, T. H., Hussein, S. A., & Hasan Abunaila, A. S. (2023). A multidimensional view of intellectual capital and dynamic innovative performance. *Journal of Risk and Financial Management, 16*(3), 139. DOI: 10.3390/jrfm16030139

Ali, M. A., Hussin, N., Haddad, H., Alkhodary, D., & Marei, A. (2021). Dynamic capabilities and their impact on intellectual capital and innovation performance. *Sustainability (Basel), 13*(18), 10028. DOI: 10.3390/su131810028

Ambrosini, V., & Bowman, C. (2009). What are dynamic capabilities and are they a useful construct in strategic management? *International Journal of Management Reviews, 11*(1), 29–49. DOI: 10.1111/j.1468-2370.2008.00251.x

Asiaei, K., O'Connor, N. G., Barani, O., & Joshi, M. (2023b). Green intellectual capital and ambidextrous green innovation and the impact on environmental performance. *Business Strategy and the Environment, 32*(1), 369–386. DOI: 10.1002/bse.3136

Barney, J. (1991). Firm resources and sustained competitive advantage. *Journal of Management, 17*(1), 99–120. DOI: 10.1177/014920639101700108

Bontis, N. (1998). Intellectual capital and an exploratory study that develops measures and models. *Management Decision, 36*(2), 63–76. DOI: 10.1108/00251749810204142

Chen, Y. Y., & Jaw, Y. L. (2014). How do business groups' small world networks effect diversification, innovation, and internationalisation? *Asia Pacific Journal of Management, 31*(4), 1019–1044. DOI: 10.1007/s10490-014-9385-9

Easterby-Smith, M., & Prieto, I. M. (2008). Dynamic capabilities and knowledge management and an integrative role for learning? *British Journal of Management, 19*(3), 235–249. DOI: 10.1111/j.1467-8551.2007.00543.x

Edvinsson, L., & Malone, M. S. (1997). *Intellectual capital realising your company's true value by finding its hidden brainpower*. HarperBusiness.

Edvinsson, L., & Sullivan, P. (1996). Developing a model for managing intellectual capital. *European Management Journal, 14*(4), 356–364. DOI: 10.1016/0263-2373(96)00022-9

Eisenhardt, K. M., & Martin, J. A. (2000). Dynamic capabilities and what are they? *Strategic Management Journal, 21*(10/11), 1105–1121. DOI: 10.1002/1097-0266(200010/11)21:10/11<1105::AID-SMJ133>3.0.CO;2-E

Felin, T., Foss, N. J., & Ployhart, R. E. (2015). The microfoundations movement in strategy and organisation theory. *The Academy of Management Annals, 9*(1), 575–632. DOI: 10.5465/19416520.2015.1007651

Han, Y., & Li, D. (2015). Effects of intellectual capital on innovative performance and the role of knowledge-based dynamic capability. *Management Decision, 53*(1), 40–56. DOI: 10.1108/MD-08-2013-0411

Helfat, C. E., & Peteraf, M. A. (2015). Managerial cognitive capabilities and the microfoundations of dynamic capabilities. *Strategic Management Journal, 36*(6), 831–850. DOI: 10.1002/smj.2247

Hsu, L. C., & Wang, C. H. (2012). Clarifying the effect of intellectual capital on performance and the mediating role of dynamic capability. *British Journal of Management, 23*(2), 179–195. DOI: 10.1111/j.1467-8551.2010.00718.x

Jia-Jun, S., & Hua-Ming, S. (2022). The impact of career growth on knowledge-based employee engagement and the mediating role of affective commitment and the moderating role of perceived organisational support. *Frontiers in Psychology, 13*, 805208. DOI: 10.3389/fpsyg.2022.805208 PMID: 35369191

Kortus, L., & Gutmann, T. (2023). How do firms build dynamic capabilities to develop sustainable products? A multiple case study in the manufacturing industry. *Journal of Cleaner Production, 415*, 137887. DOI: 10.1016/j.jclepro.2023.137887

Kraus, S., Clauss, T., Breier, M., Gast, J., Sardini, A., & Tiberius, V. (2020). The economics of COVID-19 and initial empirical evidence on how family firms in five European countries cope with the corona crisis. *International Journal of Entrepreneurial Behaviour & Research, 26*(5), 1067–1092. DOI: 10.1108/IJEBR-04-2020-0214

Lin, Y., & Wu, L. Y. (2014). Exploring the role of dynamic capabilities in firm performance under the resource-based view framework. *Journal of Business Research, 67*(3), 407–413. DOI: 10.1016/j.jbusres.2012.12.019

Millar, C. C., Groth, O., & Mahon, J. F. (2018). Management innovation in a VUCA world and challenges and recommendations. *California Management Review, 61*(1), 5–14. DOI: 10.1177/0008125618805111

Mubarik, M. S., Bontis, N., Mubarik, M., & Mahmood, T. (2022). Intellectual capital and supply chain resilience. *Journal of Intellectual Capital, 23*(3), 713–738. DOI: 10.1108/JIC-06-2020-0206

Nahapiet, J., & Ghoshal, S. (1998). Social capital, intellectual capital, and the organisational advantage. *Academy of Management Review*, *23*(2), 242–266. DOI: 10.2307/259373

Ortis-Avram, D., Ovcharova, N., & Engelmann, A. (2024). Dynamic capabilities for sustainability and toward a typology based on dimensions of sustainability-oriented innovation and stakeholder integration. *Business Strategy and the Environment*, *33*(4), 2969–3004. DOI: 10.1002/bse.3630

Pasamar, S., Cabrales, A. L., & Cabrales, R. V. (2015). Ambidexterity and intellectual capital architectures for developing dynamic capabilities and towards a research agenda. *European Journal of International Management*, *9*(1), 74–87. DOI: 10.1504/EJIM.2015.066672

Roos, G. (2019). *Optimising resource deployment within the firm and overcoming theoretical problems with a practical application* (Doctoral dissertation, University of South Australia).

Roos, G., Pike, S., & Fernström, L. (2005). *Managing Intellectual Capital in Practice*. Butterworth-Heinemann.

Roos, G., & Roos, J. (1997). Measuring your company's intellectual performance. *Long Range Planning*, *30*(3), 413–426. DOI: 10.1016/S0024-6301(97)90260-0

Roos, G., von Krogh, G., & Roos, J. (2025). *Strategi – En Innføring*, 8. utgave. Bergen. Norway: Fagbokforlaget.

Roos, J., Roos, G., Dragonetti, N. C., & Edvinsson, L. (1997). *Intellectual Capital and navigating in the new business landscape*. Macmillan. DOI: 10.1007/978-1-349-14494-5

Schoemaker, P. J., Heaton, S., & Teece, D. (2018). Innovation, dynamic capabilities, and leadership. *California Management Review*, *61*(1), 15–42. DOI: 10.1177/0008125618790246

Senaratne, C., & Wang, C. L. (2018). Organisational ambidexterity in UK high-tech SMEs and an exploratory study of key drivers and barriers. *Journal of Small Business and Enterprise Development*, *25*(6), 1025–1050. DOI: 10.1108/JSBED-04-2018-0110

Snow, C. C., Fjeldstad, Ø. D., Lettl, C., & Miles, R. E. (2011). Organising continuous product development and commercialisation and the collaborative community of firms model. *Journal of Product Innovation Management*, *28*(1), 3–16. DOI: 10.1111/j.1540-5885.2010.00777.x

Stabell, C. B., & Fjeldstad, Ø. D. (1998). Configuring value for competitive advantage on chains, shops and networks. *Strategic Management Journal*, *19*(5), 413–437. DOI: 10.1002/(SICI)1097-0266(199805)19:5<413::AID-SMJ946>3.0.CO;2-C

Subramaniam, M., & Youndt, M. A. (2005). The influence of intellectual capital on the types of innovative capabilities. *Academy of Management Journal*, *48*(3), 450–463. DOI: 10.5465/amj.2005.17407911

Teece, D. J. (2007). Explicating dynamic capabilities and the nature and microfoundations of enterprise performance. *Strategic Management Journal*, *28*(13), 1319–1350. DOI: 10.1002/smj.640

Teece, D. J., Pisano, G., & Shuen, A. (1997). Dynamic capabilities and strategic management. *Strategic Management Journal*, *18*(7), 509–533. DOI: 10.1002/(SICI)1097-0266(199708)18:7<509::AID-SMJ882>3.0.CO;2-Z

Vătămănescu, E. M., Gorgos, E. A., Ghigiu, A. M., & Pătru , M. (2019). Bridging intellectual capital and SMEs internationalisation through the lens of sustainable competitive advantage and a systematic literature review. *Sustainability (Basel)*, *11*(9), 2510. DOI: 10.3390/su11092510

Wang, C. L., & Ahmed, P. K. (2007). Dynamic capabilities and a review and research agenda. *International Journal of Management Reviews*, *9*(1), 31–51. DOI: 10.1111/j.1468-2370.2007.00201.x

Wei, F., Abbas, J., Alarifi, G., Shang, S., Adam, N. A., & de Queiros, M. J. (2023). Role of green intellectual capital and top management commitment in organisational environmental performance and reputation and moderating role of pro-environmental behaviour. *Journal of Cleaner Production*, *405*, 136847. DOI: 10.1016/j.jclepro.2023.136847

Wu, L. Y. (2010). Applicability of the resource-based and dynamic-capability views under environmental volatility. *Journal of Business Research*, *63*(1), 27–31. DOI: 10.1016/j.jbusres.2009.01.007

Yli-Renko, H., Autio, E., & Sapiensa, H. J. (2001). Social capital, knowledge acquisition, and knowledge exploitation in young technology-based firms. *Strategic Management Journal*, *22*(6-7), 587–613. DOI: 10.1002/smj.183

Yuslisa, M. Y., Yong, J. Y., Tanveer, M. I., Ramayah, T., Faesah, J. N., & Muhammad, S. (2020). A structural model of the impact of green intellectual capital on sustainable performance. *Journal of Cleaner Production*, *249*, 119334. DOI: 10.1016/j.jclepro.2019.119334

Zahra, S. A., & George, G. (2002). Absorptive capacity and a review, reconceptualisation, and extension. *Academy of Management Review*, *27*(2), 185–203. DOI: 10.2307/4134351

Zahra, S. A., Sapiensa, H. J., & Davidsson, P. (2006). Entrepreneurship and dynamic capabilities and a review, model and research agenda. *Journal of Management Studies*, *43*(4), 917–955. DOI: 10.1111/j.1467-6486.2006.00616.x

Zollo, M., & Winter, S. G. (2002). Deliberate learning and the evolution of dynamic capabilities. *Organization Science*, *13*(3), 339–351. DOI: 10.1287/orsc.13.3.339.2780

ADDITIONAL READINGS

Barney, J. B., & Arikan, A. M. (2001). The resource-based view: Origins and implications for organizational science. *Organization Science*, *12*(1), 124–136.

Bennett, N., & Lemoine, G. J. (2014). What a difference a word makes: Understanding threats to performance in a VUCA world. *Business Horizons*, *57*(3), 311–317. DOI: 10.1016/j.bushor.2014.01.001

Cohen, W. M., & Levinthal, D. A. (1990). Absorptive capacity: A new perspective on learning and innovation. *Administrative Science Quarterly*, *35*(1), 128–152. DOI: 10.2307/2393553

Eisenhardt, K. M., & Graebner, M. E. (2007). Theory building from cases: Opportunities and challenges. *Academy of Management Journal*, *50*(1), 25–32. DOI: 10.5465/amj.2007.24160888

Nonaka, I., & Takeuchi, H. (1995). *The knowledge-creating company: How Japanese companies create the dynamics of innovation*. Oxford University Press. DOI: 10.1093/oso/9780195092691.001.0001

Peteraf, M. A. (1993). The cornerstones of competitive advantage: A resource-based view. *Strategic Management Journal*, *14*(3), 179–191. DOI: 10.1002/smj.4250140303

Senge, P. M. (1990). *The fifth discipline: The art and practice of the learning organization*. Doubleday.

Wernerfelt, B. (1984). A resource-based view of the firm. *Strategic Management Journal*, *5*(2), 171–180. DOI: 10.1002/smj.4250050207

Winter, S. G. (2003). Understanding dynamic capabilities. *Strategic Management Journal*, *24*(10), 991–995. DOI: 10.1002/smj.318

KEY TERMS AND DEFINITIONS

Absorptive Capacity: The ability to absorb, process, and utilise new knowledge, which represents a sensing and learning-oriented dynamic capability.

Dynamic Capabilities: A firm's ability to integrate, build, and reconfigure internal and external competencies to address rapidly changing environments, constituting the fundamental mechanisms through which organisations adapt and evolve over time.

Dynamic Eco-capabilities: The firm's ability to integrate environmental considerations into the normal capability processes of sensing environmental risks and opportunities, seizing them by systematically innovating green solutions, and transforming business models to be more sustainable.

Green Intellectual Capital: Knowledge, skills, relationships, and systems specifically oriented towards environmental management and eco-innovation, representing a specialised subset of traditional intellectual capital focused on sustainable practices.

Human Capital Resources: The knowledge, skills, abilities, experience, and capabilities possessed by employees that provide cognitive capabilities, expertise, and learning capacity within the organisation.

ICR-EDC Framework (Intellectual Capital Resource-Enhanced Dynamic Capabilities Framework): A theoretical integration that positions intellectual capital resources as the foundational resource base from which dynamic capabilities emerge and through which SMEs achieve multi-dimensional performance outcomes in VUCA environments, operating through three interconnected layers: foundational (intellectual capital resources), capability (dynamic processes), and performance (outcome dimensions).

Intellectual: Capital: The non-financial and non-physical assets of an organisation that are not fully captured on traditional balance sheets, including both the knowledge residing in employees' minds and the structures and relationships that enable systematic value creation.

Micro-foundations: Individual-level and group-level actions, interactions, and cognitions that underlie and give rise to collective-level organisational constructs and outcomes.

Network Economic Behaviour: A characteristic of intellectual capital resources where value increases through network effects and connections rather than following traditional decreasing marginal returns.

Non-rivalry Resources: Resources that enable simultaneous use by multiple parties without depletion, a key characteristic distinguishing intellectual capital from physical resources.

Relational Capital Resources: The value derived from relationships with customers, suppliers, partners, and other external stakeholders, including reputation, trust, and network connections that extend the organisation's capabilities beyond formal boundaries.

Seizing Capabilities: The ability to mobilise and orchestrate resources to exploit identified opportunities through innovation and strategic action.

Sensing Capabilities: The ability to systematically identify and interpret environmental opportunities and threats through information gathering and analysis processes.

Structural Capital Resources: Organisational knowledge embedded in processes, systems, databases, organisational culture, intellectual property, and operational routines that remain within the organisation even when employees leave. This includes the embedded knowledge systems and institutional knowledge infrastructure.

Transforming Capabilities: The ability to support continuous organisational adaptation through learning systems and resource reconfiguration processes.

VUCA Environments: Environments characterised by volatility, uncertainty, complexity, and ambiguity that create substantial challenges through rapid technological shifts, evolving market conditions, changing consumer preferences, regulatory transformations, and intensifying competitive pressures.

Chapter 6

Minimal Resources, Maximum Impact: A Knowledge-Based Approach to Frugal Innovation

Gurpreet pal Kaur
http://orcid.org/0000-0001-7475-3548
Lovely Professional University, India

Mushtaq Ahmed Shah
http://orcid.org/0000-0002-3177-9622
Lovely Professional University, India

ABSTRACT

The chapter examines how frugal innovation has been combined with knowledge management in settings where financial, infrastructural, institutional and human resource conditions are acute. It underlines the idea that the force of impactful innovation may be motivated by expertise instead of resources. It corroborates on Knowledge-based View (KBV) of the firm and stresses the value of tacit skills, local knowledge, collective experience and general-access internet-based spaces and platforms. The chapter demonstrates the development of the frugal innovation over time using a conceptual and case-based approach and discusses creation, sharing and application of knowledge in low-resource environments. It presents a model that describes how knowledge input, knowledge management processes and collaborative effort in stakeholders are key to attaining socially relevant innovation at minimum cost. It illustrates through global and Indian case studies including Aravind Eye Care, M-Pesa, SELCO Solar, and Goonj, how radically different knowledge intensive frugal innovation is able to provide cost and scalable solutions to pertinent problems in a variety of arenas including healthcare, finance, energy, and

DOI: 10.4018/979-8-3373-6053-9.ch006

grassroots development. A subsequent theoretical contribution of the chapter is to lend plausibility to KBV as an extension of frugal innovation, furnishing practical resources and policy insights on how to nurture and develop inclusive knowledge environments. This study suggested the direction of future research opportunities, among others, on AI-enabled knowledge integration, cross-sectoral relations, and longitudinal evaluations as possible ways to sustain and spread frugal innovation.

1. INTRODUCTION

Innovation is usually associated with high levels of resources, new technologies and financed R&D settings. This viewpoint, however, misses the reality faced by most communities in the Global South, which lack resources and infrastructure in addition to often having limited financial means, which compels innovation to take a different path. Such a setting fosters simple, locally based, necessity-driven innovation, sometimes referred to as frugal innovation (Chakravarty, 2022). According to studies, frugal innovation is a resource-driven approach that creates affordable, practical solutions to address the demands of neglected markets. It usually promotes sustainable development and technology adoption in the Global South (Gandenberger et al., 2020). In order to solve regional issues and promote equitable development, this kind of innovation has been required (Nilsson et al., 2022).

Frugal innovation is the process of designing affordable, available and practical solutions that meet the needs of the population in the limitations of resource-free nature (Shivdas et al., 2021). In contrast to straightforward cost-cutting, it involves reevaluating the product's concept, features, and utility in order to maximize value while minimizing inputs (Sharmelly & Ray, 2021). They are typically ideas rooted on firsthand knowledge, real-world experiences, and creative problem-solving within common limitations (Nilsson et al., 2022). These could include low-cost medical devices (Chakravarty, 2022), renewable energy technologies (Gandenberger et al., 2020b), community-supported infrastructures, and unofficial educational programs that consider societal demands that are beyond the scope of current innovation systems (Corsini et al., 2021).

Although the concept of frugal innovation is quite a well-known concept, the essentiality of knowledge in the process of making frugal innovations possible has been considerably under-researched. Knowledge within the local artisans, frontline workers, or conventional practices develops crucial resource pool towards innovation especially in resource-starved settings (Bhattacharjya et al., 2023a). Usually this knowledge is informal, tacit, and spread deep into communities therefore difficult to grasp and use using common knowledge tools of management (Nilsson et al., 2022c). Research indicates that community-based collaboration and bricolage are very vital in promoting innovation in such settings, whereby problems are creatively resolved through procedural wisdom and mutual understanding (Steinfield & Holt, 2019).

Based on the firm's Knowledge-Based View (KBV), this chapter offers a knowledge-based strategy for frugal innovation. According to KBV, an organization's greatest strategic resource is knowledge rather than land, labor, or capital (Rehman et al., 2025; Jayabalan & Dorasamy, 2024). This theoretical viewpoint holds that an organization's effectiveness is determined by its capacity to produce, disseminate, and apply information efficiently rather than by its material resources (Dabic et al., 2022). Studying frugal innovation through the same lenses, research suggests that, when combined with systematic knowledge mobilization, frugal innovation can produce unusually powerful social and economic outcomes with minimal physical resources (Jayabalan & Dorasamy, 2024; Jiraphanumes et al., 2023).

Resource-Constrained Environments (RCEs) offer a unique setting for analyzing the dynamics of phenomena such as innovation under constrained conditions. Economic limitations, backlogs in infrastructure, and institutional deficiencies are some of the characteristics that are typically viewed as impeding innovation. However, they can also serve as catalysts for creativity, as people and communities make use of the tools, resources, and local knowledge that are available to them due to unforeseen situations (Favretto & Stringer, 2024; Pradhan et al., 2023). Performers in RCEs that possess high contextual intelligence have demonstrated resilience and flexibility despite lacking formal schooling or financial resources. Utilizing locally placed knowledge systems has the potential to produce innovative solutions that are both pertinent and long-lasting (Alayande et al., 2022).

The failure to understand the role of the Knowledge Management (KM) in fueling frugal innovation is crucial and revolutionary. KM involves the following processes of producing, storing, sharing, and implementing knowledge both in an amazing firm and community (Raphael & Matsuoka, 2024a). KM activities in small-scale, informal companies that are constrained in resources do not usually use formal documentation systems and instead are based on the practices of storytelling, peer learning, mentorship, and social networks (Bindumadhavan & Lacey, 2025). These processes allow sharing the ideas and experience and allow the communities to develop upon the previous successes, prevent repeated failure, and improve the pace of innovation. Besides, KM facilitates the introduction of various knowledge types, including scientific, technical, experiential, and indigenous, into viable yet culturally satisfactory and lasting solutions (Raphael & Matsuoka, 2024a).

The chapter is anticipated to assist with the conceptual interpretation and implementation stages of frugal innovation by proposing a Knowledge-Based Approach to frugal innovation, which would center on knowledge as the key to increasing effectiveness while using less resources. It covers fundamental issues such as how communities and organizations can use knowledge as a strategic asset in resource-constrained environments, what types of knowledge are best suited for frugal innovation and how to access, share, and apply these knowledge sources, and which knowledge management (KM) practices are appropriate in situations where formal systems are inadequate or non-existent (Kun, 2022; Umar et al., 2025). A conceptual model of links, relationships between knowledge assets, KM processes, and frugal innovation outcomes is presented in this chapter along with real-world examples of several industries, including energy, health (health care), and grassroots entrepreneurship. These illustrations show how highly knowledgeable but resource-poor situations can foster scalable and successful innovations (Zara, 2025; De Moraes et al., 2025).

This way, this chapter can help move the frugal innovation theory and knowledge management sections forward by synthesizing two conceptually related and mostly disparate areas in a systematized manner (Hossain et al., 2022; Sarkar & Mateus, 2022). It provides practical solutions to several stakeholders: to the researchers, it can give new theoretical knowledge about what drives innovation in low-resources settings (Manishimwe et al., 2024); to practitioners, it can outline how to identify, manage and deploy knowledge to solve problems efficiently (Hossain, 2022); and to the policymakers, it can remind them of the significance of enabling knowledge ecosystems which help local innovation and the inclusive development (Hossain et al., 2023). Ultimately, this chapter reframes frugal innovation as strategic creativity that lives on cooperation, learning, and adaptation, arguing that knowledge is not a luxury but a lifeline, particularly in environments with limited conventional resources (Manzi-Puertas et al., 2025). Making knowledge the focal point of frugal innovation provides a mechanism to achieve high-impact, sustainable, and a liberal solutions with less resources.

2. CONCEPTUAL FOUNDATIONS

Frugal innovation is a reality for millions of people worldwide, not simply a trendy idea. Imagine a rural health clinic repurposing outdated equipment to provide basic medical care, or a mechanic in a remote location using discarded bicycle parts to create a water pump. These are thoughtful and strategic responses to insufficiency rather than merely band-aid fixes (Hossain et al., 2022). Frugal innovation is the process of creating practical, economical, and efficient solutions that work in low-resource societies. It embodies the proverb "do more with less" (Sarkar & Mateus, 2022). Economic crises, restricted environment, and the imperative need of having an inclusive development have contributed to the evolution of the concept. The business and scientific communities learned by the early 2000s that high-quality inventions could be created in low-resource environments, in contrast to the top-down paradigms of innovation that were then in use (Hossain et al., 2023). Localized terminology such as jugaad in India, gambiarra in Brazil, and makinismo in some regions of Africa are used because of the long history of such cultural traditions of resourcefulness and adaptable innovation (Manzi-Puertas et al., 2025).

Frugal innovation is characterized by four attributes. The affordability aspect allows solutions to be affordable to the populations living at the bottom of the pyramid taking precedence on long term value and maintenance costs (Van Niekerk, 2022). Simplicity focuses on designs that are minimalized to minimum functionalities and hence enhances user-friendliness and acceptance (Omer et al., 2024). Robustness embodies the ability or capability of the products or processes to work stress-free in stiff and unpredictable situations with low maintenance (Bouvier-Patron, 2023). The focus on using renewable or recycled materials and the integration of ecological responsibility along with a social influence (Urata et al., 2023) are the attributes of sustainability.

There are several levels where frugal innovation can be seen. As examples of the product level, one can mention inexpensive water purifiers, solar lanterns, and cardboard incubators, which are affordable and capable of the main functionality (Omer et al., 2024). Some examples of innovations at the process level include shifting tasks in the manner of delivering rural healthcare or deploying community volunteers to assist in the primary sector of education (Van Niekerk, 2022). At the system level, microgrid solar energy models and low-cost telemedicine networks demonstrate how entire ecosystems can be reimagined to serve underserved communities (Urata et al., 2023). Its significance is especially noticeable in developing and emerging economies where formal markets are fragmented, income levels are low, and infrastructure is scarce. According to Bouvier-Patron (2023), inexpensive innovation democratizes the invention process by demonstrating that meaningful solutions can arise from necessity, community cooperation, and local expertise rather than requiring billion-dollar R&D funds.

2.1 Knowledge-Based View of the Firm

When frugal innovation addresses the topic of what we can create with limited resources, the firm's Knowledge-Based View (KBV) provides client-side solutions to address still another crucial question: "What do we know that can help us innovate more wisely"? KBV is an expansion of the broader resource-based approach, which holds that knowledge and other intangible assets, rather than only tangible resources, are the foundation of competitive advantage. Given the rising complexity and unpredictability that organizations face, knowledge has been identified as the most strategically significant resource for driving innovation and success (Radhakrishna et al., 2024). KBV distinguishes between two types of knowledge:

explicit information, which is easily codified and transmitted through manuals and databases, and tacit knowledge, which is experiential, personal, and challenging to codify. A farmer with practical experience in soil management or a midwife with hands-on practice in childbirth are two examples of how tacit knowledge is often more helpful than explicit information in many resource-poor contexts.

Knowledge Management (KM) is an understanding of how organisations create, store, share and use knowledge. The KM key processes involve Knowledge creation, Retention of experience, Knowledge sharing, Knowledge use. The creation of knowledge is the process of developing novel concepts through interaction, experimentation, and observation. In frugal environments, this typically happens informally through trial and error or community collaboration.

Experience retention: The ability to store knowledge that will be valuable in the future, which is frequently impossible in low-resource environments with limited institutional memory.

Knowledge sharing is the process of encouraging the exchange of information between individuals, groups, or communities through online forums, social media, or local gatherings.

Knowledge use: According to Radhakrishna et al. (2024), knowledge use is the practice of applying specific knowledge to produce newer solutions or solutions to problems, typically in quick, iterative phases within economical contexts. A knowledge-based strategy shifts the focus of innovation from the idea that there is a lack of material or financial resources to using what is understood, experienced, and collectively wisdom to enable resilience and adaptation.

2.2 Intersection of Frugality and Knowledge Management

When knowledge management (KM) and frugal innovation come together, it is important to realize that knowledge can serve as a substitute for traditional resources like cash, infrastructure, and advanced technology in order to foster innovation (Dabic et al., 2022). In every situation when formal systems are ineffective or non-existent, knowledge acts as the glue that enables adaptation and problem-solving. Another example of knowledge management in action is when young people in low-income neighbourhoods fix cell phones using web videos and peer-posted advice. This demonstrates that KM is informal, community-based, and fosters innovation outside of conventional corporate structures (Provin et al., 2024).

Furthermore, in situations of frugal innovation, there is no differentiation between people who produce and consume information. In an informal, decentralized, and iterative manner, people and society work together to produce ideas. They can also teach larger corporations valuable lessons about involvement and flexibility (De Marchi et al., 2022). From a technical standpoint, the intersection of KM and frugal living allows people to leverage their knowledge to create what they need. Innovation has come to be recognized as a collection of preexisting concepts, common experience, and cooperative problem solving rather than a characteristic of financial availability (Audretsch et al., 2025).

3. RESOURCE-CONSTRAINED ENVIRONMENTS (RCES)

Innovation is often seen as a trait that may be brought about by new technologies, money, and contemporary laboratories. However, research indicates that scarcity can also lead to innovative solutions to issues, particularly in Resource-Constrained Environments (RCEs), where improvised resilience and abundant social capital coexist with institutional lack, economic incapacity, and inadequate infrastructure. For instance, August literature shows how "jugaad," or improvisational innovation, is vital in informal settlements and how it contributes to the sustainable urban development of cities (Azunre et al., 2025). It also shows how bricolage enables social entrepreneurs to redistribute scarce resources in an emergency situation (Glasbeek, 2025). Similarly, exaptive inventions such as the use of snorkeling masks for medicinal purposes and the repurposing of COVID-19 are excellent illustrations of how a grave need can spur cost-effective innovation (Sedita et al., 2022). These findings suggest that, even in the absence of typical innovation input sources, RCEs may contribute to the development of unique, knowledge-based inventions whose roots are in common resilience and tacit abilities.

3.1 Types of Constraints

In an effort to understand how complex innovation in resource- constrained environments (RCEs) really is, it is important to acknowledge that these environments are characterized by several interdependent constraints.

Financial Constraints: The most immediate obstacles are those related to financial capital, as individuals, startups, and institutions frequently struggle to obtain financing, investments, or public assistance. Venture financing is concentrated in rapidly growing urban locations, and financial institutions do not view small-scale innovators as high-risk (Hossain et al., 2024). Investment in important areas like raw materials, skilled human resources, marketing, and research and development is hampered by this lack of funding. Paradoxically, that constraint often serves as a catalyst for innovation and compels innovators to pursue cost-effectiveness by rethinking current procedures, reusing materials, and utilizing knowledge systems (Le & Scaringella, 2025; Onsongo & Knorringa, 2020). Therefore, in these situations, money is not always used to promote innovation.

Figure 1. Resource- Constrained Environments (RCEs)

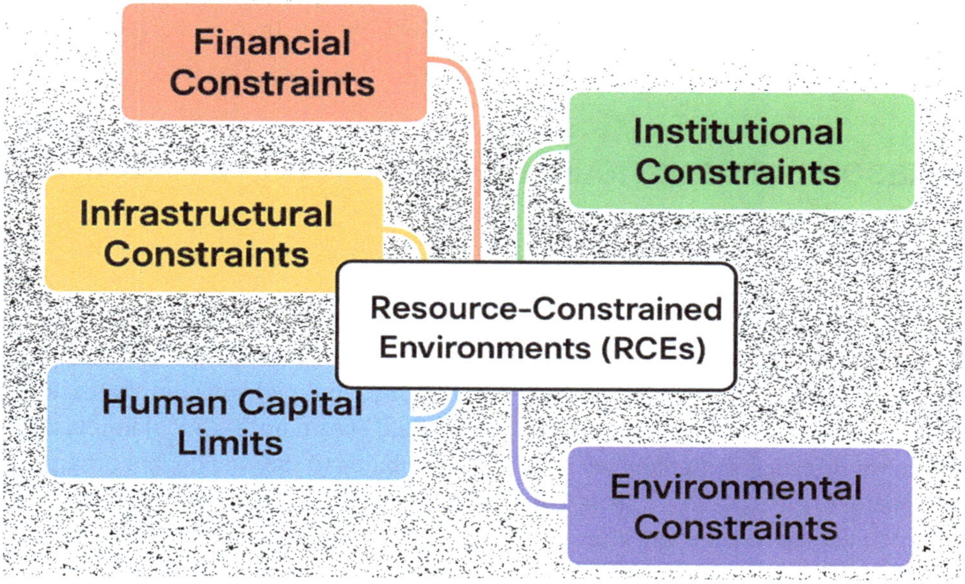

Infrastructural Constraints: Infrastructure, both digital and physical, is the foundation of development. In RCEs, this basis is either broken or inadequate. However Poor roads limit the supply chain, sporadic electricity disrupts communication and industry, and a lack of internet connectivity prevents access to digital industries. The simplest technical initiatives may be difficult to scale or deploy due to a lack of basic infrastructure. An illustration would be a rural school with digital tablets but no dependable power source for charging them. Some business owners own mobile phones, but because they are not networked, they are unable to receive mobile payments. In addition to limiting access to innovation, infrastructure deficiencies also affect livelihoods, healthcare, and education, perpetuating the cycle of exclusion.

Institutional Constraints: Although digital and physical infrastructure are important building blocks for development, they are frequently inadequate or fragmented in Resource-Constrained Environments (RCEs). Supply chains are put at risk by inefficient roads, production and communications are disrupted by frequent power outages, and impoverished people are unable to access the internet and hence are unable to fully participate in the emergence of digital economy (Le & Scaringella, 2025). In these situations of insufficient infrastructure, it is difficult to implement or build upon even basic technology initiatives. For instance, an entrepreneur may have a mobile phone but be unable to accept mobile payments due to inadequate network access, or a remote school may be given digital tablets without a dependable power source to charge them (Savant, 2025). In addition to impeding innovation, these disparities also make it difficult to obtain essential resources like health care, education, and stable employment, which reinforces exclusionary practices (Mvulirwenande & Wehn, 2020).

Human Capital Limits: The issue is that talented personnel are hard to come by in resource-constrained environments, and their ability to innovate is somewhat restricted by their access to formal education or technical training. Due to a lack of engineers, designers, and technicians, even the most innovative ideas may not succeed. Additionally, skilled individuals sometimes go to larger cities or even foreign nations where they believe they may earn more money or have more possibilities (Onsongo & Knorringa, 2020). Indigenous knowledge systems and informal learning networks are still in place, though, and community mechanics, self-taught programmers, traditional healers, and craftswomen all provide valuable implicit information. Localized competency can become essential to successful and inclusive innovations once it is recognized and integrated (Park et al., 2022; Dote-Pardo et al., 2025)

Environmental Constraints: In Resource-Constrained Environments (RCEs), environmental concerns pose a long-term and short-term danger to innovation. Agricultural seasons, transportation, and livelihood insecurity are all negatively impacted by climate change, water scarcity, soil erosion, and extreme weather (Dote-Pardo et al., 2025). Environmental pressures have been at the forefront of eco-frugal innovation, such as waste-cutting technology, low-water agricultural techniques, and solar-powered equipment, most of which is motivated by survival (Park et al., 2022). These innovations have an impact on a sustainable, context-sensitive growth trajectory because they go beyond resolving temporary environmental limitations (Mvulirwenande & Wehn, 2020).

3.2 Innovation in spite of Challenges

Resource-Constrained Environments (RCEs) have a lot of problems, but that's where most innovation has started. In and of themselves, limitations frequently act as a spur for creativity, innovation, and ground-breaking solutions when they enable communities to come up with creative and less expensive answer to challenges they face (Hossain et al., 2023). The researchers have shown that some of the most successful innovations in the world have not resulted from the availability of resources but rather from a continuous effort to break through the systematic boundaries of underserved and developing regions (Le & Scaringella, 2025; Onsongo & Knorringa, 2020).

Resource-Constrained Environments (RCE) are frequently recognized for their necessity-based design, which fosters focused thinking, risk-taking, and unrestrained creativity. In these kinds of environments, technology innovators have a keen sense of community and can therefore offer highly customized solutions that are user-focused. One well-known example is the Jaipur Foot, a lightweight, inexpensive prosthetic that met the needs of the community by enabling squatting and shoeless walking (Korsunova et al., 2022). The absence of corporate R&D or formal institutions can make community-based solutions stand out. Self-help organizations, cooperatives, and unofficial networks where ideas and talents are exchanged can transform innovation into a collaborative endeavor. These grassroots models are cost-effective and sustainable, grounded in social trust and shared ownership, and have been instrumental in advancing practices such as water harvesting and micro-enterprise training (Dabić et al., 2022).

Reverse innovation serves as an example of how cost-effective solutions created at RCEs can impact international markets beyond their place of origin. While Kenya's M-Pesa mobile payment system has influenced fintech solutions globally, GE's inexpensive portable ultrasound equipment, which were first created for rural India, are now used in ambulances in the United States (Dima et al., 2022). Furthermore, by actively embracing new technology and eschewing antiquated infrastructures, RCEs frequently outpace conventional development pathways. Examples include solar microgrids that do away with the requirement for centralized power grids and the extensive use of mobile phones in Africa (Klarin, 2019). RCEs present significant obstacles, but they also present opportunities for game-changing innovation. Instead of being viewed as a constraint, scarcity can serve as a driving force for creativity, adaptability, and sustainable growth. Communities in these settings are proactive change agents that use social networks, local knowledge, and expertise to produce low-cost, high-impact innovations (Dima et al., 2022; Korsunova et al., 2022).

4. A KNOWLEDGE-BASED APPROACH TO FRUGAL INNOVATION

Frugal innovation is based on both material and creative use of information, which is typically the most important resource in Resource-Constrained Environments (RCEs). Knowledge serves as the unseen infrastructure that enables people and communities to adapt, solve issues, and create using the resources at their disposal in situations where financial and technological resources are scarce (Iqbal et al., 2025; Precious, 2025). This knowledge, which emerges via lived experiences, experimentation, storytelling, observation, and community participation, is rarely abstract but rather practical, contextual, tacit, and collaborative (Nilsson et al., 2022; Bhattacharjya et al., 2023). Such localized knowledge is a potent lever for inclusive, sustainable, and scalable frugal innovation when it is appropriately disclosed, shared, and managed (Moreira et al., 2024; Anooja & Kumar, 2025).

Diverse knowledge inputs are used in frugal innovation, including digital commons, user insights, and indigenous methods in addition to formal institutional knowledge. For the purpose of developing reasonably priced, culturally appropriate, and robust solutions, it is imperative to acknowledge and utilize these types of knowledge (Luiz et al., 2021).

Figure 2. A Knowledge-Based Approach to Frugal Innovation

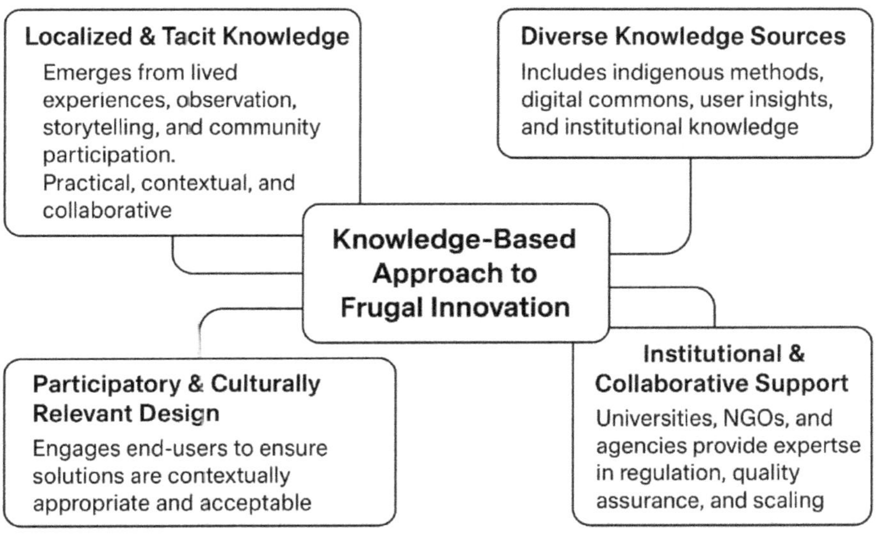

In traditional innovation systems, user knowledge—derived from lived experiences and local practices—remains underdeveloped. In resource-constrained environments, it is essential to involve users in participatory design to guarantee that solutions are both realistically relevant and culturally acceptable (Jagtap, 2022). For example, neglecting the storage practices and routines of rural populations in India can lead to the failure of a technically competent water filtering system. In order to provide sustainable and affordable alternatives to foreign technologies, communities dealing with scarcity frequently create deep-rooted indigenous knowledge in areas such as agriculture, resource management, medicine, and crafts. For instance, Peru's amunas for medicinal purposes and India's johads for water conservation ("Preface," 2023). To maintain authenticity, such information must be respectfully documented and integrated. Additionally, if grassroots innovators choose a reciprocal partnership model over a top-down delivery approach, universities, non-governmental organizations, and development agencies can offer institutional knowledge about regulation, supply chains, quality assurance, and funding, assisting them in scaling ideas and reaching wider markets (Agnihotri et al., 2023). Digital platforms, such as open-source repositories, maker communities, MOOCs, and social media, democratize access to technical know-how. Rural entrepreneurs can now access blueprints for solar cookers or join online forums for vermicomposting without formal training (Ramalingam & Kumpf, 2021). While transformative, ensuring equitable digital access remains a challenge.

4.1 Strategies for Resource-Limited Settings

In frugal contexts, knowledge flows through informal and decentralized channels such as conversations, community rituals, and mobile communication rather than through centralized databases or corporate systems. This requires Knowledge Management (KM) approaches that are flexible and socially embedded (Shepherd et al., 2022). Many Resource-Constrained Environments (RCEs) lack hierarchical bureaucracies or IT-driven KM systems; instead, family networks, artisan guilds, women's collectives, and local trade groups act as custodians of knowledge, transmitting expertise through practice, mentoring, and observation (Raphael & Matsuoka, 2024). Learning is often horizontal, with farmers sharing techniques during meetings, entrepreneurs exchanging tips in markets, and artisans teaching neighboring communities. This peer-to-peer model is cost-effective, trust-based, and scalable, and can be amplified through tools such as community radio, WhatsApp groups, maker fairs, or traveling demo vans (Fitzsimmons Frey et al., 2023). Knowledge brokers—including NGOs, teachers, village leaders, and health workers—play a crucial role in translating external information into locally relevant knowledge. Establishing small, decentralized community hubs equipped with digital access, learning materials, and local mentors can further enable culturally sensitive knowledge exchange (Raphael & Matsuoka, 2024). Despite infrastructure constraints, mobile technologies have become vital knowledge carriers in RCEs, enabling SMS-based advisory services, voice-assisted learning, mobile banking, and crowdsourced problem-solving. Simple digital KM tools such as regional language videos, voice notes, or mobile surveys can effectively capture and disseminate knowledge when designed for low bandwidth, low literacy, and local contexts (Glückler & Panitz, 2024)

Knowledge management (KM) extends beyond storing and sharing information. It is about cultivating the ability to absorb, adapt, and apply knowledge effectively. This absorptive capacity is particularly vital in frugal innovation within Resource-Constrained Environments (RCEs), determining whether communities rely solely on external aid or thrive through self-driven innovation. Absorptive capacity refers to the ability to recognize the value of new knowledge, assimilate it, and apply it to practical outcomes. In RCEs, this process often occurs through experiential learning and iterative problem-solving rather than formal training (Bindumadhavan & Lacey, 2025). Enhancing this capability requires simplifying technical concepts, offering hands-on demonstrations, and creating feedback loops to foster contextual understanding (Gray-Deh, 2025).

Training and upskilling programs tailored to local needs can strengthen this capacity. Unlike standardized curricula, modular and action-oriented programs co-created with community members ensure relevance and foster shared ownership of knowledge. For example, co-designing waste management training with local waste pickers integrates their lived experiences and practical techniques often overlooked by outsiders, empowering participants as both learners and knowledge contributors (Ehlers & Eigbrecht, 2024).

Moreover, frugal innovation typically involves diverse performers such as local producers, NGOs, micro-finance institutions, technology providers, and government agencies. Effective KM integrates knowledge across these actors by aligning goals, sharing best practices, standardizing data, and building collaborative platforms. In rural healthcare innovations, for instance, combining insights from grassroots health workers, biomedical engineers, and policymakers ensures that solutions are not only technically robust but also field-tested and policy-aligned (Petropoulos et al., 2025).

Knowledge serves as the invisible engine of frugal innovation. In RCEs, where financial and infrastructural resources are limited, knowledge provides the strategic advantage. From user insights and traditional practices to peer networks and mobile platforms, knowledge is ubiquitous and, when surfaced and nurtured, empowers communities to innovate independently. A knowledge-based approach is not about top-down expertise transfer but about enabling communities to innovate through localized wisdom, participatory design, and context-specific KM strategies ((Farazmand, 2022)

6. CASE STUDIES AND REAL-WORLD EXAMPLES

Frugal innovation is not merely theoretical but demonstrated globally, particularly in the Global South, where knowledge has become a core resource for creating affordable and scalable solutions. In renewable energy, AI-driven microgrids have enabled energy access in underserved communities, leveraging community learning and cooperation to build social capital and sustainable power systems (Beckett, 2023).

Healthcare initiatives show similar patterns, where frugal approaches transform service delivery through local knowledge and adaptive solutions, reinforcing findings that frugal innovation contributes to inclusive and sustainable growth (Hossain et al., 2022). In finance, grassroots and social entrepreneurship models utilize collective intelligence and low-cost knowledge-sharing mechanisms to empower marginalized populations, echoing principles of resourcefulness such as "jugaad" innovation (Peng, 2024). Renewable energy and grassroots innovations further demonstrate how non-corporate, locally driven models can overcome structural limitations of market-led diffusion strategies, offering more equitable pathways to sustainability (Groenewoudt & Romijn, 2022). These cases collectively highlight the pivotal role of knowledge management (KM) strategies, peer learning, community networks, and adaptive design in achieving maximum impact with minimal resources across multiple sectors.

These real-world examples offer practical validation for the Frugal Innovation–Knowledge Synergy Framework and demonstrate that impact is not bound by resources, but by the intelligence and intent with which knowledge is mobilized.

Table 1. These real-world examples

Case Study	Sector	Constraints Addressed	Knowledge Strategies Applied	Innovation Outcome
Aravind Eye Care	Healthcare	Limited access to affordable, quality eye care; shortage of skilled staff	Standardization of surgical processes, structured training systems, knowledge reuse from global best practices	High-volume, low-cost eye surgeries with global quality benchmarks
Mitticool Refrigerator	Indigenous Product	Lack of electricity in rural areas; need for affordable refrigeration	Use of traditional clay techniques and user feedback; integration of indigenous knowledge with user-centered design	Electricity-free, affordable refrigerator using local materials
M-Pesa	Financial Inclusion	Limited access to banking; infrastructural barriers in rural Kenya	Leveraging mobile technology; embedding local financial behaviors into platform design	Mobile-based money transfer and banking services for the unbanked population
SELCO Solar	Renewable Energy	Lack of electricity; affordability constraints; rural disconnect	Bottom-up KM approach; local technician training; community knowledge hubs	Affordable, customizable solar energy solutions for off-grid communities
Goonj	Social Enterprise	Urban waste accumulation; rural material poverty	Decentralized KM systems; tacit knowledge capture; community-led problem-solving	Upcycled urban waste used in rural development projects via knowledge-driven model

continued on following page

Table 1. Continued

Case Study	Sector	Constraints Addressed	Knowledge Strategies Applied	Innovation Outcome
Chotukool	Rural Appliances	Inability to afford or access traditional refrigerators in rural areas	Participatory design, ethnographic research, informal KM with NGOs and rural users	Low-cost, portable fridge using thermoelectric cooling
Digital Green	Agriculture	Low digital literacy; limited access to localized farming knowledge	Peer-to-peer video learning; farmer-created content; local language dissemination	7x higher adoption of practices through localized, participatory videos
Jaipur Foot	Prosthetics/ Healthcare	High cost of prosthetics; lack of infrastructure in rural health systems	Community knowledge integration; iterative design; local materials; free dissemination	Highly affordable prosthetic limb adopted globally

Each case, though distinct in sector and geography, reinforces a common theme: knowledge, when strategically captured, shared, and applied, can substitute for capital and infrastructure. Whether it is the clinical codification at Aravind, the vernacular ingenuity behind Mitticool, the mobile-driven inclusion of M-Pesa, or the localized learning at SELCO—frugal innovation becomes powerful when grounded in continuous, inclusive, and decentralized knowledge practices.

7. IMPLICATIONS

As the intersection of frugal innovation and knowledge management gains prominence, this chapter offers insights that extend beyond academic theory into managerial praxis and public policy. In resource-constrained environments (RCEs), traditional innovation models often fall short of delivering impact. The knowledge-based approach to frugal innovation presented here provides a pathway not only for doing more with less but also for creating resilient, context-sensitive, and inclusive innovation systems.

7.1 Theoretical Implications

Theoretically, this chapter contributes to the evolving body of literature on frugal innovation by foregrounding the role of knowledge as a central enabler of innovation under constraints. Much of the existing literature on innovation stems from high-resource, technology-intensive environments, where R&D, formal processes, and patent systems dominate. In contrast, frugal innovation often emerges in environments characterized by informality, grassroots participation, and scarcity. This necessitates a reconceptualization of what constitutes "innovation."

By integrating the Knowledge-Based View (KBV) of the firm into the discourse on frugal innovation, this work extends KBV's applicability. Traditionally, KBV emphasizes knowledge as a strategic resource that is rare, valuable, inimitable, and non-substitutable. However, this view often prioritizes codified, technical, and proprietary knowledge. This chapter expands the KBV framework to include tacit, experiential, indigenous, and community-embedded knowledge. It highlights how innovation can be driven not by cutting-edge laboratories or proprietary patents but by contextually relevant know-how, bricolage, and participatory problem-solving.

Furthermore, the chapter adds depth to innovation theory by suggesting that informal knowledge ecosystems, often overlooked in mainstream innovation models, are not only valid but essential in RCEs. These informal ecosystems include traditional artisans, local NGOs, farmer collectives, health volunteers, and community leaders who act as knowledge brokers and innovation enablers. Thus, this work invites scholars to explore new epistemologies of innovation that are decentralized, non-linear, and culturally grounded.

The Frugal Innovation–Knowledge Synergy Framework proposed here also provides a conceptual scaffold for future empirical research. It creates a basis for scholars to examine how different types of knowledge (user, institutional, digital, indigenous) interact with innovation processes in constrained environments. Moreover, the framework's emphasis on feedback loops and absorptive capacity opens avenues for longitudinal studies on knowledge maturity and innovation sustainability in such contexts.

7.2 Managerial Implications

For entrepreneurs, managers, and practitioners operating in RCEs, this chapter presents practical insights into how knowledge can be mobilized as a strategic asset for frugal innovation. Startups and small enterprises in such environments often lack access to capital-intensive resources such as advanced technology or formal R&D labs. However, they can still innovate effectively by harnessing alternative knowledge pathways.

One key implication is the importance of Knowledge Management (KM) best practices, tailored to the realities of low-resource settings. Formal KM systems may not always be feasible. Instead, informal KM mechanisms—such as storytelling, mentorship, peer learning, and community-driven knowledge exchange—can be highly effective. Organizations can establish knowledge circles, community knowledge hubs, or mobile-enabled knowledge platforms to foster learning and innovation.

These decentralized systems help accumulate, validate, and disseminate insights that are locally relevant and practically useful.

Managers should also focus on building knowledge networks that connect diverse stakeholders, including end-users, suppliers, academic institutions, and NGOs. Such networks increase the organization's absorptive capacity, enabling it to sense, adapt, and respond to challenges creatively. Knowledge networks also mitigate risk, as shared learning spreads responsibility and fosters collaborative innovation.

The role of leadership is particularly critical in creating a culture that supports frugal innovation. Leaders must champion learning mindsets, reward problem-solving, and support experimentation even when resources are limited. In such environments, transformational leadership that emphasizes shared purpose and contextual sensitivity is more impactful than transactional leadership styles. Additionally, leadership in RCEs must be multi-level, not just top-down, but also bottom-up and lateral. Grassroots leaders, field workers, and frontline staff are often closest to user needs and can drive powerful innovations when empowered.

Finally, NGOs and social enterprises can use this knowledge-based approach to scale their interventions sustainably. By documenting success stories, codifying processes, and creating knowledge toolkits, they can replicate their models across similar geographies and sectors. Monitoring and evaluation systems must also include knowledge indicators, such as learning uptake, peer exchange frequency, and knowledge dissemination reach, to assess impact beyond traditional metrics.

7.3 Policy Implications

Policy frameworks must evolve to support the unique dynamics of knowledge-driven frugal innovation. In many countries, innovation policies are still geared toward formal sectors, large corporations, or high-tech ecosystems. This chapter argues for a broader innovation policy lens—one that recognizes the value of community knowledge, indigenous wisdom, and grassroots problem-solving.

First, governments must invest in knowledge infrastructure, especially in rural and marginalized regions. This includes not only digital connectivity (internet, mobile networks) but also physical infrastructure such as community learning centers, innovation labs, and rural libraries. Policies should promote the creation of local knowledge repositories where context-specific practices can be preserved, shared, and adapted.

Second, there is a need for incentive structures that reward knowledge sharing. Current IP regimes often focus on exclusivity and monetization, which can discourage open collaboration. Policymakers should explore alternative models such as open-source licensing, innovation commons, and community patents that allow knowledge to flow freely while ensuring attribution and collective benefit.

Third, governments should actively support local innovation systems, including maker spaces, hackathons, and innovation accelerators tailored for RCEs. These platforms can act as living laboratories where innovators, students, and citizens collaborate on low-cost, high-impact solutions. Funding mechanisms such as micro-grants, innovation vouchers, and challenge prizes can further catalyse experimentation and learning.

Public procurement policies can also be aligned to favour frugal, knowledge-based solutions. For instance, hospitals and schools in underserved areas can be encouraged to adopt innovations like Jaipur Foot, Aravind Eye Care models, or SELCO solar kits. Such adoption not only validates these solutions but also creates demand-driven feedback loops that enhance their quality and relevance.

Lastly, cross-sectoral collaboration must be institutionalized. Ministries of education, technology, rural development, and health should work in tandem to build integrated knowledge systems. This requires joint policy design, data-sharing protocols, and inter-ministerial knowledge platforms. Academic institutions and think tanks must be encouraged to conduct transdisciplinary research that bridges theory and practice in frugal innovation.

In sum, the implications of a knowledge-based approach to frugal innovation are far-reaching. Theoretically, it broadens our understanding of innovation to include informal and indigenous knowledge ecosystems. Managerially, it equips practitioners with tools and frameworks to innovate in the face of constraints. Policy-wise, it calls for new governance models that democratize innovation and make it inclusive, sustainable, and responsive to local realities. As global challenges—from climate change to digital divides—continue to grow, frugal innovation backed by robust knowledge systems may offer the most resilient and equitable path forward.

8. CONCLUSION AND FUTURE DIRECTIONS

This chapter has explored the deep and dynamic interrelationship between frugal innovation and knowledge management (KM) in the context of resource-constrained environments (RCEs). In a world increasingly shaped by inequality, climate vulnerability, and digital transformation, the need to innovate with limited means has never been more pressing. Through this lens, the chapter has offered conceptual, practical, and policy-oriented insights into how knowledge—especially in its diverse, informal, and community-embedded forms—can serve as a critical enabler of innovation when traditional resources are scarce.

At the heart of the discussion lies the argument that frugal innovation is not simply about cost-cutting, but about value creation through ingenuity, relevance, and resource sensitivity. Unlike conventional innovation models that often rely on significant financial and infrastructural capital, frugal innovation emphasizes doing more with less, often relying on locally available materials, grassroots participation, and context-specific solutions. This value-centric, bottom-up orientation aligns closely with the principles of effective knowledge management—particularly those that emphasize learning from users, sharing tacit knowledge, and integrating diverse knowledge sources.

The chapter began by defining frugal innovation and KM, and establishing their relevance to environments constrained by financial, institutional, technological, or geographic limitations. It introduced a framework for understanding how various forms of knowledge—including user knowledge, indigenous knowledge, institutional memory, and digital knowledge assets—can be systematically mobilized to foster low-cost, scalable, and sustainable innovations. Importantly, the framework proposed herein highlighted the critical feedback loops between knowledge inputs, KM and innovation processes, and social and economic outcomes, thus offering a dynamic and adaptive model for knowledge-driven frugal innovation.

The chapter also offered real-world illustrations through case studies, demonstrating how organizations such as Aravind Eye Care, Mitticool, M-Pesa, SELCO Solar, Jaipur Foot, and others have successfully leveraged knowledge to innovate under constraint. These cases show that knowledge strategies—whether formal or informal—are not peripheral but central to innovation outcomes, shaping everything from product design and service delivery to system scalability and impact measurement.

From a theoretical standpoint, the integration of KM and frugal innovation provides a promising direction for extending the Knowledge-Based View (KBV) of the firm. By emphasizing the role of informal, decentralized, and non-codified knowledge in driving innovation, the chapter suggests a rethinking of dominant paradigms that prioritize technical, proprietary, or R&D-intensive forms of knowledge. It argues for a more inclusive and pluralistic knowledge ecosystem, where every stakeholder—regardless of institutional affiliation or technological capacity—has the potential to contribute to innovation processes.

From a managerial perspective, the chapter emphasized the importance of informal KM mechanisms, peer learning, mobile technologies, and community knowledge hubs as practical tools for organizations operating in constrained contexts. Leadership, too, was identified as a key driver, not only in providing direction but also in fostering a culture of frugality, collaboration, and knowledge sharing. For startups, NGOs, and social enterprises, the insights offered here can guide strategic decisions around capacity building, stakeholder engagement, and resource allocation.

On the policy front, the chapter made a case for government support in building knowledge infrastructure, offering incentives for knowledge-sharing platforms, and supporting local innovation systems such as maker spaces and grassroots accelerators.

In doing so, it envisions a shift from top-down, technocratic models of innovation to more participatory, decentralized, and knowledge-empowered systems that can thrive even in low-resource settings.

Future Directions

As the convergence of frugal innovation and knowledge management gains prominence, several promising avenues for future research and practice emerge. First, there is an urgent need to explore the role of artificial intelligence (AI) and digital knowledge management (KM) in advancing frugal innovation. With the proliferation of affordable mobile technologies and open-source platforms, AI-enabled KM tools can help organizations in resource-constrained environments access real-time insights, automate knowledge sharing, and co-create scalable solutions. Research could focus on how AI can be adapted for low-bandwidth contexts, embedded in community services, and governed responsibly to ensure inclusivity and ethical use.

Second, future studies should delve deeper into cross-sectoral knowledge integration. Many societal problems in RCEs—such as access to healthcare, clean energy, or financial inclusion—require knowledge inputs from multiple sectors. There is significant potential in exploring how hybrid knowledge systems, which blend scientific, local, indigenous, and technological know-how, can foster holistic, frugal innovations. Such integration not only enhances problem-solving capacity but also encourages collaboration across traditionally siloed domains such as academia, industry, and civil society.

Third, the field would benefit from longitudinal studies that examine the evolution and impact of knowledge-based frugal innovations over time. Many innovations begin with promise but struggle to scale or sustain without proper knowledge governance and learning mechanisms. Tracking these trajectories can yield insights into the enablers and barriers of durable innovation, the transformation of knowledge flows, and the shifting roles of stakeholders. Such research can also inform more resilient KM systems in uncertain environments.

Lastly, the issue of knowledge equity and governance deserves closer scrutiny. As frugal innovators increasingly draw upon indigenous, community-based, or informal knowledge, questions around attribution, ownership, and benefit-sharing become critical. Future research should address how to design fair and transparent systems for recognizing contributors, preventing exploitation, and ensuring that local communities are not only sources of knowledge but also beneficiaries of innovation outcomes. The development of ethical guidelines and legal frameworks for knowledge access, use, and distribution will be key to maintaining trust and sustainability in the frugal innovation ecosystem.

In sum, the future of frugal innovation lies in its ability to intelligently and ethically harness knowledge as a transformative resource. By deepening our understanding of how knowledge is created, shared, and applied across boundaries—and by leveraging emerging technologies and inclusive governance models—we can unlock new possibilities for innovation that is not only efficient but also equitable, resilient, and human-centered.

REFERENCES

Agnihotri, A., Madon, T., & Gadgil, A. J. (2023). Introduction to Development Engineering. In T. Madon, A. J. Gadgil, R. Anderson, L. Casaburi, K. Lee, & A. Rezaee (Eds.), *Introduction to Development Engineering* (pp. 1–15). Springer International Publishing. DOI: 10.1007/978-3-030-86065-3_1

Alayande, B., Chu, K. M., Jumbam, D. T., Kimto, O. E., Musa Danladi, G., Niyukuri, A., Anderson, G. A., El-Gabri, D., Miranda, E., Taye, M., Tertong, N., Yempabe, T., Ntirenganya, F., Byiringiro, J. C., Sule, A. Z., Kobusingye, O. C., Bekele, A., & Riviello, R. R. (2022). Disparities in Access to Trauma Care in Sub-Saharan Africa: A Narrative Review. *Current Trauma Reports*, *8*(3), 66–94. DOI: 10.1007/s40719-022-00229-1 PMID: 35692507

Anooja, J., & Kumar, V. (2025). Elements of innovation: A review of literature on craft-design ecosystem. *Sustainable Futures : An Applied Journal of Technology, Environment and Society*, *9*, 100670. DOI: 10.1016/j.sftr.2025.100670

Audretsch, D. B., Belitski, M., Fiedler, A., & Meurer, M. M. (2025). Values and entrepreneurship in the sustainable society: Toward a multilevel understanding of entrepreneurial value practices. *Small Business Economics*, *65*(3), 1701–1725. Advance online publication. DOI: 10.1007/s11187-025-01069-4

Azunre, G. A., Azerigyik, R. A., Amponsah, O., & Kpeebi, Y. (2025). The jugaad urbanism-sustainable circular cities nexus: Insights from sub-Saharan Africa's informal settlements. *Habitat International*, *158*, 103349. DOI: 10.1016/j.habitatint.2025.103349

(2023). Back to Common Sense: Towards Frugal Environmental Innovation (FEI). InBouvier-Patron, P. (Ed.), *Frugal Innovation and Innovative Creation* (1st ed., pp. 133–145). Wiley., DOI: 10.1002/9781394236817.ch5

Beckett, R. (2023). Affordable innovation facilitating renewable energy deployment: Two 'smart' energy poverty alleviation case examples. *Journal of Innovation Management*, *11*(2), 118–156. DOI: 10.24840/2183-0606_011.002_0005

Bhattacharjya, B. R., Bhaduri, S., & Kakoty, S. K. (2023). Co-creating community-led frugal innovation: An adapted Quadruple Helix? *Technovation*, *124*, 102752. DOI: 10.1016/j.technovation.2023.102752

Bindumadhavan, K., & Lacey, N. (Eds.). (2025). *Work Integrated Learning-Directions for the Future: Select Proceedings of ICONWIL 2024* (Vol. 1206). Springer Nature Singapore. DOI: 10.1007/978-981-96-0201-8

Chakravarty, S. (2022). Resource constrained innovation in a technology intensive sector: Frugal medical devices from manufacturing firms in South Africa. *Technovation, 112*, 102397. DOI: 10.1016/j.technovation.2021.102397

Corsini, L., Dammicco, V., & Moultrie, J. (2021). Frugal innovation in a crisis: The digital fabrication maker response to COVID-19. *R & D Management, 51*(2), 195–210. DOI: 10.1111/radm.12446

Dabić, M., Vlačić, B., Guerrero, M., & Daim, T. U. (2022). University spin-offs: The past, the present, and the future. *Studies in Higher Education, 47*(10), 2007–2021. DOI: 10.1080/03075079.2022.2122656

De Marchi, V., Pineda-Escobar, M. A., Howell, R., Verheij, M., & Knorringa, P. (2022). Frugal innovation and sustainability outcomes: Findings from a systematic literature review. *European Journal of Innovation Management, 25*(6), 984–1007. DOI: 10.1108/EJIM-02-2022-0083

De Moraes, M. A., De Moraes, G. H. S. M., Do Prado, N. B., & Fischer, B. B. (2025). Triggering Sustainable Transitions in Entrepreneurial Ecosystems: Key Enabling Conditions and Outcomes. *Sustainable Development*, sd.70005. DOI: 10.1002/sd.70005

Dima, A., Bugheanu, A.-M., Dinulescu, R., Potcovaru, A.-M., Stefanescu, C. A., & Marin, I. (2022). Exploring the Research Regarding Frugal Innovation and Business Sustainability through Bibliometric Analysis. *Sustainability (Basel), 14*(3), 1326. DOI: 10.3390/su14031326

Dote-Pardo, J., Ortiz-Cea, V., Peña-Acuña, V., Severino-González, P., Contreras-Henríquez, J. M., & Ramírez-Molina, R. I. (2025). Innovative Entrepreneurship and Sustainability: A Bibliometric Analysis in Emerging Countries. *Sustainability (Basel), 17*(2), 658. DOI: 10.3390/su17020658

Ehlers, U.-D., & Eigbrecht, L. (Eds.). (2024). *Creating the University of the Future: A Global View on Future Skills and Future Higher Education*. Springer Fachmedien Wiesbaden., DOI: 10.1007/978-3-658-42948-5

Farazmand, A. (Ed.). (2022). *Global Encyclopedia of Public Administration, Public Policy, and Governance*. Springer International Publishing., DOI: 10.1007/978-3-030-66252-3

Favretto, N., & Stringer, L. C. (2024). Climate resilient development in vulnerable geographies. *Mitigation and Adaptation Strategies for Global Change, 29*(8), 90. DOI: 10.1007/s11027-024-10187-5

Fitzsimmons Frey, H., Sefton-Green, J., & Poyntz, S. R. (2023). *Youthsites: Histories of Creativity, Care, and Learning in the City* (1st ed.). Oxford University PressNew York., DOI: 10.1093/oso/9780197555491.001.0001

Gandenberger, C., Kroll, H., & Walz, R. (2020). The role of frugal innovation in the global diffusion of green technologies. *International Journal of Technology Management, 83*(1/2/3), 97. DOI: 10.1504/IJTM.2020.109218

Glasbeek, L. (2025). Bricolage and its Strategic Connotations: A Study of Greek Social Entrepreneurs in Times of Crisis. *British Journal of Management*, *36*(3), 1003–1022. DOI: 10.1111/1467-8551.12880

Glückler, J., & Panitz, R. (Eds.). (2024). *Knowledge and Digital Technology* (Vol. 19). Springer Nature Switzerland., DOI: 10.1007/978-3-031-39101-9

Gray-Deh, F. Y. (2025). *Entrepreneurial orientation among small and medium enterprises in selected rural areas of KwaZulu-Natal* [Doctor of Philosophy Management Sciences Specialising in Business Administration, Durban University of Technology]., DOI: 10.51415/10321/6120

Groenewoudt, A. C., & Romijn, H. A. (2022). Limits of the corporate-led market approach to off-grid energy access: A review. *Environmental Innovation and Societal Transitions*, *42*, 27–43. DOI: 10.1016/j.eist.2021.10.027

Hossain, M. (2022). Frugal entrepreneurship: Resource mobilization in resource-constrained environments. *Creativity and Innovation Management*, *31*(3), 509–520. DOI: 10.1111/caim.12502

Hossain, M., Agarwal, N., Bhatti, Y., & Levänen, J. (2022). Frugal innovation: Antecedents, mediators, and consequences. *Creativity and Innovation Management*, *31*(3), 521–540. DOI: 10.1111/caim.12511

Hossain, M., Park, S., & Shahid, S. (2023). Frugal innovation for sustainable rural development. *Technological Forecasting and Social Change*, *193*, 122662. DOI: 10.1016/j.techfore.2023.122662

Hossain, M., Shahid, M. S., & Park, S. (2024). The Business Models of Frugal Enterprises for Sustainable Development in a Constrained Environment. *IEEE Transactions on Engineering Management*, *71*, 3448–3463. DOI: 10.1109/TEM.2023.3342440

Iqbal, Q., Piwowar-Sulej, K., & Kallmuenzer, A. (2025). Sustainable development through frugal innovation: The role of leadership, entrepreneurial bricolage and knowledge diversity. *Review of Managerial Science*, *19*(2), 573–594. DOI: 10.1007/s11846-024-00764-y

Jagtap, S. (2022). Codesign in resource-limited societies: Theoretical perspectives, inputs, outputs and influencing factors. *Research in Engineering Design*, *33*(2), 191–211. DOI: 10.1007/s00163-022-00384-1

Jayabalan, J., & Dorasamy, M. (2024). Revitalizing Higher Education Institutions: Embracing Frugal Innovation for Transformation. *Procedia Computer Science*, *234*, 1305–1312. DOI: 10.1016/j.procs.2024.03.128

Jiraphanumes, K., Aujirapongpan, S., & Songkajorn, Y. (2023). Influence of diagnostic and dynamic capabilities on frugal innovation development: An empirical study of the Thai auto parts industry. *Asia Pacific Management Review*, *28*(2), 229–239. DOI: 10.1016/j.apmrv.2022.10.001

Klarin, A. (2019). Mapping product and service innovation: A bibliometric analysis and a typology. *Technological Forecasting and Social Change*, *149*, 119776. DOI: 10.1016/j.techfore.2019.119776

Korsunova, A., Halme, M., Kourula, A., Levänen, J., & Lima-Toivanen, M. (2022). Necessity-driven circular economy in low-income contexts: How informal sector practices retain value for circularity. *Global Environmental Change*, *76*, 102573. DOI: 10.1016/j.gloenvcha.2022.102573

Kun, M. (2022). Linkages Between Knowledge Management Process and Corporate Sustainable Performance of Chinese Small and Medium Enterprises: Mediating Role of Frugal Innovation. *Frontiers in Psychology*, *13*, 850820. DOI: 10.3389/fpsyg.2022.850820 PMID: 35391966

Le, S. T. K., & Scaringella, L. (2025). Scarcity, Absorptive Capacity, and Social Networking—Antecedents of Self-Constructed Innovation in Vietnamese SMEs? *International Journal of Innovation Studies*, *S2096248725000244*(4), 366–382. Advance online publication. DOI: 10.1016/j.ijis.2025.07.001

Luiz, O. R., Mariano, E. B., & Silva, H. M. R. D. (2021). Pro-Poor Innovations to Promote Instrumental Freedoms: A Systematic Literature Review. *Sustainability (Basel)*, *13*(24), 13587. DOI: 10.3390/su132413587

Manishimwe, T., Frazier, D. P., & Yusuf, H. (2024). Frugal innovation and entrepreneurial university: A case study of African first development university in Africa. *Discover Education*, *3*(1), 190. DOI: 10.1007/s44217-024-00299-0

Manzi-Puertas, M. A., Agirre-Aramburu, I., & López-Pérez, S. (2025). Uncovering the hidden value of scarce resources: Frugality, resourcefulness and innovative behavior among student entrepreneurs. *Cogent Business & Management*, *12*(1), 2525500. DOI: 10.1080/23311975.2025.2525500

Moreira, G. G., Dos Santos, R. J. R., De Carvalho, V. D. H., Rosário, F. J. P., & Dos Santos, A. J. (2024). Potential for Frugal Innovation in a Brazilian Regional System: A Study Based on a Multicriteria Approach. *Societies (Basel, Switzerland)*, *14*(6), 95. DOI: 10.3390/soc14060095

Mvulirwenande, S., & Wehn, U. (2020). Analysing frugal innovation incubation programmes: A case study from the water sector. *Prometheus*, *36*(2). Advance online publication. DOI: 10.13169/prometheus.36.2.0095

Nilsson, S., Samuelsson, M., & Meyer, C. (2022). Social entrepreneurs' use of spatial bricolage to create frugal innovation in a divided urban setting. *Africa Journal of Management*, *8*(3), 298–323. DOI: 10.1080/23322373.2022.2071578

Omer, M., Kaiser, M., Buxbaum-Conradi, S., Moritz, M., & Redlich, T. (2024). Designing for replicability: A qualitative empirical study on the replication of open-source machine tools. *Design Science*, *10*, e30. DOI: 10.1017/dsj.2024.35

Onsongo, E. K., & Knorringa, P. (2020). Comparing frugality and inclusion in innovation for development: Logic, process and outcome. *Innovation and Development*, •••, 1–21. DOI: 10.1080/2157930X.2020.1811931

Park, S., Rosca, E., & Agarwal, N. (2022). Driving social impact at the bottom of the Pyramid through the internet-of-things enabled frugal innovations. *Technovation*, *118*, 102381. DOI: 10.1016/j.technovation.2021.102381

Peng, S.-H. L. (2024). An intergenerational comeback: Girls' education, development, and social capital. *Policy Futures in Education*, *22*(8), 1709–1728. DOI: 10.1177/14782103241237320

Petropoulos, F., Akkermans, H., Aksin, O. Z., Ali, I., Babai, M. Z., Barbosa-Povoa, A., Battaïa, O., Besiou, M., Boysen, N., Brammer, S., Brandon-Jones, A., Briskorn, D., Browning, T. R., Buijs, P., Centobelli, P., Chiarini, A., Cousins, P., Cudney, E. A., Davies, A., . . . Zheng, T. (2025). *Operations & Supply Chain Management: Principles and Practice* (Version 2). arXiv. DOI: 10.48550/ARXIV.2503.05749

Pradhan, N. A., Samnani, A. A. B. A., Abbas, K., & Rizvi, N. (2023). Resilience of primary healthcare system across low- and middle-income countries during COVID-19 pandemic: A scoping review. *Health Research Policy and Systems*, *21*(1), 98. DOI: 10.1186/s12961-023-01031-4 PMID: 37723533

Precious, D. (2025). The Role of Industry 4.0 Readiness, Knowledge Management Capabilities, and Sustainability Culture in Driving Circular Economy Practices. *Business Strategy & Development*, *8*(2), e70135. DOI: 10.1002/bsd2.70135

Preface. (2023). *IOP Conference Series: Earth and Environmental Science, 1211*(1), 011001. DOI: 10.1088/1755-1315/1211/1/011001

Provin, A. P., Leal Vieira Cubas, A., De Aguiar Dutra, A. R., Carneiro Mussi, C., Junges, I., Nunes, N. A., Casagrande, J. L., & Salgueirinho Osório De Andrade Guerra, J. B. (2024). Qualitative Research Parameters in Studies on Frugal Innovation. *International Journal of Qualitative Methods, 23*, 16094069241237550. DOI: 10.1177/16094069241237550

Radhakrishna, V., Ravi, H., Elango, S., Divyashree, V., Jaganathan, A., & Ponnusamy, M. (2024). Future of knowledge management in investment banking: Role of personal intelligent assistants. *Methodological Innovations, 17*(4), 229–247. DOI: 10.1177/20597991241287118

Ramalingam, B., & Kumpf, B. (2021). *COVID-19 innovation in low and middle-income countries: Lessons for development co-operation* (OECD Development Policy Papers No. 39; OECD Development Policy Papers, Vol. 39). DOI: 10.1787/24140929

Raphael, C., & Matsuoka, M. (Eds.). (2024). *Ground Truths: Community-Engaged Research for Environmental Justice*. University of California Press., DOI: 10.1525/9780520384347

Sarkar, S., & Mateus, S. (2022a). Value creation using minimal resources – A meta-synthesis of frugal innovation. *Technological Forecasting and Social Change, 179*, 121612. DOI: 10.1016/j.techfore.2022.121612

Sarkar, S., & Mateus, S. (2022b). Value creation using minimal resources – A meta-synthesis of frugal innovation. *Technological Forecasting and Social Change, 179*, 121612. DOI: 10.1016/j.techfore.2022.121612

Savant, N. V. (2025). Leveraging Surplus Android Phones in India: Scalable Use Cases in Edge Computing, Digital Health, and Smart Infrastructure. SSRN *Electronic Journal*. DOI: 10.2139/ssrn.5315514

Sedita, S. R., Blasi, S., & Ganzaroli, A. (2022). Exaptive innovation in constraint-based environments: Lessons from COVID-19 crisis. *European Journal of Innovation Management, 25*(6), 549–566. DOI: 10.1108/EJIM-07-2021-0348

Sharmelly, R., & Ray, P. K. (2021). Managing resource-constrained innovation in emerging markets: Perspectives from a business model. *Technology in Society, 65*, 101538. DOI: 10.1016/j.techsoc.2021.101538

Sheikh, F. A., Pugh, R., Wu, X., & Sarkar, S. (2024). Regional studies and frugal innovation: A missing link? *Regional Studies, 58*(4), 893–905. DOI: 10.1080/00343404.2023.2222136

Shepherd, D. A., Parida, V., & Wincent, J. (2022). *Entrepreneurial Responses to Chronic Adversity: The Bright, the Dark, and the in Between*. Springer International Publishing., DOI: 10.1007/978-3-031-04884-5

Shivdas, A., Barpanda, S., Sivakumar, S., & Bishu, R. (2021). Frugal innovation capabilities: Conceptualization and measurement. *Prometheus*, *37*(3). Advance online publication. DOI: 10.13169/prometheus.37.3.0259

Steinfield, L., & Holt, D. (2019). Toward A Theory on the Reproduction of Social Innovations in Subsistence Marketplaces. *Journal of Product Innovation Management*, *36*(6), 764–799. DOI: 10.1111/jpim.12510

Umar, S. B., Ahmad, J., Mohd Bukhori, M. A. B., Ali, K. A. M., & Hussain, W. M. H. W. (2025). Transforming Higher-Education-Intitutes: Impact of Change Management on Sustainable Performance Through Transformational Leadership and Knowledge Management. *Sustainability (Basel)*, *17*(6), 2445. DOI: 10.3390/su17062445

Urata, S., Akao, K.-I., & Washizu, A. (Eds.). (2023). *Sustainable Development Disciplines for Society: Breaking Down the 5Ps—People, Planet, Prosperity, Peace, and Partnerships*. Springer Nature Singapore., DOI: 10.1007/978-981-19-5145-9

Van Niekerk, A. J. (2022). *The Inclusive Economy: Criteria, Principles and Ubuntu* (1st ed.). UJ Press., DOI: 10.36615/9781776402366

Zara, A. R. (2025). Bridging Sectors, Catalyzing Innovation: The Role of FabLab Characteristics in Cross-sector Collaboration and Successful Collaborative Projects. SSRN *Electronic Journal*. DOI: 10.2139/ssrn.5206917

Chapter 7
Rural-Urban Disparities in SME Access to Non-Banking Financing in Colombia Post COVID-19

Hector Botello
http://orcid.org/0000-0002-7795-2590
Washington State University, USA

ABSTRACT

This chapter examines the impact of the COVID-19 pandemic on small and medium-sized enterprises' (SMEs) access to financing in Colombia, focusing on the disparities between rural and urban areas. The purpose is to understand how these businesses adapted to financial constraints by leveraging non-banking financing sources. The analysis reveals that in the post-pandemic period, SMEs were significantly more likely to utilize non-banking financing, such as microfinance and fintech, compared to traditional banking. A key finding is the existence of significant rural-urban disparities, with rural SMEs being 30.4% less likely than their urban counterparts to access non-banking financing in 2021. Younger firms and male-owned businesses demonstrated a higher likelihood of securing financing. The chapter concludes by discussing the policy implications of these findings, highlighting the need for targeted financial inclusion strategies to support rural and underserved SMEs and promote a more resilient and equitable financial ecosystem in Colombia.

DOI: 10.4018/979-8-3373-6053-9.ch007

1 INTRODUCTION

The COVID-19 pandemic caused global economic disruptions, especially impacting SMEs in developing countries due to liquidity issues and limited resources. The impact was higher in these countries due to the economic, institutional, and political challenges. This stems from the government's inability to deliver comparable assistance levels seen in developed countries. Furthermore, the pandemic shows the financial access restrictions cause from limited financial markets and asset diversity.

In Colombia, these firms play a crucial role in economic stability, contributing 99.5% of formal companies, generating 79% of the country's employment, and contributing about 40% to the annual GDP. Given the critical role of SMEs in Colombia's economic stability, understanding how these enterprises survive the crisis, mainly through alternative financing, has become an urgent research priority. Therefore, this paper explores one crucial aspect of their recovery—access to non-banking funding—and examines how disparities between rural and urban SMEs affected their ability to secure this form of financing in the aftermath of COVID-19.

However, extensive research has focused on SME access to non-banking sources globally (Beck et al., 2005; Fisman & Raturi, 2004; Nilsen, J., 2002; Petersen & Rajan, 1994, 1997). Moreover, more attention needs to be paid to the determinants of access between rural and urban SMEs after the COVID-19 pandemic. This gap is particularly pertinent regarding access to non-banking financing, which has emerged as a crucial alternative for SMEs during the pandemic. Non-banking financing offers services from non-traditional institutions like microfinance and fintech. These institutions often support small firms, especially in rural areas lacking formal banking. They provide microloans and digital services that are generally easier for SMEs to access because these companies often do not look for profit. Also, these companies do not have financial limitations imposed by the regulators, or they have more laxity norms. During the COVID-19 pandemic, non-banking financing played a crucial role in helping SMEs, especially in rural regions with limited banking options.

Non-banking financing mechanisms offered support for Colombian SMEs' post-COVID recovery, addressing gaps left by traditional bank lending constraints, as shown in Figure 1. This alternative ecosystem encompasses diverse capital sources like microfinance, crowdfunding, factoring, and leasing, providing vital liquidity and growth capital. Non-banking financial institutions (NBFIs) and fintech companies typically offer more agile, flexible financing options tailored to SME needs, such as revenue-based and digital loans. These alternatives often feature less stringent requirements and innovative risk assessment models, lowering barriers for businesses traditionally excluded from formal financial markets.

Non-banking finance stimulates economic activity in underserved areas by promoting financial inclusion through peer-to-peer lending and digital payment platforms. It also supports innovation by providing risk-tolerant capital through venture capital, private equity, and angel investors, who offer funds, valuable guidance, and networks.

Furthermore, non-banking financing complements government support programs, efficiently disbursing subsidies and guarantees. This multifaceted approach, blending alternative funding sources, fintech solutions, and policy support, fosters a more inclusive and dynamic financial ecosystem. It is crucial in enhancing SMEs' resilience, adaptability, and growth potential, contributing significantly to Colombia's broader economic recovery and development.

Figure 1. Ways non-banking supports SMEs in Colombia

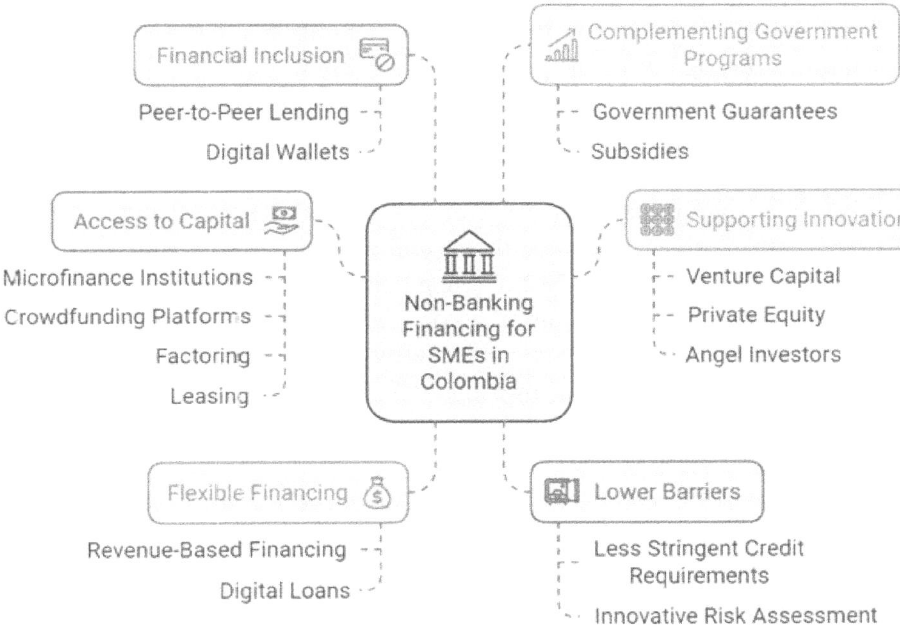

The Colombian economy suffered a contraction of 7.3% in GDP in 2020 due to the COVID-19 pandemic, followed by a recovery of about 10.6% in 2021; however, sectorial differences persisted, particularly for the micro and small firms (Prada et al., 2022). The pandemic caused 4.9 million infections and 125,000 deaths from March 2020 to October 2021. This triggered a set of government policies, including credit lines from non-commercial banks like Bancoldex.

To support financial stability, the Central Bank of Colombia reduced the benchmark interest rate from 4.25% in March 2020 to a historic low of 1.75% by September 2020. Additionally, liquidity measures were introduced, such as enhanced liquidity auctions, acceptance of new collateral types, and lowered reserve requirements for banks to stimulate lending. Therefore, Colombia presents a compelling case for studying SME recovery and access to non-banking financing for several reasons. First, its diverse geographical and economic landscape provides a unique opportunity to examine how financial inclusion and recovery differ across rural and urban regions. Second, the Colombian government and financial institutions enacted support measures for SMEs amid the pandemic, providing a valuable case study for assessing intervention efficacy. Lastly, Colombia's ongoing efforts to address rural-urban inequality add to the relevance of this study, as it provides insights into how these disparities might be mitigated through targeted financial inclusion efforts.

The study investigates the disparity in non-banking financing access between rural and urban SMEs in Colombia during COVID-19 recovery. The study has three specific objectives: (1) to evaluate the likelihood of rural and urban SMEs accessing non-banking financing during the pandemic; (2) to assess the variables of the SME that make them choose non-banking financing and (3) to identify regional disparities in financial inclusion within Colombia. By addressing these objectives, the study provides a comprehensive understanding of how Colombia's SMEs accessed alternative financing mechanisms, especially in underbanked rural areas.

To achieve these objectives, we utilize a multinomial logistic regression model to estimate the likelihood of SMEs accessing non-banking financing compared to banking or no funding. The analysis draws on a nationally representative survey of 205,796 Colombian microbusinesses conducted by the Departamento Administrativo Nacional de Estadística (DANE), covering 2019, 2021, and 2022. This time frame allows for a comparison of pre-and post-pandemic financing behaviors. The dependent variable categorizes businesses into three groups: those that access banking financing, non-banking funding, and those that do not access any form of financing (the base category). Independent variables include rural residency, business characteristics (age, size, sector), and owner characteristics (gender, age, savings behavior). An interaction term between year and rural residency is introduced to examine how the pandemic's effects on financing access differ between rural and urban SMEs.

The multinomial logistic regression results suggest significant rural-urban disparities in access to non-banking financing during the COVID-19 recovery period. Rural SMEs were 30.4% less likely than their urban counterparts to access formal non-banking financing in 2021, indicating that geographic location was critical in determining financing opportunities. Furthermore, the results show that business age significantly influenced access to non-banking financing, with younger firms (0-2 years) more likely to secure such financing than older firms (10+ years). This finding aligns with existing literature, which suggests that younger SMEs are more adaptable and willing to explore alternative financing sources during crises (Baral et al., 2021; Cowling et al., 2016).

These findings have important implications for policymakers and financial institutions. The observed rural-urban disparities highlight the need for targeted financial inclusion efforts in rural areas, where SMEs face more significant challenges accessing formal financing. Moreover, the study underscores the importance of developing non-banking financial instruments that cater specifically to the needs of rural enterprises, which are often underserved by traditional banking systems. By improving access to non-banking financing, policymakers can enhance the resilience of rural SMEs, promoting economic stability and recovery in these regions.

This study contributes to economics by providing new insights into the role of non-banking financing in SME recovery during crises, particularly in an emerging market context. By examining rural-urban disparities in financing access, the research sheds light on the geographic and sectorial factors that influence financial inclusion in economic hardship. The findings also contribute to the broader literature on labor market dynamics during crises, as SMEs are key drivers of employment in Colombia. Understanding how these businesses adapt to financial constraints during recovery periods is crucial for developing effective economic policies that support job creation and economic growth.

The remainder of the paper is structured as follows: Section 2 reviews the relevant literature on SME financing and crisis recovery, focusing on the role of non-banking financing during economic downturns. Section 3 outlines the data and methodology used in the analysis, detailing the variables, econometric model, and robustness checks. Section 4 presents the empirical results, discussing the rural-urban disparities in financing access and the role of non-banking financing in SME financial behavior. Section 5 provides a discussion of the findings, their policy implications, and directions for future research. Finally, Section 6 concludes the paper by summarizing the key contributions and offering recommendations for improving financial inclusion for SMEs in Colombia.

2 LITERATURE REVIEW

2.1 Impact of COVID-19 on SMEs and Financial Accessibility

The COVID-19 pandemic significantly affected global economies, particularly severely impacting Small and Medium Enterprises (SMEs) (Bartik et al., 2020; Pedauga et al., 2021). In the United States, for instance, there was a 22% drop in active SME businesses between February and April 2020 (Fairlie et al., 2021). SMEs faced increased financial challenges due to reduced demand and altered risk assessments (Dörr et al., 2021; Engidaw, 2022; Fairlie et al., 2021). In developing countries, SMEs encountered reduced revenue, job losses, and weakened marketing performance, necessitating financial and government support to survive the crisis (Engidaw, 2022).

Financial limitations have long been recognized as impediments to SME growth (Beck et al., 2005; Gur, 2012). Various crises can lead to credit limitations, resulting in reduced external financing options for enterprises (Berg & Schrader, 2012; Khwaja & Mian, 2008; Stiglitz & Weiss, 1981). Theoretical perspectives suggest that such limitations induce underinvestment, preventing small firms from reaching optimal scale (Cabral & Mata, 2003; McDermott et al., 2014).

Strengthening financial development is crucial for mitigating these limitations by expanding financial resources and lowering borrowing costs (Hsu et al., 2014; Levine, 2005; Manova, 2013; Rajan & Zingales, 1998) . A robust financial system can foster Schumpeterian growth by enabling emerging firms to compete with established players (Aghion et al., 2005; Laeven et al., 2015).

In financial constraints, non-banking financing has emerged as a vital alternative for SMEs, particularly during financial restrictions like those encountered during COVID-19 (Levine et al., 2018). Amid credit shortages, SMEs have demonstrated resilience by seeking alternative financing avenues (Baral et al., 2021).

Research by Carbo-Valverde et al. (2016) revealed that credit-constrained SMEs in Spain increasingly relied on trade credits during the financial crisis. McGuinness and Hogan (2016) highlighted the importance of trade credit for financially vulnerable Irish SMEs during the 2008 crisis. Sriyono et al. (2021) noted that non-banking financing significantly aided SMEs during the pandemic, fostering performance recovery and enhancing competitiveness

However, the interplay between various financing sources can be complex. McGuinness & Hogan, (2016) demonstrated that bank and commercial loans served as complementary resources for SMEs after the 2008 financial crisis, highlighting SMEs' diverse financing strategies based on specific contexts and economic conditions, this evidence has been supported for extensive literature (Beck et al., 2005; Fisman & Raturi, 2004; Nilsen, J., 2002; Petersen & Rajan, 1994, 1997)

These firms can stay resilient during crises using non-bank debt financing options like securitization, private placements, trade credit, and bonds (Carbo-Valverde et al., 2016; McGuinness & Hogan, 2016). Hossain et al. (2022) proposed two alternative financing models to address SMEs' borrowing challenges. Their empirical results support these models, indicating that sustainable financing strategies through non-banking channels can enhance SMEs' access to affordable, collateral-free loans.

2.2 Rural vs Urban SMEs: Financing Strategies and Recovery Mechanisms

The literature underscores that while SMEs globally face similar challenges during crises, local contexts significantly influence their performance and recovery strategies. Rural and urban SMEs exhibit distinct approaches to financing and recovery, shaped by their respective environments.

Rural SMEs, with limited access to formal financial institutions, often rely on local resources and community networks. Degryse et al., (2013) highlights the importance of informal networks in rural SME financing, where family and community-based support often serve as crucial sources of capital. Accordingly Kumar et al., (2010) rural firms usually depend on agricultural credit, subsidized programs, and cooperatives in developing economies to meet their financial needs. Despite these limitations, some rural SMEs have shown high resilience (Chisasa & Makina, 2015; Yadav & Sharma, 2015). Getman et al., (2018) describe how certain rural enterprises engage in extensive networking to overcome local resource constraints.

Urban SMEs benefit from a more developed financial ecosystem with diverse financing options. Beck et al., (2005) note that urban SMEs have enhanced access to formal financial institutions, venture capital, and angel investors. However, they grapple with substantial obstacles, including high collateral demands and risk perceptions from investors. The dynamics of urban financial sectors significantly influence SME financing strategies, with financial sector liberalization markedly affecting credit availability and costs (Demirgüç-Kunt & Maksimovic, 1998).

Rural SMEs typically utilize local networks and resources to recover from economic downturns. The literature emphasize that rural SMEs often aim to diversify income sources to reduce risks linked to economic challenges (Calabrese et al., 2021; Fouejieu et al., 2020; Tagoe et al., 2005). Urban SMEs, benefiting from their location in more economically diverse environments, tend to have more robust recovery mechanisms. Fouejieu et al., (2020) note that SMEs can capitalize on urban infrastructure and technology to adapt quickly to changing economic conditions.

Summarizing, the literature highlights the significant challenges SMEs face in accessing finance, particularly during economic crises like the COVID-19 pandemic. Non-banking financing emerges as a crucial alternative, with its importance varying between rural and urban contexts. The review underscores the need for tailored approaches to SME financing and recovery strategies, considering rural and urban environments' distinct characteristics and challenges. Based on the literature review and the research questions outlined in the introduction, the following are the three hypotheses that we propose:

Hypothesis 1: Rural SMEs in Colombia have less access to non-banking financing than urban SMEs before and after the COVID-19 pandemic.

Hypothesis 2: The likelihood of accessing non-banking financing increased post-COVID-19, particularly in 2021 and 2022. This is also affected by Sectoral differences.

Hypothesis 3: Businesses' age and manager characteristics are significant factors that allows the firm to access both banking and non-banking financing.

3 METHODOLOGY

This section shows the data, variables, econometric models, and methodological model utilized to investigate the determinants of non-banking financing for microbusinesses in Colombia. The analysis seek to estimate the influence of rural residency, economic sector, and firm characteristics on the propensity to secure informal versus formal non-banking financing. Research on SMEs' non-banking financing encompasses various methodologies, including firm-level surveys (Cowling et al., 2016; Ferrando & Ganoulis, 2020), panel data analyses (Demirgüç-Kunt & Maksimovic, 1998; McGuinness & Hogan, 2016), and cross-country comparisons (Levine et al., 2018). This methodological diversity allows a better comprehension of SMEs' financing difficulties while discovering the complexity of deriving universal conclusions. We conduct a series of multinomial logistic regressions, systematically incorporating control variables to affirm the robustness of the findings.

3.1.1 Data

The information for this examination derives from a nationally representative inquiry of microenterprises in Colombia conducted by the Departamento Nacional de Estadistica (DANE). The dataset encompasses comprehensive details regarding firm attributes, the socioeconomic background of proprietors, and financial behavior. The data covers a span of three years, specifically 2019, 2021, and 2022, furnishing a pre- and post-pandemic outlook. A total of 205,796 instances are utilized in the analysis, which is adjusted using the supplied expansion factors to accommodate for survey design and ensure representativeness. The analysis also aggregates standard errors by county to address within-region correlation.

3.1.2 Access to Non-Banking Financing model

This paper will utilize two models. The first model will assess access to non-banking financing by categorizing microbusinesses accordingly:

- Category 0: No financing access (base category).
- Category 1: Access to banking financing.
- Category 2: Access to non-banking financing (Supplier Credit, Pawn Shop, Microfinance Institutions, Informal Lenders, Family or Friends, or others).

Key independent variables will include temporal and geographical effects, where temporal variables will reflect financing changes pre- and post-pandemic. Additionally, an interaction of year and rural residency will be included to evaluate the pandemic's differential impact on rural versus urban businesses.

A quick view of the percentage of firms accessing banking financing (1) and non-banking financing (2) across four key sectors is projected in table 1. Urban firms generally report higher access to both banking and non-banking financing across sectors, with Retail and Industry showing the highest percentages of access to banking financing (13.77% and 11.36%, respectively) in 2019. However, this access appears to decline across all sectors in 2021, with Retail dropping to 8.77% and Industry to 6.83%. Despite a slight recovery in 2022, banking financing access remains below pre-pandemic levels in most sectors.

To progressively refine the models, a series of control variables are added to give robustness to the estimation. We include a categorical variable that classifies businesses into 12 sectors following the CIIU Rev. 4 standard. These sectors include agriculture, manufacturing, construction, commerce, transportation, services, and more. The number of workers employed by the business, used as a proxy for business size. Other variable related with the firm is the register of the firm and the number of years the business has been operating, categorized as 1-2 years, 3-4 years, 5-9 years, and 10+ years. We also include owner characteristics like the gender, age and saving behavior and the main geographical location of the firm.

3.1.3 Econometric Model

To analyze the probability of accessing non-banking financing, we estimate multinomial logistic regression models. The multinomial logit model is appropriate given the categorical nature of the dependent variable with more than two outcomes (informal financing, formal non-banking financing, no financing). This approach allows us to estimate the relative risk ratios (RRR) of accessing each financing category compared to the base category (no financing).

The general form of the multinomial logit model is as follows:

$$\Pr(Y = j) = \frac{\exp(X\beta_j}{1 + \sum_{k=1}^{2} \exp(X\beta_k)}$$

where Y represents the non-banking financing outcome (0 = no financing, 1 = banking financing, 2 = non-banking financing), X is the vector of explanatory variables, and β are the coefficients for each category j. The base outcome is Category 0 (no financing), and the coefficients are interpreted relative to this baseline. We also test for the significance of the interaction between year and rural residency to determine whether the pandemic's impact on financing differed across urban and rural areas

The estimation was made in Stata 16. Several robustness checks and diagnostic tests are conducted to ensure the validity and stability of the results. By gradually introducing control variables, we verify that the key relationships hold even after accounting for additional factors. This also helps identify whether omitted variables in earlier models biased the results.

- *Model 1:* The first model includes the interaction between year and rural residency, examining how access to financing changes over time and across geographic regions.
- *Model 2:* The second model adds regional controls to account for differences in financing patterns across Colombia's departments.
- *Model 3:* The third model introduces sectoral controls and business age, allowing for a deeper understanding of how industry and firm maturity influence financing decisions.
- *Model 4:* The final model is the most comprehensive, incorporating personal characteristics of the business owner (gender, age, savings behavior), and workforce size, alongside the variables included in the earlier models.

Each model is estimated using survey weights to ensure national representativeness and clustered standard errors by county to account for within-region correlation in financing behavior. These also ensure that the standard errors are reliable despite variations in variance across observations.

The dataset used in this analysis contains very few missing observations. In cases where data are missing, observations are dropped, and the results are checked for consistency across models. Given the large sample size, this approach ensures that the results remain robust and unaffected by any missing values.

4 RESULTS

The multinomial logistic regression results presented in table show a shift in financing patterns over the post pandemic period. SMEs were 35% less likely to access banking financing in both 2021 and 2022 compared to the pre-pandemic baseline. Conversely, access to non-banking financing increased substantially, with SMEs being 71.1% more likely to utilize these sources in the same period. This stark contrast suggests a substitution effect, with SMEs turning to alternative financing sources as traditional banking options became less accessible or desirable during the pandemic. About the interaction terms, the ratios for banking financing are no significant, suggesting that rural businesses, during the post pandemic period, were neither more nor less likely to access to banking financing compared to urban businesses. Still, for the category of non-banking financing, the odds ratio is 0.696 ($p < 0.05$), meaning rural businesses were 30.4% less likely to access formal non-banking financing compared to urban businesses in 2021. This indicates that in the aftermath of the pandemic's early phase, rural businesses had more difficulty or were less inclined to rely on formal non-banking financing compared to their urban counterparts. The coefficients are consistent across models.

Table 1. Multinomial Logistic Regression with Odds Ratios

	Model 1		Model 2		Model 3		Model 4	
Variable	Cat 1	Cat 2	Cat 1	Cat 2	Cat 1	Cat 2	Cat 1	Cat 2
YEAR (2021)	0.652***	1.711***	0.651***	1.712***	0.647***	1.713***	0.672***	1.703***
	(0.041)	(0.039)	(0.041)	(0.039)	(0.041)	(0.035)	(0.040)	(0.035)
YEAR (2022)	0.683***	1.645***	0.677***	1.671***	0.650***	1.626***	0.725***	1.626***
	(0.034)	(0.034)	(0.034)	(0.035)	(0.035)	(0.035)	(0.034)	(0.035)
Rural	1.167***	0.852**	1.152***	0.847**	1.152***	0.848**	1.155***	0.851**
	(0.041)	(0.069)	(0.041)	(0.069)	(0.053)	(0.070)	(0.057)	(0.075)
YEAR × Rural (2021)	1.080	0.732**	1.080	0.734**	1.023	0.699***	0.995	0.696***
	(0.075)	(0.099)	(0.077)	(0.099)	(0.077)	(0.086)	(0.091)	(0.086)
YEAR × Rural (2022)	1.008	0.835**	0.993	0.837**	0.979	0.767***	0.984	0.762***
	(0.061)	(0.086)	(0.061)	(0.086)	(0.062)	(0.086)	(0.063)	(0.088)
Age (1-2 years)	-	-	0.856	-	0.919	-	1.013	-
	-	-	(0.089)	-	(0.089)	-	(0.090)	-
Age (3-4 years)	-	-	1.151	0.856**	1.073	0.783**	1.053	0.729**
	-	-	(0.085)	(0.085)	(0.085)	(0.090)	(0.072)	(0.092)
Age (5-9 years)	-	-	1.025***	0.743***	1.153**	0.788**	1.177***	0.775**
	-	-	(0.053)	(0.053)	(0.090)	(0.072)	(0.097)	(0.072)
Age (10+ years)	-	-	1.213**	0.601**	1.276***	0.570***	1.238***	0.579**
	-	-	(0.085)	(0.067)	(0.086)	(0.067)	(0.087)	(0.067)
Sex of Owner	-	-	-	-	-	-	1.005	1.002
	-	-	-	-	-	-	(0.053)	(0.052)
Age of Owner	-	-	-	-	-	-	1.015***	1.011**
	-	-	-	-	-	-	(0.001)	(0.001)
Savings	-	-	-	-	-	-	0.775**	0.815**
	-	-	-	-	-	-	(0.075)	(0.065)
Personal	-	-	-	-	-	-	1.448***	1.122***
	-	-	-	-	-	-	(0.070)	(0.070)
Constant	0.159***	0.074***	0.136***	0.064***	0.145***	0.053***	0.082***	0.041***
	(0.022)	(0.027)	(0.022)	(0.027)	(0.027)	(0.027)	(0.130)	(0.013)
Observations	205,796		205,796		205,796		205,796	
Pseudo R-squared	0.0103		0.0123		0.0676		0.0795	

- Odds Ratios reported, with Standard Errors in parentheses.
- Significance levels: * $p < 0.1$, ** $p < 0.05$, *** $p < 0.01$.

The age of SMEs emerges as a critical factor, particularly for non-banking financing. While age showed no statistically significant effect on access to banking finance, older SMEs consistently demonstrated lower odds of opting for non-banking financing compared to the youngest cohort. This is consistent with the idea that older businesses, with more established credit histories and assets, have a greater ability to secure loans from banks. This trend becomes more pronounced with increasing age, suggesting that younger SMEs may be more adept at or inclined towards utilizing alternative financing sources. This inference is confirmed by the magnitude of the odds ratio for the category two around 0.775 ($p < 0.1$), meaning that businesses aged 5–9 years were 22.5% less likely to access formal non-banking financing compared to new businesses. Its also suggests that formal non-banking institutions may prioritize younger or newer businesses for financing.

Our analysis indicates that certain personal characteristics of SME owners or managers significantly influence financing access. These characteristics increased the likelihood of accessing both banking (44.8% more likely) and non-banking financing (12.1% more likely), highlighting the importance of individual factors in determining financing outcomes.

While not fully elaborated in the provided table, our analysis hints at significant sectoral differences in financing access. For instance, manufacturing SMEs showed lower odds of accessing banking financing compared to the agricultural sector. Conversely, sectors like accommodation and food services demonstrated higher odds of accessing non-banking financing. These findings underscore the heterogeneous impact of the pandemic across different economic sectors and their varying ability to secure financial resources.

The number of workers in a company positively influences access to both types of financing. Larger SMEs are 44.8% more likely to access banking finance and 12.1% more likely to access non-banking finance compared to their smaller counterparts. This suggests that having more employees may signal greater stability or capacity to lenders, facilitating easier access to various forms of financing.

Interestingly, while a company's age doesn't significantly affect its access to banking finance, it plays a notable role in non-banking finance access. Compared to the youngest firms (0-2 years old), older firms consistently show lower odds of accessing non-banking financing. This effect becomes more pronounced with age, with the oldest category (10+ years) being 39.9% less likely to use non-banking finance sources. This trend might indicate that younger firms are more adaptable or open to alternative financing options, possibly due to difficulties in accessing traditional bank loans or a greater willingness to explore innovative funding sources.

Summarizing we can answer the hypothesis statement previously. The results support Hypothesis 1, as rural SMEs were 30.4% less likely to access formal non-banking financing in 2021 compared to urban SMEs. This finding is significant ($p < 0.05$) and suggests that rural businesses faced greater challenges in accessing non-banking financing during the pandemic. However, the interaction term for banking financing was not significant, indicating that rural businesses did not differ significantly from urban businesses in terms of access to traditional banking financing.

Hypothesis 2 is also confirmed. The findings show that SMEs were 71.1% more likely to access non-banking financing in the post-pandemic period, particularly in 2021 and 2022, compared to the pre-pandemic baseline. This suggests a significant shift towards non-banking financing as traditional banking options became less available or desirable. Furthermore, the results indicate significant sectoral differences, with certain sectors, such as accommodation and food services, showing higher odds of accessing non-banking financing compared to sectors like manufacturing, which were more likely to rely on traditional banking options.

The results partly support Hypothesis 3. Younger SMEs were more likely to utilize non-banking financing, with businesses aged 5–9 years being 22.5% less likely to access formal non-banking financing compared to newer businesses. Manager characteristics, such as gender, were significant, with male business owners more likely to access both banking (44.8% more likely) and non-banking (12.1% more likely) financing. These findings confirm that personal characteristics play a crucial role in determining financing outcomes.

These findings highlight the complex interplay between firm characteristics and financing access. While larger firms generally have an advantage in accessing all types of finance, younger firms appear more inclined towards non-banking alternatives. This nuanced understanding is crucial for policymakers and financial institutions aiming to support SMEs across different stages of their lifecycle and size categories

5 DISCUSSION

Our results highlight key differences in access to financing. Rural SMEs need more barriers in non-banking funding compared to urban SMEs. Younger firms rely more on non-banking sources, while older firms prefer traditional bank loans. Male-owned businesses are more likely to access both banking and non-banking financing.

Policymakers need to address rural-urban financial inequalities. Access to non-banking finance is vital for rural businesses. Governments should expand microfinance and fintech services in rural areas. They should also offer incentives for non-banking institutions to serve these regions. Supporting younger businesses through targeted non-banking finance programs can boost their growth.

Gender disparities in finance access also require attention. Programs should reduce the gap between male and female business owners. Offering targeted financial literacy programs and reducing biases in lending practices could address this issue.

Future studies should explore how different sectors respond to non-banking finance. Examining the long-term impact of non-banking finance on business performance will also provide valuable insights. Finally, understanding how cultural and regional factors affect access to finance will contribute to more inclusive financial policies.

6 CONCLUSION

This study looks at how Colombia's small and medium-sized enterprises (SMEs) got financing during the COVID-19 pandemic. We focused on the differences between rural and urban businesses. We used survey data and statistical models to understand what factors affected SMEs' ability to get bank loans or other types of financing.

Our research adds new knowledge about SME financing in emerging economies. We examined how the pandemic, location, and business traits affect financing options. This is the first study to examine these factors for Colombian SMEs during the pandemic.

We found that rural SMEs had a more challenging time getting non-bank financing than urban SMEs, especially early in the pandemic recovery. However, rural and urban SMEs used more non-bank financing after the pandemic. We also found that a business's age, owner traits, industry, and size affected its financing chances.

These findings concern policymakers, banks, and SME support programs in Colombia and similar countries. The study underscores the need to address the financial inclusion gap between rural and urban SMEs, promote a diverse financial ecosystem that can support businesses during crises, and develop nuanced, sector-specific support mechanisms. Creating specific support tools for different industries and business sizes

The limitation of this paper is that the model does not account for unobserved factors, such as SME management quality or external market shocks, which may have influenced both financing access and business outcomes. Future research could explore these factors through more advanced econometric techniques, such as instrumental variable (IV) estimation or fixed-effects modeling.

The limitations of this study include its focus on a single country and reliance on survey data. Future research could expand on this work by conducting similar analyses across multiple countries or regions to determine the generalizability of the results and incorporating additional firm-level variables, such as profitability or debt levels, to provide a more comprehensive understanding of SME financing decisions. Finally undertaking longitudinal studies to track the long-term effects of non-banking financing on business survival and growth and exploring the optimal mix of banking and non-banking financing for SMEs in different sectors and stages of development.

In conclusion, this study shows how non-bank financing helped Colombian SMEs recover from the COVID-19 pandemic. Understanding what affects financing access can help create better strategies to support SMEs in both rural and urban areas. This research opens the door for more studies on SME financing in emerging economies and adds to discussions about financial inclusion and economic recovery during global crises.

REFERENCES

Aghion, P., Fally, T., & Scarpetta, S. (2005). Credit constraints as a barrier to the entry and post-entry growth of firms. *Economic Policy*, *20*(42), 731–779.

Baral, M. M., Singh, R., & Kazancoglu, Y. (2021). Analysis of factors impacting survivability of sustainable supply chain during COVID-19 pandemic: An empirical study in the context of SMEs. *International Journal of Logistics Management*. Advance online publication. DOI: 10.1108/IJLM-04-2021-0198

Bartik, A. W., Bertrand, M., Lin, F., Rothstein, J., & Unrath, M. (2020). *Measuring the labor market at the onset of the COVID-19 crisis* (Working Paper 27613). National Bureau of Economic Research. DOI: 10.3386/w27613

Beck, T., Demirguc-Kunt, A., & Maksimovic, V. (2005). Financial and legal constraints to firm growth: Does size matter? *The Journal of Finance*, *60*(1), 137–177. DOI: 10.1111/j.1540-6261.2005.00727.x

Berg, G., & Schrader, J. (2012). Access to credit, natural disasters, and relationship lending. *Journal of Financial Intermediation*, *21*(4), 549–568. DOI: 10.1016/j.jfi.2012.05.003

Cabral, L. M. B., & Mata, J. (2003). On the evolution of the firm size distribution: Facts and theory. *The American Economic Review*, *93*(4), 1075–1090. DOI: 10.1257/000282803769206205

Calabrese, R., Girardone, C., & Sclip, A. (2021). Financial fragmentation and SMEs' access to finance. *Small Business Economics*, *57*(4), 2041–2065. DOI: 10.1007/s11187-020-00393-1

Carbo-Valverde, S., Rodriguez-Fernandez, F., & Udell, G. F. (2016). Trade credit, the financial crisis, and SME access to finance. *Journal of Money, Credit and Banking*, *48*(1), 113–143. DOI: 10.1111/jmcb.12292

Chisasa, J., & Makina, D. (2015). Bank credit and agricultural output in South Africa: Cointegration, short run dynamics and causality. *Journal of Applied Business Research*, *31*(2), 489. DOI: 10.19030/jabr.v31i2.9148

Cowling, M., Liu, W., & Zhang, N. (2016). Access to bank finance for UK SMEs in the wake of the recent financial crisis. *International Journal of Entrepreneurial Behaviour & Research*, *22*(6), 903–932. DOI: 10.1108/IJEBR-06-2015-0126

Degryse, H., Lu, L., & Ongena, S. (2013). Informal or formal financing? Or both? First evidence on the co-funding of Chinese firms. *First Evidence on the Co-Funding of Chinese Firms (June 18, 2013). BOFIT Discussion Paper, 14.*

Demirgüç-Kunt, A., & Maksimovic, V. (1998). Law, finance, and firm growth. *The Journal of Finance*, *53*(6), 2107–2137. DOI: 10.1111/0022-1082.00084

Dörr, J. O., Licht, G., & Murmann, S. (2021). Small firms and the COVID-19 insolvency gap. *Small Business Economics*, •••, 1–31. DOI: 10.1007/s11187-021-00514-4

Engidaw, A. E. (2022). Small businesses and their challenges during COVID-19 pandemic in developing countries: In the case of Ethiopia. *Journal of Innovation and Entrepreneurship*, *11*(1), 1. Advance online publication. DOI: 10.1186/s13731-021-00191-3

Fairlie, R. W., Fairlie, R. W., Fairlie, R. W., & Fossen, F. M. (2021). The early impacts of the COVID-19 pandemic on business sales. *Small Business Economics*, •••, 1–12. DOI: 10.1007/s11187-021-00479-4

Ferrando, A., & Ganoulis, I. (2020). Firms' expectations on access to finance at the early stages of the COVID-19 pandemic. *European Central Bank Working Paper Series, 2446.*

Fisman, R., & Raturi, M. (2004). Does Competition Encourage Credit Provision? Evidence from African Trade Credit Relationships. *The Review of Economics and Statistics*, *86*(3), 545–554. DOI: 10.1162/003465304323023859

Fouejieu, M. A., Ndoye, A., & Sydorenko, T. (2020). *Unlocking access to finance for SMEs: A cross-country analysis*. International Monetary Fund. DOI: 10.5089/9781513536156.001

Getman, R., Helmi, M., Roberts, H., Yansane, A., Cutler, D., & Seymour, B. (2018). Vaccine Hesitancy and Online Information: The Influence of Digital Networks. *Health Education & Behavior*, *45*(4), 599–606. DOI: 10.1177/1090198117739673

Gur, F. A. (2012). Financial constraints, growth opportunities, and firm size: Evidence from Turkey. *International Journal of Economics and Finance*, *4*(2), 53–68.

Hossain, M. R., Akhter, F., & Sultana, M. M. (2022). SMEs in Covid-19 Crisis and Combating Strategies: A Systematic Literature Review (SLR) and A Case from Emerging Economy. *Operations Research Perspectives*, *9*, 100222. DOI: 10.1016/j.orp.2022.100222

Hsu, P.-H., Tian, X., & Xu, Y. (2014). Financial development and innovation: Cross-country evidence. *Journal of Financial Economics*, *112*(1), 116–135. DOI: 10.1016/j.jfineco.2013.12.002

Khwaja, A. I., & Mian, A. (2008). Tracing the impact of bank liquidity shocks: Evidence from an emerging market. *The American Economic Review*, *98*(4), 1413–1442. DOI: 10.1257/aer.98.4.1413

Kumar, A., Singh, K. M., & Sinha, S. (2010). Institutional credit to agriculture sector in India: Status, performance and determinants. *Agricultural Economics Research Review*, *23*(2), 253–264. DOI: 10.1177/0971344120100206

Laeven, L., Levine, R., & Michalopoulos, S. (2015). Financial innovation and endogenous growth. *Journal of Financial Intermediation*, *24*(1), 1–24. DOI: 10.1016/j.jfi.2014.04.001

Levine, R. (2005). Finance and growth: Theory and evidence. In P. Aghion & S. N. Durlauf (Eds.), *Handbook of Economic Growth* (Vol. 1A, pp. 865–934). Elsevier.

Levine, R., Lin, C., & Xie, W. (2018). Corporate resilience to banking crises: The roles of trust and trade credit. *Journal of Financial and Quantitative Analysis*, *53*(4), 1441–1477. DOI: 10.1017/S0022109018000224

Manova, K. (2013). Credit constraints, heterogeneous firms, and international trade. *The Review of Economic Studies*, *80*(2), 711–744. DOI: 10.1093/restud/rds036

McDermott, T. K. J., Barry, F., & Tol, R. S. J. (2014). Disasters and development: Natural disasters, credit constraints, and economic growth. *Oxford Economic Papers*, *66*(3), 750–773. DOI: 10.1093/oep/gpt034

McGuinness, G., & Hogan, T. (2016). Bank credit and trade credit: Evidence from SMEs over the financial crisis. *International Small Business Journal*, *34*(4), 412–445. DOI: 10.1177/0266242614558314

Nilsen, J. C. K. (2002). Trade Credit and the Bank Lending Channel. *Journal of Money, Credit and Banking*, *34*(1), 226–253. DOI: 10.1353/mcb.2002.0032

Pedauga, L. E., Sáez, F., & Delgado-Márquez, B. L. (2021). Macroeconomic lockdown and SMEs: The impact of the COVID-19 pandemic in Spain. *Small Business Economics*, •••, 1–24. DOI: 10.1007/s11187-021-00476-7

Petersen, M. A., & Rajan, R. G. (1994). The benefits of lending relationships: Evidence from small business data. *The Journal of Finance*, *49*(1), 3–37. DOI: 10.1111/j.1540-6261.1994.tb04418.x

Petersen, M. A., & Rajan, R. G. (1997). Trade Credit: Theories and Evidence. *Review of Financial Studies*, *10*(3), 661–691. DOI: 10.1093/rfs/10.3.661

Prada, S. I., Garcia-Garcia, M. P., & Guzman, J. (2022). COVID-19 response in Colombia: Hits and misses. *Health Policy and Technology*, *11*(2), 100621. DOI: 10.1016/j.hlpt.2022.100621

Rajan, R. G., & Zingales, L. (1998). Financial dependence and growth. *The American Economic Review*, *88*(3), 559–586.

Sriyono, B., Biduri, S., & Proyogi, B. (2021). Acceleration of performance recovery and competitiveness through non-banking financing in SMEs based on green economy: Impact of Covid-19 pandemic. *Journal of Innovation and Entrepreneurship*, *10*(1), 27. DOI: 10.1186/s13731-021-00166-4

Stiglitz, J. E., & Weiss, A. (1981). Credit rationing in markets with imperfect information. *The American Economic Review*, *71*(3), 393–410.

Tagoe, N., Nyarko, E., & Anuwa-Amarh, E. (2005). Financial challenges facing urban SMEs under financial sector liberalization in Ghana. *Journal of Small Business Management*, *43*(3), 331–343. DOI: 10.1111/j.1540-627X.2005.00140.x

Yadav, P., & Sharma, A. K. (2015). Agriculture credit in developing economies: A review of relevant literature. *International Journal of Economics and Finance*, *7*(12), 219–244. DOI: 10.5539/ijef.v7n12p219

Chapter 8
Strengthening Micro and Small Enterprises' (MSEs) Dynamic Capabilities Through Digital Transformation in the VUCA Era

Lucky Nugroho
http://orcid.org/0000-0002-9613-1667
Universitas Mercu Buana, Indonesia

ABSTRACT

Digital transformation is a strategic imperative for Micro and Small Enterprises (MSEs) in the VUCA era, marked by volatility, uncertainty, complexity, and ambiguity. This chapter addresses the gap between the urgency for digital adaptation and MSEs' readiness in technology, behavior, and policy by applying Dynamic Capabilities Theory (DCT) to explain how sensing, seizing, and transforming processes enhance adaptability. Using a qualitative synthesis of literature and field practices, the study identifies key success determinants: adoption of AI, IoT, and Big Data; digital behavioral readiness; inclusive public policy; and integration of ESG and CSR values. Findings highlight that effective transformation requires synergy between internal capacity and external ecosystem support through partnerships, funding, and training. The study extends DCT's application to MSEs, offering data-driven, behavioral, and policy strategies for sustainable transformation, and recommends a community-based, inclusive approach to bridge the digital divide and foster equitable growth in Indonesia.

DOI: 10.4018/979-8-3373-6053-9.ch008

BACKGROUND

Rapid social, economic, and technological changes have created new challenges for business actors worldwide, including in Indonesia (Adriansah et al., 2025; Ahmadin et al., 2023; Nugroho, 2023). The disruption phenomenon not only affects large companies but also has a significant impact on the sustainability of Micro and Small Enterprises (MSEs) (Nugroho, Utami, et al., 2024; Rani et al., 2023). The era we live in today is often described by the terms VUCA—Volatility, Uncertainty, Complexity, and Ambiguity—which was first introduced by the United States military to describe a strategic environment full of uncertainty and drastic change (Fasa & Febrianty, 2020; Nugroho, Mor, et al., 2024). Over time, the term was adopted by the business and management worlds to describe the new realities facing organizations across sectors. Volatility in the context of MSEs is reflected in rapid changes in consumer preferences, digitalization trends, and instability in raw material prices. Uncertainty arises due to global crises, such as the COVID-19 pandemic and geopolitical turmoil, which have a direct impact on market demand and supply chains. Complexity is increasing because MSE actors must now understand and manage various digital platforms, new technologies, and global competition. Meanwhile, ambiguity manifests itself in the form of confusion in decision-making due to a lack of valid information or rapidly changing data. In this context, the resilience and adaptability of MSEs are tested to the extreme.

This phenomenon demonstrates that the ability of MSEs to survive is no longer sufficient to rely solely on operational efficiency or conventional resources; they must also be able to build dynamic capabilities that enable them to respond to environmental changes quickly, innovatively, and strategically (Bai et al., 2021; Nugroho & Arafah, 2020). However, there is a gap between the environmental demands of VUCA and the actual capacity of MSEs. Many MSEs still face significant obstacles in implementing digital transformation, including limited technology literacy, insufficient capital, limited access to technology training and guidance, and organizational unpreparedness to manage data-driven change (Azizi et al., 2022; Irwansyah et al., 2021; Tambunan & Busnetti, 2024). On the other hand, technological developments such as Artificial Intelligence (AI), the Internet of Things (IoT), and Big Data present significant opportunities for MSEs to enhance their business position through more intelligent and efficient decision-making. Unfortunately, the adoption of this technology remains limited among small businesses in Indonesia, due to both technical and non-technical constraints. In addition, behavioral aspects such as attitudes towards technology, social norms in the business environment, and perceived behavioral control also influence the readiness of MSEs for complete digital transformation (Maria et al., 2022; Widodo et al., 2022). In addition to internal challenges, MSEs require the proper public policy support to undergo an inclusive and sustainable digital transformation. Policies such as digitalization incentives, technology-based coaching, and strengthening digital infrastructure should be targeted to accelerate the adoption of technology in MSEs, particularly those in rural areas or the economic periphery.

Furthermore, MSEs are now also faced with new demands to integrate ESG (Environmental, Social, and Governance) and CSR (Corporate Social Responsibility) principles in their business strategies. Digital transformation is not just about business efficiency and growth; it must also be aligned with the values of sustainability, social ethics, and environmental responsibility (Lin & Mao, 2023). Given the complexity of these challenges, a theoretical framework is needed that can explain how MSEs can systematically and sustainably build adaptive capacity. In this context, the Dynamic Capabilities Theory (DCT), developed by Teece (2007), and Teece et al. (1997), is highly relevant as the primary foundation for discussing the dynamics of MSEs' capabilities in the face of the VUCA era through digital transformation. This theory defines dynamic capability as the ability of an organization to consciously and systematically integrate, build, and reconfigure internal and external competencies in response to environmental changes. In other words, a company or organization—in this case, MSEs—is not enough to merely have resources, but must also possess capabilities that can adjust, combine, and reconstruct these resources to remain relevant in the face of uncertainty and ongoing changes. In practice, Teece (2007) divides dynamic capabilities into three main activities that can ilustrated as follows

Figure 1. Three Main Activities in Dynamic Capabilities Theory (DCT)

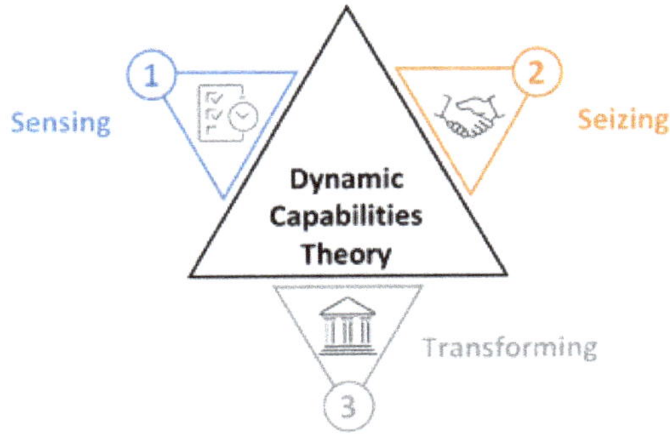

Source: Teece et al. (1997)

Moreover, according to figure 1, the explanation of three main activities in dynamic capabilities theory as follows:

- Sensing – recognizing and assessing opportunities and threats in the business environment;
- Seizing – mobilizing resources to pursue identified opportunities;
- Transforming – changing and reshaping the structure, culture, and business model to stay competitive.

For MSEs, sensing can mean the ability to read digital trends, understand changing consumer needs, and identify relevant technologies. Seizing includes efforts to invest in technology, develop human resource capacity, and establish strategic collaborations. Meanwhile, transformation requires MSEs to be able to rebuild business processes, work systems, and even organizational culture to align with the digital era and sustainability principles. DCT is also aligned with the ESG and CSR framework, as it encourages companies to adapt not only technically, but also socially and ethically. MSEs that apply sustainability principles in their digital transformation process will not only last longer but also gain stronger legitimacy from consumers and the public.

Furthermore, the DCT-based approach is also able to accommodate various external factors such as public policy, the role of the community, and digital networks as part of external enablers that support MSEs in building business resilience. This makes this theory not only a tool for academic analysis but also a basis for developing fundamental strategies for governments and other stakeholders. Therefore, the use of Dynamic Capabilities Theory in the discussion of this book chapter is the key to answering the six main questions that are the formulation of the problem, namely:

- How can MSEs build dynamic capabilities during the challenges of the VUCA era?
- How does digital transformation support the resilience of MSEs in the face of disruption?
- How are technologies such as AI, big data, and IoT used by MSEs for decision-making?
- How do attitudes, social norms, and behavioral controls affect the readiness of MSEs to digitalize?
- How can public policy accelerate inclusive and sustainable digital adoption for MSEs?
- How do MSEs integrate ESG and CSR principles in the digital transformation process?

Furthermore, following the formulation of the problem, this book chapter aims to:

- Analyze how MSEs can build dynamic capabilities in responding to the challenges of the VUCA era characterized by rapid change, uncertainty, complexity, and ambiguity.
- Analyzing how digital transformation can support MSEs' business resilience in the face of disruption
- Identifying technologies such as AI, big data, and IoT can be leveraged by MSEs for decision-making.
- Exploring behavioral factors, such as attitudes, social norms, and behavioral controls, that influence the readiness of technology adoption among MSEs.
- Evaluate relevant public policy support in accelerating the digitalization of MSEs inclusively and sustainably.
- Examining the integration of ESG and CSR values into the digital transformation process of MSEs as a business sustainability strategy.

Furthermore, this book chapter is expected to make both theoretical and practical contributions to understanding the dynamics of MSE adaptation in the VUCA era, as well as providing a basis for consideration by the government and policymakers in designing a more inclusive and adaptive MSE digitalization strategy. Recommendations developed through the DCT framework can be utilized to formulate digital training policies, provide incentives for technology adoption, establish a community-based digital ecosystem, and integrate ESG principles into MSE regulations. This book chapter also emphasizes the importance of public policies that are not only technocratic but also consider the behavioral and social aspects of MSE actors. The novelty of this paper lies in its approach, which unites the concept of dynamic capability with the context of MSEs in Indonesia as they face the challenges of the VUCA era. So far, the theory of Dynamic Capabilities has been more often applied on the scale of large companies. Still, this paper places it precisely in the micro and small business sectors, which are the most vulnerable to disruption. In addition, this approach not only focuses on technological aspects but also links them to behavioral readiness, the role of public policy, and the integration of sustainability values, such as ESG and CSR, in the digital transformation process. Thus, this paper offers a new perspective that is more comprehensive, contextual, and relevant to strengthen the resilience of MSEs strategically and sustainably.

THE INEVITABILITY OF MSES TO BUILD DYNAMIC CAPABILITIES AMID THE CHALLENGES OF THE VUCA ERA

Rapid change, high uncertainty, interconnection complexity, and information ambiguity are the hallmarks of the so-called VUCA era—Volatility, Uncertainty, Complexity, and Ambiguity. This phenomenon not only affects large corporations but also impacts the most vulnerable sector in the economy, namely Micro and Small Enterprises (MSEs). When the COVID-19 pandemic hit, MSEs in Indonesia experienced a drastic decline in turnover, disruptions in the supply of raw materials, and limited market access due to mobility restrictions. Although conditions have gradually improved, VUCA dynamics persist in other forms, such as technological disruptions, shifting digital consumer preferences, geopolitical tensions, and the climate crisis. In this context, MSEs are required not only to survive but also to adapt and build dynamic capabilities to remain relevant and competitive. Amid the onslaught of disruption, the Dynamic Capabilities Theory (DCT), introduced by Teece et al. (1997), became the proper theoretical framework for explaining how organizations, including MSEs, can manage change by building ever-evolving adaptive capacity. DCT emphasizes that long-term success does not depend solely on the resource-based view, but on the ability of organizations to integrate, rebuild, and reconfigure their competencies in response to a changing environment. Teece (2007) categorizes these dynamics into three dimensions: sensing (the ability to recognize opportunities and threats), seizing (the ability to mobilize resources to capitalize on opportunities), and transforming (the ability to reform organizational processes and structures to address environmental changes sustainably).

The application of DCT in the MSE sector is becoming increasingly relevant, given the limited capacity and flexibility of small-scale businesses, which makes them more vulnerable to external pressures. However, recent studies indicate that MSEs adopting a dynamic approach can create new competitive advantages. Research by Badakhshan et al. (2019), and Holman & Whitaker (2022) found that an organization's ability to reshape its business processes quickly is a significant factor in dealing with a volatile environment. In the context of Indonesian MSEs, a study by Hidayah et al. (2022), Minanari et al. (2024), and Zakiyah et al. (2022) shows that platform-based digitalization, the use of social media for marketing, and business community collaboration are tangible forms of the application of dynamic capabilities, especially in the sensing and seizing aspects.

Meanwhile, the characteristics of VUCA have been expanded in the post-pandemic academic literature. According to Shet (2024), Wang et al. (2022), and Zamzami et al. (2022), the VUCA challenge now emphasizes the importance of continuous learning, co-creation, and self-organization as a new approach to building resilience. Within the framework of DCT, this means that the transformation is not only structural, but also cultural. MSEs must be able to create an adaptive, collaborative, and data-based work culture. In practice, this is demonstrated through the ability of MSEs to evaluate market trends in real-time, respond quickly to changing customer preferences, and create new products or services based on technologies such as AI and IoT. For example, many food and beverage MSEs have managed to rise from the pandemic crisis because they quickly switched to online ordering services and digital payments (Maria et al., 2022). This shows the success of the sensing and seizing aspects. However, the biggest challenge lies in the transformation process—how MSEs transform traditional business models into more agile, technology-based, and sustainable models. At this point, the importance of systemic support from public policy and the digital ecosystem is evident.

The study by Dyduch et al. (2021) reinforces the importance of dynamic capabilities in vulnerable sectors. They note that drastic changes due to global uncertainties, such as the pandemic, have led to a surge in volatility across various industries, and only organizations with flexible structures and rapid learning capabilities can survive. Therefore, MSEs are required not only to rely on natural resilience or customer loyalty, but also to build a data-based adaptation system and digitalization. Furthermore, research by Doern (2014), and Osakwe et al. (2016) confirms that small organizations that actively develop sensing capabilities—through gathering market information and strengthening interactions with consumers—can strengthen the resilience of their businesses in the long run. This is important because many MSEs in Indonesia still face limitations in accessing data, technology, and competent human resources for data analysis (Gunawan & Winarto, 2024; Nugroho, Melzatia, et al., 2024). In practice, the application of technologies such as AI, big data analytics, and IoT cannot stand alone without organizational readiness (Nurdany et al., 2024). Therefore, the development of dynamic capabilities must be accompanied by a change in mindset and organizational culture that is open to learning. This aligns with a study by Cortellazzo et al. (2019), Gilch & Sieweke, (2020), and Wicaksono et al. (2024), which states that the success of digital transformation is highly dependent on elements of human behavior within the organization, rather than solely on its technological tools. Adaptive MSEs will prioritize a culture of learning, experimentation, and the courage to try new models, not just waiting for external help.

In the context of policy, the government needs to form a more integrated ecosystem to support the digital transformation of MSEs. Policies must encourage MSEs to enter the national digital supply chain through technology adoption incentives, digital skills training, and the formation of inter-MSE learning communities. A study by Machado et al. (2021) even shows that the role of policy is huge in encouraging the adoption of AI for sustainable decision-making in the MSME sector. Without inclusive and responsive policy interventions to the needs of the field, the process of strengthening dynamic capabilities will be slow and uneven. The relationship between DCT and sustainability values is also an important thing that is often overlooked in MSE studies. In an increasingly connected digital era, consumers not only demand speed and convenience, but also consider the ethical, environmental, and social aspects of the products they consume. Therefore, the integration of Environmental, Social, and Governance (ESG) and Corporate Social Responsibility (CSR) principles in the digital transformation of MSEs is no longer an option, but a must. DCT in this context serves as a tool to direct organizational change toward long-term sustainability by sensing new market values, seizing social-environmental opportunities, and transforming business processes to be more ethical and responsible.

Overall, this discussion demonstrates that the application of Dynamic Capabilities Theory in the context of Indonesian MSEs is a strategic and practical approach to addressing the challenges of the VUCA era. By linking this theory to actual phenomena such as digitalization, the post-pandemic crisis, and sustainability demands, MSEs can not only survive but also grow in an increasingly complex and uncertain economic ecosystem. This theory can also serve as a practical guide for MSEs, policymakers, and academics in designing long-term strategies that are not only adaptive but also competitive and sustainable.

DIGITAL TRANSFORMATION ENHANCES THE BUSINESS RESILIENCE OF MSES IN THE FACE OF DISRUPTION.

Uncertainty has become an integral part of today's business dynamics, especially in the Micro and Small Enterprises (MSEs) ecosystem, which is very vulnerable to external changes. The disruptions that come one after another—both technological, social, and economic—force MSE actors not only to survive but also to build a solid foundation for adaptation and development. It is in this context that digital transformation becomes more than just a tool for operations. It has become a catalyst for change and a source of business strength. On closer inspection, this process can be explained in depth through the lens of Dynamic Capabilities Theory, which emphasizes the importance of an organization's capacity to continuously adapt and reconfigure its competencies amid a rapidly changing environment. The phenomenon of disruption is no longer something surprising, but has become a daily reality. The COVID-19 pandemic has become an obvious turning point in how MSEs that previously relied on conventional business models must change drastically to survive. Many business actors who initially relied on physical stores began to switch to digital platforms, application-based delivery services, and digital payment systems. However, digital transformation is not enough to stop at the adoption of surface technologies. More important is how the process creates new capabilities to read opportunities, respond quickly, and reshape business strategies across the board. This is the essence of dynamic capabilities discussed by Teece et al. (1997), where sensing, seizing, and transforming capabilities are the main components in maintaining competitiveness and business resilience.

Therefore, through their sensing skills, MSEs are required to recognize signals of market changes, understand evolving customer needs, and pay attention to relevant digital trends. In the age of abundant data, access to information is no longer a significant problem. The challenge lies precisely in how MSE actors can filter, understand, and interpret data into strategic insights. This is where technologies such as Big Data and Artificial Intelligence (AI) play a crucial role. With increasingly sophisticated analytics capabilities, MSEs can predict purchasing trends, identify new market segments, and even design more targeted marketing strategies. A study by Dong et al. (2016), and Wong & Ngai (2023) demonstrates that data-driven sensing capabilities can enhance business adaptability in responding to economic crises and technological disruptions. Once the opportunity is identified, the next crucial step is to seize it. At this stage, MSEs need to be able to mobilize resources, both human, capital, and infrastructure, to respond quickly and efficiently to existing opportunities. Digital transformation supports this stage through the adoption of technologies such as the Internet of Things (IoT), e-commerce platforms, and small-scale Enterprise Resource Planning (ERP) systems, which enable process automation, cost efficiency, and increased productivity. For example, MSEs in the culinary sector that implement digital ordering systems and application-based logistics integration have proven to be able to maintain sales volumes during crisis times. This is reinforced by research by (Browder et al., 2023; Kretschmer & Khashabi, 2020), which states that small organizations that successfully integrate digital technology in their operations have a higher chance of surviving amid market shocks. However, the most challenging stage in the dynamic capability framework is transforming—that is, how MSEs reshape organizational processes, structures, and cultures to align with the demands of the digital age. This is where many MSEs stutter, because the transformation process requires a change in mentality, long-term investment, and the courage to abandon old habits. This transformation involves changing business models from previously linear to more digital ecosystem-based, altering leadership structures to be more agile and collaborative, and implementing a culture of continuous learning. The study by Panjaitan (2022), and Nugroho (2022) said that transforming will only be effective if MSEs also build organizational learning capacity and adopt the principle of co-creation in responding to external challenges.

In reality, the digital transformation process is also closely tied to the social and cultural context. Many MSEs operate in a community environment with a distinctive value system, including a preference for face-to-face relationships, family management patterns, and reliance on informal resources. Therefore, the success of digital transformation requires a contextual and participatory approach. Digital training, for example, will be more effective if it is tailored to the specific needs of the business sector, uses local language, and is directly linked to the daily challenges faced by business actors. This finding aligns with the research results of Choerudin et al. (2023), and Nugroho & Tamala (2018), which emphasize the importance of a community-based approach in supporting MSE digital literacy. It is also important to note that successful digital transformation is not only determined by internal factors of MSEs, but also highly dependent on their supporting ecosystems. The government has a strategic role in building equitable digital infrastructure, creating inclusive regulations, and providing incentives for technology adoption. In addition, the role of private partners, such as technology startups, digital platforms, and microfinance institutions, is crucial in expanding MSEs' access to relevant and affordable digital solutions. This cross-actor collaboration creates a kind of 'external capability' that strengthens the resilience of MSEs from the outside. This aligns with Teece (2007) notion that dynamic capabilities are not always internal, but are also influenced by interactions and collaborations within external networks.

The context of sustainability is also increasingly demanding that the digital transformation carried out by MSEs not only enhances business efficiency but also supports the principles of social and environmental responsibility. In this case, the integration of ESG (Environmental, Social, Governance) values in the practice of digital MSEs is becoming increasingly relevant. Technology can facilitate transparent social impact reporting, drive energy efficiency, and foster fairer relationships with partners and customers. Business resilience is not only measured in terms of profitability, but also in terms of the extent to which MSEs can survive ethically and sustainably in the midst of the complexity of the modern business world. When MSEs effectively combine sensing, seizing, and transforming capabilities with the support of digital technology and a strong ecosystem, business resilience is no longer just a hope, but a reality. Digital transformation is a sustainable process that strengthens the business foundation to face various forms of disruption in the future, including technological, economic, and social changes. With a Dynamic Capabilities Theory-based approach, MSEs have a strong framework to not only understand change but also reshape themselves as resilient, innovative, and relevant actors in the ever-changing business landscape.

MSES USE TECHNOLOGIES SUCH AS AI, BIG DATA, AND IOT FOR DECISION-MAKING.

In an era marked by uncertainty and rapid change, micro and small enterprises (MSEs) face significant challenges in maintaining their sustainability and competitiveness. The VUCA phenomenon—Volatility, Uncertainty, Complexity, and Ambiguity—has become a widely used conceptual framework for describing the contemporary business environment. MSEs as the dominant sector in the national economic structure need to adapt to this dynamic through technology-based strategies. This is where the role of digital transformation becomes very vital, especially with the emergence of technologies such as Artificial Intelligence (AI), Internet of Things (IoT), and Big Data, which can be optimized as catalysts for more agile, predictive, and data-driven decision-making. Digital transformation is no longer just an option; it has become a strategic necessity inherent in the MSE business process. Digital technology allows MSEs to access market information in real-time, monitor consumer trends, and manage operations and supply chains efficiently. The use of AI, for example, can help MSEs in forecasting market demand, automating customer service, and analyzing consumer behavior. Meanwhile, IoT enables the monitoring of production or logistics equipment, helping to create a work system that is responsive to changing business environmental conditions. Big Data enables MSEs to process large volumes of data from various sources, yielding in-depth business insights, and thus making decision-making more evidence-based.

However, the main challenge in implementing this technology is the internal readiness of the MSE organization, particularly in terms of digital capabilities, human resources, and the adaptive decision-making process structure. Therefore, Dynamic Capabilities Theory is a relevant approach to understanding how MSEs can develop the ability to sense environmental changes (sensing), seize opportunities, and reconfigure internal resources (reconfiguring) to remain relevant and competitive amid market turbulence. Sensing capabilities are the first and crucial step for MSEs in building technology-based excellence. In this context, AI and Big Data technology play an essential role in detecting consumer behavior patterns, competitor movements, and changes in market trends. By applying machine learning algorithms, MSEs can obtain predictive information that was previously only accessible to large companies. For example, through social media analytics, MSEs can monitor customer sentiment towards their products and adjust promotional strategies in real-time. This creates anticipatory capabilities that were previously difficult to realize in conventional ways. A study by Jin et al. (2023) demonstrates that the application of AI and Big Data in the MSE manufacturing sector can enhance responsiveness to demand dynamics and help prevent overproduction or excess inventory.

Within the framework of Dynamic Capabilities, after MSEs recognize the existence of digital opportunities, the next step is to seize or take advantage of these opportunities concretely. IoT technology can play a role in this stage, particularly in the production process and supply chain management. Through sensor devices and continuous connectivity, MSEs can optimize the production process, detect early disturbances in the machine system, and efficiently manage the delivery of goods.

The implementation of IoT has been proven to help reduce operational costs and increase productivity, particularly in the agribusiness and household industries. As an illustration, a local food processing MSE using IoT sensors can automatically adjust the temperature of the refrigerant according to food safety standards, thereby reducing the risk of damage and lowering storage costs. In addition, Big Data Analytics-based technology supports the seizing process through more accurate mapping of customer preferences. MSEs can segment the market more precisely based on purchasing behavior, geographical location, and customer digital interaction. Thus, marketing strategies and product offerings can be tailored to better align with the needs of target consumers. Research from Kitchin & McArdle (2016), and Sanchez-Hughet et al. (2022) confirms that Big Data-based analytics help small organizations develop a competitive advantage by providing a granular understanding of the market, which previously could only be achieved by large companies with strong market research capabilities.

Furthermore, within the framework of Dynamic Capabilities, transformation is the ability to reconfigure organizational structures, internal processes, and business strategies to suit the demands of a new environment. This is where the biggest challenge for MSEs lies. Although technologies such as AI, Big Data, and IoT are available, not all MSEs can completely overhaul their work processes. This transformation requires not only technical understanding but also a change in organizational mindset and culture. Many MSEs still rely on intuition in decision-making, while the data they have has not been utilized optimally. The literature shows that companies that successfully adopt a data-driven approach have better business resilience in the face of crises and market volatility(Adekola & Clelland, 2019). The use of technology to transform MSE business processes requires a vital role from business leaders. Digital leadership that is adaptive and open to learning is a determining factor for the success of this change. MSE leaders need to have the ability to recognize the potential of technology, build a digital vision, and involve the entire team in the change process. In practice, this can start with small steps, such as integrating a cloud-based Point of Sale (POS) system to monitor daily transactions in real-time, connecting the inventory system to sales, and automating financial reports. That way, business decisions can be made with accurate and up-to-date data, rather than relying solely on estimates or outdated habits. A study by Mikalef et al. (2019) confirms that the success of digital transformation depends on the organization's capabilities in managing data, developing digital infrastructure, and fostering an analytics-based culture. For MSEs, this means building a simple yet effective information system, familiarizing staff with the use of digital dashboards, and utilizing data as a tool for reflection and learning. This transformation may not occur instantly, but it can begin with gradual steps tailored to the business's capacity and characteristics.

Furthermore, the integration between AI, IoT, and Big Data not only strengthens decision-making at the strategic level but also drives operational efficiency at the micro level. For example, the use of AI for product recommendations can be applied to local e-commerce sites owned by MSEs, allowing customers to enjoy a more personalized shopping experience. IoT can be used to monitor energy usage and reduce waste, while Big Data helps compile automated financial reports and analysis of sales trends. The three complement each other in creating a data ecosystem that supports rapid responses and measurable decisions. In addition, in the context of business resilience, the adoption of technologies such as AI, Big Data, and IoT is not only a means of increasing efficiency but also a strategic foundation for building sustainable, adaptive capabilities. Resilience here includes more than just surviving an economic crisis or market pressures. He reflects the capacity of MSEs to continue developing, learning, and updating business strategies dynamically. Digital technology provides opportunities for MSEs not only to survive but also to create a competitive advantage through data-driven innovation, cost savings, and speed in responding to market changes.

However, the success of implementing this technology is greatly influenced by the organization's readiness, both in terms of culture, decision-making structure, and support from external ecosystems. The government and technology partners need to provide assistance, training, and access to affordable technology for MSE actors. Initiatives such as digital business incubators, sector-based digital transformation training, and tax incentives or financing for technology investments can be important catalysts. In this way, the digital transformation process is not exclusive but open and inclusive for MSE actors in various regions and sectors. On the other hand, from the internal side, MSEs must build a learning culture that is open to innovation. The use of data should be part of the organization's reflective and evaluative process. Every decision—whether it's marketing strategy, product diversification, or market expansion—must be backed by credible and measurable analytics. This aligns with Teece's (2007) view that organizations with dynamic capabilities are those that can learn from their environment, respond quickly, and continuously adapt to external demands. Therefore, when AI, Big Data, and IoT are not only used as technical tools but are also developed as an integral part of the decision-making system, MSEs will have the advantage of surviving and growing in a challenging environment. Digital transformation is no longer just a tool for modernization, but a new way of building a resilient, adaptive, and knowledge-based organization. According to the Dynamic Capabilities Theory approach, we can understand that business resilience is not the result of chance, but rather the outcome of a long process of learning, strengthening capabilities, and continuous technology integration.

ATTITUDES, SOCIAL NORMS, AND BEHAVIORAL CONTROLS HAVE THE POTENTIAL TO AFFECT THE READINESS OF MSE DIGITALIZATION.

During global disruptions and increasing economic uncertainty, MSEs are required not only to survive but also to transform to remain relevant. The era of VUCA Volatility, Uncertainty, Complexity, Ambiguity) has created an unstable and unpredictable business environment (Nugroho, Mor, et al., 2024). This condition requires organizations, including MSEs, to have high adaptability and readiness to face change, including in terms of digital technology adoption. However, this readiness does not depend only on the availability of technology itself, but also on the behavioral dimensions of MSE actors, who are the leading actors in the technology decision-making process. Behavioral factors, such as attitudes towards technology, social norms that develop within the MSE environment, and perceptions of the ability to use technology, are crucial. A positive attitude towards innovation, driven by the belief that technology brings benefits, can encourage MSE actors to be more open to digitalization. On the contrary, a pessimistic or skeptical attitude can be a significant obstacle. Social norms also play a significant role: when the MSE community views the use of technology as commonplace and expected, individuals will be encouraged to follow the trend. On the other hand, if the collective culture still prioritizes traditional methods, then the adoption of technology will be hampered. In addition, the perception of behavioral control, or self-efficacy, which refers to the extent to which business actors feel capable of implementing technology in their business, significantly influences the success of the digital transformation process.

Dynamic Capabilities Theory (DCT) offers a robust framework for understanding how these behavioral factors can be developed as part of MSEs' adaptive strategies in responding to the challenges of the VUCA era. David Teece (D. J. Teece, 1996; D. J. Teece et al., 1997), introduced this theory in the late 1990s to answer the need for organizations to manage rapid change. In DCT, there are three main pillars: sensing (detecting opportunities or threats), seizing (capturing opportunities through strategic decision-making), and transforming (adjusting and adapting organizational structures to address change). Therefore, from DCT's point of view, MSEs' attitudes towards technology can affect their sensing ability to digital opportunities. MSEs that have a proactive and open attitude to innovation are better able to recognize the benefits of technology that can increase efficiency, expand the market, and improve customer service. In the seizing process, social norms serve as a reinforcement in collective decision-making, especially among MSEs that are managed communally or family-owned. Strong social support can accelerate the decision-making process for adopting certain technologies.

Meanwhile, high behavioral control allows MSE actors to transform their organizations internally. Those who have confidence in themselves and their teams will be more confident in overhauling work systems, introducing new digital processes, and training the workforce to operate technological devices. This aligns with research by Yang & Gan (2020), and Wilhelm et al. (2015), who stated that dynamic capabilities are not only sourced from tangible assets, but also from human resources and the way organizations build continuous learning processes. Empirical research also strengthens the relationship between behavioral factors and readiness for technology adoption. Studies by Chen et al. (2015) show that innovation in technology-based services relies heavily on the acceptance and active participation of internal users of the organization. Meanwhile, research from Zornoza & Forés (2010), and Chaudhary (2019) proves that the ability to absorb, process, and internalize new knowledge—which is particularly relevant in the context of digital transformation—is closely related to open and flexible organizational behavioral factors.

Field conditions in Indonesia reveal that many MSEs are facing difficulties not because technology is unavailable, but due to a lack of self-confidence, a scarcity of success examples, and a lack of a digital culture that encourages technology exploration. Some MSEs are reluctant to switch from manual methods due to fear of failure, perceive technology as too complicated, or are concerned about losing control over the business process. Therefore, interventions are not enough to be structural, such as device assistance or training subsidies, but must target changes in individual mindsets and attitudes. In this context, experience-based training, mentoring from fellow MSE actors, and the provision of learning communities can be effective strategies for enhancing the skills of MSE actors. Therefore, in the context of dynamic capability frameworks, such interventions not only increase individual readiness but also strengthen the overall organizational mechanism. MSEs that collectively learn from experience, try to evaluate new technologies, and gradually form digital behavior patterns will have higher resilience in facing future challenges. A transformation that begins with behavioral changes will have an impact on organizational structures, work systems, and foster a more strategic way of thinking.

Thus, the exploration of behavioral factors in the readiness of technology adoption not only plays a role in explaining the phenomenon of delays in the digitalization of MSEs but also becomes a critical entry point in building their dynamic capabilities. In this context, DCT theory becomes a conceptual foundation that bridges aspects of organizational behavior and strategy. The integration between behavioral approaches and organizational capabilities is key to ensuring that digital transformation is not only symbolic but truly forms long-term resilience for MSEs in the VUCA era.

PUBLIC POLICIES CAN ACCELERATE INCLUSIVE AND SUSTAINABLE DIGITAL ADOPTION FOR MSES

Amid the pressure of the VUCA era marked by uncertainty, rapid change, complexity, and ambiguity, micro and small enterprises (MSEs) face extraordinary challenges in maintaining business continuity. Digital transformation, which was once considered a competitive advantage, has now become a basic necessity for survival and growth. MSEs are no longer able to rely solely on conventional methods; changes in consumer behavior, the digitization of transactions, and the emergence of new technologies such as artificial intelligence and big data have demanded that MSEs adapt quickly. However, the reality on the ground reveals a significant gap between the potential for digitalization and its actual implementation among MSEs. Many MSE actors have not been impacted by the digitalization program, either due to limited infrastructure, low digital literacy, a fear of change, or a lack of concrete incentives. This is where the role of public policy becomes crucial, not only as a technical facilitator, but also as a provider of strategic direction and a guarantor of equitable access in the digital transformation process. The digitalization of MSEs will not succeed if it is driven solely by market forces; it is necessary to have the presence of the state and policies that are actively on their side.

In a theoretical framework, Dynamic Capabilities Theory (DCT) provides an essential foundation for explaining how MSEs can develop adaptive capabilities in response to disruptive environmental changes. Introduced by Teece (1996), and Teece et al. (1997), DCT emphasizes three key capabilities that organizations must possess: sensing (the ability to recognize opportunities and threats), seizing (the ability to capitalize on opportunities effectively), and transforming (the ability to implement sustainable internal changes). Effective public policy should foster the development of these three capabilities within the context of MSEs. First, at the sensing stage, public policy can play a role in expanding the awareness of MSE actors to the urgency of digitalization. This can be done through national-scale digital literacy programs, the dissemination of data-based information, and the creation of a public narrative that mainstreams technology as an integral part of MSE management. When MSEs recognize the importance of digitalization, they will be more open to innovation and more easily identify opportunities that can be leveraged. Second, during the seizing stage, public policies must provide concrete support that enables MSEs to capture digital opportunities in real terms. This includes providing fiscal incentives for technology investments, digital training subsidies, and strengthening access to technology-based financing. Programs such as digital vouchers, cloud grants, or soft credits for digitalization can accelerate the process of adopting technology more widely and evenly.

On the other hand, strategic partnerships between the government and digital platforms can also open up access to the digital market for MSEs. Third, in the transforming stage, the role of public policy is to create an ecosystem that supports MSEs in changing their internal structure to be compatible with digital systems. This includes integrating digital payment systems, automating financial record-keeping, implementing technology-based inventory management, and enhancing customer relationship management (CRM) systems. This transformation requires not only technological advancements but also a shift in mindset and organizational structure. Therefore, the sustainability of training, tiered coaching, and digital certification schemes is essential so that the transformation does not stop on the surface.

Previous research supports the importance of public policy in boosting the digital capabilities of MSEs. A study by Pongtanalert & Assarut (2022) shows that countries with a regulatory framework that favors small businesses, including in terms of digitalization, tend to have a more resilient MSE sector during a crisis. Meanwhile, research by Tang et al. (2023) highlights that the involvement of MSEs in digital platforms increases significantly when governments provide adequate digital infrastructure and fiscal incentives. In Indonesia, several programs, such as Bangga Made in Indonesia, PaDi MSMEs, and digital training for MSMEs, initiated by the Ministry of Cooperatives and SMEs, are reasonable first steps; however, they still need to be expanded and strengthened with a cross-sectoral and data-driven approach.

Public policies that encourage digitalization must also ensure the principles of inclusivity and sustainability. Inclusivity means that every MSE actor, regardless of geographic location, gender, age, or education level, has equal opportunities to access technology and training. Sustainability means that policies are not just temporary or symbolic, but create long-term systemic change. This can be achieved by integrating MSE digital policies into regional development planning documents (RPJMD), strengthening cooperation between ministries, and establishing measurable performance indicators for the progress of MSE digitalization.

Furthermore, policies must consider the dynamics of technological change itself. In the context of VUCA, regulations that are too rigid or slow in responding to technological changes can be an obstacle. Therefore, a flexible and continuous evaluation-based adaptive policy approach needs to be implemented. The government can form a special unit that focuses on MSE digital policy innovation, involving industry players, academics, and the MSE community in the policy formulation process. This collaboration will ensure that policies are not only responsive but also relevant to the field's needs. Therefore, the acceleration of MSE digitalization cannot be separated from the strategic role of public policy. Within the framework of Dynamic Capabilities Theory, policies that encourage sensing, seizing, and transforming processes will strengthen the competitiveness and resilience of MSEs in the face of the challenges of the VUCA era. However, the effectiveness of such policies is primarily determined by the extent to which they are inclusive, sustainable, and adaptive to change. Therefore, synergy between stakeholders, strong political commitment, and data-driven policy approaches are necessary to create a digital ecosystem that supports the overall progress of MSEs.

MSES INTEGRATE ESG AND CSR PRINCIPLES IN THE DIGITAL TRANSFORMATION PROCESS.

In an era of disruption characterized by uncertainty, complexity, and accelerating technological change, micro and small enterprises (MSEs) face both significant challenges and opportunities. One of the increasingly critical strategic approaches in this context is the integration of Environmental, Social, and Governance (ESG) and Corporate Social Responsibility (CSR) values into the digital transformation process. Digital transformation is not only a technical tool for improving efficiency and productivity, but also a vehicle for creating sustainable long-term value. Therefore, the study of how ESG and CSR can be integrated into the MSE digitalization agenda is highly relevant and urgent to discuss. The disruption phenomenon that has arisen due to global crises, such as the COVID-19 pandemic, clearly shows how vulnerable MSEs are to external shocks. Resilience and sustainability are key issues that demand rapid adaptation. In this context, the concept of VUCA (Volatility, Uncertainty, Complexity, Ambiguity) is increasingly evident and demands a strategic response based on dynamic capabilities. MSEs are required to capture opportunities (sensing), take advantage of opportunities (seizing), and reconfigure resources (transforming) in an agile manner. The integration of ESG and CSR into the digital transformation framework provides a strategic direction that enables MSEs not only to survive but also to grow inclusively and responsibly.

The theory of Dynamic Capabilities introduced by Teece et al. (1997) is the primary theoretical foundation to understand how organizations, including MSEs, can manage and transform their resources effectively in the face of rapidly changing environmental dynamics. Within this framework, ESG and CSR are no longer positioned as external obligations or additional programs, but rather as the core of a strategic innovation process that strengthens the adaptive capabilities of MSEs. Sensing in this context includes the ability of MSEs to identify social and environmental needs, including awareness of sustainability issues. Seizing means their ability to align business models and digital strategies that take into account the principles of social and environmental responsibility. Transforming demonstrates the readiness of MSEs to transform their organizational culture and operational processes, thereby embedding ESG and CSR values in every strategic decision.

Several studies show that digitalization can be an enabler for achieving sustainability goals. For example, a study by Moodaley & Telukdarie (2023) demonstrates that the adoption of digital technologies, such as big data analytics, e-commerce platforms, and artificial intelligence, can enhance corporate sustainability reporting and social accountability. At the MSE level, the use of technology allows for energy efficiency, waste reduction, and increased transparency in the supply chain. Additionally, digitalization can be a tool to empower local communities through engagement in digital platform-based CSR initiatives, such as online social campaigns or app-based training programs. The integration of ESG and CSR in digital transformation also affects the reputation and legitimacy of MSEs in the eyes of customers and business partners. Today's consumers are increasingly concerned about ethical and sustainable business practices, especially the younger generation, who are the main drivers of the digital economy. By adopting ESG principles, MSEs can build public trust and expand the market through values that align with the expectations of modern consumers. For example, MSEs that adopt renewable energy or use eco-friendly materials in their production can leverage digital channels to promote their sustainable practices to a broader audience.

However, the challenges of integrating ESG and CSR in the digital transformation process of MSEs cannot be ignored. Many MSE actors still have limitations in terms of digital literacy, understanding of ESG principles, and access to resources and mentoring. This is where the role of the supporting ecosystem, including government agencies, universities, and financial institutions, comes in. Inclusive and adaptive public policies are essential for creating an environment conducive to integrating ESG and CSR into the digital business practices of MSEs. Training programs, fiscal incentives, access to green funding, and policies for the procurement of goods and services that support sustainable business actors need to be expanded. Conceptually, ESG and CSR are not only normative aspects but also an integral part of competitive advantage. More over Teece et al. (2016) emphasizes that dynamic capabilities encompass an organization's ability to innovate and sustainably respond to stakeholder needs. Within the framework of MSEs, this capability needs to be developed through organizational learning, cross-sector collaboration, and the adaptation of technology tailored to the local context. Thus, ESG and CSR are not only a response to external demands, but also the foundation for the formation of new value-driven business models.

Recent literature also indicates that integrating ESG and CSR into digital strategies can enhance organizational resilience. A study by Darid (2023) suggests that companies with structured sustainability initiatives tend to exhibit higher resilience in the face of economic crises and technological disruptions. On the MSE scale, this can be observed in how some MSEs with high social awareness are actually better able to retain customers, maintain relationships with the community, and innovate during times of crisis. Furthermore, the sustainability principles inherent in ESG and CSR allow for the creation of a balance between profit orientation and social value. This is particularly important for MSEs operating in local communities, where social legitimacy plays a significant role in determining business continuity. Consistent implementation of ESG enables MSEs to become agents of change in sustainable development, particularly in the informal sector, which is often overlooked in national policy agendas. Therefore, MSEs that strategically embed ESG and CSR principles into their digitalization process not only improve internal performance but also expand their holistic contribution to economic and social development. Digital transformation also opens up opportunities for MSEs to connect with global networks, including international e-commerce platforms and sustainable funding networks. Through ESG integration, MSEs can enhance their competitiveness in a global market that is increasingly emphasizing sustainable business practices. This aligns with a shift in the global paradigm that demands transparency, accountability, and compliance with international environmental and social standards. In this context, digitalization serves as a bridge between MSEs and a more transparent and inclusive global business ecosystem.

CONCLUSION

This book chapter emphasizes that the development of dynamic capabilities is essential for MSEs to survive and grow in the pressure of the VUCA era. Digital transformation is no longer an optional choice, but has evolved into a core strategy that leverages the internal strengths of MSEs in conjunction with technology-based external opportunities. Through the Dynamic Capabilities Theory (DCT) approach, this paper describes how sensing, seizing, and transforming capabilities are the key for MSEs to respond to disruption adaptively and strategically. In this context, technologies such as AI, Big Data, and IoT are acting as accelerators, not only in operational efficiency but also in data-driven decision-making.

Nevertheless, the gap between potential and realization remains a significant challenge. Many MSEs lack the structural and cultural readiness to adopt technology fully. A skeptical attitude towards technology, low social norms that support digitalization, and a limited perception of one's ability are significant behavioral barriers. In addition, limited access to training, infrastructure, and financing also hindered the transformation process. Therefore, this book chapter emphasizes the importance of inclusive, adaptive, and responsive public policies in creating a digital ecosystem that supports MSEs from upstream to downstream.

The theoretical implications of this study extend the application of DCT to the MSE sector, which has been largely neglected in the adaptive strategy literature. This approach provides a new lens that integrates aspects of organizational capabilities with behavioral and sustainability factors. Meanwhile, from a practical perspective, MSEs are encouraged to develop a culture of learning, community collaboration, and build a data-driven decision-making system, starting with small but consistent steps. The government and strategic partners are also advised to develop contextual training programs, digitalization incentives, and integrate ESG and CSR into the MSE development agenda.

The limitations in this writing lie in the lack of in-depth field empirical data and limited generalizations across MSE sectors. For this reason, follow-up studies that combine quantitative and qualitative approaches are needed to test the effectiveness of dynamic capability models in a more applicable manner. In the future, collaboration between sectors is needed to formulate policies that are not only technical but also strengthen the adaptive behavior and sustainability ethos of MSEs in the face of increasingly complex global challenges.

REFERENCES

Adekola, J., & Clelland, D. (2019). Two Sides of the Same Coin: Business Resilience and Community Resilience. *Journal of Contingencies and Crisis Management*, *28*(1), 50–60. DOI: 10.1111/1468-5973.12275

Adriansah, A., Ulya, Z., Maulina, D., Awaludin, D. T., Lastinawati, E., Kairupan, D. J. I., Sari, N. M. W., Lestari, P. F. K., Achmad, F. S., Atmaja, U., & Nugroho, L. (2025). EKONOMI MANAJERIAL. In Damayanti, E. (Ed.), *CV WIDINA MEDIA UTAMA*. CV WIDINA MEDIA UTAMA.

Ahmadin, A., Nugroho, L., Sari, E. J., Mustopa, M., Hasbi, I., Islam, N., Kurniawan, A., Jermias, E. O., Dey, N. P. H., Rahman, A., Putra, A. E., Amane, A. P. O., Subandi, Y., & Djumaty, B. L. (2023). SOSIOLOGI RUANG VIRTUAL. In A. Ahmadin (Ed.), *CV WIDINA MEDIA UTAMA*. CV WIDINA MEDIA UTAMA. https://repository.penerbitwidina.com/media/publications/559113-sosiologi-ruang-virtual-e4f161f0.pdf

Azizi, M., Umiyati, H., Nugroho, L., Utami, A. R., Sudirman, A., Aryani, L., Irwansyah, R., Purbowo, P., Mardiana, S., Witi, F. L., Pratiwi, C. P., Syahputra, S., Hanika, I. M., & Johassan, D. M. R. Y. (2022). Effective Digital Marketing. In Putri, D. E., & Sari, E. P. (Eds.), *Widina Media Utama*. Widina Media Utama.

Badakhshan, P., Conboy, K., Grisold, T., & vom Brocke, J. (2019). Agile Business Process Management. *Business Process Management Journal*, *26*(6), 1505–1523. DOI: 10.1108/BPMJ-12-2018-0347

Bai, C., Quayson, M., & Sarkis, J. (2021). COVID-19 Pandemic Digitization Lessons for Sustainable Development of Micro-and Small- Enterprises. *Sustainable Production and Consumption*, *27*, 1989–2001. DOI: 10.1016/j.spc.2021.04.035 PMID: 34722843

Browder, R. E., Dwyer, S. M., & Koch, H. (2023). Upgrading Adaptation: How Digital Transformation Promotes Organizational Resilience. *Strategic Entrepreneurship Journal*, *18*(1), 128–164. DOI: 10.1002/sej.1483

Chaudhary, S. (2019). Implications of Strategic Flexibility in Small Firms: The Moderating Role of Absorptive Capacity. *South Asian Journal of Business Studies*, *8*(3), 370–386. DOI: 10.1108/SAJBS-10-2018-0104

Chen, Y., Wang, Y., Nevo, S., Benítez-Amado, J., & Kou, G. (2015). IT Capabilities and Product Innovation Performance: The Roles of Corporate Entrepreneurship and Competitive Intensity. *Information & Management*, *52*(6), 643–657. DOI: 10.1016/j.im.2015.05.003

Choerudin, A., Zulfachry, Widyaswati, R., Khasanah, L. D. W. J. S. N., Harto, B., Nita Fauziah Oktaviani, M. I. S., Nugroho, L., Suharsono, J., & Paramita, V. S. (2023). *Literasi keuangan* (Issue June). PT GLOBAL EKSEKUTIF TEKNOLOGI.

Cortellazzo, L., Bruni, E., & Zampieri, R. (2019). The Role of Leadership in a Digitalized World: A Review. *Frontiers in Psychology*, *10*, 1938. Advance online publication. DOI: 10.3389/fpsyg.2019.01938 PMID: 31507494

Darid, A.-H. (2023). Overcoming Global Economic Challenges: The Imperative of Diversification and Sustainable Development. *Vìsnik Marìupol s kogo Deržavnogo Unìversitetu Serìâ Ekonomìka*, *13*(26), 14–21. DOI: 10.34079/2226-2822-2023-13-26-14-21

Doern, R. (2014). Entrepreneurship and Crisis Management: The Experiences of Small Businesses During the London 2011 Riots. *International Small Business Journal*, *34*(3), 276–302. DOI: 10.1177/0266242614553863

Dong, A., Garbuio, M., & Lovallo, D. (2016). Generative Sensing: A Design Perspective on the Microfoundations of Sensing Capabilities. *California Management Review*, *58*(4), 97–117. DOI: 10.1525/cmr.2016.58.4.97

Dyduch, W., Chudziński, P., Cyfert, S., & Zastempowski, M. (2021). Dynamic Capabilities, Value Creation and Value Capture: Evidence From SMEs Under Covid-19 Lockdown in Poland. *PLoS One*, *16*(6), e0252423. DOI: 10.1371/journal.pone.0252423 PMID: 34129597

Fasa, M. I., & Febrianty, F. (2020). *Eksistensi Bisnis Islami di Era Revolusi Industri 4.0*. Widina Bhakti Persada. https://books.google.co.id/books?hl=en&lr=&id=omDcDwAAQBAJ&oi=fnd&pg=PR3&ots=-c_XgwtKNA&sig=aEdIDy7rMH3J_bPAGr2R3lDy19o&redir_esc=y#v=onepage&q&f=false

Gilch, P. M., & Sieweke, J. (2020). Recruiting Digital Talent: The Strategic Role of Recruitment in Organisations' Digital Transformation. *German Journal of Human Resource Management Zeitschrift Für Personalforschung*, *35*(1), 53–82. DOI: 10.1177/2397002220952734

Gunawan, A. W., & Winarto, S. H. (2024). Strategy for Improving Business Performance in Micro and Small Enterprises Through Innovation and Digitalization. *International Journal of Social and Human*, *1*(2), 97–105. DOI: 10.59613/qtcfze12

Hidayah, N., Nugroho, L., Suharman, H., & Ali, A. J. (2022). Exploring the Benefit of Introducing Accounting and Finance Knowledge for Micro and Small Entrepreneurs During the COVID-19 Pandemic. *ASEAN Journal of Community*, *6*(2), 335–346.

Holman, B., & Whitaker, C. (2022). COVID-19 Pandemic and Research on the Mediating Role of Absorptive Capacity on the Relationship Between Business Analytics Capability and Small-to-Medium-Sized Enterprise Performance. *Business Management Research and Applications a Cross-Disciplinary Journal, 1*(1), 37–59. DOI: 10.54093/bmra.v1i1.2122

Irwansyah, R., Syahputra, D., Ningsih, S., Hasan, M., Kristanto, T., Nugroho, L., Triwardhani, D., & Marwan, D. Febrianty, Sudarmanto, E., Abdurohim BS, D., Sudirman, A., & S.Maggabarani, A. (2021). Marketing Digital Usaha Mikro. In *Paper Knowledge. Toward a Media History of Documents* (Vol. 5, Issue 2). www .penerbitwidina.com

Jin, Y., Zhang, S., & Lei, X. (2023). Evolutionary Game Analysis of the Impact of Big Data Credit Technology on the Credit Rationing of Micro and Small Enterprises (MSEs). *Journal of Theoretical and Applied Electronic Commerce Research, 18*(4), 1926–1954. DOI: 10.3390/jtaer18040097

Kitchin, R., & McArdle, G. (2016). What Makes Big Data, Big Data? Exploring the Ontological Characteristics of 26 Datasets. *Big Data & Society, 3*(1), 2053951716631130. Advance online publication. DOI: 10.1177/2053951716631130

Kretschmer, T., & Khashabi, P. (2020). Digital Transformation and Organization Design: An Integrated Approach. *California Management Review, 62*(4), 86–104. DOI: 10.1177/0008125620940296

Lin, J., & Mao, M. J. (2023). How Does Digital Transformation Affect Sustainable Innovation Performance? The Pivotal Roles of Digital Technology-business Alignment and Environmental Uncertainty. *Sustainable Development (Bradford), 32*(4), 3163–3181. DOI: 10.1002/sd.2830

Machado, E., Scavarda, L. F., Caiado, R. G. G., & Thomé, A. M. T. (2021). Barriers and Enablers for the Integration of Industry 4.0 and Sustainability in Supply Chains of MSMEs. *Sustainability (Basel), 13*(21), 11664. DOI: 10.3390/su132111664

Maria, K., Kasmo, A. B. P., & Nugroho, L. (2022). Kajian Penggunaan Aplikasi Digital dalam Meningkatkan Pendapatan UMKM pada Sektor Makanan (Studi Kasus Ayam Gepuk Pak Gembus). *Jurnal Cakrawala Ilmiah, 2*(4), 1669–1678. DOI: 10.53625/jcijurnalcakrawalailmiah.v2i4.4564

Mikalef, P., Boura, M., Lekakos, G., & Krogstie, J. (2019). Big Data Analytics Capabilities and Innovation: The Mediating Role of Dynamic Capabilities and Moderating Effect of the Environment. *British Journal of Management, 30*(2), 272–298. DOI: 10.1111/1467-8551.12343

Minanari, M., Nugroho, L., Nurhasanah, N., Safira, S., & Nugraha, E. (2024). Financial distress determinants factors of retail companies with profitability as moderating (Indonesia cases 2016-2021). *Business Economics and Management Research Journal, 7*(1), 29–47. DOI: 10.58308/bemarej.1324931

Moodaley, W., & Telukdarie, A. (2023). Greenwashing, Sustainability Reporting, and Artificial Intelligence: A Systematic Literature Review. *Sustainability (Basel), 15*(2), 1481. DOI: 10.3390/su15021481

Nugroho, L. (2022). *Peran Corporate University dalam Mempertahankan Kinerja yang Berkelanjutan (Implementasi Pada Bank Syariah Mandiri)* (W. Utami (ed.)). Deepublish. https://deepublishstore.com/shop/buku-peran-corporate/

Nugroho, L. (2023). Reshaping the Mindset of Halal Entrepreneurs Toward Sustainable Business: The Case of Indonesia. In *Contemporary Discourse of Halal and Islamic Entrepreneurship* (pp. 207–221). Springer. DOI: 10.1007/978-981-99-6427-7_14

Nugroho, L., & Arafah, W. (2020). Eksistensi Dan Tantangan Usaha Mikro, Kecil Dan Menengah (UMKM) Pada Era Globalisasi. In Sumitro, A. S., & Nurhayati, S. (Eds.), *Manajemen Hasil Pemikiran dari Para Dosen Perguruan Tinggi di Indonesia: Vol. First* (pp. 172–187). Sihsawit Labuhan Batu., DOI: 10.1017/CBO9781107415324.004

Nugroho, L., Melzatia, H. H., & Abidin, M. I. (2024). Digitalizing Rural Development in Indonesia : Unveiling Concepts and Strategies for Building Sustainable Digital Villages. *Proceeding of The First International Annual Conference on Economics, Management, Business and Accounting*, 61–74.

Nugroho, L., Mor, S., Iskandar, D., Setiany, E., Asih, D., & Mellin, F. (2024). The Urgency of Digitalization Vis-a-Vis Business Trends (Indonesia Case). *Proceeding International Annual Conference Economics, Management, Business, and Accounting, 1*(1 SE-Articles), 1–13. https://proceeding.inacemba.org/index.php/eproceeding-inacemba/article/view/1

Nugroho, L., & Tamala, D. (2018). Persepsi pengusaha umkm terhadap peran bank syariah. *Jurnal SIKAP (Sistem Informasi, Keuangan, Auditing Dan Perpajakan), 3*(1), 49–62.

Nugroho, L., Utami, W., & Kasmo, A. B. P. (2024). *BUKU REFERENSI MANAJEMEN STRATEGI DI ERA DIGITALISASI ISU-ISU TERKINI*. Widina Media Utama.

Nurdany, A., Nugroho, L., & Shahirah, N. A. Nikamtuzzahra, Musyarofah, A. N., Bandiyah, A. N., Ali, J., Kurnia, R., Nafisa, A., & Putri, A. Z. (2024). DIGITAL ECONOMY DISRUPTION (Unveiling the Dynamic View of Islamic Finance, Digital Asset, Financial Crime and Cybersecurity). In *Widina Media Utama*. Widina Media Utama.

Osakwe, C. N., Chovancova, M., & Ogbonna, B. U. (2016). Linking SMEs Profitability to Brand Orientation and Market-Sensing Capability: A Service Sector Evidence. *Periodica Polytechnica Social and Management Sciences*, *24*(1), 34–40. DOI: 10.3311/PPso.8069

Panjaitan, R. (2022). Towards Resilient MSMEs: The Role of Organizational Resilience and Entrepreneurial Resilience. *Jurnal Manajemen Dan Keuangan*, *11*(1), 97–111. DOI: 10.33059/jmk.v11i1.5035

Pongtanalert, K., & Assarut, N. (2022). Entrepreneur Mindset, Social Capital and Adaptive Capacity for Tourism SME Resilience and Transformation During the COVID-19 Pandemic. *Sustainability (Basel)*, *14*(19), 12675. DOI: 10.3390/su141912675

Rani, D. Y., Nugroho, L., & Zulfahmi. (2023). Kajian Faktor Internal dan Eksternal UMKM Wanita di Sektor Fashion pada Kecamatan Ngunut, Kabupaten Tulungagung, Jawa Timur. *SAMMAJIVA : Jurnal Penelitian Bisnis Dan Manajemen*, *1*(2), 227–241.

Sanchez-Hughet, C., Aramendia-Muneta, M. E., & Erro-Garcés, A. (2022). Seizing Opportunities in Europe: A Roadmap for Efficient Big Data Implementation in Spanish SMEs. *Digital Policy Regulation and Governance*, *24*(5), 463–478. DOI: 10.1108/DPRG-02-2022-0019

Shet, S. V. (2024). A VUCA-ready Workforce: Exploring Employee Competencies and Learning and Development Implications. *Personnel Review*, *53*(3), 674–703. DOI: 10.1108/PR-10-2023-0873

Tambunan, T. T., & Busnetti, I. (2024). Recent Evidence on the Digitalization Process in Indonesia's Micro and Small Enterprises. *International Journal of Current Science Research and Review*, *07*(08). Advance online publication. DOI: 10.47191/ijcsrr/V7-i8-18

Tang, L., Jiang, H., Hou, S., Zheng, J., & Miao, L. (2023). The Effect of Enterprise Digital Transformation on Green Technology Innovation: A Quantitative Study on Chinese Listed Companies. *Sustainability (Basel)*, *15*(13), 10036. DOI: 10.3390/su151310036

Teece, D., Peteraf, M., & Leih, S. (2016). Dynamic capabilities and organizational agility: Risk, uncertainty, and strategy in the innovation economy. *California Management Review*, *58*(4), 13–35. DOI: 10.1525/cmr.2016.58.4.13

Teece, D. J. (1996). Firm organization, industrial structure, and technological innovation. *Journal of Economic Behavior & Organization*, *31*(2), 193–224. DOI: 10.1016/S0167-2681(96)00895-5

Teece, D. J. (2007). Explicating Dynamic Capabilities: The Nature and Microfoundations of (Sustainable) Enterprise Performance. *Strategic Management Journal*, *28*(13), 1319–1350. DOI: 10.1002/smj.640

Teece, D. J., Pisano, G., & Shuen, A. (1997). Dynamic Capabilities and Strategic Management. *Strategic Management Journal*, *18*(7), 509–533. DOI: 10.1002/(SICI)1097-0266(199708)18:7<509::AID-SMJ882>3.0.CO;2-Z

Wang, N., Cui, D., & Jin, C. (2022). The Value of Internal Control During a Crisis: Evidence From Enterprise Resilience. *Sustainability (Basel)*, *15*(1), 513. DOI: 10.3390/su15010513

Wicaksono, T., Wiraguna, S. A., Violin, V., Sudirman, A., Nugroho, L., Rizkiawan, R., Krisnanik, E., & Djumrianti, D. (2024). *KONSEP DAN TEORI E-BUSINESS & E-COMMERCE*. CV WIDINA MEDIA UTAMA.

Widodo, Z. D., Purwaningrum, J. P., Purbasari, I., Rini, G. P., Putra, A. R., Uran, B. E. K. R., Mulyani, M., Soegoto, A. S., Nugroho, L., Nurzianti, R., Nugroho, H., Sudirman, A., Santosa, S., Novianti, R., Pattiapon, M. L., Pinem, D., & Ridwan, N. H. (2022). Manajemen Koperasi dan UMKM. In Sari, E. P., & Putri, D. E. (Eds.), *Widina Bhakti Persada*. Widina Bhakti Persada.

Wilhelm, H., Schlömer, M., & Maurer, I. (2015). How Dynamic Capabilities Affect the Effectiveness and Efficiency of Operating Routines Under High and Low Levels of Environmental Dynamism. *British Journal of Management*, *26*(2), 327–345. DOI: 10.1111/1467-8551.12085

Wong, D. T. W., & Ngai, E. W. T. (2023). The Effects of Analytics Capability and Sensing Capability on Operations Performance: The Moderating Role of Data-Driven Culture. *Annals of Operations Research*. Advance online publication. DOI: 10.1007/s10479-023-05241-5 PMID: 37361097

Yang, L., & Gan, C. (2020). Cooperative Goals and Dynamic Capability: The Mediating Role of Strategic Flexibility and the Moderating Role of Human Resource Flexibility. *Journal of Business and Industrial Marketing*, *36*(5), 782–795. DOI: 10.1108/JBIM-11-2019-0495

Zakiyah, E. F., Kasmo, A. B. P., & Nugroho, L. (2022). Peran Dan Fungsi Usaha Mikro Kecil Dan Menengah (UMKM) Dalam Memitigasi Resesi Ekonomi Global 2023. *Jurnal Cakrawala Ilmiah*, *2*(4), 1–12.

Zamzami, A. H., Mahliza, F., Ali, A. J., & Nugroho, L. (2022). Pandemic Covid-19, Revolution Industry 4.0 and Digital Entrepreneur Trending. [JIESS]. *Journal of Islamic Economics and Social Science*, *2*(2), 133. DOI: 10.22441/jiess.2021.v2i2.007

Zornoza, C. C., & Forés, B. (2010). Knowledge Absorptive Capacity: New Insights for Its Conceptualization and Measurement. *Journal of Business Research*, *63*(7), 707–715. DOI: 10.1016/j.jbusres.2009.04.022

Compilation of References

Abawari, A. M., Debela, K. L., & Abegaz, M. B. (2024). The effects of organizational culture on change management in Oromia public sectors: The mediating role of leadership styles. *Cogent Business & Management*, *11*(1), 2375623. DOI: 10.1080/23311975.2024.2375623

Abdul-Azeez, O., Ogadimma, A., & Idemudia, C. (2024). Optimizing supply chain management: strategic business models and solutions using SAP S/4HANA. *Magna Scientia Advanced Research and Reviews*. .DOI: 10.30574/msarr.2024.11.1.0097

Adekola, J., & Clelland, D. (2019). Two Sides of the Same Coin: Business Resilience and Community Resilience. *Journal of Contingencies and Crisis Management*, *28*(1), 50–60. DOI: 10.1111/1468-5973.12275

Adriansah, A., Ulya, Z., Maulina, D., Awaludin, D. T., Lastinawati, E., Kairupan, D. J. I., Sari, N. M. W., Lestari, P. F. K., Achmad, F. S., Atmaja, U., & Nugroho, L. (2025). EKONOMI MANAJERIAL. In Damayanti, E. (Ed.), *CV WIDINA MEDIA UTAMA*. CV WIDINA MEDIA UTAMA.

Adu-Gyamfi, Y., & Adjei, B. (2018). *Skills development, knowledge and innovation at Suame Magazine, Kumasi* (Open AIR Working Paper No. 16). Open African Innovation Research. (Working paper discusses how artisans acquire skills through apprenticeships and share knowledge and innovation within the Suame cluster.) https://openair.africa/wp-content/uploads/2020/05/WP-16-Skills-Development-Knowledge-and-Innovation-at-Suame-Magazine-Kumasi.pdf

Adula, M., Kant, S., Badi, S., & Kumari, M. (2025). Abusive Work Environment Effect on Female Entrepreneurs' Emotional Wellbeing by Mediation of Social and Moral Values in the Horn of Africa. In *Supporting Psychological and Emotional Wellbeing Among Entrepreneurs* (pp. 1-22). IGI Global Scientific Publishing.

Aghion, P., Fally, T., & Scarpetta, S. (2005). Credit constraints as a barrier to the entry and post-entry growth of firms. *Economic Policy*, *20*(42), 731–779.

Agho, M., Eyo-Udo, N., Onukwulu, E., Sule, A., & Azubuike, C. (2025). Digital Twin Technology for Real Time Monitoring of Energy Supply Chains. *International Journal of Research and Innovation in Applied Science*. .DOI: 10.51584/IJRIAS.2024.912049

Agnihotri, A., Madon, T., & Gadgil, A. J. (2023). Introduction to Development Engineering. In T. Madon, A. J. Gadgil, R. Anderson, L. Casaburi, K. Lee, & A. Rezaee (Eds.), *Introduction to Development Engineering* (pp. 1–15). Springer International Publishing. DOI: 10.1007/978-3-030-86065-3_1

Agostini, L., Nosella, A., & Filippini, R. (2017). Does intellectual capital allow improving innovation performance? A quantitative analysis in the SME context. *Journal of Intellectual Capital*, *18*(2), 400–418. DOI: 10.1108/JIC-05-2016-0056

Aguenza, B. (2024). *Readiness of Local Educational Institution for ISO 9001:2015 Quality Management System Certification: A Comprehensive Analysis*. Education Policy and Development., DOI: 10.31098/epd.v2i1.1804

Agyapong, D., & Attram, A. B. (2019). Effect of owner-manager's financial literacy on the performance of SMEs in the Cape Coast Metropolis in Ghana. *Journal of Global Entrepreneurship Research*, *9*(67), 1–13. DOI: 10.1186/s40497-019-0191-1

Ahmadin, A., Nugroho, L., Sari, E. J., Mustopa, M., Hasbi, I., Islam, N., Kurniawan, A., Jermias, E. O., Dey, N. P. H., Rahman, A., Putra, A. E., Amane, A. P. O., Subandi, Y., & Djumaty, B. L. (2023). SOSIOLOGI RUANG VIRTUAL. In A. Ahmadin (Ed.), *CV WIDINA MEDIA UTAMA*. CV WIDINA MEDIA UTAMA. https://repository.penerbitwidina.com/media/publications/559113-sosiologi-ruang-virtual-e4f161f0.pdf

Ahmed, S., & Ruth, D. (2024). *The benefits of iso 9001 certification for small to medium-sized engineering firMS*. Performance Improvement Journal., DOI: 10.56811/PFI-24-0010

AlAnazi, A. A., Kura, K. M., Suleiman, E. S., & Abubakar, R. A. (2022). Mediating effect of organisational innovation in the prediction of change-oriented leadership on organisational performance. *International Journal of Innovation Science*, *14*(1), 138–156. DOI: 10.1108/IJIS-03-2021-0051

Alayande, B., Chu, K. M., Jumbam, D. T., Kimto, O. E., Musa Danladi, G., Niyukuri, A., Anderson, G. A., El-Gabri, D., Miranda, E., Taye, M., Tertong, N., Yempabe, T., Ntirenganya, F., Byiringiro, J. C., Sule, A. Z., Kobusingye, O. C., Bekele, A., & Riviello, R. R. (2022). Disparities in Access to Trauma Care in Sub-Saharan Africa: A Narrative Review. *Current Trauma Reports*, *8*(3), 66–94. DOI: 10.1007/s40719-022-00229-1 PMID: 35692507

Al-Balushi, M. (2024). The impact of quality management systems on organizational resilience. *International Journal of Quality & Reliability Management*. Advance online publication. DOI: 10.1108/IJQRM-05-2023-0169

Alherian, N., Spasojević-Brkić, V., Perišić, M., & Alsharif, A. (2021). *Integrated risk management model implementation's contextual dependence on company size*. Tehnika., DOI: 10.5937/tehnika2103361A

Ali, M. A., Hussin, N., Flayyih, H. H., Haddad, H., Al-Ramahi, N. M., Almubaydeen, T. H., Hussein, S. A., & Hasan Abunaila, A. S. (2023). A multidimensional view of intellectual capital and dynamic innovative performance. *Journal of Risk and Financial Management, 16*(3), 139. DOI: 10.3390/jrfm16030139

Ali, M. A., Hussin, N., Haddad, H., Alkhodary, D., & Marei, A. (2021). Dynamic capabilities and their impact on intellectual capital and innovation performance. *Sustainability (Basel), 13*(18), 10028. DOI: 10.3390/su131810028

Alshahrani, M., & Husain, K. (2023). The effectiveness of the implementation of ISO 9001 on SMEs performance: The case of an emerging economy. *International Journal of Quality & Reliability Management*. Advance online publication. DOI: 10.1108/IJQRM-08-2022-0233

Ambrosini, V., & Bowman, C. (2009). What are dynamic capabilities and are they a useful construct in strategic management? *International Journal of Management Reviews, 11*(1), 29–49. DOI: 10.1111/j.1468-2370.2008.00251.x

Anooja, J., & Kumar, V. (2025). Elements of innovation: A review of literature on craft-design ecosystem. *Sustainable Futures : An Applied Journal of Technology, Environment and Society, 9*, 100670. DOI: 10.1016/j.sftr.2025.100670

Anwer, A., 2024. ISO 9000: (1987-2016) A trend's Review. *Journal of Policy Research*. .DOI: 10.61506/02.00236

Armbrust, M., Fox, A., Griffith, R., Joseph, A. D., Katz, R., Konwinski, A., Lee, G., Patterson, D., Rabkin, A., Stoica, I., & Zaharia, M. (2010). A view of cloud computing. *Communications of the ACM, 53*(4), 50–58. DOI: 10.1145/1721654.1721672

Asiaei, K., O'Connor, N. G., Barani, O., & Joshi, M. (2023b). Green intellectual capital and ambidextrous green innovation and the impact on environmental performance. *Business Strategy and the Environment, 32*(1), 369–386. DOI: 10.1002/bse.3136

Attanayake, A., & Ratnayake, R. (2024). Transitioning to Circular Economy in Power Distribution Utilities: A Framework Integrating ISO 9001 Quality Management Standards. *2024 IEEE International Conference on Industrial Engineering and Engineering Management* (IEEM), 760-764. DOI: 10.1109/IEEM62345.2024.10857066

Audretsch, D. B., Belitski, M., Fiedler, A., & Meurer, M. M. (2025). Values and entrepreneurship in the sustainable society: Toward a multilevel understanding of entrepreneurial value practices. *Small Business Economics*, *65*(3), 1701–1725. Advance online publication. DOI: 10.1007/s11187-025-01069-4

Avilés-Sacoto, H., Avilés-González, J., & García-Reyes, S. (2021). A Model to Become a Supply Chain 4.0 Based on a Digital Maturity Perspective. 1058-1067. .DOI: 10.1016/j.procs.2022.01.305

Ayub, A. (2022). Motivation and benefits of iso 9001:2015 implementation and maintenance in a Malaysian legal firm. https://www.qjssh.com/index.php/qjssh/article/view/107

Azizi, M., Umiyati, H., Nugroho, L., Utami, A. R., Sudirman, A., Aryani, L., Irwansyah, R., Purbowo, P., Mardiana, S., Witi, F. L., Pratiwi, C. P., Syahputra, S., Hanika, I. M., & Johassan, D. M. R. Y. (2022). Effective Digital Marketing. In Putri, D. E., & Sari, E. P. (Eds.), *Widina Media Utama*. Widina Media Utama.

Azunre, G. A., Azerigyik, R. A., Amponsah, O., & Kpeebi, Y. (2025). The jugaad urbanism-sustainable circular cities nexus: Insights from sub-Saharan Africa's informal settlements. *Habitat International*, *158*, 103349. DOI: 10.1016/j.habitatint.2025.103349

Badakhshan, P., Conboy, K., Grisold, T., & vom Brocke, J. (2019). Agile Business Process Management. *Business Process Management Journal*, *26*(6), 1505–1523. DOI: 10.1108/BPMJ-12-2018-0347

Bai, C., Quayson, M., & Sarkis, J. (2021). COVID-19 Pandemic Digitization Lessons for Sustainable Development of Micro-and Small- Enterprises. *Sustainable Production and Consumption*, *27*, 1989–2001. DOI: 10.1016/j.spc.2021.04.035 PMID: 34722843

Baral, M. M., Singh, R., & Kazancoglu, Y. (2021). Analysis of factors impacting survivability of sustainable supply chain during COVID-19 pandemic: An empirical study in the context of SMEs. *International Journal of Logistics Management*. Advance online publication. DOI: 10.1108/IJLM-04-2021-0198

Barasa, E., Mbau, R., & Gilson, L. (2018). What Is Resilience and How Can It Be Nurtured? A Systematic Review of Empirical Literature on Organizational Resilience. *International Journal of Health Policy and Management*, *7*(6), 491–503. DOI: 10.15171/ijhpm.2018.06 PMID: 29935126

Barney, J. (1991). Firm resources and sustained competitive advantage. *Journal of Management*, *17*(1), 99–120. DOI: 10.1177/014920639101700108

Barnhart, C. (2023). Data and connectivity as key building blocks for effective collaboration with supply chain partners. *Journal of Supply Chain Management, Logistics and Procurement*. .DOI: 10.69554/FTSR7867

Bartik, A. W., Bertrand, M., Lin, F., Rothstein, J., & Unrath, M. (2020). *Measuring the labor market at the onset of the COVID-19 crisis* (Working Paper 27613). National Bureau of Economic Research. DOI: 10.3386/w27613

Basiru, J., Ejiofor, C., Onukwulu, E., & Attah, R. (2025). Sustainable Procurement in Multinational Corporations: A Conceptual Framework for Aligning Business and Environmental Goals. *International Journal of Multidisciplinary Research and Growth Evaluation*. .DOI: 10.54660/.IJMRGE.2023.4.1.774-787

Beckett, R. (2023). Affordable innovation facilitating renewable energy deployment: Two 'smart' energy poverty alleviation case examples. *Journal of Innovation Management, 11*(2), 118–156. DOI: 10.24840/2183-0606_011.002_0005

Beck, T., Demirguc-Kunt, A., & Maksimovic, V. (2005). Financial and legal constraints to firm growth: Does size matter? *The Journal of Finance, 60*(1), 137–177. DOI: 10.1111/j.1540-6261.2005.00727.x

Bedi, K., Singh, P., Kohli, N., Kaur, H., Angra, P., & Cheema, G. (2024). Effectiveness of IoT (Internet of Things) in Real-Time Supply Chain Monitoring and Management. *2024 Second International Conference Computational and Characterization Techniques in Engineering & Sciences (IC3TES),* 1-5. DOI: 10.1109/IC3TES62412.2024.10877555

Berg, G., & Schrader, J. (2012). Access to credit, natural disasters, and relationship lending. *Journal of Financial Intermediation, 21*(4), 549–568. DOI: 10.1016/j.jfi.2012.05.003

Bhattacharjya, B. R., Bhaduri, S., & Kakoty, S. K. (2023). Co-creating community-led frugal innovation: An adapted Quadruple Helix? *Technovation, 124*, 102752. DOI: 10.1016/j.technovation.2023.102752

Bindumadhavan, K., & Lacey, N. (Eds.). (2025). *Work Integrated Learning-Directions for the Future: Select Proceedings of ICONWIL 2024* (Vol. 1206). Springer Nature Singapore. DOI: 10.1007/978-981-96-0201-8

Bisha, A. (2025). Frugal innovation – new paradigm in innovation management. *Balkan Journal of Interdisciplinary Research, 11*(1), 35–47. DOI: 10.2478/bjir-2025-0003

Boçe, M., & Hoxha, J. (2024). *Blockchain Technology as a Catalyst for Sustainable Development: Exploring Economic, Social, and Environmental Synergies*. Academic Journal of Interdisciplinary Studies., DOI: 10.36941/ajis-2024-0041

Bondarenko, S. (2024). Quality management of business processes in the context of achieving sustainable development of fashion industry enterprises. *Management*, *37*(1), 94–105. Advance online publication. DOI: 10.30857/2415-3206.2023.1.9

Bontis, N. (1998). Intellectual capital and an exploratory study that develops measures and models. *Management Decision*, *36*(2), 63–76. DOI: 10.1108/00251749810204142

Bound, K., & Thornton, I. (2012). *Our Frugal Future: Lessons from India's Innovation System*. Nesta.

Bravi, L., & Murmura, F. (2021). Evidences about ISO 9001:2015 and ISO 9004:2018 implementation in different-size organisations. *Total Quality Management & Business Excellence*, *33*(11-12), 1366–1386. DOI: 10.1080/14783363.2021.1954900

Bravim, M., Lira, T., De Freitas, R., & Xavier, T. (2020). A evolução nos estudos da gestão da qualidade baseado na norma iso 9001:2015: um estudo bibliométrico: the evolution in quality management studies based on iso 9001: 2015 standard: a bibliometric study. *Brazilian Journal of Production Engineering* - BJPE, 88-106. https://dialnet.unirioja.es/servlet/articulo?codigo=8698522

Browder, R. E., Dwyer, S. M., & Koch, H. (2023). Upgrading Adaptation: How Digital Transformation Promotes Organizational Resilience. *Strategic Entrepreneurship Journal*, *18*(1), 128–164. DOI: 10.1002/sej.1483

Brynjolfsson, E., & McAfee, A. (2014). *The Second Machine Age: Work, Progress, and Prosperity in a Time of Brilliant Technologies*. W. W. Norton & Company.

Buenrostro, H., & Domínguez, N. (2023). *Propuesta de Categorías Para la Medición de la Sustentabilidad Portuaria a Través de la Metodología FuzzyDelphi. European Scientific Journal*. ESJ., DOI: 10.19044/esj.2023.v19n37p174

Business Management Systems. (2025). What might be changed in ISO 9001:2026? Business Management Systems Ltd. https://businessmanagementsystems.ltd.uk/what-might-be-changed-in-iso-90012026/

Cabral, L. M. B., & Mata, J. (2003). On the evolution of the firm size distribution: Facts and theory. *The American Economic Review*, *93*(4), 1075–1090. DOI: 10.1257/000282803769206205

Cadavid, V., Duque, D., & Carabalí, L. (2021)... *Modelo Multicriterio para el Diseño de Cadenas de Suministro Considerando Opciones Reales para el Tratamiento de la Incertidumbre.*, *26*, 159–166. DOI: 10.22517/23447214.24543

Calabrese, R., Girardone, C., & Sclip, A. (2021). Financial fragmentation and SMEs' access to finance. *Small Business Economics*, *57*(4), 2041–2065. DOI: 10.1007/s11187-020-00393-1

Campbell, J. W. (2025). Change management, performance feedback, and public service motivation: Cultivating change-oriented behaviour in public organisations. *Asia Pacific Journal of Public Administration*, *47*(2), 140–164. DOI: 10.1080/23276665.2024.2382092

Carbo-Valverde, S., Rodriguez-Fernandez, F., & Udell, G. F. (2016). Trade credit, the financial crisis, and SME access to finance. *Journal of Money, Credit and Banking*, *48*(1), 113–143. DOI: 10.1111/jmcb.12292

Cerroblanco-Vázquez, V., López-Mateo, C., & Macías, D. (2021). Asociatividad y cadenas de valor: estudio de caso de una marca colectiva de mezcal en Guanajuato, México (Associativity and Value Chains: A Case Study of a Collective Brand of Mezcal in Guanajuato, México). *PSN: Other International Political Economy: Trade Policy (Topic)*. .DOI: 10.29393/RAN7-2ACCL20002

Chakravarty, S. (2022). Resource constrained innovation in a technology intensive sector: Frugal medical devices from manufacturing firms in South Africa. *Technovation*, *112*, 102397. DOI: 10.1016/j.technovation.2021.102397

Chaudhary, S. (2019). Implications of Strategic Flexibility in Small Firms: The Moderating Role of Absorptive Capacity. *South Asian Journal of Business Studies*, *8*(3), 370–386. DOI: 10.1108/SAJBS-10-2018-0104

Chavan, V., Joshi, A., & Jha, D. 2024. Strategic Integration of HR, Organizational Management, Big Data, IoT, and AI: A Comprehensive Framework for Future-Ready Enterprises. *2024 Ninth International Conference on Science Technology Engineering and Mathematics (ICONSTEM)*, pp. 1-6. DOI: 10.1109/ICONSTEM60960.2024.10568704

Chen, S. (2025). Research on Supply Chain Logistics Prediction and Decision Optimization Driven by Artificial Intelligence. *Academic Journal of Business & Management*. .DOI: 10.25236/AJBM.2025.070218

Chen, C., Duan, J., & Peng, Y. (2024). How does sense of power influence change-oriented organizational citizenship behavior? Evidence from China. *Public Performance & Management Review*, *47*(3), 732–760. DOI: 10.1080/15309576.2023.2298414

Chen, K. K., & Mandiberg, J. M. (2024). Legitimizing organizations via research: Facilitating possibilities through the study of relational, emergent, transformative, and change-oriented organizations (RETCOs). *Public Integrity*, *26*(3), 360–373. DOI: 10.1080/10999922.2023.2262212

Chen, Y. Y., & Jaw, Y. L. (2014). How do business groups' small world networks effect diversification, innovation, and internationalisation? *Asia Pacific Journal of Management*, *31*(4), 1019–1044. DOI: 10.1007/s10490-014-9385-9

Chen, Y., Wang, Y., Nevo, S., Benítez-Amado, J., & Kou, G. (2015). IT Capabilities and Product Innovation Performance: The Roles of Corporate Entrepreneurship and Competitive Intensity. *Information & Management*, *52*(6), 643–657. DOI: 10.1016/j.im.2015.05.003

Chisasa, J., & Makina, D. (2015). Bank credit and agricultural output in South Africa: Cointegration, short run dynamics and causality. *Journal of Applied Business Research*, *31*(2), 489. DOI: 10.19030/jabr.v31i2.9148

Choerudin, A., Zulfachry, Widyaswati, R., Khasanah, L. D. W. J. S. N., Harto, B., Nita Fauziah Oktaviani, M. I. S., Nugroho, L., Suharsono, J., & Paramita, V. S. (2023). *Literasi keuangan* (Issue June). PT GLOBAL EKSEKUTIF TEKNOLOGI.

Chowdhary, Y., & Kumar, B., 2023. Advancement and benefits associated with ISO 9000 series. Asian Journal of Pharmaceutical Research. .DOI: 10.52711/2231-5691.2023.00008

Chowdhury, A. (2025). A systematic review of risk-based procurement strategies in retail supply chains: sourcing flexibility and vendor disruption management. *American Journal of Advanced Technology and Engineering Solutions*. .DOI: 10.63125/jr03rv07

Cohen, W. M., & Levinthal, D. A. (1990). Absorptive capacity: A new perspective on learning and innovation. *Administrative Science Quarterly*, *35*(1), 128–152. DOI: 10.2307/2393553

Corsini, L., Dammicco, V., & Moultrie, J. (2021). Frugal innovation in a crisis: The digital fabrication maker response to COVID-19. *R & D Management*, *51*(2), 195–210. DOI: 10.1111/radm.12446

Cortellazzo, L., Bruni, E., & Zampieri, R. (2019). The Role of Leadership in a Digitalized World: A Review. *Frontiers in Psychology, 10*, 1938. Advance online publication. DOI: 10.3389/fpsyg.2019.01938 PMID: 31507494

Cowling, M., Liu, W., & Zhang, N. (2016). Access to bank finance for UK SMEs in the wake of the recent financial crisis. *International Journal of Entrepreneurial Behaviour & Research, 22*(6), 903–932. DOI: 10.1108/IJEBR-06-2015-0126

Cunningham, W. (1992). *The WyCash portfolio management system. Addendum to the proceedings of the OOPSLA '92 conference on Object-oriented programming systems, languages, and applications*. ACM.

Curkovic, S., Scannell, T., & Wagner, B. (2013). Using FMEA for Supply Chain Risk Management. *Using FMEA for Supply Chain Risk Management., 1*, 251. DOI: 10.1201/b18610-3

Dabić, M., Vlačić, B., Guerrero, M., & Daim, T. U. (2022). University spin-offs: The past, the present, and the future. *Studies in Higher Education, 47*(10), 2007–2021. DOI: 10.1080/03075079.2022.2122656

Dalkir, K. (2017). *Knowledge management in theory and practice* (3rd ed.). MIT Press.

David, A.-H. (2023). Overcoming Global Economic Challenges: The Imperative of Diversification and Sustainable Development. *Vìsnik Marìupol s kogo Deržavnogo Unìversitetu Serìâ Ekonomìka, 13*(26), 14–21. DOI: 10.34079/2226-2822-2023-13-26-14-21

De Marchi, V., Pineda-Escobar, M. A., Howell, R., Verheij, M., & Knorringa, P. (2022). Frugal innovation and sustainability outcomes: Findings from a systematic literature review. *European Journal of Innovation Management, 25*(6), 984–1007. DOI: 10.1108/EJIM-02-2022-0083

De Moraes, M. A., De Moraes, G. H. S. M., Do Prado, N. B., & Fischer, B. B. (2025). Triggering Sustainable Transitions in Entrepreneurial Ecosystems: Key Enabling Conditions and Outcomes. *Sustainable Development*, sd.70005. DOI: 10.1002/sd.70005

Degryse, H., Lu, L., & Ongena, S. (2013). Informal or formal financing? Or both? First evidence on the co-funding of Chinese firms. *First Evidence on the Co-Funding of Chinese Firms (June 18, 2013). BOFIT Discussion Paper, 14.*

Deming, W. E. (1986). *Out of the Crisis*. MIT Press.

Demircioglu, M. A., & Chowdhury, F. (2021). Entrepreneurship in public organizations: The role of leadership behavior. *Small Business Economics*, *57*(3), 1107–1123. DOI: 10.1007/s11187-020-00328-w

Demirgüç-Kunt, A., & Maksimovic, V. (1998). Law, finance, and firm growth. *The Journal of Finance*, *53*(6), 2107–2137. DOI: 10.1111/0022-1082.00084

Deresso, J. W., Karo, C. A., & Kant, S. (2026). Organizational Culture Effect on Employees' Learning and Growth by Mediation of Employee Commitment in the Ethiopian Public Sector. In *Leading Inclusive Workplaces Through Digital Transformation and Organizational Change* (pp. 251-280). IGI Global Scientific Publishing.

Dey, A. (2022). Network wide visibility and Orchestration for Supply Chain. https://www.sciencedirect.com/science/article/pii/S2667344422000081

Diakova, A., Bagrationi, K., & Gordienko, O. (2024, November). Change-oriented Leadership in the Context of Transitioning to Strategic Autonomy. In *European Conference on Management, Leadership & Governance* (pp. 114-123). Academic Conferences International Limited. DOI: 10.34190/ecmlg.20.1.2962

Díaz-Arancibia, J., Hochstetter-Diez, J., Bustamante-Mora, A., Sepúlveda-Cuevas, S., Albayay, I., & Arango-López, J. (2024). Navigating digital transformation and technology adoption: A literature review from small and medium-sized enterprises in developing countries. *Sustainability (Basel)*, *16*(14), 5946. DOI: 10.3390/su16145946

Dima, A., Bugheanu, A.-M., Dinulescu, R., Potcovaru, A.-M., Stefanescu, C. A., & Marin, I. (2022). Exploring the Research Regarding Frugal Innovation and Business Sustainability through Bibliometric Analysis. *Sustainability (Basel)*, *14*(3), 1326. DOI: 10.3390/su14031326

Doern, R. (2014). Entrepreneurship and Crisis Management: The Experiences of Small Businesses During the London 2011 Riots. *International Small Business Journal*, *34*(3), 276–302. DOI: 10.1177/0266242614553863

Dong, A., Garbuio, M., & Lovallo, D. (2016). Generative Sensing: A Design Perspective on the Microfoundations of Sensing Capabilities. *California Management Review*, *58*(4), 97–117. DOI: 10.1525/cmr.2016.58.4.97

Doran, G. T. (1981). There's a S.M.A.R.T. way to write management's goals and objectives. *Management Review*, *70*(11), 35–36.

Dörr, J. O., Licht, G., & Murmann, S. (2021). Small firms and the COVID-19 insolvency gap. *Small Business Economics*, •••, 1–31. DOI: 10.1007/s11187-021-00514-4

Dote-Pardo, J., Ortiz-Cea, V., Peña-Acuña, V., Severino-González, P., Contreras-Henríquez, J. M., & Ramírez-Molina, R. I. (2025). Innovative Entrepreneurship and Sustainability: A Bibliometric Analysis in Emerging Countries. *Sustainability (Basel), 17*(2), 658. DOI: 10.3390/su17020658

Dyduch, W., Chudziński, P., Cyfert, S., & Zastempowski, M. (2021). Dynamic Capabilities, Value Creation and Value Capture: Evidence From SMEs Under Covid-19 Lockdown in Poland. *PLoS One, 16*(6), e0252423. DOI: 10.1371/journal.pone.0252423 PMID: 34129597

Dzenopoljac, V., Dzenopoljac, A., Ognjanovic, J., Kraus, S., & Puumalainen, K. (2025). From sharing to shaping: Role of knowledge quality and ambidexterity in SME innovation performance. *Journal of Innovation & Knowledge, 10*(100838), 100838. Advance online publication. DOI: 10.1016/j.jik.2025.100838

Dziedzic, S., Warmińska, A., & Wyrwa, D., 2023. Perspectives of the analysis of organisation's context in the light of the ISO 9001:2015 standard and the subject literature. *Scientific Papers of Silesian University of Technology. Organization and Management Series.* .DOI: 10.29119/1641-3466.2023.181.7

Easterby-Smith, M., & Prieto, I. M. (2008). Dynamic capabilities and knowledge management and an integrative role for learning? *British Journal of Management, 19*(3), 235–249. DOI: 10.1111/j.1467-8551.2007.00543.x

Echeverría, E. (2024). Supply Chain Resilience And Risk Management: Strategies For Mitigating Global Supply Chain Disruptions. *Educational Administration: Theory and Practice.* .DOI: 10.53555/kuey.v30i6.5680

Edmondson, A. C. (2018). *The Fearless Organization: Creating Psychological Safety in the Workplace for Learning, Innovation, and Growth.* John Wiley & Sons.

Edvinsson, L., & Malone, M. S. (1997). *Intellectual capital realising your company's true value by finding its hidden brainpower.* HarperBusiness.

Edvinsson, L., & Sullivan, P. (1996). Developing a model for managing intellectual capital. *European Management Journal, 14*(4), 356–364. DOI: 10.1016/0263-2373(96)00022-9

Egbumokei, P., Dienagha, I., Digitemie, W., Onukwulu, E., & Oladipo, O. (2024). The role of digital transformation in enhancing sustainability in oil and gas business operations. *International Journal of Multidisciplinary Research and Growth Evaluation*. .DOI: 10.54660/.IJMRGE.2024.5.5.1029-1041

Ehlers, U.-D., & Eigbrecht, L. (Eds.). (2024). *Creating the University of the Future: A Global View on Future Skills and Future Higher Education*. Springer Fachmedien Wiesbaden., DOI: 10.1007/978-3-658-42948-5

Eisenhardt, K. M., & Martin, J. A. (2000). Dynamic capabilities and what are they? *Strategic Management Journal*, *21*(10/11), 1105–1121. DOI: 10.1002/1097-0266(200010/11)21:10/11<1105::AID-SMJ133>3.0.CO;2-E

Engidaw, A. E. (2022). Small businesses and their challenges during COVID-19 pandemic in developing countries: In the case of Ethiopia. *Journal of Innovation and Entrepreneurship*, *11*(1), 1. Advance online publication. DOI: 10.1186/s13731-021-00191-3

ENISA (European Union Agency for Cybersecurity). (2021). *ENISA Threat Landscape for SMEs*. ENISA Publications.

Escot, L. Domínguez-Quiñones, I., & Aliende. (2025). Application of data science for building corporate reputation strategy: An analysis in business intangibles scoping review. *Corporate and Business Strategy Review*. .DOI: 10.22495/cbsrv6i2art10

Escudero-Cipriani, C., García-del Junco, J., Chafloque-Céspedes, R., & Alvarez-Risco, A. (2024). Frugal innovation in the business environment: A literature review and future perspectives. *Frontiers in Artificial Intelligence*, *7*, 1385522. Advance online publication. DOI: 10.3389/frai.2024.1385522 PMID: 39712468

Ezekwu, E. (2025). Sustainable supply chain practices: Driving efficiency, reducing waste, and promoting circular economy models. *International Journal of Science and Research Archive*. DOI: 10.30574/ijsra.2025.14.1.0206

Fainshmidt, S., Wenger, L., Pezeshkan, A., & Mallon, M. R. (2019). When do dynamic capabilities lead to competitive advantage? The importance of strategic fit. *Journal of Management Studies*, *56*(4), 758–787. DOI: 10.1111/joms.12415

Fairlie, R. W., Fairlie, R. W., Fairlie, R. W., & Fossen, F. M. (2021). The early impacts of the COVID-19 pandemic on business sales. *Small Business Economics*, •••, 1–12. DOI: 10.1007/s11187-021-00479-4

Fang, Y., Liu, Y., Yu, P., & Chen, N. (2024). How does narcissistic leadership influence change-oriented organizational citizenship behavior? Empirical evidence from China. *Humanities & Social Sciences Communications*, *11*(1), 1–11. DOI: 10.1057/s41599-024-03159-2

Farazi, R., & Zahidur, M. (2024). Designing circular supply chains with digital technologies for competitive sustainability: An operation management perspective. *International Journal of Science and Research Archive*. .DOI: 10.30574/ijsra.2024.13.1.1928

Farazmand, A. (Ed.). (2022). *Global Encyclopedia of Public Administration, Public Policy, and Governance*. Springer International Publishing., DOI: 10.1007/978-3-030-66252-3

Fares, O. (2024). *Falta de seguridad en la gestión de la cadena de suministros en la agroindustria ecuatoriana*. Revista Científica Sapientia Technological., DOI: 10.58515/028RSPT

Fasa, M. I., & Febrianty, F. (2020). *Eksistensi Bisnis Islami di Era Revolusi Industri 4.0*. Widina Bhakti Persada. https://books.google.co.id/books?hl=en&lr=&id=omDcDwAAQBAJ&oi=fnd&pg=PR3&ots=-c_XgwtKNA&sig=aEdIDy7rMH3J_bPAGr2R3lDy19o&redir_esc=y#v=onepage&q&f=false

Favretto, N., & Stringer, L. C. (2024). Climate resilient development in vulnerable geographies. *Mitigation and Adaptation Strategies for Global Change*, *29*(8), 90. DOI: 10.1007/s11027-024-10187-5

Felin, T., Foss, N. J., & Ployhart, R. E. (2015). The microfoundations movement in strategy and organisation theory. *The Academy of Management Annals*, *9*(1), 575–632. DOI: 10.5465/19416520.2015.1007651

Ferrando, A., & Ganoulis, I. (2020). Firms' expectations on access to finance at the early stages of the COVID-19 pandemic. *European Central Bank Working Paper Series, 2446*.

Fesobi, B., Fesobi, M., & Ogungbeje, O. (2024). Implementing agile supply chain strategy for improved response to market volatility: a systematic literature review. *South Florida Journal of Development*. .DOI: 10.46932/sfjdv5n12-057

Figueirêdo Da, S. M. (2024, September 08). S., De Araujo Filho, J., Rocha, T., De Paula Filho, F., & Cavalcanti, M. (2024). Sustainability Indicators in the Integrated Management of Industries with Galvanic Activities. *Journal of Management and Sustainability*, *14*(2), 53. Advance online publication. DOI: 10.5539/jms.v14n2p53

Fisman, R., & Raturi, M. (2004). Does Competition Encourage Credit Provision? Evidence from African Trade Credit Relationships. *The Review of Economics and Statistics*, *86*(3), 545–554. DOI: 10.1162/003465304323023859

Fitzgerald, B. (2006). The transformation of open-source software. *Management Information Systems Quarterly*, *30*(3), 587–598. DOI: 10.2307/25148740

Fitzsimmons Frey, H., Sefton-Green, J., & Poyntz, S. R. (2023). *Youthsites: Histories of Creativity, Care, and Learning in the City* (1st ed.). Oxford University PressNew York., DOI: 10.1093/oso/9780197555491.001.0001

Fouejieu, M. A., Ndoye, A., & Sydorenko, T. (2020). *Unlocking access to finance for SMEs: A cross-country analysis.* International Monetary Fund. DOI: 10.5089/9781513536156.001

Fu, Q., Rahman, A., Jiang, H., Abbas, J., & Comite, U. (2022). Sustainable Supply Chain and Business Performance: *The Impact of Strategy, Network Design, Information Systems, and Organizational Structure*. https://www.mdpi.com/2071-1050/14/3/1080

Gabriel, L., Da Silva, C., Sampaio, P., & Martins, Y. (2021). ISO 9001:2015 and risk-based thinking: scientific research insights. *Total Quality Management & Business Excellence, 33*(11-12), 1326–1343. DOI: 10.1080/14783363.2021.1954898

Gamboa, J., Castro, J., & Mantilla, C. (2020). The Sustainable Supply Chain: Concepts, Optimization and Simulation Models, and Trends. . .DOI: 10.14483/23448393.16926

Gandenberger, C., Kroll, H., & Walz, R. (2020). The role of frugal innovation in the global diffusion of green technologies. *International Journal of Technology Management, 83*(1/2/3), 97. DOI: 10.1504/IJTM.2020.109218

Gartner, Inc. (2020). *Managing SaaS Costs and Risks in the Age of App Sprawl.* Gartner Research.

Gartner, Inc. (2021). *Gartner Forecasts Worldwide Low-Code Development Technologies Market to Grow 23% in 2021.* Gartner Press Release.

George, E. (2025). *Business model innovation in a post-pandemic world: How companies are redefining value creation.* International Journal For Multidisciplinary Research., DOI: 10.36948/ijfmr.2025.v07i01.36703

Getman, R., Helmi, M., Roberts, H., Yansane, A., Cutler, D., & Seymour, B. (2018). Vaccine Hesitancy and Online Information: The Influence of Digital Networks. *Health Education & Behavior, 45*(4), 599–606. DOI: 10.1177/1090198117739673

Gilch, P. M., & Sieweke, J. (2020). Recruiting Digital Talent: The Strategic Role of Recruitment in Organisations' Digital Transformation. *German Journal of Human Resource Management Zeitschrift Für Personalforschung, 35*(1), 53–82. DOI: 10.1177/2397002220952734

Gitau, T. (2025). The Role of Industry 4.0 Technologies in Shaping Sustainable Digital Business Models: An Integrated Approach to Innovation and Strategic Capability Development: An Empirical Literature Review. *The International Journal of Humanities & Social Studies*. .DOI: 10.24940/theijhss/2025/v13/i1/HS2501-004

Glasbeek, L. (2025). Bricolage and its Strategic Connotations: A Study of Greek Social Entrepreneurs in Times of Crisis. *British Journal of Management*, *36*(3), 1003–1022. DOI: 10.1111/1467-8551.12880

Glogovac, M., Ruso, J., & Maričić, M. (2020). ISO 9004 maturity model for quality in industry 4.0. *Total Quality Management & Business Excellence*, *33*(5-6), 529–547. DOI: 10.1080/14783363.2020.1865793

Glückler, J., & Panitz, R. (Eds.). (2024). *Knowledge and Digital Technology* (Vol. 19). Springer Nature Switzerland., DOI: 10.1007/978-3-031-39101-9

Gosan, M., & Kosasih, W. (2020). Quality Management System in Automatic Machine Construction Based on ISO 9001. *IOP Conference Series. Materials Science and Engineering*, *1007*(1), 012064. Advance online publication. DOI: 10.1088/1757-899X/1007/1/012064

Grant, R. M. (1996). Toward a knowledge-based theory of the firm. *Strategic Management Journal*, *17*(S2), 109–122. DOI: 10.1002/smj.4250171110

Gray-Deh, F. Y. (2025). *Entrepreneurial orientation among small and medium enterprises in selected rural areas of KwaZulu-Natal* [Doctor of Philosophy Management Sciences Specialising in Business Administration, Durban University of Technology]., DOI: 10.51415/10321/6120

Groenewoudt, A. C., & Romijn, H. A. (2022). Limits of the corporate-led market approach to off-grid energy access: A review. *Environmental Innovation and Societal Transitions*, *42*, 27–43. DOI: 10.1016/j.eist.2021.10.027

Gueorguiev, T. (2024). *The PDCA cycle in innovation management systems based on ISO 56001:2024*. Unitech – Selected Papers., DOI: 10.70456/UIFI9691

Guirette-Barbosa, O. A., Castañeda-Burciaga, S., Ramírez-Salazar, M. A., Cruz-Domínguez, O., Carrera-Escobedo, J. L., Velázquez-Macías, J. D. J., Lara-Torres, C. G., Celaya-Padilla, J. M., & Durán-Muñoz, H. A. (2025). Transforming Quality into Results: A Multivariate Analysis with Hotelling's T2 on the Impact of ISO 9001. *Systems*, *13*(4), 226. DOI: 10.3390/systems13040226

Gunawan, A. W., & Winarto, S. H. (2024). Strategy for Improving Business Performance in Micro and Small Enterprises Through Innovation and Digitalization. *International Journal of Social and Human*, *1*(2), 97–105. DOI: 10.59613/qtcfze12

Gur, F. A. (2012). Financial constraints, growth opportunities, and firm size: Evidence from Turkey. *International Journal of Economics and Finance*, *4*(2), 53–68.

Han, Y., & Li, D. (2015). Effects of intellectual capital on innovative performance and the role of knowledge-based dynamic capability. *Management Decision*, *53*(1), 40–56. DOI: 10.1108/MD-08-2013-0411

Haouat, Z., Essalih, S., Bennouna, F., & Amegouz, D. (2025). Development of a Global Framework for an Integrated Life Cycle Assessment (LCA) Model in Quality, Safety and Environmental (QSE) Management Systems: Improving Environmental, Social and Economic Sustainability Performance. *Sustainability (Basel)*, *17*(8), 3521. Advance online publication. DOI: 10.3390/su17083521

Hekneby, T., & Olsen, T. (2024). The role of leadership in organizational learning in multinational companies. *The Learning Organization*, *31*(2), 141–162. Advance online publication. DOI: 10.1108/TLO-09-2022-0101

Helfat, C. E., & Peteraf, M. A. (2015). Managerial cognitive capabilities and the microfoundations of dynamic capabilities. *Strategic Management Journal*, *36*(6), 831–850. DOI: 10.1002/smj.2247

Hidayah, N., Nugroho, L., Suharman, H., & Ali, A. J. (2022). Exploring the Benefit of Introducing Accounting and Finance Knowledge for Micro and Small Entrepreneurs During the COVID-19 Pandemic. *ASEAN Journal of Community*, *6*(2), 335–346.

Holman, B., & Whitaker, C. (2022). COVID-19 Pandemic and Research on the Mediating Role of Absorptive Capacity on the Relationship Between Business Analytics Capability and Small-to-Medium-Sized Enterprise Performance. *Business Management Research and Applications a Cross-Disciplinary Journal*, *1*(1), 37–59. DOI: 10.54093/bmra.v1i1.2122

Homayoun, S., Velashani, M. A. B., Abbas Alkhafaji, B. K., & Jabbar Mezher, S. (2023). The effect of COVID-19 on the performance of SMEs in emerging markets in Iran, Iraq and Jordan. *Sustainability (Basel)*, *15*(10), 7847. DOI: 10.3390/su15107847

Hossain, M. (2018). Frugal innovation: A review and research agenda. *Journal of Cleaner Production*, *182*, 926–936. DOI: 10.1016/j.jclepro.2018.02.091

Hossain, M. (2022). Frugal entrepreneurship: Resource mobilization in resource-constrained environments. *Creativity and Innovation Management*, *31*(3), 509–520. DOI: 10.1111/caim.12502

Hossain, M. R., Akhter, F., & Sultana, M. M. (2022). SMEs in Covid-19 Crisis and Combating Strategies: A Systematic Literature Review (SLR) and A Case from Emerging Economy. *Operations Research Perspectives*, *9*, 100222. DOI: 10.1016/j.orp.2022.100222

Hossain, M., Agarwal, N., Bhatti, Y., & Levänen, J. (2022). Frugal innovation: Antecedents, mediators, and consequences. *Creativity and Innovation Management*, *31*(3), 521–540. DOI: 10.1111/caim.12511

Hossain, M., Park, S., & Shahid, S. (2023). Frugal innovation for sustainable rural development. *Technological Forecasting and Social Change*, *193*, 122662. DOI: 10.1016/j.techfore.2023.122662

Hossain, M., Shahid, M. S., & Park, S. (2024). The Business Models of Frugal Enterprises for Sustainable Development in a Constrained Environment. *IEEE Transactions on Engineering Management*, *71*, 3448–3463. DOI: 10.1109/TEM.2023.3342440

Hsu, L. C., & Wang, C. H. (2012). Clarifying the effect of intellectual capital on performance and the mediating role of dynamic capability. *British Journal of Management*, *23*(2), 179–195. DOI: 10.1111/j.1467-8551.2010.00718.x

Hsu, P.-H., Tian, X., & Xu, Y. (2014). Financial development and innovation: Cross-country evidence. *Journal of Financial Economics*, *112*(1), 116–135. DOI: 10.1016/j.jfineco.2013.12.002

Iansiti, M., & Lakhani, K. R. (2020). *Competing in the Age of AI: Strategy and Leadership When Algorithms and Networks Run the World*. Harvard Business Review Press.

Ibiyemi, M., & Olutimehin, D. (2024). Cybersecurity in supply chains: Addressing emerging threats with strategic measures. *International Journal of Management & Entrepreneurship Research*. .DOI: 10.51594/ijmer.v6i6.1241

Ijiri, G., Chilicaus, G., Licapa-Redolfo, G., Ballesteros, M., Otazú, C., Miranda, S., Castillo, M., De Los Ángeles Guzmán Valle, M., & Castillo, J. (2025). Digital Transformation and Sustainability in Post-Pandemic Supply Chains: *A Global Bibliometric Analysis of Technological Evolution and Research Patterns (2020–2024). Sustainability (Basel)*, *17*(7), 3009. Advance online publication. DOI: 10.3390/su17073009

Iqbal, Q., Piwowar-Sulej, K., & Kallmuenzer, A. (2025). Sustainable development through frugal innovation: The role of leadership, entrepreneurial bricolage and knowledge diversity. *Review of Managerial Science*, *19*(2), 573–594. DOI: 10.1007/s11846-024-00764-y

Irwansyah, R., Syahputra, D., Ningsih, S., Hasan, M., Kristanto, T., Nugroho, L., Triwardhani, D., & Marwan, D. Febrianty, Sudarmanto, E., Abdurohim BS, D., Sudirman, A., & S.Maggabarani, A. (2021). Marketing Digital Usaha Mikro. In *Paper Knowledge. Toward a Media History of Documents* (Vol. 5, Issue 2). www .penerbitwidina.com

ISO. (2023). *The ISO Survey of Management System Standard Certifications (latest available results for ISO 9001)*. International Organization for Standardization.

Ito, K., Umeda, S., & Sekiya, H. (2020). Impact of Intangibles on Corporate Value. *Journal of Human Resource and Sustainability Studies*, *8*(2), 131–150. Advance online publication. DOI: 10.4236/jhrss.2020.82008

Jagtap, S. (2022). Codesign in resource-limited societies: Theoretical perspectives, inputs, outputs and influencing factors. *Research in Engineering Design*, *33*(2), 191–211. DOI: 10.1007/s00163-022-00384-1

Jarrett, J. (2022). Update and Acceleration of Health Care Using Artificial Intelligence in Medical Treatments and Diagnostics. *Advances in Social Sciences Research Journal*, *8*(12), 394–400. Advance online publication. DOI: 10.14738/assrj.812.11425

Javed, A., Basit, A., Ejaz, F., Hameed, A., Fodor, Z., & Hossain, M. (2024). The role of advanced technologies and supply chain collaboration: During COVID-19 on sustainable supply chain performance. *Discover Sustainability*, *5*(1), 46. Advance online publication. DOI: 10.1007/s43621-024-00228-z

Jayabalan, J., & Dorasamy, M. (2024). Revitalizing Higher Education Institutions: Embracing Frugal Innovation for Transformation. *Procedia Computer Science*, *234*, 1305–1312. DOI: 10.1016/j.procs.2024.03.128

Jia-Jun, S., & Hua-Ming, S. (2022). The impact of career growth on knowledge-based employee engagement and the mediating role of affective commitment and the moderating role of perceived organisational support. *Frontiers in Psychology*, *13*, 805208. DOI: 10.3389/fpsyg.2022.805208 PMID: 35369191

Jinga, A. A., Hussen, J. O., Negash, H. G., & Estifanos, A. B. (2024). Leadership behavior and organizational change management in selected public universities of Ethiopia: Exploring the impact of leadership influences and change processes. *Heliyon*, *10*(19), e37149. DOI: 10.1016/j.heliyon.2024.e37149 PMID: 39398013

Jin, Y., Zhang, S., & Lei, X. (2023). Evolutionary Game Analysis of the Impact of Big Data Credit Technology on the Credit Rationing of Micro and Small Enterprises (MSEs). *Journal of Theoretical and Applied Electronic Commerce Research*, *18*(4), 1926–1954. DOI: 10.3390/jtaer18040097

Jio, W., Kant, S., & Lemi, K. (2025). Ethical Leadership: Effect on Future of Organizational Citizenship Behavior by Mediation of Organizational Culture in Ethiopia. In *Generation Alpha and Next Generation Leadership for Greener Futures* (pp. 41-62). IGI Global Scientific Publishing.

Jiraphanumes, K., Aujirapongpan, S., & Songkajorn, Y. (2023). Influence of diagnostic and dynamic capabilities on frugal innovation development: An empirical study of the Thai auto parts industry. *Asia Pacific Management Review, 28*(2), 229–239. DOI: 10.1016/j.apmrv.2022.10.001

Kant, S., Niguse, T., Terefe, A., Jio, W., & Adula, M. (2025). Ethical Leadership's Role in Promoting Resilience Among Employees by Mediation of Building a Resilient Organizational Culture in the Horn of Africa. In *Enhancing Resilience in Business Continuity Management* (pp. 219–244). IGI Global Scientific Publishing. DOI: 10.4018/979-8-3693-8809-9.ch007

Kant, S., Terefe, A., Alemu, Z. K., & Takaro, G. S. (2025). Unlocking the Potential of Smart Logistics by Enhancing Business Leadership Through Human Capital in the Horn of Africa. In *Understanding Human Decision-Making in Economic Models* (pp. 81–110). IGI Global Scientific Publishing. DOI: 10.4018/979-8-3693-8166-3.ch004

Karminska-Bielobrova, M., & Shmatko, N. (2021). Risk-management as an aspect of operational management. *Bulletin of the National Technical University "Kharkiv Polytechnic Institute" (economic sciences).* DOI: 10.20998/2519-4461.2021.1.36

Karnsomdee, P., & Phongkaew, P. (2023). The influence of entrepreneurial leadership and public entrepreneurship on organizational performance of local administrative organizations in the northeastern region of Thailand. *Russian Law Journal, 11*(6S), 238–252.

Karo, C. A., Deresso, J. W., & Kant, S. (2025). Organizational Culture Effect on Enhancing Workplace Productivity Through Women Employees' Normative Commitment in the Ethiopian Public Sector. In *Enhancing Workplace Productivity Through Gender Equity and Intergenerational Communication* (pp. 137-166). IGI Global Scientific Publishing.

Khairunnisa, N., Christiani, F., & Prawiyogi, A. (2024). Supply Chain Transparency: Exploring Blockchain Solutions for Enhanced Traceability and Efficiency. *Blockchain Frontier Technology.* .DOI: 10.34306/bfront.v4i1.569

Khanna, T., & Palepu, K. G. (1997). Why focused strategies may be wrong for emerging markets. *Harvard Business Review, 75*(4), 41–51.

Khatib, M., Zeyoudi, A., & Shaqar, S. (2020). The Influence of Integrating ISO and TQM on Project Risk Management. *American Journal of Industrial and Business Management*. .DOI: 10.4236/ajibm.2020.1012118

Khoa, B., Nguyen, H., Anh, D., & Ngoc, N. (2024). Impact of Artificial Intelligence's Part in Supply Chain Planning and Decision Making Optimization. *International Journal of Multidisciplinary Research and Growth Evaluation*. .DOI: 10.54660/. IJMRGE.2024.5.6.837-856

Khwaja, A. I., & Mian, A. (2008). Tracing the impact of bank liquidity shocks: Evidence from an emerging market. *The American Economic Review*, *98*(4), 1413–1442. DOI: 10.1257/aer.98.4.1413

Kilic, H., Canbakis, S., Karabas, M., Koseoglu, S., Unal, E., & Kalender, Z. (2023). Integrated Supply Chain Risk Assessment Methodology Based on Modified FMEA. *Journal of Risk Analysis and Crisis Response*, *13*(2). Advance online publication. DOI: 10.54560/jracr.v13i2.359

Kitchin, R., & McArdle, G. (2016). What Makes Big Data, Big Data? Exploring the Ontological Characteristics of 26 Datasets. *Big Data & Society*, *3*(1), 2053951716631130. Advance online publication. DOI: 10.1177/2053951716631130

Klarin, A. (2019). Mapping product and service innovation: A bibliometric analysis and a typology. *Technological Forecasting and Social Change*, *149*, 119776. DOI: 10.1016/j.techfore.2019.119776

Koch, R. (2008). *The 80/20 Principle: The Secret to Achieving More with Less*. Crown Business.

Korsunova, A., Halme, M., Kourula, A., Levänen, J., & Lima-Toivanen, M. (2022). Necessity-driven circular economy in low-income contexts: How informal sector practices retain value for circularity. *Global Environmental Change*, *76*, 102573. DOI: 10.1016/j.gloenvcha.2022.102573

Kortus, L., & Gutmann, T. (2023). How do firms build dynamic capabilities to develop sustainable products? A multiple case study in the manufacturing industry. *Journal of Cleaner Production*, *415*, 137887. DOI: 10.1016/j.jclepro.2023.137887

Kotte, K., Thammareddi, L., Kodi, D., Anumolu, V. K. A., & Joshi, S. (2025). Integration of Process Optimization and Automation: A Way to AI Powered Digital Transformation. *2025 First International Conference on Advances in Computer Science, Electrical, Electronics, and Communication Technologies (CE2CT)*, 1133-1138. DOI: 10.1109/CE2CT64011.2025.10939966

Kotter, J. P. (1996). *Leading Change*. Harvard Business School Press.

Kraus, S., Clauss, T., Breier, M., Gast, J., Sardini, A., & Tiberius, V. (2020). The economics of COVID-19 and initial empirical evidence on how family firms in five European countries cope with the corona crisis. *International Journal of Entrepreneurial Behaviour & Research*, *26*(5), 1067–1092. DOI: 10.1108/IJEBR-04-2020-0214

Kretschmer, T., & Khashabi, P. (2020). Digital Transformation and Organization Design: An Integrated Approach. *California Management Review*, *62*(4), 86–104. DOI: 10.1177/0008125620940296

Kumar, A., Singh, K. M., & Sinha, S. (2010). Institutional credit to agriculture sector in India: Status, performance and determinants. *Agricultural Economics Research Review*, *23*(2), 253–264. DOI: 10.1177/0971344120100206

Kumari, V., Tiwari, A., & Mendiratta, A. (2025). Does Inclusive Leadership Promote Rule Breaking for Positive Change? Exploring Psychological Empowerment and Change-oriented Citizenship Behavior. *Business Perspectives and Research*, 22785337251357736.

Kun, M. (2022). Linkages Between Knowledge Management Process and Corporate Sustainable Performance of Chinese Small and Medium Enterprises: Mediating Role of Frugal Innovation. *Frontiers in Psychology*, *13*, 850820. DOI: 10.3389/fpsyg.2022.850820 PMID: 35391966

Kyeong, K. (2025). Do Transformational Leadership and Innovative Climate Always Enhance Employees' Innovative Behavior? Focusing on the Moderated Mediating Role of Innovative Climate on Change-Oriented Organizational Citizenship Behavior. *Public Personnel Management*, *54*(4), 00910260251325269. DOI: 10.1177/00910260251325269

Laeven, L., Levine, R., & Michalopoulos, S. (2015). Financial innovation and endogenous growth. *Journal of Financial Intermediation*, *24*(1), 1–24. DOI: 10.1016/j.jfi.2014.04.001

Latan, H., Jabbour, C., Jabbour, A., Fiorini, P., & Foropon, C. (2020). Innovative efforts of ISO 9001certified manufacturing firms: Evidence of links between determinants of innovation, continuous innovation and firm performance. *International Journal of Production Economics*, *223*, 107526. Advance online publication. DOI: 10.1016/j.ijpe.2019.107526

Lee, C., Sohn, D., Sang, M., & Lee, C. (2025). Empirical Analysis of Barriers to Collaborative Information Sharing in Maritime Logistics Using Fuzzy AHP Approach. *Sustainability (Basel)*, *17*(4), 1721. Advance online publication. DOI: 10.3390/su17041721

Lee, J., & Shin, H. (2024). Effects of Inclusive leadership on the diversity climate and change-oriented organizational citizenship behavior. *Behavioral Sciences (Basel, Switzerland), 14*(6), 491. DOI: 10.3390/bs14060491 PMID: 38920823

Lemi, K., Kant, S., & Jio, W. (2025). Greener Hospital Future in the Horn of Africa by Transactional Leadership: Outcome on Altruism Through Adaptability. In *Generation Alpha and Next Generation Leadership for Greener Futures* (pp. 1-22). IGI Global Scientific Publishing.

Le, S. T. K., & Scaringella, L. (2025). Scarcity, Absorptive Capacity, and Social Networking—Antecedents of Self-Constructed Innovation in Vietnamese SMEs? *International Journal of Innovation Studies, S2096248725000244*(4), 366–382. Advance online publication. DOI: 10.1016/j.ijis.2025.07.001

Le, T., Hsu, C., & Chen, W. (2022). A Hybrid Blockchain-Based Log Management Scheme With Nonrepudiation for Smart Grids. *IEEE Transactions on Industrial Informatics, 18*(9), 5771–5782. DOI: 10.1109/TII.2021.3136580

Levine, R. (2005). Finance and growth: Theory and evidence. In P. Aghion & S. N. Durlauf (Eds.), *Handbook of Economic Growth* (Vol. 1A, pp. 865–934). Elsevier.

Levine, R., Lin, C., & Xie, W. (2018). Corporate resilience to banking crises: The roles of trust and trade credit. *Journal of Financial and Quantitative Analysis, 53*(4), 1441–1477. DOI: 10.1017/S0022109018000224

Lim, C., & Fujimoto, T. (2019). Frugal innovation and design changes expanding the cost-performance frontier: A Schumpeterian approach. *Research Policy, 48*(4), 1016–1029. DOI: 10.1016/j.respol.2018.10.014

Ling, B., Yao, Q., Liu, Y., & Chen, D. (2024). Fairness matters for change: A multilevel study on organizational change fairness, proactive motivation, and change-oriented OCB. *PLoS One, 19*(10), e0312886. DOI: 10.1371/journal.pone.0312886 PMID: 39480783

Lin, J., & Mao, M. J. (2023). How Does Digital Transformation Affect Sustainable Innovation Performance? The Pivotal Roles of Digital Technology-business Alignment and Environmental Uncertainty. *Sustainable Development (Bradford), 32*(4), 3163–3181. DOI: 10.1002/sd.2830

Lin, Y., & Wu, L. Y. (2014). Exploring the role of dynamic capabilities in firm performance under the resource-based view framework. *Journal of Business Research, 67*(3), 407–413. DOI: 10.1016/j.jbusres.2012.12.019

Lita, P., & Rosa, I. (2020). Perbandingan ISO 31000 dan COBIT 5 for Risk sebagai framework risk management pasca implementasi Enterprise Resource Planning (Studi kasus: PT Pupuk Indonesia (Persero)) [Tesis sarjana, Universitas Negeri Padang]. Repository Universitas Negeri Padang. http://repo.unp.ac.id/31018/

Liu, W., Zhang, X., & Chen, H. (2025). Improving Supply Chain Transparency through Blockchain Technology. *Optimizations in Applied Machine Learning*. .DOI: 10.71070/oaml.v5i1.89

Libre Lončarević, Z., Rebersek, S., Sela, S., Skvarč, J., Ude, A., & Gams, A. (2024). Adaptive Visual Quality Inspection Based on Defect Prediction From Production Parameters. *IEEE Access : Practical Innovations, Open Solutions*, *12*, 93899–93910. DOI: 10.1109/ACCESS.2024.3424664

Lotfi, M., & Larmour, A. (2021). Supply chain resilience in the face of uncertainty: how horizontal and vertical collaboration can help?. *Continuity & Resilience Review*. .DOI: 10.1108/CRR-04-2021-0016

Loukopoulos, A., Papadimitriou, D., & Glaveli, N. (2025). Rising to the challenge: Job stress, role overload, and change-oriented organizational citizenship behavior in the public sector. *International Public Management Journal*, •••, 1–20. DOI: 10.1080/10967494.2025.2513369

Luiz, O. R., Mariano, E. B., & Silva, H. M. R. D. (2021). Pro-Poor Innovations to Promote Instrumental Freedoms: A Systematic Literature Review. *Sustainability (Basel)*, *13*(24), 13587. DOI: 10.3390/su132413587

Machado, E., Scavarda, L. F., Caiado, R. G. G., & Thomé, A. M. T. (2021). Barriers and Enablers for the Integration of Industry 4.0 and Sustainability in Supply Chains of MSMEs. *Sustainability (Basel)*, *13*(21), 11664. DOI: 10.3390/su132111664

Magallanes, M. (2020). Impacto de la gestión de sustentabilidad empresarial en la cultura organizacional. 12, 45-56. .DOI: 10.20983/novarua.2020.20.3

Mahankali, R. (2025). *Digital twins and enterprise architecture: a framework for real time manufacturing decision support*. International Journal Of Computer Engineering And Technology., DOI: 10.34218/IJCET_16_01_049

Malhotra, Y. (2023). Augmented AI-Knowledge Driven Intelligent Systems for Adversarial-Dynamic Uncertainty and Complexity. SSRN *Electronic Journ*al. DOI: 10.2139/ssrn.4380524

Manishimwe, T., Frazier, D. P., & Yusuf, H. (2024). Frugal innovation and entrepreneurial university: A case study of African first development university in Africa. *Discover Education*, *3*(1), 190. DOI: 10.1007/s44217-024-00299-0

Manova, K. (2013). Credit constraints, heterogeneous firms, and international trade. *The Review of Economic Studies*, *80*(2), 711–744. DOI: 10.1093/restud/rds036

Manzi-Puertas, M. A., Agirre-Aramburu, I., & López-Pérez, S. (2025). Uncovering the hidden value of scarce resources: Frugality, resourcefulness and innovative behavior among student entrepreneurs. *Cogent Business & Management*, *12*(1), 2525500. DOI: 10.1080/23311975.2025.2525500

Maria, K., Kasmo, A. B. P., & Nugroho, L. (2022). Kajian Penggunaan Aplikasi Digital dalam Meningkatkan Pendapatan UMKM pada Sektor Makanan (Studi Kasus Ayam Gepuk Pak Gembus). *Jurnal Cakrawala Ilmiah*, *2*(4), 1669–1678. DOI: 10.53625/jcijurnalcakrawalailmiah.v2i4.4564

Martusewicz, J., Wierzbic, A., & Łukaszewicz, M. (2024). Strategic Transformation and Sustainability: Unveiling the EFQM Model 2025. *Sustainability (Basel)*, *16*(20), 9106. Advance online publication. DOI: 10.3390/su16209106

Ma, S., Ding, W., Liu, Y., Ren, S., & Yang, H. (2022). Digital twin and big data-driven sustainable smart manufacturing based on information management systems for energy intensive industries. *Applied Energy*, *326*, 119986. Advance online publication. DOI: 10.1016/j.apenergy.2022.119986

Masanet, E., Shehabi, A., Ramakrishnan, L., Liang, J., Ma, X., Walker, B., & Mantha, P. (2013). *The Energy Efficiency Potential of Cloud-Based Software: A U.S. Case Study*. Lawrence Berkeley National Laboratory. DOI: 10.2172/1171159

Masih, S., Punchanathan, U. E., Naqshbandi, M. M., & Ahmed, F. (2025). How inclusive leadership drives change-oriented extra-role behaviors via leader-member exchange and trust in leadership. *Global Knowledge, Memory and Communication*. Advance online publication. DOI: 10.1108/GKMC-05-2024-0276

Maula, S. S. A. Z., Syurofa, S. S., Aulia, S., Aulia, P., & Fauzi, R. Z. (2025). Adaptive Leadership and Organizational Agility: Managing Change and Fostering Entrepreneurship in Uncertain Times. *Oikos*, *17*(2), 303–322.

McDermott, T. K. J., Barry, F., & Tol, R. S. J. (2014). Disasters and development: Natural disasters, credit constraints, and economic growth. *Oxford Economic Papers*, *66*(3), 750–773. DOI: 10.1093/oep/gpt034

McGuinness, G., & Hogan, T. (2016). Bank credit and trade credit: Evidence from SMEs over the financial crisis. *International Small Business Journal*, *34*(4), 412–445. DOI: 10.1177/0266242614558314

Medase, S. K., & Abdul-Basit, S. (2020). External knowledge modes and firm-level innovation performance: Empirical evidence from sub-Saharan Africa. *Journal of Innovation & Knowledge*, *5*(2), 81–95. DOI: 10.1016/j.jik.2019.08.001

Medina, E., Lara, M., Dávila, J., & Velarde, R. (2020). Gestión eficiente de las economías locales a través de estrategias administrativas/Efficient management of local economies through administrative strategies., 654–673-654–673. .DOI: 10.18502/keg.v5i2.6288

Meena, M., Mishra, Y., Dusad, C., Dangayach, G., Sarkar, P., & Singh, A. (2024). Navigating Uncertainty: Cutting Edge Approaches in Process Control and Monitoring for Risk Mitigation in Supply Chain Management. *The 3rd International Electronic Conference on Processes*. DOI: 10.3390/engproc2024067074

Mikalef, P., Boura, M., Lekakos, G., & Krogstie, J. (2019). Big Data Analytics Capabilities and Innovation: The Mediating Role of Dynamic Capabilities and Moderating Effect of the Environment. *British Journal of Management*, *30*(2), 272–298. DOI: 10.1111/1467-8551.12343

Millar, C. C., Groth, O., & Mahon, J. F. (2018). Management innovation in a VUCA world and challenges and recommendations. *California Management Review*, *61*(1), 5–14. DOI: 10.1177/0008125618805111

Milovanović, G., Milovanović, S., & Popović, G. (2022). The role of Industry 4.0 in digitalization of production and supply chains. *Ekonomika (Nis)*, *68*(2), 1–14. Advance online publication. DOI: 10.5937/ekonomika2202001M

Minanari, M., Nugroho, L., Nurhasanah, N., Safira, S., & Nugraha, E. (2024). Financial distress determinants factors of retail companies with profitability as moderating (Indonesia cases 2016-2021). *Business Economics and Management Research Journal*, *7*(1), 29–47. DOI: 10.58308/bemarej.1324931

Mohan, V.Vijay Mohan, Keerthana N. (2025). Integrated AI Models for Simultaneous Quality Improvement and Risk Reduction in Production Processes. *Journal of Information Systems Engineering & Management*, *10*(18s), 499–512. Advance online publication. DOI: 10.52783/jisem.v10i18s.2935

Moodaley, W., & Telukdarie, A. (2023). Greenwashing, Sustainability Reporting, and Artificial Intelligence: A Systematic Literature Review. *Sustainability (Basel)*, *15*(2), 1481. DOI: 10.3390/su15021481

Moreira, G. G., Dos Santos, R. J. R., De Carvalho, V. D. H., Rosário, F. J. P., & Dos Santos, A. J. (2024). Potential for Frugal Innovation in a Brazilian Regional System: A Study Based on a Multicriteria Approach. *Societies (Basel, Switzerland), 14*(6), 95. DOI: 10.3390/soc14060095

Mubarik, M. S., Bontis, N., Mubarik, M., & Mahmood, T. (2022). Intellectual capital and supply chain resilience. *Journal of Intellectual Capital*, *23*(3), 713–738. DOI: 10.1108/JIC-06-2020-0206

Mullapudi, L. (2025). Optimizing Supply Chain Management with Real Time Data Integration Platform. *International Journal of Scientific Research in Computer Science, Engineering and Information Technology*. .DOI: 10.32628/CSEIT25111243

Muruganandham, R., Venkatesh, K., Devadasan, S., & Harish, V. (2022). TQM through the integration of blockchain with ISO 9001:2015 standard based quality management system. *Total Quality Management & Business Excellence*, *34*(3-4), 291–311. DOI: 10.1080/14783363.2022.2054318

Mvulirwenande, S., & Wehn, U. (2020). Analysing frugal innovation incubation programmes: A case study from the water sector. *Prometheus*, *36*(2). Advance online publication. DOI: 10.13169/prometheus.36.2.0095

Nagy, G., & Szentesi, S. (2024). *Collaborative logistics: An innovative strategy to address future logistics challenges*. Advanced Logistic Systems Theory and Practice., DOI: 10.32971/als.2024.031

Nahapiet, J., & Ghoshal, S. (1998). Social capital, intellectual capital, and the organisational advantage. *Academy of Management Review*, *23*(2), 242–266. DOI: 10.2307/259373

Nathany, D. (2022). Impact of COVID-19 on Supply Chain: A Comprehensive Analysis. *Interantional journal of scientific research in engineering and management*. .DOI: 10.55041/IJSREM16967

Naveen, K., Selvan, C., & Senanayake, R. (2022). Assessment of Risk and Opportunity in Accordance With ISO 9001. *International Journal of Social Ecology and Sustainable Development*, *13*(5), 1–16. Advance online publication. DOI: 10.4018/IJSESD.292037

Nilsen, J. C. K. (2002). Trade Credit and the Bank Lending Channel. *Journal of Money, Credit and Banking*, *34*(1), 226–253. DOI: 10.1353/mcb.2002.0032

Nilsson, S., Samuelsson, M., & Meyer, C. (2022). Social entrepreneurs' use of spatial bricolage to create frugal innovation in a divided urban setting. *Africa Journal of Management*, *8*(3), 298–323. DOI: 10.1080/23322373.2022.2071578

Nugroho, L. (2022). *Peran Corporate University dalam Mempertahankan Kinerja yang Berkelanjutan (Implementasi Pada Bank Syariah Mandiri)* (W. Utami (ed.)). Deepublish. https://deepublishstore.com/shop/buku-peran-corporate/

Nugroho, L. (2023). Reshaping the Mindset of Halal Entrepreneurs Toward Sustainable Business: The Case of Indonesia. In *Contemporary Discourse of Halal and Islamic Entrepreneurship* (pp. 207–221). Springer. DOI: 10.1007/978-981-99-6427-7_14

Nugroho, L., & Tamala, D. (2018). Persepsi pengusaha umkm terhadap peran bank syariah. *Jurnal SIKAP (Sistem Informasi, Keuangan, Auditing Dan Perpajakan), 3*(1), 49–62.

Nugroho, L., Mor, S., Iskandar, D., Setiany, E., Asih, D., & Mellin, F. (2024). The Urgency of Digitalization Vis-a-Vis Business Trends (Indonesia Case). *Proceeding International Annual Conference Economics, Management, Business, and Accounting, 1*(1 SE-Articles), 1–13. https://proceeding.inacemba.org/index.php/eproceeding-inacemba/article/view/1

Nugroho, L., Utami, W., & Kasmo, A. B. P. (2024). *BUKU REFERENSI MANAJEMEN STRATEGI DI ERA DIGITALISASI ISU-ISU TERKINI*. Widina Media Utama.

Nugroho, L., & Arafah, W. (2020). Eksistensi Dan Tantangan Usaha Mikro, Kecil Dan Menengah (UMKM) Pada Era Globalisasi. In Sumitro, A. S., & Nurhayati, S. (Eds.), *Manajemen Hasil Pemikiran dari Para Dosen Perguruan Tinggi di Indonesia: Vol. First* (pp. 172–187). Sihsawit Labuhan Batu., DOI: 10.1017/CBO9781107415324.004

Nugroho, L., Melzatia, H. H., & Abidin, M. I. (2024). Digitalizing Rural Development in Indonesia : Unveiling Concepts and Strategies for Building Sustainable Digital Villages. *Proceeding of The First International Annual Conference on Economics, Management, Business and Accounting*, 61–74.

Nurdany, A., Nugroho, L., & Shahirah, N. A. Nikamtuzzahra, Musyarofah, A. N., Bandiyah, A. N., Ali, J., Kurnia, R., Nafisa, A., & Putri, A. Z. (2024). DIGITAL ECONOMY DISRUPTION (Unveiling the Dynamic View of Islamic Finance, Digital Asset, Financial Crime and Cybersecurity). In *Widina Media Utama*. Widina Media Utama.

Nweje, U., & Taiwo, M. (2025). Leveraging Artificial Intelligence for predictive supply chain management, focus on how AI- driven tools are revolutionizing demand forecasting and inventory optimization. *International Journal of Science and Research Archive*. .DOI: 10.30574/ijsra.2025.14.1.0027

Omer, M., Kaiser, M., Buxbaum-Conradi, S., Moritz, M., & Redlich, T. (2024). Designing for replicability: A qualitative empirical study on the replication of open-source machine tools. *Design Science*, *10*, e30. DOI: 10.1017/dsj.2024.35

Onsongo, E. K., & Knorringa, P. (2020). Comparing frugality and inclusion in innovation for development: Logic, process and outcome. *Innovation and Development*, •••, 1–21. DOI: 10.1080/2157930X.2020.1811931

Orelj, A., & Torfason, M. T. (2022). They didn't ask: Online innovation communities as a latent dynamic capability. *Technological Forecasting and Social Change*, *180*, 121738. Advance online publication. DOI: 10.1016/j.techfore.2022.121738

Organisation for Economic Co-operation and Development. (2023). *OECD SME and entrepreneurship outlook 2023*. OECD Publishing. https://www.oecd.org/content/dam/oecd/en/publications/reports/2023/06/oecd-sme-and-entrepreneurship-outlook-2023_c5ac21d0/342b8564-en.pdf

Ortis-Avram, D., Ovcharova, N., & Engelmann, A. (2024). Dynamic capabilities for sustainability and toward a typology based on dimensions of sustainability-oriented innovation and stakeholder integration. *Business Strategy and the Environment*, *33*(4), 2969–3004. DOI: 10.1002/bse.3630

Orzáez, H., & Moreno, G. (2021). Risk management methodology in the supply chain: A case study applied. *Annals of Operations Research*, *313*(2), 1051–1075. DOI: 10.1007/s10479-021-04220-y

Osakwe, C. N., Chovancova, M., & Ogbonna, B. U. (2016). Linking SMEs Profitability to Brand Orientation and Market-Sensing Capability: A Service Sector Evidence. *Periodica Polytechnica Social and Management Sciences*, *24*(1), 34–40. DOI: 10.3311/PPso.8069

Osho, G., J., & Omisola, J., Shiyanbola., 2024. A Systems-Based Framework for ISO 9000 Compliance: Applying Statistical Quality Control and Continuous Improvement Tools in U.S. Manufacturing. *International Journal of Advanced Multidisciplinary Research and Studies*. .DOI: 10.62225/2583049X.2024.4.6.4052

Owusu-Berko, L. (2025). Advanced supply chain analytics: Leveraging digital twins, IoT and blockchain for resilient, data-driven business operations. *World Journal of Advanced Research and Reviews*. .DOI: 10.30574/wjarr.2025.25.2.0572

Özkan, B. (2021). Analysing Effects of ISO 9001:2015 Quality Management System on Organizational Communication Structure. *Open Journal of Social Sciences*, *9*(10), 85–96. Advance online publication. DOI: 10.4236/jss.2021.910006

Pal, P., Hens, A., Behera, N., & Lahiri, S. (2025). Digital twins: Transforming the chemical process industry A review. *Canadian Journal of Chemical Engineering*, *103*(8), 3611–3636. Advance online publication. DOI: 10.1002/cjce.25611

Panjaitan, R. (2022). Towards Resilient MSMEs: The Role of Organizational Resilience and Entrepreneurial Resilience. *Jurnal Manajemen Dan Keuangan*, *11*(1), 97–111. DOI: 10.33059/jmk.v11i1.5035

Park, S., Rosca, E., & Agarwal, N. (2022). Driving social impact at the bottom of the Pyramid through the internet-of-things enabled frugal innovations. *Technovation*, *118*, 102381. DOI: 10.1016/j.technovation.2021.102381

Parra, Y., Veloz, M., Ávila, G., Veloz, M., Rochina, P., & Parra, E. (2025). Risk Management in Process Management in the Contemporary Organization that Meets Sustainable Development Goals (SDG). *Journal of Lifestyle and SDGs Review*. .DOI: 10.47172/2965-730X.SDGsReview.v5.n02.pe04175

Pasamar, S., Cabrales, A. L., & Cabrales, R. V. (2015). Ambidexterity and intellectual capital architectures for developing dynamic capabilities and towards a research agenda. *European Journal of International Management*, *9*(1), 74–87. DOI: 10.1504/EJIM.2015.066672

Pedauga, L. E., Sáez, F., & Delgado-Márquez, B. L. (2021). Macroeconomic lockdown and SMEs: The impact of the COVID-19 pandemic in Spain. *Small Business Economics*, •••, 1–24. DOI: 10.1007/s11187-021-00476-7

Peet's, J. D. E. (2024). Supplier Self-Assessment Form 2024. https://www.jdepeets.com/siteassets/home/sustainability/responsible-sourcing/jde-peets-supplier-self-assessment-form-2024.pdf

Peng, S.-H. L. (2024). An intergenerational comeback: Girls' education, development, and social capital. *Policy Futures in Education*, *22*(8), 1709–1728. DOI: 10.1177/14782103241237320

Petersen, M. A., & Rajan, R. G. (1994). The benefits of lending relationships: Evidence from small business data. *The Journal of Finance*, *49*(1), 3–37. DOI: 10.1111/j.1540-6261.1994.tb04418.x

Petersen, M. A., & Rajan, R. G. (1997). Trade Credit: Theories and Evidence. *Review of Financial Studies*, *10*(3), 661–691. DOI: 10.1093/rfs/10.3.661

Petropoulos, F., Akkermans, H., Aksin, O. Z., Ali, I., Babai, M. Z., Barbosa-Povoa, A., Battaïa, O., Besiou, M., Boysen, N., Brammer, S., Brandon-Jones, A., Briskorn, D., Browning, T. R., Buijs, P., Centobelli, P., Chiarini, A., Cousins, P., Cudney, E. A., Davies, A., . . . Zheng, T. (2025). *Operations & Supply Chain Management: Principles and Practice* (Version 2). arXiv. DOI: 10.48550/ARXIV.2503.05749

Pirrone, G., & Milotta, M. (2024). Entrepreneurial Culture and Continuous Improvement to Handle Environmental Turbulence. *Proceedings of the International Conference on Business Excellence*, 18, 1465 - 1476. DOI: 10.2478/picbe-2024-0120

Piwowar-Sulej, K., & Iqbal, Q. (2025). Workplace envy as an inhibitor of change-oriented organizational citizenship behavior: The role of sustainable leadership. *Journal of Organizational Change Management*, *38*(1), 103–122. DOI: 10.1108/JOCM-02-2024-0086

Pongtanalert, K., & Assarut, N. (2022). Entrepreneur Mindset, Social Capital and Adaptive Capacity for Tourism SME Resilience and Transformation During the COVID-19 Pandemic. *Sustainability (Basel)*, *14*(19), 12675. DOI: 10.3390/su141912675

Potipiroon, W., & Thawornprasert, W. (2024). Local government managers' change-oriented leadership and employees' change-supportive behaviour during COVID-19: Utilizing the theory of planned behaviour. *Asia Pacific Journal of Public Administration*, *46*(2), 139–158. DOI: 10.1080/23276665.2023.2207833

Prada, S. I., Garcia-Garcia, M. P., & Guzman, J. (2022). COVID-19 response in Colombia: Hits and misses. *Health Policy and Technology*, *11*(2), 100621. DOI: 10.1016/j.hlpt.2022.100621

Pradhan, N. A., Samnani, A. A. B. A., Abbas, K., & Rizvi, N. (2023). Resilience of primary healthcare system across low- and middle-income countries during COVID-19 pandemic: A scoping review. *Health Research Policy and Systems*, *21*(1), 98. DOI: 10.1186/s12961-023-01031-4 PMID: 37723533

Prahalad, C. K. (2004). *The fortune at the bottom of the pyramid: Eradicating poverty through profits*. Wharton School Publishing.

Prameswari, A., Riezky, R., & Sudrajat, D. (2025). Supply chain 4.0 maturity, agility, resilience and absorptive capacity: an empirical study in Indonesia. *Jurnal Teknik Industri*. .DOI: 10.14710/jati.20.1.33-41

Precious, D. (2025). The Role of Industry 4.0 Readiness, Knowledge Management Capabilities, and Sustainability Culture in Driving Circular Economy Practices. *Business Strategy & Development*, *8*(2), e70135. DOI: 10.1002/bsd2.70135

Preface. (2023). *IOP Conference Series: Earth and Environmental Science, 1211*(1), 011001. DOI: 10.1088/1755-1315/1211/1/011001

Provin, A. P., Leal Vieira Cubas, A., De Aguiar Dutra, A. R., Carneiro Mussi, C., Junges, I., Nunes, N. A., Casagrande, J. L., & Salgueirinho Osório De Andrade Guerra, J. B. (2024). Qualitative Research Parameters in Studies on Frugal Innovation. *International Journal of Qualitative Methods, 23*, 16094069241237550. DOI: 10.1177/16094069241237550

Puglieri, F., Ferreira, M., Júnior, A., Piekarski, C., & Silva, D. (2024). How to consider life cycle thinking into ISO 14001? A step-by-step method for small and medium sized companies and a case study in waste management. *Gestão & Produção*. DOI: 10.1590/1806-9649-2024v31e8723

Pylypchuk, V., Holitsyn, A., & Vasilkova, N. (2025). *International standards of the ISO 9000-9004 series in the system of marketing management*. Marketing and Digital Technologies., DOI: 10.15276/mdt.9.1.2025.7

Radhakrishna, V., Ravi, H., Elango, S., Divyashree, V., Jaganathan, A., & Ponnusamy, M. (2024). Future of knowledge management in investment banking: Role of personal intelligent assistants. *Methodological Innovations, 17*(4), 229–247. DOI: 10.1177/20597991241287118

Radjou, N., & Prabhu, J. (2015). *Frugal Innovation: How to Do More with Less*. PublicAffairs.

Radke, A., Wuest, T., & Romero, D. (2021). Developing Digital Supply Network's Visibility Towards Transparency and Predictability. 13-21. .DOI: 10.1007/978-3-030-85902-2_2

Rahardjo, B., Wang, F., Lo, S., & Chu, T. (2023). A Sustainable Innovation Framework Based on Lean Six Sigma and Industry 5.0. *Arabian Journal for Science and Engineering*. Advance online publication. DOI: 10.1007/s13369-023-08565-3

Rajan, R. G., & Zingales, L. (1998). Financial dependence and growth. *The American Economic Review, 88*(3), 559–586.

Ramalingam, B., & Kumpf, B. (2021). *COVID-19 innovation in low and middle-income countries: Lessons for development co-operation* (OECD Development Policy Papers No. 39; OECD Development Policy Papers, Vol. 39). DOI: 10.1787/24140929

Ramos-González, M., Rubio-Andrés, M., & Sastre-Castillo, M. (2021). Effects of socially responsible human resource management (SR-HRM) on innovation and reputation in entrepreneurial SMEs. *The International Entrepreneurship and Management Journal, 18*(3), 1205–1233. DOI: 10.1007/s11365-020-00720-8

Rani, D. Y., Nugroho, L., & Zulfahmi. (2023). Kajian Faktor Internal dan Eksternal UMKM Wanita di Sektor Fashion pada Kecamatan Ngunut, Kabupaten Tulungagung, Jawa Timur. *SAMMAJIVA : Jurnal Penelitian Bisnis Dan Manajemen, 1*(2), 227–241.

Raphael, C., & Matsuoka, M. (Eds.). (2024). *Ground Truths: Community-Engaged Research for Environmental Justice*. University of California Press., DOI: 10.1525/9780520384347

Rehman, K. U., Anwar, R. S., Antohi, V. M., Ali, U., Fortea, C., & Zlati, M. L. (2024). Driving frugal innovation in SMEs: How sustainable leadership, knowledge sources and information credibility make a difference. *Frontiers in Sociology, 9*, 1344704. Advance online publication. DOI: 10.3389/fsoc.2024.1344704 PMID: 38497083

Ries, E. (2011). *The Lean Startup: How Today's Entrepreneurs Use Continuous Innovation to Create Radically Successful Businesses*. Crown Business.

Rimmer, P. & Kam, B., (2022). Consumer connectivity: forging supply chain success in the digital ecosystem. . .DOI: 10.4337/9781789905731.00012

Rodríguez, J. (2020). La gestión de recursos humanos en contextos de individualización., 16, 15. .DOI: 10.15332/22563067.5551

Rodríguez-García, M., Galindo-Manrique, A., Cortez-Alejandro, K. A., & Méndez-Sáenz, A.-B. (2022). Eco-efficiency and financial performance in Latin American countries: An environmental intensity approach. *Research in International Business and Finance, 59*, 101547. Advance online publication. DOI: 10.1016/j.ribaf.2021.101547

Rogers, D. L. (2016). *The Digital Transformation Playbook: Rethink Your Business for the Digital Age*. Columbia Business School Publishing. DOI: 10.7312/roge17544

Roos, G. (2019). *Optimising resource deployment within the firm and overcoming theoretical problems with a practical application* (Doctoral dissertation, University of South Australia).

Roos, G., von Krogh, G., & Roos, J. (2025). *Strategi – En Innføring*, 8. utgave. Bergen. Norway: Fagbokforlaget.

Roos, G., Pike, S., & Fernström, L. (2005). *Managing Intellectual Capital in Practice*. Butterworth-Heinemann.

Roos, G., & Roos, J. (1997). Measuring your company's intellectual performance. *Long Range Planning, 30*(3), 413–426. DOI: 10.1016/S0024-6301(97)90260-0

Roos, J., Roos, G., Dragonetti, N. C., & Edvinsson, L. (1997). *Intellectual Capital and navigating in the new business landscape*. Macmillan. DOI: 10.1007/978-1-349-14494-5

Sah, B., Hasan, M., Shofiullah, S., & Faysal, S. (2024). AI-Driven IoT And Blockchain Integration In Industry 5.0 A Systematic Review Of Supply Chain Transformation. *Innovatech Engineering Journal*. .DOI: 10.70937/itej.v1i01.12

Sallam, K., Mohamed, M., & Mohamed, A. (2023). Internet of Things (IoT) in Supply Chain Management: Challenges, Opportunities, and Best Practices. *Sustainable Machine Intelligence Journal*. .DOI: 10.61185/SMIJ.2023.22103

Sanchez-Hughet, C., Aramendia-Muneta, M. E., & Erro-Garcés, A. (2022). Seizing Opportunities in Europe: A Roadmap for Efficient Big Data Implementation in Spanish SMEs. *Digital Policy Regulation and Governance*, *24*(5), 463–478. DOI: 10.1108/DPRG-02-2022-0019

Sârb, A., Udrea, C., Onita, D., Itul, L., & Popa, M. (2021). Prediction of defects using machine learning techniques in order to improve quality management system A case study. *MATEC Web of Conferences*. DOI: 10.1051/matecconf/202134305010

Sarkar, S., & Mateus, S. (2022a). Value creation using minimal resources – A meta-synthesis of frugal innovation. *Technological Forecasting and Social Change*, *179*, 121612. DOI: 10.1016/j.techfore.2022.121612

Savant, N. V. (2025). Leveraging Surplus Android Phones in India: Scalable Use Cases in Edge Computing, Digital Health, and Smart Infrastructure. SSRN *Electronic Journal*. DOI: 10.2139/ssrn.5315514

Saygılı, M., & Çiğal, E. (2022). Using Lean Six Sigma for Sustainability in Inbound Logistics: An Application in The Automotive Industry. *International Journal of Environment and Geoinformatics*, *9*(2), 108–119. Advance online publication. DOI: 10.30897/ijegeo.975066

Scanlan, M. (2021). *Sustainable by Design*. Prosperity in the Fossil-Free Economy., DOI: 10.12987/yale/9780300253993.003.0006

Schoemaker, P. J., Heaton, S., & Teece, D. (2018). Innovation, dynamic capabilities, and leadership. *California Management Review*, *61*(1), 15–42. DOI: 10.1177/0008125618790246

Sedita, S. R., Blasi, S., & Ganzaroli, A. (2022). Exaptive innovation in constraint-based environments: Lessons from COVID-19 crisis. *European Journal of Innovation Management*, *25*(6), 549–566. DOI: 10.1108/EJIM-07-2021-0348

Senaratne, C., & Wang, C. L. (2018). Organisational ambidexterity in UK high-tech SMEs and an exploratory study of key drivers and barriers. *Journal of Small Business and Enterprise Development*, *25*(6), 1025–1050. DOI: 10.1108/JSBED-04-2018-0110

Shao, B., Kuang, X., & Wang, H. (2024). Digital knowledge management and technological innovation of manufacturing enterprises: The perspective of dynamic capabilities. *Keji Jinbu Yu Duice*, *41*(14), 111–121. DOI: 10.6049/kjjbydc.2023030519

Sharma, S., & Pratap, R. (2023). A case study of risks prioritization using FMEA method. International Journal of Engineering Research and, 12(5), 449–453. DOI: 10.17577/IJERTV12IS050170

Sharmelly, R., & Ray, P. K. (2021). Managing resource-constrained innovation in emerging markets: Perspectives from a business model. *Technology in Society*, *65*, 101538. DOI: 10.1016/j.techsoc.2021.101538

Sheikh, F. A., Pugh, R., Wu, X., & Sarkar, S. (2024). Regional studies and frugal innovation: A missing link? *Regional Studies*, *58*(4), 893–905. DOI: 10.1080/00343404.2023.2222136

Shepherd, D. A., Parida, V., & Wincent, J. (2022). *Entrepreneurial Responses to Chronic Adversity: The Bright, the Dark, and the in Between*. Springer International Publishing., DOI: 10.1007/978-3-031-04884-5

Sheth, A., Roy, K., Gaur, M., & Sheth, A. (2023). Neurosymbolic Artificial Intelligence (Why, What, and How). *IEEE Intelligent Systems*, *38*(3), 56–62. DOI: 10.1109/MIS.2023.3268724

Shet, S. V. (2024). A VUCA-ready Workforce: Exploring Employee Competencies and Learning and Development Implications. *Personnel Review*, *53*(3), 674–703. DOI: 10.1108/PR-10-2023-0873

Shivdas, A., Barpanda, S., Sivakumar, S., & Bishu, R. (2021). Frugal innovation capabilities: Conceptualization and measurement. *Prometheus*, *37*(3). Advance online publication. DOI: 10.13169/prometheus.37.3.0259

Shovon, M., Amjad, M., & Hasan, A. (2024). Examining the integration of industry 4.0 technologies in manufacturing. *Academic journal on science, technology, engineering & mathematics education*. .DOI: 10.69593/ajsteme.v4i04.137

Silvério, J., & Pestana, G. (2022). Integrated Risk Monitoring in the Quality Management System., 3-12. .DOI: 10.1007/978-3-031-04829-6_1

Simão, V., Bonina, N., Lima, G., & Gonçalves, O. (2020). Comparative analysis between ABNT NBR ISO 9001:2015 and ABNT NBR ISO 31000:2009: The risk mindset in quality management systems. *Brazilian Journal of Development*, *6*(3), 10872–10887. DOI: 10.34117/bjdv6n3-320

Singh, G. (2020). Developing a maintenance management system based on integrated approach of ISO 9001:2015 and TQM philosophy. *Industrial Engineering and Management*, *9*(1), 1–4. DOI: 10.4172/2169-0316.1000295

Singh, P. (2024). Measuring the Broader Value Proposition of Digital Transformation in Supply Chains. *International. The Journal of Supply Chain Management*, *13*(1), 16–24. Advance online publication. DOI: 10.59160/ijscm.v13i1.6222

Singh, R. (2025). Transforming humanitarian supply chains with digital twin technology: A study on resilience and agility. *International Journal of Logistics Management*, *36*(4), 1119–1135. Advance online publication. DOI: 10.1108/IJLM-08-2024-0504

Siougle, E., Dimelis, S., & Malevris, N. (2023). Does personal data protection matter for ISO 9001 certification and firm performance? *International Journal of Productivity and Performance Management*. Advance online publication. DOI: 10.1108/IJPPM-07-2022-0345

Snow, C. C., Fjeldstad, Ø. D., Lettl, C., & Miles, R. E. (2011). Organising continuous product development and commercialisation and the collaborative community of firms model. *Journal of Product Innovation Management*, *28*(1), 3–16. DOI: 10.1111/j.1540-5885.2010.00777.x

Solonytska, I., Popel, O., Mardar, M., & Ganchev, S. (2024). *Evolution of quality control systems: from taylor to modern standards*. Scientific Works., DOI: 10.15673/swonaft.v88i2.3055

Soori, M., Arezoo, B., & Dastres, R. (2023). Internet of things for smart factories in industry 4.0, a review. *Internet of Things and Cyber-Physical Systems*, *3*, 192–204. Advance online publication. DOI: 10.1016/j.iotcps.2023.04.006

Sørensen, P., & Lindholst, A. C. (2025). Does long-term management education change behaviors? A study of change in self-perceived leadership behaviors among participants in a three-year Danish diploma program. *International Journal of Public Sector Management*, *38*(4), 507–523. DOI: 10.1108/IJPSM-05-2023-0167

Sriyono, B., Biduri, S., & Proyogi, B. (2021). Acceleration of performance recovery and competitiveness through non-banking financing in SMEs based on green economy: Impact of Covid-19 pandemic. *Journal of Innovation and Entrepreneurship*, *10*(1), 27. DOI: 10.1186/s13731-021-00166-4

Stabell, C. B., & Fjeldstad, Ø. D. (1998). Configuring value for competitive advantage on chains, shops and networks. *Strategic Management Journal*, *19*(5), 413–437. DOI: 10.1002/(SICI)1097-0266(199805)19:5<413::AID-SMJ946>3.0.CO;2-C

Stefanova-Stoyanova, V., & Danov, P. 2022. Comparative Analysis of Specialized Standards and Methods on Increasing the Effectiveness and Role of PDCA for Risk Control in Management Syste*ms*. 2022 10th International Scientific Conference on Computer Science (COMSCI), pp. 1-4. DOI: 10.1109/COMSCI55378.2022.9912583

Steinfield, L., & Holt, D. (2019). Toward A Theory on the Reproduction of Social Innovations in Subsistence Marketplaces. *Journal of Product Innovation Management*, *36*(6), 764–799. DOI: 10.1111/jpim.12510

Stiglitz, J. E., & Weiss, A. (1981). Credit rationing in markets with imperfect information. *The American Economic Review*, *71*(3), 393–410.

Stovpnyk, O., 2024. Building integrated management systems: achieving synergy and sustainability in modern organizations. *Вісник Східноукраїнського національного університету імені Володимира Даля*. .DOI: 10.33216/1998-7927-2024-284-4-89-95

Study, I. S. O. (2021). *International Organization for Standardization. (2021). Economic impact of standards – Methodological guidance* [PDF]. ISO.

Subrahmanyam, S. (2025). Talent Management in Startups and SMEs. In Al Daraai, S., Al Abri, S., & Alhamar Alkathiri, N. (Eds.), *Aligning Talent Management and Organizational Innovation Goals* (pp. 359–392). IGI Global Scientific Publishing., DOI: 10.4018/979-8-3373-0015-3.ch013

Subrahmanyam, S., Aishwaryalaxmi, N. S., Khalife, D., Shaikh, I. A. K., Faldu, R., & Asthana, N. (2024). Impact of Knowledge Management and Big Data Analytics Capabilities on Firm Performance. In *2024 Ninth International Conference on Science Technology Engineering and Mathematics (ICONSTEM)* (pp. 1-5). IEEE. https://doi.org/DOI: 10.1109/ICONSTEM60960.2024.10568874

Subramaniam, M., & Youndt, M. A. (2005). The influence of intellectual capital on the types of innovative capabilities. *Academy of Management Journal*, *48*(3), 450–463. DOI: 10.5465/amj.2005.17407911

Sun, J. (2024). How to Green the Supply Chain Through Daily Necessities Packaging Management from the Perspective of Consumers' Habits. *Advances in Economics, Management and Political Science*s. .DOI: 10.54254/2754-1169/66/20241216

Systems, E. P. A. M. (2023). Driving sustainable impact for JDE Peet's. https://www.epam.com/services/client-work/driving-sustainable-impact-for-jde-peets

Tagoe, N., Nyarko, E., & Anuwa-Amarh, E. (2005). Financial challenges facing urban SMEs under financial sector liberalization in Ghana. *Journal of Small Business Management, 43*(3), 331–343. DOI: 10.1111/j.1540-627X.2005.00140.x

Tambunan, T. T., & Busnetti, I. (2024). Recent Evidence on the Digitalization Process in Indonesia's Micro and Small Enterprises. *International Journal of Current Science Research and Review, 07*(08). Advance online publication. DOI: 10.47191/ijcsrr/V7-i8-18

Tang, L., Jiang, H., Hou, S., Zheng, J., & Miao, L. (2023). The Effect of Enterprise Digital Transformation on Green Technology Innovation: A Quantitative Study on Chinese Listed Companies. *Sustainability (Basel), 15*(13), 10036. DOI: 10.3390/su151310036

Teece, D. J. (1996). Firm organization, industrial structure, and technological innovation. *Journal of Economic Behavior & Organization, 31*(2), 193–224. DOI: 10.1016/S0167-2681(96)00895-5

Teece, D. J. (2007). Explicating dynamic capabilities and the nature and microfoundations of enterprise performance. *Strategic Management Journal, 28*(13), 1319–1350. DOI: 10.1002/smj.640

Teece, D. J., Pisano, G., & Shuen, A. (1997). Dynamic capabilities and strategic management. *Strategic Management Journal, 18*(7), 509–533. https://www.jstor.org/stable/3088148. DOI: 10.1002/(SICI)1097-0266(199708)18:7<509::AID-SMJ882>3.0.CO;2-Z

Teece, D., Peteraf, M., & Leih, S. (2016). Dynamic capabilities and organizational agility: Risk, uncertainty, and strategy in the innovation economy. *California Management Review, 58*(4), 13–35. DOI: 10.1525/cmr.2016.58.4.13

Thakur, V. (2024). Collaborative supply chain network: Confusion or way ahead. International *Journal of Multidisciplinary Research and Growth Evaluation*. .DOI: 10.54660/.IJMRGE.2024.5.4.688-694

Țîmbaliuc, N. (2024). Organizational resilience in conditions of uncertainty. *EcoSoEn*. .DOI: 10.54481/ecosoen.2023.3.14

Tim, Y., Cui, L., & Sheng, Z. (2020). Digital resilience: How rural communities leapfrogged into sustainable development. *Information Systems Journal, 31*(2), 323–345. DOI: 10.1111/isj.12312

Tiwari, M., Bidanda, B., Geunes, J., Fernandes, K., & Dolgui, A. (2024). Supply chain digitisation and management. *International Journal of Production Research, 62*(8), 2918–2926. DOI: 10.1080/00207543.2024.2316476

Torcică, G., & Georgescu, D. (2022). Analysis of the Quality-Risk Correlation in the Educational Organization. *LUMEN Proceedings*. DOI: 10.18662/lumproc/gidtp2022/04

Toromade, A., Soyombo, D., Kupa, E., & Ijomah, T. (2024). Technological innovations in accounting for food supply chain management. *Finance & Accounting Research Journal*. .DOI: 10.51594/farj.v6i7.1315

Tufa, G., Kinde, Z., & Kant, S. (2025). Strategic Leadership: Effect on Employee Performance With Mediation of Dynamic Capabilities in Case of Ethiopian Public Organizations. In *Generation Alpha and Next Generation Leadership for Greener Futures* (pp. 115-138). IGI Global Scientific Publishing.

Umar, S. B., Ahmad, J., Mohd Bukhori, M. A. B., Ali, K. A. M., & Hussain, W. M. H. W. (2025). Transforming Higher-Education-Intitutes: Impact of Change Management on Sustainable Performance Through Transformational Leadership and Knowledge Management. *Sustainability (Basel)*, *17*(6), 2445. DOI: 10.3390/su17062445

Urata, S., Akao, K.-I., & Washizu, A. (Eds.). (2023). *Sustainable Development Disciplines for Society: Breaking Down the 5Ps—People, Planet, Prosperity, Peace, and Partnerships*. Springer Nature Singapore., DOI: 10.1007/978-981-19-5145-9

Van Niekerk, A. J. (2022). *The Inclusive Economy: Criteria, Principles and Ubuntu* (1st ed.). UJ Press., DOI: 10.36615/9781776402366

Varatharaj, M. (2024). *Enterprise Data-Driven Decision Making: A Framework for Digital Transformation and Organizational Excellence*. International Journal For Multidisciplinary Research., DOI: 10.36948/ijfmr.2024.v06i06.34279

Vătămănescu, E. M., Gorgos, E. A., Ghigiu, A. M., & Pătru , M. (2019). Bridging intellectual capital and SMEs internationalisation through the lens of sustainable competitive advantage and a systematic literature review. *Sustainability (Basel)*, *11*(9), 2510. DOI: 10.3390/su11092510

Vivona, R. (2024). The new era leadership for the public sector? Entrepreneurship, effectiveness, and democracy. *Public Management Review*, *26*(6), 1566–1582. DOI: 10.1080/14719037.2022.2162957

Wang, C. L., & Ahmed, P. K. (2007). Dynamic capabilities and a review and research agenda. *International Journal of Management Reviews*, *9*(1), 31–51. DOI: 10.1111/j.1468-2370.2007.00201.x

Wang, N., Cui, D., & Jin, C. (2022). The Value of Internal Control During a Crisis: Evidence From Enterprise Resilience. *Sustainability (Basel)*, *15*(1), 513. DOI: 10.3390/su15010513

Wei, F., Abbas, J., Alarifi, G., Shang, S., Adam, N. A., & de Queiros, M. J. (2023). Role of green intellectual capital and top management commitment in organisational environmental performance and reputation and moderating role of pro-environmental behaviour. *Journal of Cleaner Production*, *405*, 136847. DOI: 10.1016/j.jclepro.2023.136847

Wernerfelt, B. (1984). A resource-based view of the firm. *Strategic Management Journal*, *5*(2), 171–180. DOI: 10.1002/smj.4250050207

Westerman, G., Bonnet, D., & McAfee, A. (2014). *Leading Digital: Turning Technology into Business Transformation*. Harvard Business Review Press.

Weyrauch, T., & Herstatt, C. (2016). What is frugal innovation? Three defining criteria. *Journal of Frugal Innovation*, *2*(1), 1. Advance online publication. DOI: 10.1186/s40669-016-0005-y

Wicaksono, T., Wiraguna, S. A., Violin, V., Sudirman, A., Nugroho, L., Rizkiawan, R., Krisnanik, E., & Djumrianti, D. (2024). *KONSEP DAN TEORI E-BUSINESS & E-COMMERCE*. CV WIDINA MEDIA UTAMA.

Widianti, T., Firdaus, H., & Rakhmawati, T. (2024). Mapping the landscape: A bibliometric analysis of ISO 31000. *International Journal of Quality & Reliability Management*, *41*(7), 1783–1810. Advance online publication. DOI: 10.1108/IJQRM-09-2023-0287

Widodo, Z. D., Purwaningrum, J. P., Purbasari, I., Rini, G. P., Putra, A. R., Uran, B. E. K. R., Mulyani, M., Soegoto, A. S., Nugroho, L., Nurzianti, R., Nugroho, H., Sudirman, A., Santosa, S., Novianti, R., Pattiapon, M. L., Pinem, D., & Ridwan, N. H. (2022). Manajemen Koperasi dan UMKM. In Sari, E. P., & Putri, D. E. (Eds.), *Widina Bhakti Persada*. Widina Bhakti Persada.

Wigren-Kristoferson, C., Brundin, E., Hellerstedt, K., Stevenson, A., & Aggestam, M. (2022). Rethinking embeddedness: A review and research agenda. *Entrepreneurship and Regional Development*, *34*(1–2), 32–56. DOI: 10.1080/08985626.2021.2021298

Wilhelm, H., Schlömer, M., & Maurer, I. (2015). How Dynamic Capabilities Affect the Effectiveness and Efficiency of Operating Routines Under High and Low Levels of Environmental Dynamism. *British Journal of Management*, *26*(2), 327–345. DOI: 10.1111/1467-8551.12085

Wong, D. T. W., & Ngai, E. W. T. (2023). The Effects of Analytics Capability and Sensing Capability on Operations Performance: The Moderating Role of Data-Driven Culture. *Annals of Operations Research*. Advance online publication. DOI: 10.1007/s10479-023-05241-5 PMID: 37361097

World Bank. (2021). *Small and Medium Enterprises (SMEs) Finance*. Retrieved from https://www.worldbank.org/en/topic/smefinance

Wu, L. Y. (2010). Applicability of the resource-based and dynamic-capability views under environmental volatility. *Journal of Business Research*, *63*(1), 27–31. DOI: 10.1016/j.jbusres.2009.01.007

Xu, J. (2025). Research on the Strategies and Methods for Improving the Efficiency of Logistics Supply Chain. *Advances in Economics, Management and Political Sciences*. .DOI: 10.54254/2754-1169/2024.GA19140

Xue, J., Li, G., & Ivanov, D. (2025). Digital transformation in the blockchain era: Balancing efficiency and resilience in operations management. *International Journal of Production Economics*, *282*, 109525. Advance online publication. DOI: 10.1016/j.ijpe.2025.109525

Yadav, P., & Sharma, A. K. (2015). Agriculture credit in developing economies: A review of relevant literature. *International Journal of Economics and Finance*, *7*(12), 219–244. DOI: 10.5539/ijef.v7n12p219

Yang, L., & Gan, C. (2020). Cooperative Goals and Dynamic Capability: The Mediating Role of Strategic Flexibility and the Moderating Role of Human Resource Flexibility. *Journal of Business and Industrial Marketing*, *36*(5), 782–795. DOI: 10.1108/JBIM-11-2019-0495

Yazo-Cabuya, E., Ibeas, A., & Rey-Caballero, R. (2025). Multi-Criteria Decision Making for Risk Management in Quality Management Systems. *Sustainability (Basel)*, *17*(3), 1092. Advance online publication. DOI: 10.3390/su17031092

Yekeen, A., Ewim, C., & Sam-Bulya, N. (2024). Enhancing supply chain security and transparency with ai and blockchain integration for future-proof solutions. *International Journal of Frontline Research in Science and Technology*. .DOI: 10.56355/ijfrst.2024.4.1.0052

Yli-Renko, H., Autio, E., & Sapiensa, H. J. (2001). Social capital, knowledge acquisition, and knowledge exploitation in young technology-based firms. *Strategic Management Journal*, *22*(6-7), 587–613. DOI: 10.1002/smj.183

Yuslisa, M. Y., Yong, J. Y., Tanveer, M. I., Ramayah, T., Faesah, J. N., & Muhammad, S. (2020). A structural model of the impact of green intellectual capital on sustainable performance. *Journal of Cleaner Production, 249*, 119334. DOI: 10.1016/j.jclepro.2019.119334

Zahra, S. A., & George, G. (2002). Absorptive capacity and a review, reconceptualisation, and extension. *Academy of Management Review, 27*(2), 185–203. DOI: 10.2307/4134351

Zahra, S. A., Sapiensa, H. J., & Davidsson, P. (2006). Entrepreneurship and dynamic capabilities and a review, model and research agenda. *Journal of Management Studies, 43*(4), 917–955. DOI: 10.1111/j.1467-6486.2006.00616.x

Zakiyah, E. F., Kasmo, A. B. P., & Nugroho, L. (2022). Peran Dan Fungsi Usaha Mikro Kecil Dan Menengah (UMKM) Dalam Memitigasi Resesi Ekonomi Global 2023. *Jurnal Cakrawala Ilmiah, 2*(4), 1–12.

Zamzami, A. H., Mahliza, F., Ali, A. J., & Nugroho, L. (2022). Pandemic Covid-19, Revolution Industry 4.0 and Digital Entrepreneur Trending. [JIESS]. *Journal of Islamic Economics and Social Science, 2*(2), 133. DOI: 10.22441/jiess.2021.v2i2.007

Zara, A. R. (2025). Bridging Sectors, Catalyzing Innovation: The Role of FabLab Characteristics in Cross-sector Collaboration and Successful Collaborative Projects. SSRN *Electronic Journal*. DOI: 10.2139/ssrn.5206917

Zollo, M., & Winter, S. G. (2002). Deliberate learning and the evolution of dynamic capabilities. *Organization Science, 13*(3), 339–351. DOI: 10.1287/orsc.13.3.339.2780

Zornoza, C. C., & Forés, B. (2010). Knowledge Absorptive Capacity: New Insights for Its Conceptualization and Measurement. *Journal of Business Research, 63*(7), 707–715. DOI: 10.1016/j.jbusres.2009.04.022

About the Contributors

José De Jesús Reyes-Sánchez, Ph.D. in senior management, has six master's degrees, in education, in management, professional soccer technique, in physical preparation, in professional soccer, in physical rehabilitation sciences, in sports sciences, as well as in coaching and integral well-being, who is a research professor at the TECNM Instituto Tecnológico Superior De Fresnillo, with more than 20 years of teaching experience, PRODEP profile and coordinator of the academic body with vast experience in conferences and workshops, currently novelist and writer.

Mario García-Camacho Teacher and researcher with more than 15 years of experience, Educational Psychologist and Master in Education, as well as a PhD candidate in Senior Management. Professor at the TecNM Fresnillo Campus, he has promoted academic and human development in areas such as leadership and business management. It combines teaching, research and culture to promote education and competitiveness in globalised environments.

***

Gurpreet Pal Kaur is an Assistant Professor at Lovely Professional University, specializing in innovation, accounting, artificial intelligence in business, market orientation, and learning orientation. With a strong academic and research background, she has authored over 10 publications in reputed journals and contributed to multiple book chapters. Her work bridges theory and practice, focusing on how emerging technologies and strategic orientations drive business performance and sustainable growth. Dr. Kaur is actively engaged in interdisciplinary research, bringing fresh perspectives to the integration of AI, frugal innovation, and financial management, while also mentoring students and collaborating with industry partners to translate research into impactful solutions.

Geetha Manoharan is currently working in Telangana as an assistant professor at SR University. She is the university-level PhD program coordinator and has also been given the additional responsibility of In Charge Director of Publications and Patents under the Research Division at SR University.

Lucky Nugroho is a senior expert in Islamic banking, financial strategy, and microfinance with over 20 years of combined experience in the banking sector and academia. His career began at Bank Rakyat Indonesia (BRI) in 2002, where he served as a Rural Account Officer and MSME Officer until 2007, gaining hands-on experience in rural finance and microenterprise development. In August 2007, he joined Bank Syariah Mandiri. He continued through the merger into Bank Syariah Indonesia in February 2021, serving in key roles including corporate planning, financial analysis, microbanking development, and treasury. He retired in November 2022 after 15 years of impactful contributions to Islamic banking. Currently, he is an Associate Professor at Universitas Mercu Buana and Universitas Terbuka, focusing on Islamic finance, sustainability, and digital transformation. He holds advanced degrees from leading institutions in Indonesia, Belgium, and the Netherlands, and is certified as a CHRP and Risk Management Level 3. His research is centered on Islamic banking and finance, with a special interest in MSME empowerment, the circular economy, financial literacy, green finance, the halal industry

Göran Roos is a globally recognised expert in intellectual capital management, manufacturing competitiveness, industry policy, and innovation systems. With around 19,000 Google citations and more than 300 publications, he has established himself as a leading authority on strategic management, economic complexity, and sustainable industrial development. Academic Credentials and Appointments Professor Roos holds a PhD from the University of South Australia (2019), an MBA from INSEAD (1989), and an MSc in Engineering Physics from Chalmers University of Technology (1982). His current academic positions and fellowships include: • Adjunct Professor at the Institute for Sustainability, Energy and Resources (ISER), The University of Adelaide (2023-2025) • Fellow of the Australian Academy of Technological Sciences and Engineering (ATSE) since 2014 • Fellow of the Royal Swedish Academy of Engineering Sciences (IVA) since 2015 Areas of Expertise Intellectual Capital and Knowledge Management Professor Roos is a world-renowned expert in intellectual capital, having developed theories and implemented practical solutions that have shaped the

Mushtaq Ahmad Shah is a finance expert with a PhD in Infrastructure Finance. He teaches banking, finance and economics at Lovely Professional University in India. Dr. Shah has over 8 years of experience teaching and researching at various institutions. He's written articles in academic journals and presented his work at conferences on banking, partnerships between public and private sectors, and behavioral finance.

Satya Subrahmanyam is a distinguished academic leader, researcher, and institutional strategist with over 28 years of experience in higher education, business research, leadership and management. He holds two PhDs and a Postdoctoral qualification from the Polytechnic Institute of Leiria, Portugal. Currently serving as Professor and Dean (Research) at Holy Spirit University of Kaslik (USEK), Lebanon, he spearheads research initiatives that enhance academic excellence and institutional reputation. He played a pivotal role in the development of the Catholic University in Erbil, Kurdistan, where he established new departments, led research programs, and collaborated on international educational projects. As a founding member and Managing Partner of Vignan Institute of Technology and Management, India, he contributed to its transformation into a premier institution. With expertise in AI-driven business strategies, HR analytics, and leadership in technology adoption, he has published extensively, guided PhD research, and led training programs in corporate and academic settings.

Index

A

Artificial Intelligence (AI) 22, 27, 36, 37, 42, 44, 52, 56, 59, 62, 64, 121, 178, 206, 213, 215, 220, 223, 229

C

Change-Oriented Organizational Culture 69, 70, 71, 73, 77, 78, 79, 80, 81, 82, 83, 84, 85, 87, 88, 89, 91
COVID-19 23, 47, 48, 59, 62, 96, 103, 122, 152, 165, 184, 185, 187, 188, 189, 190, 191, 192, 193, 194, 200, 201, 202, 203, 204, 206, 210, 212, 222, 226, 227, 228, 230, 232

D

DANE 190, 194
Decision-making 1, 28, 33, 36, 44, 45, 71, 74, 79, 81, 90, 92, 94, 97, 124, 126, 137, 142, 206, 208, 209, 211, 214, 215, 216, 217, 218, 224, 225
Digital Tools 8, 16, 18, 48, 114, 116, 117
Digital Transformation 1, 2, 3, 4, 5, 8, 12, 15, 16, 17, 18, 20, 22, 23, 25, 28, 30, 32, 36, 50, 57, 59, 60, 65, 66, 67, 93, 121, 176, 205, 206, 207, 208, 209, 211, 212, 213, 214, 215, 216, 217, 218, 219, 220, 222, 223, 224, 226, 227, 228, 230
Dynamic Capabilities 27, 96, 99, 102, 103, 108, 120, 122, 123, 124, 125, 126, 127, 130, 131, 132, 133, 134, 135, 136, 137, 139, 140, 141, 143, 144, 145, 147, 148, 149, 151, 152, 153, 154, 155, 156, 183, 205, 206, 207, 208, 209, 210, 211, 212, 213, 214, 215, 216, 217, 218, 219, 220, 221, 222, 223, 224, 227, 228, 231

E

Economic Recovery 189, 200
Emerging Markets 122, 185
Entrepreneurial Leadership 69, 70, 71, 72, 73, 74, 75, 76, 77, 78, 80, 81, 82, 83, 84, 85, 87, 88, 89, 90, 91, 92, 94, 96

F

Financial Inclusion 172, 178, 187, 188, 190, 191, 200
Fintech 168, 187, 188, 189, 199
Frugal Innovation 3, 16, 18, 25, 99, 100, 101, 102, 103, 104, 105, 106, 107, 108, 109, 110, 111, 113, 114, 115, 117, 118, 119, 120, 121, 122, 123, 124, 159, 160, 161, 162, 163, 164, 167, 168, 169, 170, 171, 172, 173, 174, 175, 176, 177, 178, 179, 180, 181, 182, 183, 184, 185, 186

H

Human Capital 94, 125, 126, 127, 129, 131, 133, 135, 136, 137, 138, 139, 140, 141, 142, 143, 144, 145, 147, 148, 149, 150, 156, 167

I

Informal Learning 167
Intellectual Capital 125, 126, 127, 129, 130, 131, 132, 136, 137, 138, 139, 140, 141, 142, 143, 144, 147, 148, 149, 150, 151, 152, 153, 154, 156
Internet of Things (IoT) 27, 37, 44, 45, 52, 55, 64, 65, 206, 213, 215
ISO 9001:2026 27, 28, 30, 31, 33, 35, 37, 38, 39, 40, 41, 43, 44, 45, 47, 48, 49, 50, 51, 52, 53, 56

K

Knowledge-Based View (KBV) 102, 103, 159, 161, 163, 174, 177
Knowledge Management 99, 100, 101, 102,

103, 104, 105, 106, 107, 108, 109, 110, 111, 112, 113, 114, 115, 116, 117, 118, 119, 120, 121, 122, 123, 124, 134, 140, 144, 146, 147, 151, 159, 161, 162, 164, 170, 172, 173, 174, 176, 177, 178, 183, 184, 185, 186

M

Microfinance 187, 188, 195, 199, 214
MSEs 205, 206, 207, 208, 209, 210, 211, 212, 213, 214, 215, 216, 217, 218, 219, 220, 221, 222, 223, 224, 225, 228
Multi-Dimensional Performance 125, 137, 147, 148, 149, 156
Multinomial Logistic Regression 190, 195, 196, 197

N

Non-Banking Financing 187, 188, 189, 190, 191, 192, 193, 194, 195, 196, 197, 198, 199, 200, 204

O

Organisational Learning 103, 107, 130

P

Participatory Governance 69, 70, 71, 72, 73, 74, 75, 76, 77, 78, 79, 80, 81, 82, 83, 84, 85, 87, 88, 89, 90, 91, 92, 96, 97
Policy Implications 99, 119, 175, 187, 191

R

Relational Capital 116, 125, 127, 131, 132, 135, 136, 137, 139, 140, 141, 142, 143, 144, 146, 147, 149, 157
Resource Constraints 133, 140, 148, 193
Rural-Urban Disparities 187, 190, 191

S

SMEs 1, 2, 3, 4, 6, 7, 8, 9, 10, 11, 12, 14, 17, 18, 21, 22, 23, 24, 25, 27, 28, 52, 54, 63, 99, 100, 101, 102, 103, 104, 105, 106, 107, 108, 109, 110, 111, 113, 114, 115, 116, 118, 119, 120, 121, 122, 123, 124, 125, 126, 132, 133, 135, 136, 137, 139, 140, 141, 142, 144, 148, 149, 150, 153, 154, 156, 183, 187, 188, 189, 190, 191, 192, 193, 194, 196, 197, 198, 199, 200, 201, 202, 203, 204, 221, 227, 230
Structural Capital 125, 127, 131, 132, 134, 136, 137, 138, 139, 140, 141, 143, 144, 146, 147, 149, 157
Supply Chain 27, 28, 29, 31, 32, 35, 37, 38, 39, 40, 41, 43, 44, 46, 47, 48, 54, 55, 56, 57, 58, 59, 60, 61, 62, 63, 64, 65, 66, 67, 103, 110, 135, 141, 152, 166, 184, 201, 211, 215, 223

V

VUCA Environment 137, 142, 144, 148
VUCA Era 205, 207, 208, 209, 210, 212, 218, 219, 220, 221, 224

www.ingramcontent.com/pod-product-compliance
Lightning Source LLC
LaVergne TN
LVHW081521300926
849161LV00006B/1253
9798337360539